Marriage and Work
in America

Marriage and Work in America

A Study of Motives and Roles

JOSEPH VEROFF
University of Michigan

SHEILA FELD
University of Michigan

VAN NOSTRAND REINHOLD COMPANY

New York   Cincinnati   Toronto   London   Melbourne

Van Nostrand Reinhold Company Regional Offices:
Cincinnati   New York   Chicago   Millbrae   Dallas
Van Nostrand Reinhold Company Foreign Offices:
London   Toronto   Melbourne

Published by Van Nostrand Reinhold Company
450 West 33rd Street, New York, N. Y. 10001

Published simultaneously in Canada by
D. Van Nostrand Company (Canada), Ltd.

12   11   10   9   8   7   6   5   4   3   2   1

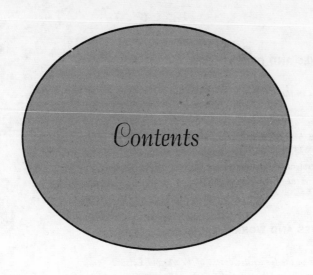

Contents

Contents

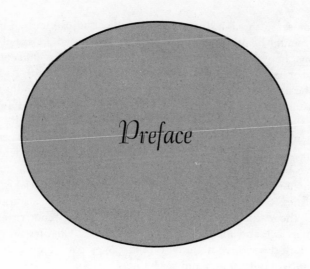

Preface

Social scientists interested in personality characteristics rarely have the opportunity to test the generalizability of their findings and theories based on college students or clinic patients to broadly diversified adult subjects. This book is based on a national study that provided one of those rare opportunities. Because we felt grateful for that opportunity, we felt obliged to share the findings as fully as possible with interested colleagues.

The personality characteristics we selected for study were three important social motives — the motives for affiliation, achievement and power. Our conceptualizations of these motives were rooted in the motivational theories of Henry Murray, David McClelland, and John W. Atkinson. We therefore conceive of motives as specific personality characteristics that affect the direction of a person's behavior, his choice of goals, and the satisfactions he experiences. Since we view social behavior as a joint function of the person and his social environment, we were interested in studying these motives in specified social situations. In the present study, the environmental influences on behavior were specified in terms of three broad social roles that most adults experience — marriage, parenthood, and work. In this book we are trying to answer the question of how these motives interact with role characteristics to affect the experience of fulfillment and frustration in these roles.

In one sense this is a study of psychological adjustment, of the forces affecting mental health and illness. We are interested in specifying the interactions between personality and cultural factors that affect the experience of happiness and stress in normal American adults. As such, the book can be used to supplement courses in the psychology of adjustment or of human motivation. The theoretical chapters (1 and 6) and any one or all of the three data chapters (3, 4, and 5) can be used in this way. In another sense this is a study of American character— the personality dispositions, social attitudes, and social behaviors that characterize our nation. We believe that however inadequate this set of data may be, it provides a unique addition to our knowledge about American national characteristics. Seen in this light, we view the book as an appropriate addition to the reading list in a wide variety of sociology courses, especially those in marriage and the family. In these courses, Chapters 3, 4, and 5, which contain descriptive material on marriage, parenthood, and work, can be read without the remaining chapters.

Viewed from either the perspective of research on mental health or the perspective of research on national character, this is not a study designed to test a clearly delimited set of specific hypotheses about motives and roles. This book reports a frankly exploratory study that we feel has provided us with a number of important insights about the significance of human motivation on the one hand, and the significance of three important social roles on the other. Although we recognize the exploratory nature of this research undertaking, we also are rather committed to some of the theoretical ideas it has generated, and are prepared to present them for serious consideration and to defend them if attacked, unless empirical evidence to the contrary is offered.

Our major interest in undertaking this exploratory research was to generate a useful theoretical orientation to the study of personality-role interaction. The description of our original theoretical ideas and the relevant past research, in Chapter 1, and our conclusions in this area, stated in Chapter 6, should be especially valuable for students in social psychology courses. We were also intrigued by the descriptive data about the motivational dispositions and role adjustments prevalent in different social groups in 1957 when these data were obtained. These data seem to us to make a major contribution to the study of American national character. We feel that our characterization of the American scene at the end of the 1950's will be relatively valid at the end of the 1970's, and perhaps later. Furthermore, we feel that codifying these data about Americans in 1957 will help draw the guidelines for data collection and analysis in future studies of national character. With such studies, by noting changes over a period of time, we would be able to place both sets of results in their proper historical perspective, and by noting consistencies we would be able to identify permanent social-psychological functions that may be involved in personality-role interactions.

The present volume is dependent on the collaboration of many persons and institutions whose names do not appear on the title page, and we would like to acknowledge our debt to them. This study grew out of a survey originally sponsored by the Joint Commission on Mental Illness and Health, as authorized by the U.S. Congress in 1955. Further financial support was later received from the National Institute of Mental Health (M2181, Veroff, Principal Investigator; M2280, Gurin, Principal Investigator) and the University of Michigan's Rackham School of Graduate Studies (Veroff, Principal Investigator). That survey was designed primarily to assess people's own evalutations of their mental health and the ways they had handled problems of mental ill health. It was carried out by the Survey Research Center at the Institute for Social Research of the University of Michigan under the direction of Angus Campbell. Gerald Gurin was the project director, and the present authors were the other staff participants in this undertaking. In conducting the survey we benefited from the help of many of our colleagues on the staff of the Institute, and we are heavily indebted to everyone connected with the earlier phases of the overall project. We would especially like to recognize the contributions to the present undertaking of three colleagues: Elizabeth Douvan, who provided general intellectual stimulation and personal encouragement; Gerald Gurin, who helped develop the theoretical ideas about personality and culture basic to the present volume; and John W. Atkinson, who served as a consultant to the entire project and was intimately involved in our early thinking about the motivational implications of the study.

Most of the work done specifically for the present volume was done after the authors were no longer associated with the original project, and while they were in the midst of other major commitments. We are therefore particularly grateful to those persons and institutions who helped us during this period. The Survey Research Center made it possible for us to complete the data analyses at their computer facility, and we wish to thank the Center and especially its director, Angus Campbell, for being patient with this slowly evolving work. The completion of the final draft of the book was facilitated by a sabbatical leave granted to the senior author in 1967–68 by the University of Michigan and supplemented by a Special Fellowship from the National Institute of Mental Health for a tenure at the Institute of Human Development at Berkeley. Throughout this period Dr. Feld was on the staff of the Mental Health Study Center at the National Institute of Mental Health where she received important administrative support, especially from James G. Kelly, James Osberg, Herbert Rooney, and Quentin Rae-Grant, that enabled her to devote time to this project and to receive valuable clerical support from Alvin Davenberg, Gertrude Peller, Esther Soloman, and Joan Vieler.

The thoughtful comments of our colleagues Wanda Bronson and Howard Ehrlich on earlier drafts of the manuscript are especially appreciated. The manuscript also benefited from the editorial review of Yetta Stern, who with Betty Jennings, typed most of the final copy. Finally, we owe thanks to Professor Veroff's entire family: to the children, Susie, Matt, Dan, Paul and Dave, who grew up accepting our disappearing to work on "the book" during various supposed vacation periods, and who provided many amusing respites during these endeavors; and to Jody, who in her roles as wife and friend offered psychological support throughout, and who in her role as colleague was a gentle but perceptive critic in frequent discussions of our ideas and in repeated readings of drafts of the manuscript.

Joseph Veroff
Sheila Feld

Marriage and Work
in America

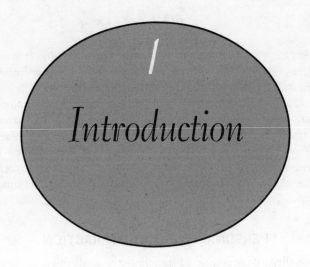

1

Introduction

This book is about the activities of men and women in
modern society that contribute to their experiences of joy and
their feelings of distress. This book is about work, marriage, and parenthood: how men and women with different personal
motivations react to these important social roles. It is not meant to be
a final work on this set of problems, nor a test of sharply focused hypotheses about the personal significance of social roles. Rather,
this book is an exploratory compilation of data from an
unusual national survey. We hope that our presentation will
provoke other social scientists to offer either supportive or contradictory evidence for some of the tentative
conclusions we have drawn. We hope it will
stimulate researchers to carry out intensive data collection, and
that it will inspire further theoretical
developments. Or, if nothing else, we hope it will exist for a
while as a storehouse of data that could corroborate some pet ideas of
social observers. If this book does any of these things,
its writing will be justified.

In this book we will be relating two kinds of data obtained from a
representative sample of men and women from the
population of the United States—their subjective reactions to three life roles (see Gurin, Veroff and
Feld, 1960) and their motivations for affiliation, achievement,

and power (see Veroff, Atkinson, Feld, and Gurin, 1960). It is our general hope that this analysis will provide some fresh insights into the relationship between personality and reactions to social roles.

The validity of the scientific undertaking rests on two major assumptions: first, that our measures of personality are valid, and second, that self-reports on feelings of satisfaction and dissatisfaction are significant aspects of role adjustment. We will be discussing the evidence for these assumptions and their implications in Chapter 2. In this chapter we will discuss the theoretical rationale for putting these two realms of data together.

PERSONALITY-ROLE INTERACTION

Personality, a province of psychology, and roles, a province of sociology, are two broad ways of conceptualizing portions of human behavior systems. While these conceptual schemas can be and are separately applied to efforts to understand human behavior, their presumed consequences interlock in determining complex social behaviors. Personality, as a schematization of the stable, persistent, internal organization of a person, has its effects within the constraints of the roles a person occupies; and roles, as a schematization of certain properties of social positions, have their effects within the constraints of the personality of the persons occupying or reacting to the roles. In our consideration of the interactions between personality and roles, we recognize the three kinds of relationships that can be assumed to exist between personality variables and social system variables: (1) personality can influence role behavior; (2) roles can influence personality; and (3) the interaction between roles and persons with specific personalities can influence observed behavior. Smelser and Smelser (1963) recently attempted to organize, under this type of trichotomy, a representative group of articles from the field of social psychology that linked personality and social systems. One general thesis of the Smelsers' book is that there are aspects of social systems that strongly affect the personal motivation of individuals, and another is that the evolution of work and social roles depends, to some extent, upon the motivational characteristics of the role occupants, or of the people reacting to the roles. Amalgamating these two general hypotheses, the present book will expand on this position and will also attempt to examine personality and roles as they interact.

As soon as we adopt an overview of human behavior that calls for an integration of social structural and personality variables, we begin to swim in muddy waters. An interactional position posits that roles influence personality, and personalities interpret roles. If so, when can the scientist intervene and assert that in a given moment in time the interaction is

2

frozen, so that the independent effects directly attributable to roles or to personality can be assessed? To handle questions like these, we have to clarify what we mean by each term and how we would differentiate one from the other when they interact.

THE CONCEPT OF ROLE

To help us establish the boundaries between a personality system and a social role, we will adopt a fairly specialized view of what a role is. There has been great diversity in the definition of the much-used concept of "role." Biddle and Thomas' (1966) recent survey of the variety of uses of the term is an overwhelming catalogue for the social scientist. In a recent review of the role construct as it relates to personality variables, Thomas concludes that there may be one major common definition: "If there is a common definition, it is that role is the set of prescriptions defining what the behavior of the position member should be" (Thomas, 1966, p. 4). This is only a minimal definition, however.

We define a *role* as a *set of expectations that has an objective concrete reality and that impinges on individuals because they hold a given social position*. We define a *position* as a *location of a person or a set of persons in a network of social relationships*. Roles, conceived of as sets of expectations, can include more than prescriptions; roles can entail expectations about rewards and punishments, expectations about potential gratifications and frustrations in social positions, as well as expectations about prescribed and proscribed behaviors.

Some role theorists would take exception to our view that roles are social *realities*, and assert that the more useful way of looking at roles would be to investigate role *perceptions*. These role theorists would assert that the scientist should examine each person's subjective appraisal about a role to know how a role operates to determine his behavior. From the start we rejected this phenomenological emphasis.

We assumed that it was meaningful to talk about the demands of parenthood, the possible gratifications of marriage, the definitions of work, as shared conceptions that exist for a fairly large group of subjects. Like Mead (1934), we would contend that roles are the articulations of the social system, organized for successful maintenance of common interests. Like Parsons and White (1961), we would contend that dramatic changes in the character structure of a group in our society are often preceded by new kinds of demands that come from changing roles. With mushrooming industrialization and the steady decline of agriculture in our social system, a new proliferation of technical occupational roles has emerged. Adequate performance in these new jobs has required an upgrading and specialization of competences. The modern American family has adapted its functioning to meet its responsibility to socialize children in ways that prepare them for these changing demands in occupational roles. Parsons and White

3

noted that the apparent independence that American adolescents show with respect to their parents, accompanied by their flexible orientation to their peer culture, may have resulted from a needed preparation for such occupational changes.

We did not equate role characteristics with individual *perceptions* of these characteristics. The latter are more subjective, more determined by the personal characteristics of each individual. We recognize that role perceptions do influence behavior, but that is another problem to investigate. We adopted the position that a role is a *common, objective* set of stimuli that elicits the behavior of *all* persons in a given social position, and that this set of stimuli remains relatively constant over short periods of time. People can perceptually distort roles, but we assumed that, in some form or other, identical stimuli impinge upon each role occupant's informational system. At any moment in time we can freeze this social reality and ask how all role occupants react to it.

In this research study we selected three aspects of roles to examine in interaction with the personality of role occupants. These characteristics are: role demands, role gratifications, and role ambiguity. Let us examine each in turn.

Role demands   The common, shared expectations about the behavior *required* of persons in a certain position is what we mean by role demands. For most sociologists, the role concept alone is used to connote demands (see Catton, 1964). We would like to view role requirements as only one aspect of the expectations that define a role. Demands are obligations, and obligations are usually assumed to be the burdens of the social contract permitting people to meet their needs while at the same time receiving societal approval. Men have to earn money in our society to fulfill marital obligations. Women have to take care of young children in our society to fulfill parental obligations. Men have to perform certain duties on the job in order to fulfill their job requirements. Seeing role demands as burdens represents a social philosophy heavily steeped in the moral traditions of religious doctrines according to which man is born capricious and must be tamed for social living. Role demands are often seen as socializing tools of the society.

Role demands are conceptualized as prescriptions that often interfere with personal goals. In a highly provocative analysis of business organizations, Argyris (1962) traces the effects that business organizations have on their members, and vice versa. In his view, the principles on which an organization is founded are antithetical to the needs of a person within it. A person's needs are basically self-actualizing ones, according to Argyris, and so men seek meaning and dignity from their labors through "authentic" experiences with the social world. To find outlets for these needs is a goal that Argyris finds incompatible with a "rational model" of effec-

4

tive organizations. Business organizations set up according to this rational model are established with the assumptions that job specialization is a functional necessity and that clearly defined chains of responsibility should be operating at all times. Under these conditions, a man's self-actualizing tendencies are severely limited, because the organization demands behaviors from the individual that are not gratifying. It is in this sense that Argyris' ideas about "rational" organizations come close to our ideas about the burdensome characteristics of role demands.

A further distinction can be made between *essential* and *secondary* role demands. An essential role demand is an obligation that must be met. This type of role demand has sometimes been called a role prescription. A person could lose the prerogatives of being in a given position if he fails to meet essential role demands. Women must provide for the physical health of their children in our society or face the possibility of being declared unfit mothers. Alice Rossi (1967) has recently noted that American women generally "go it alone," without much help from the extended family or their husbands. Many other societies provide such assistance. Rossi contends that meeting their essential role demands under these conditions might thus be very psychologically debilitating for American women.

Men must be at work for prescribed times in order to retain most jobs in our society. But beyond such minimal time requirements, there are other essential role demands for each job. Hughes (1958) has discussed some peculiar "mandates" that certain professions have, often dangerous mandates, or ones requiring awesome decisions. Doctors are entrusted with ethical mandates in decisions about maintaining the life of their patients; lawyers are bound by "the law." Hughes suggests that to carry out such mandates certain professions are given license to do things that others are not privileged to do. Doctors and lawyers hear personal details of their clients' lives that under ordinary circumstances would be kept private. The acquisition of such "guilty knowledge" would be impossible if it were not part of a clear and essential role requirement for doctors and lawyers.

Secondary role demands permit more flexibility in role performance; sometimes they are called role expectations. Usually it is more difficult to evaluate whether a person has fulfilled a secondary role demand than it is to evaluate whether he has fulfilled an essential role demand. Misconduct with regard to a secondary demand does not necessarily imply that the role occupant is a severe failure. Although affectionate behavior is seen to be an important role demand for a woman in relationship to both her children and her husband, occasional outbursts of anger are not entirely destructive of favorable role evaluation. Indeed, sometimes misconduct vis à vis essential role obligations can be incorporated as an elaboration of a role demand, as a way of siphoning off pressures that may exist for meeting burdensome requirements of the role. In our present society many enlightened women

5

believe that it is almost necessary to get away from their children on occasion in order to permit them to be successful mothers, although emotional contact with the children is an essential role obligation.

Role gratifications Although men commonly acknowledge that there are rights or privileges included in certain roles, they usually ignore the fact that the social behaviors entailed in meeting role demands do not consist only of burdens. Some obligations attendant to filling a role also offer direct possibilities for certain gratifications. In addition to tedium and toil, work offers a possibility for developing one's creative powers, for having commerce with the world, for feeling a part of an environment. A stress on the burdens attendant to role performance in marriage and parenthood, for example, ignores the fact that the roles of husband or wife and mother or father allow people to satisfy certain interpersonal wishes and physical needs that perhaps can be satisfied in no other way.

Thus, we conceive of roles as offering people certain satisfactions as well as obligations. Part of the stimuli defined by roles, then, can be thought of as incentives—both negative incentives such as nongratifying role obligations, and positive incentives, which we will call *role gratifications*.

Two sources of role gratifications should be considered—*attaining the position* and *enacting the role*. Attaining certain positions brings prestige. Becoming a lawyer, getting married, bearing a child are attainments that mark a person's arrival into important social positions. Sociologists have pointed out the status, prestige, or the attendant satisfactions that stem from having clear privileges in certain positions. The medical profession in American society has a respect accorded it that can gratify doctors' power needs. There are more subtle examples. Being married permits men and women access to certain privileges. Bachelors often complain about the presumptuous attitudes that their married friends have about the unmarried man's social activities. In our society, being married means that others usually act respectfully with regard to the couple's social calendar, while being single means that others may be casual about the person's social schedule. A bachelor can be asked to a party at the last minute more easily than can a couple.

The roles that accrue from entering into positions often imply a commitment to new kinds of social collectivities. If we assume that men have a basic need for collective experience, as Bion (1961) does, then the mere acquisition of new social roles can be gratifying in and of itself. Being in a new social group extends a person's social network. Long ago Simmel (1955) described the new kind of personality integration that occurs when men extend their "web of affiliation." It enables a person to feel more of a participant in society, independent of the special quality of that participation. A woman who becomes a mother has a strong sense of participation in a traditional social role even if she finds the particular demands in the role distasteful.

Over and above the gratifications from role acquisition is the set of gratifications that comes from performing the role. There may be a honeymoon period in most roles that has its special sets of gratifications (see Rapaport and Rapaport, 1964). But we are thinking primarily of the gratifications after the honeymoon period, or what Rossi (1967) calls the plateau period of a role, the gratifications that accrue from performing the day-to-day functions of a role, before a person becomes disengaged from it. A parent obtains affection from a child, an employer secures subservience from an employee, a wife elicits sexual interest from her husband. These kinds of gratifications will be the major focus of our inquiry about role gratification.

Role ambiguity Two kinds of role ambiguity are important in our consideration of role characteristics in interaction with motives. These can be defined in terms of the two other characteristics of roles that we have described, namely role demands and role gratifications.

There may be ambiguity with regard to what the role demands are. This ambiguity can emerge in a number of ways. First, there may be lack of consensus *among* the relevant reference groups about the role demands, although within each group there may be clarity about the demands. Gross, Mason, and McEachern (1958) have explored the conflicting sanctions and obligations that exist for the school superintendent. This is a good example of the kind of ambiguity we are talking about. The school superintendent feels pressures from the school board that are different from what he himself thinks is required. This ambiguity is especially marked if there is little consensus among the school board members.

Secondly, ambiguity may exist because the role demands are themselves diffusely characterized by many or all the relevant reference groups. The current demands for the proper child-rearing practices are ambiguous in this way. Rossi (1967) has noted that among the avant-garde families in particular, there is a growing awareness that the effects of any particular child-rearing technique are unknown. There is no one scientific authority to turn to for advice. There are as many sets of advice as there are conflicting views on child development. This puts a particular burden on this mother to resolve the ambiguity in her actual role behavior.

Bott (1957) has also mentioned this type of ambiguity about role demands, this time with respect to the marital role. She studied the differences in the conjugal relationship found in urban English men and women who lived in "highly connected" social networks, where there is considerable overlap between family life, acquaintanceships, and work relationships, as opposed to the conjugal relationship found among those from "dispersed" networks, where there was little overlap in these reference groups. What she found was a rigid division of labor for the couples who lived in a highly connected network. This was not so for the couples in a dispersed network; they tended to develop mutual participations in activities and decision-making. In the present context, we would say that there was little ambiguity in the role demands for couples from the highly connected social world; there was no conflict, no need to be diffuse. For persons in the dispersed type of network, there was little communication between their disparate reference groups. There may have been some very clear norms within these different reference groups, but, more than likely, these heterogeneous groups did not have uniform norms. Exposure to diverse role demands concerning the marital relationship probably prevents these couples from adopting crystallized role behaviors. A couple from this kind of network encounters many different types of marriages. Which is the "right one"? Such ambiguity can lead to severe questioning of one's role and it may be upon this questioning that a more mutual marital relation can be founded. It is interesting to note that Bott reports that couples from dispersed networks, when asked to describe the ideal marital relationship, tended to project their own personal solution to this problem, rather than using any general notions.

Thirdly, a role demand may be ambiguous because the same reference group has conflicting obligations for the role occupant to fulfill. For example, if expected to be both assertive with his underlings in some situations and supportive to them in others, a business executive has conflicts that induce this type of ambiguity. A teacher is expected to both nourish the creative potential of a student and at the same time be available as an authority. In what situation shall he take a "hands off—let the child learn by his own failure" policy? In what situations should he direct the student?

A related form of role conflict is "role overload," a term that Kahn and his colleagues (1964) used in their investigations of organizational stresses on individuals. Although a person may be requested to perform behaviors that are compatible with one another, there may simply be limitations to a person's time and attention. A "good" housewife may have to attend to keeping a neat house, fostering creativity in her children, gardening, being a gourmet cook, and participating in social affairs in the community. She often has to choose which one of these she has time to do. Thus, these demands create their own ambiguities for her; the hierarchy of demands may shift from day to day. She experiences role overload.

Ambiguity with regard to role gratification potential may either be independent of, or dependent on, ambiguity in the role demands. It is apparent that if there are conflicting sets of expectations about role obligations, or if the expectations about role obligations are diffuse, the expectations about the kinds of gratifications available in the attainment or maintenance of the role would also be ambiguous. Take the boss who is supposed to be assertive and demanding in some situations, but supportive and warm in others. Does his job allow for gratification of assertive wishes? Nurturant wishes? Even in instances where the kinds of behaviors required

latter, power motivation. In addition, social psychologists also make a distinction between task and emotional aspects of social behavior. Parsons and Bales (1955) distinguish the instrumental and expressive components of family roles. The instrumental component summarizes the nonemotional tasks a family faces—getting things done in the home or meeting the demands from the outside. Financial support of the family would be a prime example of an instrumental demand in the family role. The expressive component summarizes the directly emotional features of family life—maintaining love and support, regulating tensions. In 46 out of 56 societies that Parsons and Bales examined, the instrumental component was delegated to the husband-father role, the expressive component to the wife-mother role. In effect, this distinction recognized the importance of achievement orientations (instrumental), along with the affiliative and power orientations (expressive), in accounting for social phenomena.

In attempting to link personality accommodations to roles, sociologists have characterized roles in more complicated terms than merely whether they are "instrumental" or "expressive." Parsons and Bales also attend to the specificity of the role demand, and make it a major dimension for characterizing roles—how "universal" (or general), or how "particularistic" (or specific) a role demand is. Jobs are particularly easy to think of along this dimension. A scientist has more generalized demands in a search for knowledge; hence his job is more universalistic. A dentist's job is very circumscribed; hence his job places more particularistic demands upon him.

Family roles can also be characterized along the universalistic-particularistic dimension. A father who is asked to socialize his child to the general social norms has a more universalistic role demand than the mother who is asked to regulate the child's behavior within the specific family. By and large, the more universalistic roles will be less personal and more likely to engage the achievement and power motives; the more particularistic roles will require more intimate personal associations, and will be more likely to engage the affiliation motive.

There have been other role categorizations that have implications for personality functioning. Some of the most interesting of these are the ones that Hess and Handel (1959) have enumerated in their discussion of the family as a psychosocial organization. They propose that there are five essential role characteristics to consider in the family, each of which would have implications for the engagement of certain aspects of personality: (1) a family is organized around themes which can be the foundation of general values (religion, achievement); (2) a family gives its members an orientation to their outside experiences; (3) a family demands a certain level of separation and cohesion between each of the family members; (4) a family demands some congruence of family images among the family members, some perceptual unity; (5) the family sets up clear alignments of power—coalitions and antagonisms. Clearly, the first and second characteristics can affect the achievement orientation expected from a family member, and the third, fourth, and fifth can affect the expression of the affiliation and power motives of family members. These characteristics, however, would affect a variety of other motives as well. With affiliation, achievement, and power motivation, we are sampling the domains of personality that have been highlighted by both psychologists and sociologists in their attempts to simplify our comprehensions of social behavior.

TWO GUIDING PRINCIPLES ABOUT THE INTERACTION OF MOTIVES AND ROLES IN THE RESEARCH STUDY

Two major principles guided this exploratory research relating dimensions of role stimuli to the motives of men and women performing various roles. These principles provided the general theoretical framework we used in examining the data. The sensitization principle refers to how role occupants may handle role stimuli that are either ambiguous or are in conflict with their personal motivation. The congruence principle concerns an individual's reactions to a role that is compatible or incompatible with a given motive.

The sensitization principle   When there is ambiguity about goal attainment in roles, individual dispositional characteristics like motives can become effective determinants of expectancies in the situation. We would assume that the more motivated a person is with respect to certain incentives, the more disposed he is to expect these incentives in *any* situation he faces. The general sensitization principle then is: *in motivationally ambiguous roles, the strength of a man's motives will affect the quality of the demands, frustrations and gratifications that he perceives in these roles.* When the role is clear and explicit with regard to the possibilities of motive gratification or the kind of incentive available in role enactment, then the effect of motive dispositions on perceptions of the role is not easily predictable. If there is some ambiguity in role gratification in the sense that a number of different motive-incentive systems are clearly gratifiable by role enactment then a strong motive can sensitize an individual to that incentive possibility in the role. When the role requirements are explicit, there can be distortions that enhance the congruence with the motive strength, but the direction of the distortions may not be directly predictable from knowledge of the strength of the motive alone. If the motive is important to a person and he finds gratification for the motive in the role, he may exaggerate this aspect of the role. However, if the motive is important to an individual but he is not gratifying this motive, he may very well minimize the significance of this aspect of the role.

We are well aware that role demands or gratifications can sometimes elicit unconscious reactions in men and women. Being an assertive husband or a disciplinarian to one's children can make a man anxious. For example, these feelings can interact with the strength of his power motivation to induce him to minimize his influence potential as husband or father. In a similar manner, we will anticipate that each of the roles—but, in particular, marriage and parenthood—will stimulate unconscious reactions that will condition the specific way the sensitization principle will be evident.

The sensitization principle rests on the assumption that motives sensitize people's perceptions and help them *interpret* qualities about the roles to which they must respond. Thus, the sensitization principle deals with the interaction of motives and perception. We will use it to predict the relationship of motive to role perceptions. There is considerable evidence to support this general principle: Klein's work (1954) on motivational styles and perceptual distortion; Newcomb's studies (1961) of how college students' perceptions of each other help to maintain balanced interaction; Atkinson and McClelland's study (1948) showing that under ambiguous situations those objects instrumental to food attainment are perceived more often by hungry than by satiated subjects. Evidence for it also comes from work on the particular motives used in this study. McClelland and Liberman (1948) reported that among those subjects high in measured achievement motive compared to those low in achievement motive, there was a greater recognition of mastery words under ambiguous levels of tachistoscopic presentation. Byrne (1961b) showed that there was a greater perception of similarity between oneself and other persons for subjects with high affiliation motive than for those with low affiliation motive. Subjects who are high in the affiliation motive are also especially sensitive to perceiving human faces as compared to nonhuman stimuli (Atkinson and Walker, 1956). Browning (1961) showed that high power-motivated politicians are especially quick to recognize the influence gratification from political activity. There are other relevant results, but these serve to illustrate for the present the kinds of evidence relevant for the sensitization principle based on the motive measures to be employed in this book. A sensitization principle also has been used by Weinstein and Deutschberger (1963) to describe individual effects on role phenomena, but in a slightly different form. They have talked about a process called *altercasting* or "projecting an identity, to be assumed by other(s) with whom one is in interaction, which is congruent with one's own goals." The self-reflexive altercasting process is in miniature the kind of process suggested by the sensitization principle.

The congruence principle   The other major principle that has guided our work is: *to the extent there is congruence between the strength of a motive and the possibilities for the motive to be gratified in the role, there will be satisfaction and ease in role performance, and to the extent there is poor meshing, there will be problems in the way individuals react to the role.* The plug-socket analogy is not inappropriate: where the plug does not fit, there will be a short circuit. We will be looking for such smooth flows of current and short circuits. This is only a crude analogy, but it is one that communicates the sense of the principle. While we will be examining the effects of motives on role perception in the sensitization principle, we will be examining the effects of motives on *role performance, role choices,* and *feelings* about the role, in the congruence principle.

The job role has been the focus of most of the research and speculative thinking about the congruence principle. One of the central ideas in Getzels and Guba's (1957) broad theoretical approach to administration concerns the effects of congruence or disparity between behavior required by the social system and the need dispositions of the individual role performer. The congruence principle is similar to one that has been used in the work setting (Brophy, 1957; Vroom, 1959; Williams, 1961) in exploring the consequences of personality characteristics and role requirements for both satisfaction and efficiency in work. Wilensky (1956) implicitly uses a congruence principle in discussing the behavior of intellectuals in the labor union.

While the congruence principle has been stated above in terms of the effects upon behavior *within a given role situation,* a direct corollary is relevant to the *choice behavior* that leads an individual to select or attain a given position, or to stay in it. Men and women should seek out positions that are congruent with their motive dispositions, and should select themselves out of positions that are incongruent with their personality. In examining predictions of vocational choice from personality characteristics, researchers such as Roe (1956) and Thorndike (1949) have implicitly used the assumption that people will choose jobs that fit their personality. Such a view also underlies Nachman (1960), Segal (1961), and Bordin and Beale's (1964) work investigating the personality determinations of such occupational choices as dentistry, social work, engineering, law, or business. The choices of these occupations are assumed to represent choices congruent with ongoing pregenital personality needs. For example, there is some evidence that oral sadism can be involved in choosing dentistry as a career.

Experimental studies can serve as a possible analogy to the kinds of instrumental behavior assumed to occur when predicting vocational choice from knowledge of the personal needs of the subject. For example, Hare and Bales (1963) performed an interesting experiment demonstrating that college students with high status needs will select central seats in the arrangements of a discussion group.

Evidence for the congruence principle in job selection can also be found among employers who successfully select their employees through the implicit use of such a congruence principle. Argyris (1954) has shown how bank executives use very select criteria in determining who will be chosen as bank tellers. Generally speaking, the persons selected exhibit personality characteristics that mesh well with the kinds of activities that are required.

The evidence for self-selection out from incompatible positions is less numerous than that for selection in. Ross and Zander (1957) showed that need satisfaction was related to job turnover in one large utility company. Women who resigned received less gratification of their needs for recognition, achievement, and autonomy than a matched group who remained at their jobs.

One study that has come to our attention attempted to consider selection of appropriate marital roles that are congruent with one's personality. Backman and Secord (1965) reported a study of the expressed preference of women for one of three types of marital roles—wife and mother, companion, or partner. Their prediction was that choices would be toward congruence between the role and self-concept. Self-ratings on a set of adjectives were made by the women, and each of the roles was rated on the same adjectives by independent judges. Their findings generally supported a congruence principle for marital role selection.

In spite of the positive findings used above, we would conclude that it is especially difficult to find evidence for the congruence principle in research about the interpersonal roles of marriage or parenthood. A major reason for this condition is that it is difficult to specify clearly what congruence entails in these roles.

This difficulty stems from a number of sources. In studies of motive-job role congruence, the specific requirements of the job role under study can fairly readily be delimited on the basis of the occupational category under study or of the particular industrial organization in which the role is found. Although we do assume that there are certain broad categories of role demands and role gratifications that are common for all American marriages, and for all American parents, there are also variations within these broad roles delimited by the role occupant's social class, religion, education, and generation. Full descriptions of the role requirements would have to take these variations into account.

In addition, the sphere of behavior covered by the marital and parental roles is much broader than for most job roles. Therefore, the marital and parental role demands may be more complex, both with regard to the time and space limitations under which they occur and with respect to the kinds of behavior covered by the role demands. The broad scope of the role demands for these primary social roles gives them a diffuseness that makes it difficult to determine what motivational characteristics of individuals would or would not be congruent with them.

Another reason for the lack of research on the congruence principle in marital and parental roles is probably that more personalistic definitions of the demands for gratification can exist in marriage and parenthood. Perhaps it is within the social system that evolves in a *single* family that the scientist most appropriately looks for indications of personality-role congruence. Much of the thinking and research on marriage, in particular, has been concerned with the meshing of two personalities. Winch (1958) has noted that complementary traits can account for marital choice and stability. Bermann (1964) has used a similar idea in considering the stability of friendship. But for these researchers the implicit congruence hypothesis in their work implies personalistic meshing that is considered quite individually rather than the meshing of a personality with a socially defined role. The strong value that twentieth century Americans place on "psychological" aspects of living implies that in their interpersonal behavior men and women should seek *individualized* expression. Role expectations about marriage and parenthood have become more ambiguous. Men and women are expected to *adapt to each other*. Marriages are sometimes said to be satisfying and appropriate even if traditional roles are reversed, if the man is submissive and the woman dominant, as long as each fulfills the other's special needs. Nevertheless, it also seems reasonable to assume that there are shared expectations about the good wife, husband, mother, or father, for all marriages in a given social strata (Duvall, 1946; Elder, 1949; Stendler, 1950). Our efforts to apply the congruence principle to the marital and parental roles will be based on this assumption.

A congruence principle has also been implicit in some research on one of the motives of our study—the achievement motive—but within a very different kind of role, the student role. O'Connor, Atkinson, and Horner (1966) worked from the assumption that persons strongly motivated for achievement prefer situations of intermediate probabilities of success. They found that there was high satisfaction with school among elementary-school children with high achievement motives who were in classes based on homogeneous ability grouping. The challenge of this classroom, where the student role involved competing with others of similar ability, was viewed as compatible to the requirements for satisfaction of achievement goals. The children with high achievement motive in a heterogeneously grouped classroom, where the student role presumably involved less evenly matched competition, were less satisfied with school.

Thomas' (1966) examination of the experimental literature on personality-role incongruence led him to conclude that "the presumed adverse effects of person-role incongruence on member satisfaction and productivity have not been demonstrated." The four studies he cited evidenced only partial support for a congruence principle.

Borgatta (1961) found that the personality characteristic of assertiveness appears to facilitate a variety of demanded role-playing behaviors. In that experiment, subjects who were rated high in the personality syndrome of assertiveness, on the basis of past group performance, were more likely to perform well in both nonassertive and assertive roles. Furthermore, satisfaction in playing the roles was not related to congruence.

The Moos and Speisman (1962) experiment concerned a similar personality trait, dominance-submission. While not all the results were significantly supportive of the congruence principle in all six bases for comparison, role performance was better where there was a compatibility of subjects with the roles that they were selected to perform than where there was incompatibility.

Smelser (1961) found that dominant subjects, irrespective of whether or not they were assigned to dominant or submissive roles, tended to perform more effectively than submissive subjects. This result is in keeping with those of Borgotta. Smelser also found no adverse effects of incongruence of personality-role meshing on performance. What may be important to note about this study is that repeated performance led to improvement in role performance, so that the difference in effectiveness initially associated with personality characteristics of the subjects was no longer evident. In this case practice seemed to produce greater role efficiency. This result suggests that in some roles, even if there is initial incompatibility with personality, role performance may still become effective after practice.

In the Trow (1957) experiment, a limited congruence effect was found. Individuals high in need for autonomy were lowest in job satisfaction about a task when placed in a dependent position, whereas they were high in satisfaction when they were placed in an autonomous position. But for those who were low in autonomy, no differences in satisfaction were found when they were assigned to autonomous or dependent experimental treatments. Thus, there is evidence in the Trow experiment for the congruence principle, but only for certain people.

These studies certainly did not yield wholehearted support for the congruence principle with experimental data. But perhaps the laboratory is not a good setting in which to test the congruence principle. Perhaps in the more naturalistic observations of the survey setting, the congruence principle may prove more fruitful. Why should this be so? Why should the congruence principle be more useful in observing everyday behavior than in the laboratory? First, experimental studies emphasize the performance rather than affective aspects of role behavior. Even when affective reactions are solicited, the relative unimportance of the situation to the subjects should limit its affective consequences. In our data we will be dealing primarily with affective reactions to major life roles. Second, experimental studies require role performances that are highly constrained by the laboratory setting. In our data, we will be dealing with ambiguous requirements for adequate performances in roles. Perhaps this should permit personality characteristics to manifest their effect upon performance. Third, the short-term nature of experimental settings often leads to the use of performance requirements in which there can be a clear demonstration of improved performance, with only small amounts of practice. In our data we will be dealing with long-term expectations about performances that require considerable practice for improvement. Personality factors are more likely to affect increased performance in complex social role learning than in more simple circumscribed tasks of the laboratory. For all these reasons, we were not dismayed by the negative evidence about the congruence principle from experimental settings and were still optimistic about its usefulness in the present study. Because of the experimental findings, however, our optimism was somewhat tempered.

In applying the congruence principle to the job, parental, and marital roles, we will occasionally widen our perspective beyond the congruence of the three motives to the role demands, role gratifications, and role ambiguity of each role. Particularly, we will consider the idea that performing certain role demands and obtaining certain role gratifications within one role can have an effect upon meeting demands and obtaining gratifications in another role.

One role can compensate for another, and thereby affect the resulting congruence or lack of congruence. For example, compensation effects might be noted in a man's marital role reactions if incongruence prevents motivational satisfaction in work. A man with a high power motive who has a job that prevents satisfaction of this goal might place greater importance on the potential power satisfactions in marriage, thus investing himself more in marriage than he might have otherwise.

Roles can also conflict with one another, and thereby affect the resulting congruence or incongruence. For example, the role requirements of a job with high achievement gratification potential that demands hard work, long hours, and ego involvement, may conflict with a man's role requirements for companionate involvement with his wife and children. Thus, the demands of the marital role could be incongruent for a man with strong achievement motivation.

We are also aware that types of person-role incongruence other than the lack of meshing of motives and roles are important; a lack of meshing of skills, values, identities, and other personality characteristics may occur in relationship to roles. We will not be dealing with this type of incongruence systematically, but on occasion we will recognize its importance.

18

Again we will be aware that important unconscious reactions are often attached to certain role demands, especially in marriage and parenthood. In addition, to the extent that certain values, skills, or identities are related to the motives that we have measured, we will, by implication, employ these in considering the motive-role congruence hypothesis.

We recognize, too, that by their sanctions, roles *socialize* adults. There may thus be the possibility for personality change within a role. Etzioni (1964) has been an advocate of the proposition that the social role re-socializes the personality of the people performing that role. A man's personality characteristics perhaps can change while he is in a job that provides rewards or punishments for certain behaviors. In the course of marriage men and women shift their personal characteristics in directions that can aid in maintaining a stable relationship. Kelly (1955) has noted how changes in personality can occur in marital partners over a number of years. We would assume that these changes are in the direction of role congruence, permitting husbands and wives to mesh better with each other and with their roles. Caplow (1964) has identified socialization into industrial organizations. A new incumbent in an organization can learn to mesh with his role in a variety of ways: he may be required to change his behavior, he may change his self-image, he experiences new networks of individuals to interact with, he acquires new values, and accomplishes new things, all of which imply potential changes in personality structure.

Although we recognize that personality may change as adults are socialized, we will hold firmly to a view that such change is negligible. We agree with Brim (1966) that most adult socialization concerns changes in overt behavior in the role rather than changes in basic motivation. Linton (1945) and H. Becker (1964) have indicated that adults learn ways of resolving conflicts that avoid direct clashes between varying role demands or between personal needs and role demands. Therefore, rather than looking for changes in personality that facilitate coordination with roles, we will be assuming little in the way of personality change during adulthood. We assume that people enter positions with certain personality characteristics and that these remain relatively intact during the period of role occupancy. We will be looking for differential effects of roles on different personality types. A father with high power motivation perhaps can find gratification from influencing children when they are young, but then finds himself unprepared to cope with his influence position as his children grow older. He may then find his children have minds of their own and that this relationship no longer satisfies his power motive. We will generally assume that his power motive does not abate with the role change. However, we will be aware that such discontinuities and developmental changes in roles may play havoc with our assumption.

THE THREE MOTIVES:
AFFILIATION, ACHIEVEMENT, AND POWER

It is possible to specify with some precision what is meant by the affiliation motive, the achievement motive, and the power motive in light of the accumulation of research findings on these motives. We will briefly summarize each set of results.

THE AFFILIATION MOTIVE

The affiliation motive is the disposition to strive to establish, maintain, and restore positive affective relationships with other people (Shipley and Veroff, 1952). Not as much work has gone into its characteristics as with the achievement motive, and so let us examine the results that have been accumulated over the last decade in greater detail than we will for achievement motivation.

Separation from others is anxiety-provoking for persons who are strongly motivated to affiliate (Shipley and Veroff, 1952). Some research has shown that college students view their peers with strong affiliation motives as being approval-seeking (Atkinson, Heyns, and Veroff, 1954). Both of these results suggest that people with high affiliation motive are attracted to interpersonal relationships as a dominant force in their lives. In studies of Air Force personnel, French (1956) has shown that persons who are high in the motive to affiliate, but weak in the achievement motive would prefer an unsuccessful friend to a successful stranger as a work partner in solving a complex problem. On the other hand, the successful stranger is preferred to the unsuccessful friend as a work partner by people who are highly motivated to achieve but weak in affiliation motivation. Sundheim (1963) found that college women majoring in elementary education had higher affiliation motivation scores than science majors; science majors were strongly motivated for achievement. Lansing and Heyns (1959) found that strength of the affiliation motive was correlated with making and receiving local telephone calls and writing letters to friends and relatives.

The kinds of instrumental activities that may lead to affiliative goals are diverse. Experiments have shown that effortful performance sometimes was a consequence of a strong affiliation motive, particularly when working hard was clearly perceived as instrumental to friendly acceptance by another person (Atkinsona nd O'Connor, 1966; Atkinson and Raphelson, 1956; Atkinson and Reitman, 1958).

At this stage of knowledge about the affiliation motive, it is hard to estimate whether or not a person high in this motive is likely to be successful in his attempts to affiliate with others. Whether stronger affiliation motive implies behavioral characteristics conducive to establishing affiliative gratification is still an open question. The data available so far mainly indicate that strong affiliation concerns may produce approval-seeking behaviors which can hinder rather than enhance the possibility of acceptance by others (Atkinson, Heyns, and Veroff, 1954; Groesbeck, 1958; Shipley and Veroff, 1952). However, in one study, women with high affiliation motivation were described more positively by their sorority sisters (Vogel, 1954) and in another study (Fishman, 1966), women with high affiliation motivation were more friendly if they also had positive anticipations of acceptance. Fishman's study showed the importance of knowing the person's optimism about acceptance before making clear behavioral predictions in the social setting.

It is also not clear whether high scores on the measure of affiliation motive reflect approach motivation as opposed to two important negative aspects of affiliation: avoidance of isolation and fear of rejection. Byrne, McDonald, and Mikawa (1963) have evidence suggesting that very high affiliation motive scores represent approach motivation, moderate affiliation scores represent conflict between approach and avoidance tendencies, and low scores imply true low affiliation motivation. The relative weight given in the measuring instrument to the approach for affiliation or avoidance-of-rejection poles of the general affiliation motive is an important question to consider. Answers to this question would affect predictions about how people with high or low affiliation motives perceive certain events and react to different roles. Some overt behaviors may be seen as instrumental for either the approach or the avoidance pole of the motive, but other behaviors may be affected differently by the approach or avoidance types of affiliation motivation. For example, Rosenfeld and Franklin (1966) recently suggested that following a severe rejection experience, students produced fantasy responses that appeared to reflect approach affiliation. But on closer examination, some fantasy peculiar to avoidance motivation was evident in their stories. They interpret this as consistent with the view that activities directed toward obtaining positive affective relationships accompany both the approach (hope of acceptance) and avoidance (fear of rejection) components of affiliation motivation, although the two can otherwise be distinguished.

The development of both positive and negative poles of this affiliation disposition may in large part be determined by the quality of early conditions of social deprivation. It generally has been assumed in the research on the affiliation motive that the high measured affiliation motive is associated with the early experience of strong positive social contacts that keep the individual actively engaged in striving for affiliation.

Besides the two major components of the affiliation motive already mentioned—positive affiliation and fear of isolation or fear of rejection—

21

another important component might be a fear of intimacy—a fear of affiliation because of other negative consequences of affiliation. One way to avoid intimacy is to maintain a number of *different* affiliative contacts, to engage in extensive affectionate contacts rather than intensive friendships or love relationships. The overt behaviors of individuals motivated by fear of intimacy and positive affiliation might be characteristically different. But thus far the research on the affiliation motive measure has not produced any way to distinguish between extensive versus intensive interests in affiliation contacts, or between intimate and casual affiliative relationships. Results relating affiliation motivation to conformity suggest that individuals with high affiliation motivation are more affected by pressure from friends than they are by general social pressures. These results suggest that the usual measure of affiliation motive assesses the motivation for intimate, intensive relationships rather than the motivation for extensive social relationships. We will be alert to the distinction between these types of affiliative goals in our characterization of role relationships, some of which demand an intimate contact with another person, even though our measuring device may be insensitive to the distinction.

THE ACHIEVEMENT MOTIVE

Much work has gone into the delineation of the achievement motive (Atkinson, 1958b; Atkinson and Feather, 1966; McClelland, 1961; McClelland, Atkinson, Clark, and Lowell, 1953). Since these researches have been summarized a number of times, the description of this motive can be brief. The achievement motive is conceived of as a disposition to strive for the sense of pride in accomplishment that accompanies favorable evaluation of performance on a difficult task (McClelland, Clark, Roby, and Atkinson, 1949). This disposition promotes interest in activities that demand successful exercise of ability and a preference for setting intermediate or realistic goals, rather than aspirations that are too high to attain or aspirations that are so easy that they guarantee success. The achievement motive produces effort and persistence in achievement activities when the individual is faced with obstacles and when the goal of the activity is clearly a sense of personal accomplishment. For a person seeking achievement gratification, his own effort is required, but he can accept help if it is the only route toward accomplishment (Koenig, 1963). Achievement motive has been found to affect sensitivity to perceiving achievement-related words (McClelland and Liberman, 1948). It also affects behavior outside of the academic setting usually examined in relationship to achievement motivation—entrepreneurial activity (McClelland, 1961), volunteering (Burdick, 1956), withstanding conformity pressures (McClelland et al., 1953). It has *not* been found to relate systematically to social performances, however.

THE POWER MOTIVE

The body of experimental data is much sparser for the power motive than for the other two motives being investigated. The power motive presumably reflects a disposition to strive for control of the means of influencing another person or a group of persons (Veroff, 1958). Earlier studies have shown that college students who are highly motivated for power are more argumentative and more frequently try to get their opinions across to other group members than do individuals who are weak in the power motive (Veroff, 1957).

As with affiliation motivation, there is no clear-cut empirical evidence to answer the question of whether a high power motive enhances or hinders a person's chances of attaining a position of influence. One study (Veroff, 1956) has shown that in a two-person group, a person with high power motivation is more likely to influence a joint decision than a person with low power motivation. Another study (Lindman, 1958) has shown that power-oriented, high-school boys indicated a preference for occupations that were either very high or very low in power potential more frequently than high-school boys who were low in power motive. This result suggests that some persons who are high in the power need might prefer a situation where the potential for power is minimal. Indeed, the power motive may enhance successful performance only when the rules for attaining power and status are ambiguous. Skolnick (1966) has found that high power motivation is associated with assertiveness, prestige, and popularity among adolescent boys. Could the reason for this positive association between power motivation and being influential, in adolescent boys, be related to the fact that the rules for power and status are ambiguous for them? The dominance-dependence theme in adolescence has not yet crystallized as a basic dimension for overt evaluation of oneself. Clearly, issues of dominance and dependence are important to adolescents, but it is not until late adolescence, that they become fully aware of what these issues are, and how they should be reflected in their overt social goals. The callowness of youth often refers to the fact that the bases for esteem at adolescence are often shifting and superficial.

To corroborate this sort of thinking in another setting, let us cite a study of the job role. Andrews (1967) has found that high power motivation is associated with lack of success in a business organization if job advancement in that organization is clearly determined by autonomous achievement. In a business where job advancement is based on a vague general conformity to the organization, rather than on specific individual accomplishment, then high power motivation is predictive of *success* in that organization. Again we would assert that if the social system has more ambiguous rules for social relations, then high power motivation may predict successful influence behavior, but if the social system is clearly focused on the rules of successful role performance, then high power motivation may predict unsuccessful influence.

One result by Joanne Veroff (1959) suggests that the types of behaviors that may be linked to the power motive may not appear to be influence attempts. She found that fathers with high power motivation were more likely than fathers with low power motivation to be affectionate with their sons. If one assumed that affectionateness was an instrumental behavior maintaining influence with their sons, then this can be interpreted as a power assertive behavior. But on the face of it, affectionateness by itself does not seem to be a power assertive behavior. In thinking about the relationship of the power motive to role behaviors, it is therefore especially important to think of what channels there are for people to assert influences in their roles.

THE THREE ROLES: MARRIAGE, PARENTHOOD, AND WORK

In considering broad social roles as stimuli that interact with motives to influence role reactions, we used a wide perspective in defining the characteristics of these roles. In order to arrive at the general stimulus patterns that characterize these roles, we used our own intuitions, perceptions of people performing the role or directly affected by it, classifications by experts, and theoretical deductions about objective criteria that are salient to understanding how people define roles. While we have used a variety of these sources to arrive at definitions of roles, we have assumed that a broad common configuration exists for each person in a position. What are these commonly shared defining characteristics of the roles we have set ourselves to consider? What is it about marriage, parenthood, and work that gets fed into the individual's information center, is coded, and perhaps distorted, and is transmitted along with motivational dispositions to evoke certain affective or instrumental behaviors? Let us attempt to answer this question about each of the roles separately. Our answers will be oversimplified, since we have not accounted for all nuances about the role. We tried to select only those skeletal aspects of these roles that we expected to interact with the affiliation, achievement, and power motives in understanding role reactions.

MARRIAGE

The requirement of the marital contract is for personal devotion to a person of the opposite sex. Devotion can take on many facets and these facets undoubtedly shift from time to time and from group to group. But unlike parenthood, where fads for parental role obligation have markedly shifted from one generation to another, marital obligations seem to have maintained a greater uniformity even though new lights are often cast upon them. Reproduction legitimately occurs within marriage. Intimate devotion of some type is required. It is difficult to characterize the devotion required of, or satisfying to a man, the devotion given by a woman for pleasure or from a sense of duty. Such characterizations do vary subtly in different social groups and change from one generation to another. In our society, marital role demands and gratifications that have remained relatively constant have been that a husband financially support his wife, that a wife tend the home, that each sexually gratify and emotionally support the other, and that each take on the responsibilities for children.

It has been common in the sociological literature (Blood, 1953) to make a distinction between a traditional concept of marriage and a more modern, equalitarian one, and yet it is hard to date this change in the American family system. The shift has evolved slowly. Traditional marital relationships have been characterized by the husband's dominance and the wife's submission. There are obviously other possibilities in the characterization of the power structure of a family. Parson and Bales (1955) enumerate a typology of marital power structure, based on three questions: To how many different domains a given power structure applies (for example, does a husband's dominance apply to all decisions or to some and not to others)? How much joint decision-making is there, no matter who the dominant spouse is? Does the husband, wife, or neither have the upper hand in decisions? Zelditch (1964) has noted that there are many logical types emerging from these dimensions, but empirically, the critical types are reduced to a few. Herbst (1952) has suggested a promising typology that is similar to one Blood and Wolfe (1960) examined in their research. Herbst lists four basic patterns: the *autonomic pattern*, where separateness in the husband's and wife's approach to life is emphasized, and where the husband and wife have very little to do with each other psychologically, so that decision-making, whether it is husband-dominated, wife-dominated, or jointly determined, is not an issue; *husband-dominated marriage*, where most decisions are in the hands of the husband; *wife-dominated marriage*, where most decisions are in the hands of the wife; and *syncratic marriage*, where there is a mutuality in decisions. In these terms, what we have called a traditional marriage would be called husband-dominated, and what we have called equalitarian would be a syncratic marriage.

There are other qualities to a description of the marital role besides the power structure; there are other important demands. Parallel to the active-passive or initiation-receptive orientation of the sexual behaviors that are at the core of marital obligation and satisfaction, has been the view of the husband as the achiever, the doer, the decision-maker in the marital life, and the wife as the emotional supporter, the listener who makes a comfortable home for the man to come home to after the important daily life is finished. From this perspective, marriage itself is not salient for the husband. The events of the business world and progress made in an achieving society are what get special attention from him. Nevertheless, for a man, as well as for a woman, marriage is still the institution that best serves his needs for adult status, sexual gratification, emotional support, and establishment of a family. If anything, a bachelor in our society is looked on with more suspicion than a single woman. Marriage may be a necessary position for a man, but once attained, it does not seem to be as centrally important to him as to a woman.

Views of marriage are undoubtedly different in different social strata. However, the differences in specific social strata are not well documented. Some research studies support the conclusion that husbands from higher status groups actually enter into more dominant decision-making than husbands from lower status groups (Hoffman and Lippitt, 1960). However, Kohn (1959) reported no difference between working-class and middle-class mothers' reports of the relative role of men and women in making either day-to-day decisions or major family decisions. It may be that lower status groups are more likely to espouse the traditional view of marriage in expressing their attitudes, and upper status groups are more likely to espouse the egalitarian view. But when it comes to actual role behaviors, male dominance may be more in evidence in upper status families. The lower status marriage may be more female dominated, not because of men being submissive, but because these men may be disengaged from the marital role in general.

This traditional view undoubtedly still pervades much of western civilization, but this century has created a revised conception of marriage. Where marriage was once subservient to other roles or just the emotional support of men in their achieving world, it is now a major focus for many people, both men and women. The occupation role has for many reasons receded from the exalted position in the hierarchy of roles; the status of the marital role has been steadily mounting. There have been many theories about why this role shift has occurred. One of the most promising is that increased bureaucratization of occupational settings has reduced the involvement in job roles. Furthermore, there has been an increased trend for women to take over certain of the occupational obligations. The sizable numbers of women in the work force considerably changes the perspective on the male as the gallant breadwinner. Women in the achieving world make men less special and women's relegation to the home less attractive. Major sources of ambiguity in American marriages can, therefore, center on how much women are allowed to work outside the home, and how much men are expected to contribute to the maintenance of day-to-day household responsibilities.

These changing factors in women's and men's roles have converged on a more equalitarian view of marriage. In this conception, the husband should be less dominant over the wife and more communicative with her. As there is a need for increased communication in the marital relationship, affiliative dependency of men on women increases. Where power problems were once minimal in the traditional roles, they loom larger because there is more freedom allowed to women. Affiliation satisfactions shift from prescribed patterns of relationships to less articulated but more demanding interactions. Achievement gratification for men perhaps becomes less concentrated in the job role and more possible within the sphere of marriage, and vice versa, for women.

The traditional view of marriage undoubtedly remains an active part of the demands of marriages in older groups while the modern role is more often part of the expectations of younger couples. The new look in marriage is more likely to occur among the highly educated and the upper middle-class status groups. The traditional view of marriage might be as firmly entrenched in the perceptions of marriages among the aristocratic and lower classes where the separation of the sexes and their proper roles are more sharply defined. However, the shifting prescriptions for marital relationships are probably reflected in decreased consensus in all social groups. It is not surprising that disagreements between spouses about the equalitarian attitude toward the husband-wife relationship has been found to be more characteristic of divorced than married couples (Jacobson, 1952).

The switch to a more equalitarian view of marriage should be most prominent in the group that is on the move, where mobility aspirations become prominent for both men and women. Indeed, the picture of a wife eagerly cheering her husband on in his career, being an active coach, and perhaps doing her active bit in the job itself are now very noticeable in certain occupational strata. Nowadays, a man may not bring his worries home with him because the job has become less central to him, but if he does take his worries home with him, he is very likely to consult his wife about her opinions. The general amalgamation of home and work pervades large portions of the business and professional world. Such a state of affairs will undoubtedly have profound implications for the marital role. Furthermore, changing patterns of the marital role will also influence perceptions of work. These two roles can become very interdependent.

Using these characterizations of the marital role in American society, we can now specify some aspects of the marital role which, earlier in this chapter, we outlined for consideration with respect to each role. Our view of the major demands, gratifications, and ambiguities within the marital role in American society are summarized in Table 1.1.

In addition to the major dimensions of the marital role listed in Table 1.1, we will also be considering the role conflicts that exist between

TABLE 1-1 CHARACTERISTICS OF THE MARITAL ROLE

Role Characteristic	Description
Marital role demands	*Primary* To provide for the physical and emotional needs of the spouse: this includes financial support by the husband, and care of the home by the wife; sexual gratification of partner; emotional support of partner. To take responsibility for children resulting from legitimized reproduction. *Secondary* To handle decision-making in the prescribed fashion: through dominance of husband and submission of wife in the traditional view of marriage; through an equalitarian orientation in the modern view of marriage.
Marital role gratifications	Parental needs satisfied for both husband and wife; recognition of adult status in our society; emotional support for men; physical and emotional support for women; sexual gratification for both.
Marital role ambiguities	Conflict about women's role outside and inside the home in certain social groups (based on a lack of consensus); conflict of how many household tasks a man should perform (based on lack of consensus).

marriage and parenthood and marriage and work. In particular, we have looked at interrole conflict of marriage and work; we recognize that a man's orientation to home can interfere with his work, and vice versa.

PARENTHOOD

The role of parent has also assumed increasing importance within the day-to-day awareness of people in America. Fathers and mothers are today more self-conscious about being parents than they were a century ago. Social observers often attribute this change, along with other changes emphasizing the psychological view of men in their social world, to the removal of the American frontier, and to the resulting urbanization and bureaucratization of our society. The increased complexity of our living conditions limits the freedom for active living that typified the nineteenth century in this country. With no real frontier, men and women turn inward, they contemplate what they have been doing, they introspect about where they are going and especially whither go their children. Thus, parenthood becomes a self-conscious role. Furthermore, as our society becomes more affluent, parents can meet the physical aspects of their role functions without effort and the emphasis can shift to meeting psychological role requirements. Social scientists could easily characterize the last two decades as ones when "the child" has reigned supreme, perhaps because fathers and mothers have taken so seriously their roles as teachers, disciplinarians, and loving supporters of their children.

The Freudian revolution has placed in the hands of the parents a potent psychological weapon—their ways of raising children. Whether for good or for evil, whether self-confidently or with self-doubt, parents are extraordinarily sensitized to the psychological hypothesis that the child is father of the man. It is thus easy for the parent to believe that what he says and does and feels can be extraordinarily important to his child.

In discussing the parental role, it would be hard to avoid talking of the motivation for becoming a parent, the motivation for having children. Undoubtedly, many men and women see children as a means to some external goals—in particular, as a means for perpetuation of their beings in times to come—an often expressed view on the nature of immortality. But at least as often, attaining parenthood probably signifies the initiation of a man or woman into full adult status—his virility or her femininity is finally vindicated in the acts of conceiving and then bearing a child. Parenthood is such a virtuous state for the married couple that they often do not let themselves feel negative about it at all. Rossi's excellent discussion (1967) of the distressing transitions faced by men and women in becoming suddenly and irrevocably responsible for another human being is an insightful articulation of what many parents, especially women, have undoubtedly experienced. Being a parent brings adulthood, but with this, adulthood can become an overwhelming burden.

For some couples, having many children might be the most important reward to aspire to in parenthood. Especially for a woman, to bear children may be a justification for her being. She may feel that the more children she has, the greater her nobility.

Although having children can be thought of as a fulfillment of certain adult obligations, it should also be noted that through children one can relieve and satisfy unfulfilled needs. The kinds of adults children turn out to be are seen as reflections of the parent. If the children achieve, such achievement can be attributed to inheritance from the parents. Children can be the accomplishment of the parent in another way. The success of children can demonstrate parental competence in handling role obligations. However, there are probably as many different views of what an excellent product of parental guidance would be like, as there are general value orientations. If people strongly value achievement, then an accomplishing child is a demonstration of parental worth. If people value affiliation highly, then a friendly, giving, likable child is a demonstration of competence, and if power is strongly valued, a self-reliant, strong, influential child is the mark of success for the parent.

One special note about the gratification in parenthood. Children are smaller, weaker, and more naive than parents. What a perfect recipient of influence! There can be a great many unspoken satisfactions found in being a parent that are unobtainable in any other role. For most other social intercourse, such delegation of power and authority into the hands of a man or a woman is rare. The parent has at his disposal one of the most powerful positions imaginable.

What obligations are defined in this important role? Love and support, teaching and guiding, all enter into the demands commonly expected in parental behavior in households across the country. These are really quite diverse functions. To love and to discipline are seen by many parents as contradictory behavior. How can you teach a child right from wrong and still communicate your love to him? This may be an important conflict inherent in the role of the parent—the conflict of affiliation and power goals.

That the critical parental responsibility is for the care, protection, and upbringing of the human being he has brought into the world needs little elaboration. The predominant characteristic of such responsibility is the necessity for the parent to perform the tasks of socialization, to teach the societal norms for good behavior, as well as the skills, attitudes, and values necessary for adulthood. This responsibility to influence their children cannot be avoided by most parents, and parental recognition of it often quickly changes preconceptions of parenthood as a role that demands unrelenting fondness.

Critical to the course of parental adjustment is some adaptation to this conflict between loving and socializing. Should a parent minimize one or the other aspect of his duty? Should one parent choose one function, and the other parent the conflicting function? Should one of these functions be delegated to someone outside of the immediate family? How should these functions change as children mature? These conflicts lead to considerable ambiguities in role demands and gratifications.

Americans have been moving in the direction of assuming total responsibility for both functions in both parents. The division of the parental role into that of father as disciplinarian and mother as emotional supporter of a child is slowly giving way to more similar role expectations for both mothers and fathers (Kohn and Carroll, 1960). It would seem that there is, therefore, more room for idiosyncratic adaptations to the roles than there was before such role changes began, and this greater flexibility would lead us to expect that personality factors such as motives have a great effect on adjustment to the parental role. Since this shift appears to be still underway, we would also expect to find greater ambiguity in role demands and gratifications.

To complicate even further the already ambiguous demand that a parent socialize his child, parents quickly realize that they do not share total responsibility for socialization. But the range of other people's and other institutions' responsibilities in this same area are not well defined.

TABLE 1-2	CHARACTERISTICS OF THE PARENTAL ROLE

Role Characteristic	Description
Parental role demands	*Primary* To nurture the child: this includes providing shelter and food, and general financial support by the father, and attending to both the psychological and physical health of the child by the mother. *Secondary* To influence the socialization of the child for his adult role in society.
Parental role gratifications	Adult status and sexual status of being feminine or masculine through reaching the status of parenthood; affiliative and power gratification in relationship to their children; achievement gratification from performing the appropriate parental role obligations well and from vicarious experiences of achievements of their children.
Parental role ambiguities	Conflicting ideologies about socialization of the child (based on a lack of consensus about child rearing); conflict between attaining socialization through authoritarian conveyance of rules, or through moral generalization from warm acceptance; conflict about age of relinquishing control of child.

Schools can present ideologies different from that of the parents. Conflicting views about basic values can thus interfere with a parent's attempts to carry out his role. A parent is often caught in a number of cross-pressures of this sort.

As the child grows up, the parents' socializing relationship to the child changes. With the increasing adult status for the child, the role demands and gratifications for parents change, but the time at which such changes should occur is often ambiguous. The acceptance of these shifts may be difficult. The role of mother of a young child and mother of an adolescent is quite different. One of the most poignant conflicts experienced by a parent is the conflict of expectations he has about his child as a child and about his child as an adult. The "Sturm and Drang" of adolescence in our society may reflect the fact that there is "Sturm und Drang" for *parents* of adolescents.

Our discussion of the parental role is summarized in Table 1.2, in which we highlight the demands, gratifications, and ambiguities in parenthood that seem to exist in American society today.

WORK

Men at work *perform*. When they perform, they can be *evaluated*. In this cycle of performance and evaluation is portrayed the major demand for

men at work. Each job requires some specific activity that needs to be performed and that potentially can be evaluated. Usually some type of social
behavior is required at work, but we will consider it a secondary role requirement, unless social behavior is a special part of a specific type of job
that is the focus for evaluation.

In performing a job, a man obtains many types of gratification. From
the mere status of being employed, a man fulfills adult obligations to
society, which can give him some satisfaction. But perhaps more important
are the direct gratifications that a man gets from performing his particular
job: a sense of achievement from putting together a tool well, a sense of
power from having directed a team of construction workers, a sense of
companionship from helping a client through a difficult law case, a fulfillment of curiosity from discovering new chemical reactions, and so on.
Moreover, in performing his job, a man can contribute to the financial and
emotional support of others to whom he has obligations. With all these
potential gratifications, it is little wonder that the job role has been so
central to man.

However, in discussing the interdependence of the job and marital
roles, we have noted that the job role may have diminished in its centrality
for a good many workers. We can note three potential factors contributing
to the decline of the job role in American society. First, industrialization—
the automation of certain highly skilled jobs may have cut down the
personal investment or, at least, the personal satisfaction that men get from
the products of their achievement. Secondly, bureaucratization removes
from many the necessity for making decisions. Even in managerial roles
there is probably more division of labor and less free rein in decision-
making. Thirdly, with changing technology and marketing requirements,
there is little room for individual entrepreneurial achievement. The
wide-open market for business that existed years ago, when ventures of a
small businessman had a reasonable probability for being successful, has
given way to the supercorporations that have cut many inroads into individualized businesses. This is especially noteworthy in difficulties en-
countered by the small retail businessman and the small farmer. Big
business has taken over many farming areas; the supermarket is cutting
into local grocery stores. New types of occupations with bright futures
sometimes develop (laundromats, automatic car washes), but even these
often do not have the creative day-to-day demands for achievement.
Success in business now demands efficient automation rather than personal
ingenuity.

With the decline of the role of the craftsman and the ready availability
of cheap, easily obtained products on the market, the values attached to
skill may eventually diminish. At this point, however, a high value is still
attached to being a skilled worker. Even in our present economy, geared to

mass consumption rather than quality production, one can still recognize the joys that come through the exercise of human decisions and talents reflecting excellence. Kornhauser and Reid (1965) have recently shown that factory workers' dissatisfaction with the way their abilities are used on their jobs is significantly associated with poor mental health on a variety of indices. The attainment of excellence in work is still valued and the sense of a man's well-being is still tied to his work.

The focus on achievement of a difficult task as a major ongoing gratification and as a demand for work nevertheless seems dimmed in our society today. However, considerable attention still seems placed on the status of one's work—the extent to which a job gives the person and his family financial security and prestige in a community. With the focus on these gratifications, it is almost as if society's attention has shifted from considering what day-to-day activities occur at work, to considering the significance of having arrived at a given occupational position. Occupational attainment and career choice then become important manifestations of motivational goals, but once in the desired position, a person may have only minimal achievement aspiration centered on the daily work itself. As one of our colleagues has said, the business of achievement motivation may be confined to "getting into orbit," but once there, behavior may have altogether different motivational consequences. The symbolic value of work may still be very important, but how a man goes about doing what he has to do may have diminished in importance. This is not to deny that men still can satisfy their achievement or curiosity goals in work. But for some men, leisure activities can become the outlets for the achievement and curiosity motivations that once were attached to work.

What perhaps does remain as an important gratification to men in their daily activity at work, even with automation, is the sense of affiliation. Work provides a place for friendships and a place to exercise interpersonal influence. Certain jobs allow for these possibilities more than others. Work forces men to interact, throws men together where they might have been separate.

Role demands are especially ambiguous in difficult jobs. Difficult jobs often involve frequent decision-making about matters that are not easily anticipated. Thus, the greater the leeway a role occupant has in his work, the more likely his job is perceived to be creative.

Another type of ambiguity we have already mentioned is one that comes out of cross pressures from different people related to the role occupant in his actual role functioning. Role overload, which requires an occupant to do too many things at one time, and role conflict, which stems from lack of consensus about role requirements by people affected by the role, can produce this kind of role ambiguity for the role occupant (see Kahn et al., 1964).

Conflict of the role of work with other social roles has already been discussed in relationship to the marital role; it can also be seen in relationship to the parental role. In addition, cross pressures from more personal roles can affect the salience of the occupational role for a man. A behavior that is becoming more salient in American society is leisure activity. As the society moves to institutionalize the performance of leisure activities, an additional set of conflicting pressures will be brought to bear on the job role.

A summary of our discussion about the job role can be found in Table 1.3. That table points up the fact that we have to specify particular job activity before we can get a good leverage on the important role characteristics we need to consider. Unlike the other roles, we have to know more about a particular job before we can begin to list role gratifications and specific role demands. We will use such information in our further specification of the job role in Chapter 5.

TABLE 1-3 CHARACTERISTICS OF THE JOB ROLE

Role Characteristic	Description
Job role demands	*Primary* To perform the specific work activity at a minimal level of competence. *Secondary* To engage in social interaction that facilitates the specific work activity.
Job role gratifications	Financial security and emotional support of others; status gratification from merely *being in* the occupational position of an employed man; affiliation, achievement, power, independence, mastery, and curiosity in specific jobs depending on the *type of activity* that is required.
Job role ambiguities	Conflicting role demands coming from role overload, differing expectations from different role senders, and lack of structured expectation about performance.

THE PLAN OF THE BOOK

Each of the roles—marriage, parenthood, and work—will be considered in consecutive chapters, after a more detailed presentation of our methodology in Chapter 2. Within each of those succeeding chapters, we will first discuss our exploratory hunches about the relationship of motivations of affiliation, achievement, and power to the kinds of role information we could get from the interview. Then we will describe the types of measures used and our understanding of their general significance, and will present some previous data on the measures of both role characteristics and role reactions. It is at this point that we will look at the data on role reactions to various motive-role combinations. The presentation will be exploratory. We will not discuss each of the possible empirical relationships that can be worked out between motive and role variables. We will only be reporting results that seem to present some consistent picture, results that offer puzzling but provocative patterns, and results that might invalidate certain hypotheses. The tolerant reader will always have to remember that these results are subject to and require a further examination in other work. We offer these results because they are based on unique data that can serve as an impetus for those who want to investigate any aspect of it more intensively and with greater fact-finding assurance. As a result, when we present these data we will suggest a number of interpretations of them and often go on to point up areas of research that seem to be especially suggested. We hope that what follows will be the catalyst for a number of investigations of the interaction of personality characteristics with aspects of significant life roles. In the concluding chapter, we will point out the effects these data have had upon our conceptions of the marital, parental, and job roles, the motives for affiliation, achievement, and power, and the interaction of motives and roles.

2

Methodology

In each of the next three chapters we will be examining
one major life role—marriage, parenthood, or work—in order
to consider the ways that a person's motivational characteristics affect
how he reacts to the demands, the gratifications, or
the ambiguities that exist within each role. In this chapter we will
describe the subjects for the study, the operations used to measure motives
and reactions to roles, and our bases for inferring the nature of the
role characteristics that face occupants of these three
major life positions. As regards both the reactions to roles and
role characteristics, this chapter will provide an
overview only. The details about each role will be presented in
the succeeding chapters, since different operations were used to measure reactions to each role and different
information was available to infer the
demands, gratifications, and ambiguities of these three roles.

SUBJECTS

The subjects dealt with in the succeeding chapters are subsets of a
representative sample of the adult American popula-
tion interviewed in 1957. That total sample consisted of 2,460 respondents interviewed in a nationwide study of mental health
(Gurin et al., 1960) conducted by the Survey Research Center
of The University of Michigan under the sponsorship of the Joint

Commission on Mental Illness and Health. The sample was chosen by means of area probability sampling to be representative of United States adults 21 years of age and older, residing in private households. (For further details see Appendix A, Section I.) A multi-staged stratification procedure was used to insure that the sample had the same characteristics as the total population. For this purpose 66 strata were formed and one county from each stratum was included in the sample. Within each county, probability sampling techniques were used to select the specific dwelling units where interviews were to be taken, and the specific household resident to be interviewed. No substitutions were permitted. Each household unit in which a respondent was to be interviewed received in the mail a letter from the Director of the Survey Research Center of The University of Michigan describing the study, and informing them that an interviewer would call at their home within the next month to six weeks. The study, and the respondent selection were described as follows:

... we have been asked to conduct a survey to explore some of the problems of modern living in this country. Many experts have talked about the strains and pressures under which we live today. Some people feel the rapid pace may be unhealthy, while others claim that the stress of modern life is not too great.

Such a matter is of vital concern in assessing the productivity and health of the American people as a nation. Congress and the United States Public Health Service are sufficiently concerned about this question to appropriate funds for studies in this area. Our survey is part of this program of research.

We have selected several thousand addresses, chosen by a scientific method to represent an accurate cross-section of the nation. Your address has turned up as one of those to be visited by our interviewers. The interviews are entirely confidential. All of the information will be combined in statistical totals so that no individual can be identified.

Despite repeated calls, 5 percent of the selected respondents were not found at home, and were not interviewed. Another 8 percent of the selected respondents refused to be interviewed, leaving a total of 87 percent of the selected sample who were interviewed.

The overall study used three interview forms, and each interview form was assigned randomly to one-third of the selected respondents throughout all primary sampling units. This technique enabled us to use a wide variety of questions. Many questions were asked on all three forms, but some were asked on only two forms, and some on only one. The measurement of affiliation, achievement, and power motives occurred on only two interview forms. Most of the other measures used in the present study also were available on both of these interview forms. These two interview forms were used to elicit data from 1619 respondents (715 men and 904 women). Unfortunately, approximately 17 percent of these men and 14 percent of these women did not adequately complete the tasks used to assess the three motives. (The reasons for this will be discussed in a succeeding section of this chapter.) Therefore, the maximum sample available for the present study was 1371 (597 men and 774 women).

Data presented earlier (Veroff et al., 1960) suggested that those respondents who adequately completed the tasks used to assess motivation no longer comprise a totally representative sample. A comparison between the total sample ($N = 2460$) and the portion of the two-thirds random subsample that gave adequate responses for assessing motivation ($N = 1371$) is presented in Table 2.1. There it can be seen that the respondents who gave adequate responses for assessing motivation were younger, and had substantially higher educational backgrounds, and slightly larger incomes[1] than the eliminated subjects. Within any given social group, the percentage of subjects who did not adequately complete the tasks was not usually very high. The most sizable loss was among the men and women who had little or no schooling (6th grade education or less). For this group, approximately 30 percent did not give adequate responses for the measurement of motivation. Although we will talk as if we were generalizing from our analysis of these data to the American society at large, we recognize at this point that we should make these generalizations with some caution, especially to persons at the lowest educational level.

Despite these limitations, we had at our disposal a set of heterogeneous respondents from all walks of life who lived throughout the United States. We were interested in maintaining a broad sampling of Americans, one that approximated a representative sample, and reflected diversity in the roles of marriage, parenthood and work. Although we will use the diverse characteristics of the sample to make inferences about variations within each of these three general roles, our major interest is in whether there are general patterns of motive-role interaction that are characteristic of these roles in American society, despite the diversity among the subjects. However, the life situations of our white and nonwhite (predominantly Negro) respondents seemed so disparate as to preclude joint consideration. The number of Negro subjects who told stories adequate for scoring the motives was too small (31 men and 60 women) to retain for separate analysis; therefore, we limited all analyses reported here to white respondents.

By limiting our study to white subjects, we reduced the sample to $N = 1226$ (538 men and 688 women). In each of the three succeeding chapters, that portion of these 1236 subjects who occupied the position

[1]The median family income reported by the total sample was $4,613; for the present sample the figure was $4,802. Both these figures are very close to the total dollar income for families in the United States in 1957, when our survey was conducted, which was $4,791; in 1966 this is equivalent to $5,727 (U.S. Bureau of the Census, 1967, p. 2).

TABLE 2-1 SELECTED DEMOGRAPHIC CHARACTERISTICS OF TOTAL SAMPLE AND PRESENT SAMPLE

Characteristic	Total Sample		Present Sample	
	Men	**Women**	**Men**	**Women**
Age				
21–24	6.1	7.1	5.4	6.9
25–34	23.4	25.1	27.7	26.7
35–44	22.4	22.4	19.9	23.9
45–54	19.5	18.2	20.6	19.8
55–64	13.6	13.3	13.7	12.7
65 plus	15.0	13.9	12.7	10.0
Total	100.0%	100.0%	100.0%	100.0%
Base N^a	(1074)	(1373)	(597)	(769)
Education				
Grade school	34.1	31.7	29.7	28.8
High school	43.2	52.7	45.7	54.7
College	22.7	15.6	24.6	16.5
Total	100.0%	100.0%	100.0%	100.0%
Base N^a	(1068)	(1364)	(593)	(771)
Family income				
Under $1,999	13.9	19.5	11.2	16.2
$2,000–3,999	19.9	25.4	19.4	24.9
$4,000–4,999	16.9	15.8	17.0	16.6
$5,000–6,999	26.3	21.1	27.0	22.6
$7,000–9,999	13.3	11.9	15.2	12.8
$10,000 and above	9.7	6.3	10.2	6.9
Total	100.0%	100.0%	100.0%	100.0%
Base N^a	(1056)	(1334)	(587)	(752)

[a]Base Ns exclude subjects with missing data for the characteristic being tabulated.

associated with the role under discussion was used as the sample: the 464 men and 514 women who were married and living with their spouse at the time of the interview were the subjects for the analysis of reactions to the marital role; the 433 men and 564 women who had a living child at the time of the interview were the subjects for the analysis of reactions to the parental role; and the 466 men who held a full-time job at the time of the interview were used in the analysis of reactions to the job role.

INTERVIEW SITUATION

A member of the field staff of the Survey Research Center interviewed all respondents in their home. The interviewers, 27 men and 132 women, were regularly employed by the Survey Research Center to conduct structured interviews. Their regular training procedures included instruction and supervised practicum experience in the use of nondirective interviewing techniques. The interviewers are trained to ask questions exactly as worded in the questionnaire, to use only certain nondirective probes, and as much as possible, to record answers in their entirety (Survey Research Center, 1960). All interviewers received detailed written instructions concerning the overall purposes of the study, as well as instructions concerning each question in the interview schedule. (See Appendix A, for the interview schedule.) In addition, because of the unusually personal nature of part of the interview, which concerned mental health problems, immediately before the interviewing began in April 1957, regional meetings were held throughout the country. These meetings were attended by two-thirds of the interviewers. At these conferences, special attention was given to ways of introducing the interview and establishing initial rapport, to the proper procedures for administering the novel technique of assessing motivation, and to problems of emotional disturbances that might be aroused in the interview.

Once the interviewing began, the interview schedules were returned to the Survey Research Center as they were completed, where they were carefully reviewed for completeness or any indications that the interviewers were not properly following the interview schedule. Feedback to interviewers about adequacy of interviews was continually provided.

So far as we could tell, rapport was generally good, as judged from the interviewers' impressions and from reading the interviews. These impressions were corroborated by the answers to a questionnaire sent to the respondents after their interviews had reached our office. These responses indicated no unusual criticism of the personal character of the questions and showed a generally favorable attitude to the interview experience.

MOTIVE MEASURES[2]

The measures of affiliation, achievement, and power motivation were based on the coding of stories respondents told about six pictures. Such techniques have been called tests of thematic apperception. The use of this thematic apperception task is rooted in the work of McClelland and his colleagues on achievement motivation (McClelland et al., 1953), and in the earlier work of Murray (1943) on the Thematic Apperception Test. These approaches are based on the assumption that when faced with an ambiguous task, such as telling a story about persons in a picture,

[2]More detailed description of these procedures and the rationale for their development are presented in Appendix A, Section III.

the subject will project his own feelings and desires onto the characters in the story, and these projected feelings will be reflected in the themes of the story. Two important types of research findings have supported the validity of motive assessment through such techniques: (1) experimentally induced motivational states influence the content of imaginative thought in ways that can be reliably coded, and (2) individual differences in the strengths of the affiliation, achievement, and power motivation measured in this way meaningfully relate to other variables. The results of this past research relevant to the present study have been summarized in Chapter 1.

The present assessment procedures were an adaptation of the procedures developed in laboratory settings[3] to the survey interview situation. We will first describe our interview procedures, then the coding procedures and reliability, the elimination of subjects due to missing data, and finally, the validity of the method.

INTERVIEW PROCEDURES

After several questions about leisure-time activities, used to establish rapport and to avoid what might have otherwise been too abrupt a beginning if the imaginative test had been given first, the story-telling procedure was introduced to the respondents as another way of finding out what people think about situations that may come up in life. The interviewer then showed the respondent the first picture and gave him about twenty seconds to look at the picture before beginning the following series of questions:

1. Who are these people? (Who is this person?) What are they (is he/she) doing?
2. What has led up to this—what went on before?
3. What do they (does he/she) want—how do they (does he/she) feel?
4. What will happen? How will it end?

The picture remained in front of the respondent as he told the story. The interviewers were instructed to write in verbatim transcript the story told about each picture as responses to each of the questions. If the

[3]In the usual laboratory procedure, the data are collected in group settings. A large picture is shown to the subjects for 20 seconds, and the subjects write their own stories on a single sheet of paper provided for each story. On each page are four sets of questions that help to remind the subjects to cover all elements of the plots. The experimenter controls the amount of time spent on each story; the usual limit with college students is four minutes. Since the content of imaginative stories is highly susceptible to conditions immediately preceding the story-telling procedure, the experimenter controls this by either inducing certain types of motivational states, such as achievement arousal, or uses a "neutral" testing condition. In the latter case, the experimenter makes no deliberate attempts to arouse or relax a particular kind of motivation. A more detailed discussion of these standard procedures can be found in Atkinson, 1958b, Appendix III.

Figure 2.1 Male Form of the thematic apperception test

1

Figure 2.1: **1.** From *The Achievement Motive* by David C. McClelland, John W. Atkinson, Russell A. Clark and Edgar L. Lowell. Copyright © 1953, Meredith Corporation. Reprinted by permission of Appleton-Century-Crofts. **2., 3., 6.** Drawing by Mrs. Charles Bisdee. **5.** From Harold Guetzkow, "Group projection sketches for the study of small groups," *Journal of Social Psychology*, 33 (1951), pp. 77–102. Copyright © 1951 by the University of Michigan.
Figure 2.2: **1., 3., 5., 6.** Drawing by Mrs. Charles Bisdee.

2

3

4

5

6

Figure 2.2 Female Form of the thematic apperception test

1

2

3

4

5

6

respondent answered the question at all, no matter how briefly, no probes were used. Probes were permitted only under limited circumstances.[4]

The pictures were printed on 4″ × 6″ cards, and were shown to the subjects one at a time.[5] A different set of pictures was used for men and women. The picture sets were designed to elicit a balanced set of scores on the three motives. They were also designed to portray a *variety* of life situations with which, in one way or another, most people in this country have had some direct contact—for example, different types of work situations and interpersonal situations.[6]

The pictures are reproduced in Figures 2.1 (male set) and 2.2 (female set), and a brief description of each is listed below, in the order of presentation. (Numbers in parentheses refer to the list in Appendix III, Atkinson, 1958b.)

Male Form

1. Two men (inventors) in a shop working at a machine. (2)
2. Four men seated at a table with coffee cups. One man is writing on a sheaf of papers. (101)
3. Man (father) and children seated at breakfast table. (102)
4. Man seated at drafting board. (28)
5. Conference group: seven men variously grouped around a conference table. (83)
6. Woman in foreground with man standing behind and to the left. (103)

Female Form

1. Two women standing by a table and one woman is working with test tubes.
2. Woman (mother) seated by girl reclining in chair.
3. Group of four women, one standing, the others seated facing each other.
4. Woman kneeling and applying a cover to a chair.
5. Two women preparing food in the kitchen.
6. Same as 6 above, for males.

[4]These circumstances were described in a set of detailed written instructions received by each interviewer: (a) If the person immediately rejects the whole task by saying "I can't do this" or "I just have no imagination," resort to something like: "Well, just try to make up anything you want. Remember there are no right or wrong answers." (b) If, in reply to one of the questions in the story form, the person says, "I've already told you that," you can say, "Can you tell me some more about that?" (c) When a respondent says "I don't know" in reply to any of the questions about the pictures, again you might say, "You can make up anything you want. There are no right or wrong answers."

[5]These forms are available (4″ × 6″ pictures). They may be obtained by writing to the Survey Research Center, Institute for Social Research, Box 1248, Ann Arbor Michigan 48104. Price $1.00.

[6]The sets were selected after pretest data were collected from both college students and a residence survey in a major metropolitan area. For information on the selection criteria and characteristics of the selected pictures see Veroff et al. (1960, pp. 2-5).

CODING THE STORIES FOR THE AFFILIATION, ACHIEVEMENT, AND POWER MOTIVES

The stories told to each picture were scored for each of the three motives, although most pictures contained more themes relevant for one of the motives than for the other two. The coding was done according to the previously developed scoring manuals for achievement motivation, affiliation motivation and power motivation (Atkinson, 1958b, Ch. 12, 13, 14), supplemented by some new conventions adopted to handle responses from novel pictures.[7] Scores were summed across the six pictures to yield a total score for each motive.

Three scorers were trained to code each motive, using the method prescribed by Feld and Smith (1958). Then each received special training and experience in coding stories about two pictures from the male form and two pictures from the female form, and subsequently coded only these pictures. In this way the scoring of each individual coder contributed to potentially one-third of a particular motive score for each sample. As a result, we ruled out bias of total scores attributable to the scoring idiosyncracies of a particular coder.

Coding reliabilities were determined in two ways for total motive scores from a subsample of subjects. The coders' total motive scores, based on the six-story protocols, were correlated with experts' total motive scores for these same protocols. The "expert" coders (the authors) had had many years of experience coding the protocols. Then the coders and experts discussed their disagreements and arrived at a consensus. The coder's original total scores were then correlated with final total scores based on the consensus. (A detailed description of this procedure is found in Appendix A, Section IV-B.)

All of the total score reliabilities (median = .77) fall within the range found in published experimental studies, but only two are above the median of coding reliabilities reported in smaller-scale studies, (which is .89). Considering the anticipated loss in coding reliability attributable to the use of several novel pictures, we were encouraged by these results. Nevertheless we anticipate some loss in sensitivity of the measuring instruments due to some coding unreliability.

To give the reader some sense of what kinds of stories were coded for each of the motives, we present three examples of stories saturated with imagery coded for each motive.

Stories coded for affiliation motivation A 40-year-old college-educated woman told this story coded for *affiliation imagery*, in response to the picture of the woman and girl:

[7]These conventions appear in Appendix A, Section IV-A.

A lady and a child without a home. Lady is talking to the girl who is deep in thought. The girl has been left homeless and is in the lady's house. Girl has a lost feeling. Lonely. They are talking over what might be done to help the girl find a home. She will be placed in a good home to be happy.

A 25-year-old truck mechanic who left high school after his sophomore year told this story coded for *affiliation imagery*, in response to the picture of a group of men:

Gosh, they're too young to be at a board meeting. I guess they're college students having a discussion, or foreign exchange students and they're discussing various things. I suppose they just came out of class and they're having a study period of some kind and decided to get together and have a bull session. Probably they are just passing time. They're completely relaxed, having a discussion and go back to their classes. They'll have gotten better acquainted and go back to their classes in good spirits because they're relaxed.

Stories coded for achievement motivation   A 36-year-old woman with a grade-school education told this story coded for *achievement imagery*, in response to the picture of the woman upholstering the chair:

She is covering a chair. Well for one thing the chair was probably worn out and needed new covering. Well she wants to repair it. It looks like she is doing a good job and she seems well pleased with the job, I'd say.

A 50-year-old superintendent in a paint factory with a high-school diploma told the following story coded for *achievement imagery*, in response to the picture of two men at the machine:

They must be mechanics working in a machine shop, not a big machine shop. One man, the man standing with his hands on his hips is an instructor. Well they might have been a couple of business partners and they decided to get together and work on some kind of invention. They want to invent some kind of motor for a machine, they feel happy and seem to be getting what they want. When they get through they will have accomplished the invention and will maybe take out a patent on this invention.

Stories coded for power motivation   An 80-year-old widow with less than a high-school education told this story coded for *power imagery*, in response to the picture of the man and woman:

She has her back up. He is trying to convince her. Had a disagreement. He thinks he is right. She is giving in to him, I think. He's a man, she will have to give in to him.

A 50-year-old man with a grade-school education told this story coded for *power imagery*, in response to the picture of the man and children:

Father telling son what to do—at breakfast. He has gotten a little unruly and father is talking to him about it. The boy wants change to buy him something. Father wants to give him a piece of his mind. I think it will end OK if he listens to his father and I think he will.

ELIMINATION OF SUBJECTS WITH INADEQUATE STORIES

At the outset of scoring the protocols it was clear that some *S*s gave responses which had to be considered inadequate for arriving at valid motivation scores. A few *S*s tended to reject the whole undertaking, some refused to give stories to some of the pictures, some were unable or unwilling to give answers to certain questions within a story. In order to deal with this problem, the coders were instructed to keep a detailed record of "inadequate responses"—not answering certain questions in a story, saying "I don't know," or "It's hard to tell," or the like. For any *S* there are 24 possibilities for an inadequate response—four sets of questions about each of six stories. An inadequate response means that the person gave no imaginative content that could possibly be scored for motivational content. The person, for whatever reason, has prevented the measuring instrument from being applied. It was necessary to decide how many unanswered questions would seriously interfere with an adequate measure of motivation. In light of our experience with practices informally employed in experimental studies, we only used protocols when at least half the stories were complete and answers to no more than one set of questions was omitted from any or all of the remaining stories. This criterion led to the elimination of 17 percent of the men and 14 percent of the women.

Two things should be kept in mind in appraising the significance of this number of rejected protocols. First, we deliberately adopted a fairly stringent criterion for elimination. Secondly, these *S*s were eliminated not on the basis of just one set of responses to one picture, but on the basis of inadequacy of response *on any one of six pictures*. Consequently, we judge that the rejection of subjects due to inadequate protocols is not different from what would be required if we used any set of six complex open-ended questions in a nationwide survey setting and eliminated *S*s giving an inadequate response on any *one* of the set of six questions.

As we have previously indicated, the eliminated subjects were unevenly distributed by educational level. This is not surprising since verbal fluency is obviously related to ability to tell stories about pictures. What these data suggest, therefore, is that the measuring device as here employed in a survey setting is less appropriate for certain segments of the population. This is hardly a startling result. Practically any verbal measure encounters the same difficulty. Inadequate responses to open-ended attitude questions tend to stem largely from uneducated groups; inadequate answers (response sets) on certain forced choice questionnaires also are most apparent in uneducated groups (Christie, 1958).

We suspect that a failure to produce a meaningful protocol may also reflect deficiencies in the kinds of social motivation that are being assessed in this study—particularly achievement motivation. Hence, we may be overestimating the average level of motivation in any group from which a great many *S*s are removed because of their inadequate protocols. However, since our interest is not in absolute level of motivation, but rather in the relationship between motivation and other variables, this possible bias may not be so important.

CORRECTING MOTIVE SCORES FOR VARIATIONS IN NUMBER OF WORDS IN STORIES

Although the correlation between motivation scores and length of stories has been negligible in studies with college students when 4 minutes are allowed for writing stories (Atkinson, 1950, p. 27), at least five studies have shown significant relationships, requiring some sort of correction, when somewhat different test conditions were employed (Child, Storm, and Veroff, 1958; Ricciuti, 1954; Ricciuti and Sadacca, 1955; Skolnick, 1966; Walker and Atkinson, 1958). We had reason to anticipate that in this heterogeneous sample there would be gross differences in the length of stories, which might be attributed to gross differences in verbal ability of *S*s and/or to uncontrolled differences in the behavior of interviewers.

Considering only those subjects who told adequate stories, the number of words in the six stories ranged from 80 to 823. The median number of words was 291 for men and 279 for women, or about 46–48 words per story. This was the same length obtained by Ricciuti and Sadacca (1955) from 2.5-minute stories written by high school students, but it is approximately half the length usually obtained in studies with college students when 4 minutes are allotted for writing each story.

The raw achievement, affiliation, and power motive scores obtained from the content analysis were correlated with total number of words in the protocol (length of protocol) separately for men and women. The results show the anticipated significant relationships between length of protocol and raw motive scores, product-moment correlations ranging between .21 and .28 ($p < .001$ for all correlations based on 597 men and 774 women). Clearly, some correction of the raw scores was necessary to eliminate the obvious fact that a person who tells longer stories stands a greater chance of obtaining a high score based on a frequency count of particular kinds of motivational content in what he has said.

The procedures used to remove this bias in the scores was to add a correction factor to all scores that were too low because the protocols on which they were based were too short, and to subtract a correction factor from scores that were too high because of lengthy protocols. These procedures were based on analyses of regression of average motive scores on length of protocols. (For details of this procedure, see Appendix A, Section IV, C.)

The effect of this correction was to remove the systematic difference in motivation scores as a function of the number of words in the six stories. The correlations between length of protocol and the final corrected motivation scores were all low and insignificant ($-.01$ to $.05$). Thus, the effect of verbal fluency on motivation scores was effectively eliminated.

In the present report, these corrected motive scores were divided as nearly as possible at the quartiles, within each sex. The four-point ranking of motive scores was used in all data analyses.

THE EFFECT OF INTERVIEWERS ON MOTIVE SCORES

Although we made a serious effort to standardize the interviewing procedure, a group of 159 different interviewers necessarily introduced some variability into the measures that has hitherto been minimal when all protocols are collected at one time in a group administration. An estimate of the extent of this interviewer variability was therefore desirable. It was difficult to establish such an estimate. A valid test of the effect of different interviewers requires random assignment from the population of respondents to the interviewers. This was decidedly not the case.

While the selection of respondents was completely determined at the central office of the Survey Research Center by probability sampling techniques, the respondents were not assigned to interviewers at random. To the degree that the assignment was not random, systematic differences in responses obtained by various interviewers could have stemmed from differences in the composition of the samples interviewed, rather than from differences attributable to the interviewers themselves. In spite of this danger of finding effects that are really attributable to respondents, we wanted to arrive at some estimate of interviewer effect. We therefore designed an analysis of "possible" interviewer effects which, because it cannot clearly separate interviewer and respondent differences, will tend to overestimate interviewer effects.

For this analysis we identified all interviewers who had obtained an adequate motive assessment from at least four males, or at least four females. Then from these interviewers, we obtained all pairs of interviewers within a primary sampling unit who met the criterion. The motive scores of respondents interviewed by these 23 pairs of interviewers were subjected to analysis of variance, and we found that interviewer differences had negligible effects on motive scores. One reason these maximal estimates of interviewer effects on motivation scores were low was that the motivation scores had been corrected for length of protocol. As a result of these analyses, we feel safe in concluding that a sufficient degree of standardization of interviewing techniques was maintained. (See Appendix A, Section IV-D, for the details of these analyses.)

EVALUATION OF MOTIVE MEASURES

We recognize that the adaptation of the thematic apperception technique to a nationwide survey has added new sources of unreliability— due to interviewer effects and lower reliability in coding stories written to different pictures than those used in developing the original scoring manuals. However, since neither of these sources of unreliability seemed to be major problems, we assume that these measures are reliable enough to use. The increase in unreliability may mean that the obtained relationships between motive scores and other variables will be conservative estimates of these relationships.

The adaptation of this technique to the sample survey also raises certain questions about the validity of the measure obtained under different circumstances and from a more diverse sample of subjects. A potential validity problem was the wide variability in verbal fluency among the subjects. However, the relationship between motivation scores and number of words in stories was effectively reduced to zero by our correction procedures.

A more difficult problem was whether the pictures selected provided a fair opportunity for persons in all strata of American society to express their motives. There is no clear answer to that question. We have shown elsewhere (Veroff, Feld, and Crockett, 1966) that the predictive potential of achievement motive scores is related to the pictures used to elicit stories from which the motive scores were derived. It was found that for predicting upward occupational mobility from high achievement imagery, the picture of a motoric type of occupational setting was more effective for men holding jobs that demanded a conceptual orientation and the picture with a conceptual setting was more effective for men whose jobs involved a motoric orientation. Thus, pictures of familiar work settings yielded less valid indices of achievement motivation in men than did pictures of more familiar work settings when occupational mobility was used as the criterion. These data suggest, however, that by using a *set* of heterogeneous pictures to elicit motivational imagery for persons from widely differing social backgrounds, we may have obtained motivation scores with similar validity for persons from different social groups. Basing motive scores on stories told to a number of different pictures, each describing settings that have differential validity for different groups, may have the effect of eliminating differences in the overall validity of total motive scores. It is as if we added together components of a motive that are measured somewhat differently in different groups. If we assume that the components are fairly measured in all groups, even if they are measured differently by different pictures, then we can assume that the measure has a similar validity for all groups.

We have generally assumed, in the analyses to follow, that the thematic apperceptive technique measured similar motivational states in each of the social groups that we considered within the different life roles. This assumption is necessary in order to use the data to generate substantive inferences about the interplay of motives and roles. How valid is this assumption? In considering the methodological problems with these data we have elsewhere concluded that:

Differences in motivation scores in various subgroups of the population can be variously interpreted to reflect differences in personality, life situation, and the significance of the picture for various groups. The relative importance of each of these interpretations may be evaluated only by further inquiry into the kinds of variables related to these scores within different subgroups. A particular network of interrelationships may be suggestive of which of these views may be supported. It might very well be that the interpretations of the scores will vary depending on which social group is being investigated. Or one conclusion that seems likely is that for each social group the motivation score can be partially interpreted as personality assessment and partially as an assessment of reactions to ongoing life situations. There is evidence in the survey data that each of these interpretations may be operating in the scores (Veroff et al., 1960, p. 29).

In making the assumption about the similarity of meaning of motive measures in different subgroups, we thus have to disregard other interpretations. We hope that future studies of the assessment procedures for these motive measures will be directed to making clearer the distinction between assessment of personality and assessment of reactions to life roles. They are entangled in the present assessment. For simplicity we are usually going to use the interpretation that the motive scores represent *similar* personality assessments for different social groups.

The crucial test of this assumption and of the general validity of the motive scores rests with the construct validity of the measures. We can point to several studies using portions of these data that have shown theoretically meaningful relationships between these motive scores and other variables (Baruch, 1967; Crockett, 1962; Feld, 1960; Veroff, 1961; Veroff et al., 1960; Veroff, Feld, and Gurin, 1962a; Veroff et al., 1966). The present study provides another empirical test of the validity of these motive scores.

INTERRELATIONS AMONG MOTIVE SCORES

In most experimental studies where more than one of these three motives have been assessed, these motives have been found to be uncorrelated. In our data we essentially find the same thing. For each of the major subsamples (married men, married women, fathers, mothers, employed men) there were negligible correlations[8] between each pair of motives. Thus we can safely assume that these are three independent motivational tendencies in most people. It is important to know whether these motive measures are independent because in the present study we have correlated all three of the motives with a given role reaction.

Although the three motive scores were uncorrelated in our major subsamples, there were some consistent relationships within certain specific segments of these subsamples.

Among certain subgroups of our male sample, affiliation motivation was significantly negatively correlated with both power motivation (college-educated husbands and fathers, young employed men and skilled workers) and achievement motivation (college-educated husbands and fathers, younger married men with living children), while achievement and power motivation were positively correlated (college-educated husbands and fathers, younger married men with living children, salesmen, and clerical workers). We view these significant interrelationships as reflecting the differentiation and integration of these three types of motivation in these groups. For men, friendship (affiliation) and influential (power) relationships with other persons seem to be clearly differentiated. For them the active assertive goal-directed behaviors implicit in power and achievement motivation seem to be similar. But why in these groups in particular? It seems easy to explain these results for the college-educated men, whom we assume have spent long years in preparation for their occupational role in society, and who have perhaps been forced into the differentiation and integration of these motivational goals in order to successfully prepare for and perform their occupational roles. But an explanation for these significant associations among the younger group of fathers or among certain of the occupational groups is not apparent, nor is the pattern of association among the three motives as clear-cut. In any event, because of these significant relationships among the motives in certain subgroups of the men, we shall have to be cautious in interpreting parallel relationships between the various measures of motivation and role reactions, especially in the college-educated men and the younger men with children.

In contrast to the results for men, the significant interrelationships

[8]Tau Beta rank order correlations were used.

between the motives for women did not form as clear a pattern. A significant positive relationship was found between affiliation and achievement motivation among the grade-school-educated wives in our oldest age grouping (50 and older) and the mothers of school-age children. For these women achievement motivation may be more integrated into their family existence and therefore more compatible with a high level of affiliation motivation. However, for mothers of preschool-age children there was a significant negative association between affiliation and achievement motivation; for married women with living children, there was a significant negative relationship between affiliation motivation and power motivation. These relationships were comparable to those found for the college-educated husbands and fathers, and for the young married men with children. It is possible that this pattern of relationships between affiliation and achievement or power motivation signifies a more active involvement in the maternal role and that this kind of involvement fosters the separation of affiliation goals from those of achievement or power. Regardless of their cause, for these subgroups of women, the intercorrelations between motives will have to be taken into account in subsequent chapters.

MEASURES OF ROLE REACTIONS

We based our measures of role reactions on replies to a series of interview questions concerning marriage, parenthood, and work.[9] Within each role area, a number of different questions were used to elicit self-descriptions of satisfactions and dissatisfactions. In constructing the interview schedule, we assumed that it was likely that several dimensions of self-evaluation existed within each role area. Therefore, in each area we obtained a series of evaluations concerning feelings of unhappiness, a sense of inadequacy, problems in fulfilling the role, and so forth. The specific questions used in each role area will be described in the succeeding relevant chapters. At this point we would simply like to indicate the general kinds of evaluations obtained and the general interpretation we will give them. For an orientation to our assessment of role reactions, we turn to our previous work on the dimensions of subjective adjustment. For, in addition to the questions about functioning in specific positions that are used in the present study, questions concerning other aspects of adjustment and distress were included in the interview, and have been discussed elsewhere (Gurin et al., 1960; Veroff, Feld, and Gurin, 1962b). This previous work gives us some insights into the potential assessments of role reactions for the present study.

[9]The entire list of questions in the interview schedule is reproduced in Appendix A, Section III.

Indices of subjective evaluations of adjustment, established on a priori grounds, were subjected to a factor analysis (Veroff et al., 1962b), for two groups of subjects: married women with children ($N = 542$) and employed married men with children ($N = 255$). The results of the factor analyses suggested that these subjective reactions to one's life reflected at least four major dimensions of self-evaluations. Two of these dimensions are particularly relevant to reactions within life roles, the *Unhappiness Factor* and the *Social Inadequacy Factor*. The *Unhappiness Factor* was most strongly reflected in questions asking about general feelings of happiness, but it was also evidenced in reports of marital unhappiness. However, men and women differed somewhat on the further measures that reflected this factor. Men's reports of the experience of problems with their children and to a lesser extent with marriage, were correlated with this factor. For women, however, only problems in marriage were an important aspect of the *Unhappiness Factor*. The *Unhappiness Factor* was interpreted as a dimension of adjustment signifying reactions of men and women to what "happens to them" rather than reactions to what "men and women do." This factor represents reactions to one's life where the responsibility for difficulty is not attached to the self. This interpretation seemed consistent with the correlations between this factor and problems with children for men and problems with marriage for men and women. As a parent, men presumably react passively to their children's behavior while women are more likely to take the responsibility for raising their children. In contrast, the position of a married woman is presumably less assertive than that of a married man.

Another important dimension emerging from the factor analysis of subjective feelings of adjustment was the *Social Inadequacy Factor*—reflected in feelings of lack of satisfaction with one's own performance in marriage and parenthood, and in work (for men). We assumed that this factor reflects feelings of inadequate performance where the responsibility for the difficulty lies with one's self, rather than with an environmental stress.

In the main we will be looking at role reactions in each of the chapters that reflect these two different types of reactions—feelings of unhappiness and feelings of inadequacy. The role reactions reflecting these two factors will be the major basis for our investigation of the congruence principle. We will be interested in determining whether motive-role congruence is related to role reactions reflecting both the degree of felt unhappiness and inadequacy, or whether congruence is more relevant to one or another of these dimensions of self-evaluation.

In each role area we also measured types of role reactions other than those directly reflecting the two major factors of adjustment. For example, we will be looking at how personalized or how distant the role seems to be for the individual, or the extent to which the role is seen as burdensome or restrictive. These are qualities in the experiences of a role that often reflect how salient that role is to the respondent. In the same way, we also will be considering the reasons given for unhappiness, sources of feelings of inadequacy, and types of satisfactions and dissatisfactions mentioned. Such reactions may tell us about the qualitative experience within roles, and their relationships to the respondent's motives may also help expand our view of the significance of various types of motivation. Because these reactions are of a more qualitative nature, they had not been included in the previous factor-analytic study. These more qualitative kinds of role reactions will be the basis for our investigation of the sensitization principle. We will be interested in determining whether persons with different levels of achievement, affiliation, and power motivation differ in their characterizations of the sources of role satisfactions and dissatisfactions.

Earlier, we noted that one of the basic assumptions underlying this research is that self-reports of feelings of satisfaction or discontent are significant aspects of role functioning. Two kinds of questions can be raised about this assumption: (1) were the respondents honest with the interviewers, and (2) are subjective reports about role functioning important variables to consider in studying the interactive effects of motives and roles? The problem of honesty of response is a persistent one in all research with human beings. We tried to deal with this problem in the training of our interviewers, in construction of the interview schedule, and in the phrasing of the questions. Some of the techniques used may be illustrated by the handling of the questions on marriage. (See Appendix A, Section III, for questions 27 to 40.) We first approached this potentially sensitive area by asking a question phrased in very general terms (question 27—"How is a woman's [man's] life changed by being married?"). We prefaced a question probing for the unsatisfying aspects of a marriage (question 32) with "Every marriage has its good points and bad points," and only after having allowed people to talk about the "nicest things" in their marriage did we ask about dissatisfactions. We allowed a person to express qualifications about his marriage by using the alternative "average" (question 34) instead of presenting him only with "happy" or "unhappy" alternatives.

It is difficult, of course, to assign a rating to the degree of success attained in meeting this problem in any given interview survey. Perhaps the most convincing evidence derives from a reading of the interviews; in this study, as in others, they reflect the surprising frankness with which people seem willing to talk to a survey interviewer about their problems and dissatisfactions as well as their successes and sources of joy. We can also point to the meaningful way in which these data have been used in a variety of researches (Feld, 1963; Gurin et al., 1960; Jackson, 1962; Jackson and Burke, 1965; Veroff et al., 1962b), which we view as the ultimate basis for assessing the validity of any measurement technique. It is also to this source that we turn to deal with the second question, of the value of studying self-appraisals. That man's awareness of his own experiences is the proper province of science we hold to be a basic tenet of modern psychology. The specific self-appraisals used here interrelate in meaningful ways, vary in predictable ways with demographic characteristics, and are consistent with data from other types of assessments of role adjustment. Whether our measures of role reactions generate meaningful relationships in the analysis of motives and roles in interaction remains to be seen in the present study.

Measures of the reliability of the coding of the indices used to measure role reactions are not available because of the coding procedures used. Except for the questions used to assess motives, each interview was coded by a single coder. Between 20 and 30 coders were employed at this task at any one time. They were members of the staff of the coding section of the Survey Research Center, who were carefully trained in the general procedures of content analysis. Detailed coding schedules were prepared by the authors, and training sessions were held. Throughout the coding period, about six months, the authors recoded a 10% sample of the interviews, and discussed any differences with the original coders. No simple coding reliability index was used, since (a) the number of questions asked of any respondent varied according to his sex, his marital, parental, and work status, as well as his answers to certain interview questions, and (b) the number of categories used to code replies to different questions varied drastically. The reader will have to rely on our judgment that the careful training and supervision of the coders and the detailed coding instructions resulted in adequate coding reliability for the measures of role reactions.

INFERRING ROLE CHARACTERISTICS

So far in this chapter we have described the procedures used to measure one category of independent variables—motives—and the set of dependent variables—role reactions. However, our interest is not simply in the relationship between motives and role reactions, but rather in the nature of these relationships under different conditions of role demands, gratifications, and ambiguities. These role characteristics, then, can be considered another category of independent variables in this study. They comprise the set of expectations associated with a given social position. Unlike the other independent variables, or the dependent variables, the role characteristics were not directly measured by questions in the interview schedule. Instead, we first proposed that occupants of the positions of spouse, parent, or employed man each held a common set of expectations that defined the role demands, gratifications, and ambiguities.

These characteristics were described in some detail in Chapter 1. Those descriptions were based on our interpretation of previous research and theory concerning the marital, parental, and job roles in American society. However, we did indicate that a variety of factors could influence the specific set of expectations that define these roles for a given individual, such as his sex, social status, age, stage of the family life cycle, or the specific job a man holds. In the succeeding chapters, we will use these kinds of characteristics of individuals to help specify the demands, gratifications, and ambiguities they face in their marital, parental, and job roles. At this point we will indicate the various kinds of data we have used to infer role characteristics, and the general kinds of distinctions they led to. In each chapter devoted to a given role, we will be more specific about how each distinction applies to that role.

SEX AS A BASIS FOR INFERRING ROLE CHARACTERISTICS

While it is possible to specify certain characteristics associated with the positions of marriage partner, parent, and job-holder, it is also apparent that the role demands, gratifications, and ambiguities of marriage, parenthood, and work are different for men and women. Therefore, in all analyses and tabulations of the relationships between motives and role reactions in marriage and parenthood men and women will be kept separate. We shall deal with both the general roles of spouse and parent and the specific roles of husband and wife, and mother and father. We will look only at male respondents in the chapter on work, since we consider this role has an important influence on male behavior but generally not so important an influence on female behavior. We will take female employment into account in the parenthood chapter, considering that work for women so often represents a life situation that can be in conflict with maternal demands.

Not only are the expectations for marriage and parenthood different for men and women, but perhaps consonant with general sex role differences, their instinctive reactions to any social role may also differ. Recent work suggests that congenital factors may contribute to behavioral differences between men and women. Newborn female infants show greater tactile sensitivity and basal skin conductance while male infants show greater muscle strength (Bell and Costello, 1964; Bell and Darling, 1965; Weller and Bell, 1965). These and other sex differences at birth might have important implications for the quality of basic developments in both behavior and motives in men and women. The personality traits of dependency and aggressiveness seem to differ for boys and girls, with dependency being a more consistent characteristic of girls over time and aggressiveness a more consistent one for boys over time (Yarrow and Yarrow, 1964). Do these results imply that in addition to sex role differences that are learned, men are more innately able to assume the assertive role and that women are more innately endowed to be socially responsive? If so, we could suggest that males and females in very early development may have different orientations to such things as affiliation, achievement, and power motivations—the personality characteristics that are the foci of our present investigation. Furthermore, the possibility of early stronger assertiveness in males and social responsiveness in females could have important implications for the meaning that each sex attaches to marriage and parenthood.

EDUCATION AS A BASIS FOR INFERRING ROLE CHARACTERISTICS

The educational level a person has attained not only defines his level of interest, his general capacities, and the values that influence his motivational dispositions, but also defines the character of demands, gratifications, and ambiguities that exists for him in a particular role. Let us examine this assertion within the context of marriage and parenthood.

We assume that college-educated persons enter social streams that are different from those entered by persons with a high-school education or by grade-school-educated men and women; in turn, these social groupings create their own role demands. Particularly important are the conceptions of marriage and parenthood that exist for many college-educated Americans. Intellectual understanding of interpersonal behavior is a focus of study in the social sciences in the modern college classroom. Regardless of its merit, such intellectual pursuit undoubtedly affects the attitudes and expectations about social roles that college students have when they emerge from the campus. Traditional views of the authority of the father or the husband have been questioned in recent thinking about interpersonal relationships in these roles: wives are to have more influence in decision making; fathers are expected to share in caretaking for the child. As a result, the views of marriage and parenthood in the avant-garde college group often exist in defiance of certain traditional views of role obligations. When the college student assumes his or her adult role in the world, it may be necessary to fit into a more traditional view, but one can safely say that their views of parenthood or of marriage are considerably different from those who enter directly into the adult social world after high school.

It might be argued that other measures of social status would more appropriately have been used to differentiate subjects with traditional and companionate views of marriage—family income, occupation, or some combination of these with education, something that describes social class. It is true that educational level is not as complex a variable as social class, but we hope its interpretation is clearer. In earlier reports of some of these data (Gurin et al., 1960; Veroff et al., 1962b) different relationships were obtained with role reactions depending on whether social status was measured by education, by occupation, or by income. Each of these variables had slightly different impacts on subjective feelings of adjustment and on reactions to problems in adjustment. Therefore, we were unwilling to use a single combined index of social status.

We found that educational level was the single most important social-status variable related to differences in marital and parental role reactions; therefore, we used this variable for the study of marriage and parenthood in this book. A threefold classification of educational background of a respondent was used: whether a person was minimally educated (no more than grade-school education), whether he had a moderate amount of education (some high school or a high-school degree), or whether he was highly educated (some college or a college degree). We used these three educational levels to infer certain differing role characteristics in our analysis of the roles of marriage and parenthood. All analyses of the relationships between motives and role reactions are presented separately within each educational level.

In the chapter on the job role, we used the prestige of the occupation that a man is in to gauge his social-status group and to infer certain characteristics of his job role. We will present our reasons for using occupational prestige rather than educational level in a subsequent section of this chapter.

AGE AS A BASIS FOR INFERRING ROLE CHARACTERISTICS

The roles of marriage, parenthood, and work are not static; they have a natural cycle of development and change that is related in a general way to the age of the person holding the position.

In the marital role, for example, young people are immersed in the problem of learning to adjust two lives together, sexually and interpersonally. In the early years of a marriage a couple is very dependent on one another for personal contact. In subsequent years, children can serve as a focus of personal contact that perhaps detracts from the strong intimacy of early marriage. Later in life, when children are grown, marital partners are thrown together again, often to reevaluate their past and to face the prospect of each or both of their deaths. Therefore, in Chapter 3 we present the relationships between motives and marital role reactions separately for persons at three age levels: young (21–34), middle-aged (35–49), and old (50 and older).

For the parental role, we used the age range of a parent's children to infer certain variations in role characteristics because we assumed that the age of one's children should have more psychological impact on developmental changes in the parental role than the chronological age of the parent. We assumed that the stimuli from each of these life stages with children are distinctive. Preschoolers, for example, because of their limited intellectual and motor development, are extremely dependent on parents for care and in American society, and are under the care of the mother a great deal of the time. Adolescence also presents unique problems for parents. The physical and psychological changes at adolescence not only raise issues for the adolescents but also present special problems that often test a parent's maturity. A parent has to give up most but not all of his ties to the child at this time. Similar sorts of peculiar demands of parenthood exist at other points in the parental cycle. Therefore, the relationships between motives and parental reactions will be separately presented for parents of preschoolers, school-age children, adolescent children, and adult children.

Age is also a useful key to differentiating changes in the role characteristics of work. At younger ages, men face the task of attaining the kind of occupational position that they desire. They are most able to change their job at this point in their lives if the role characteristics are incongruent with their needs. During middle-age, a man is more likely to be committed to a particular job and to have to adapt to any incongruence between his motives and the job characteristics. The oldest men may have so fully adapted to their job demands that there is a reduced investment in work. To take account of the inferred differences in job-role characteristics associated with age, the relationships between motives and job-role reactions will be presented separately for young, middle-aged, and old men.

A final note of caution should be sounded about the difficulties of using age of respondent or children as a variable to represent life cycle variance in a cross-sectional survey. Age differences imply generation differences as well as stages of the life cycle. Let us illustrate this problem within the context of the present survey. In a previous study using the motive measures in this national survey (Veroff et al., 1962a), we found that the age of a man may be critically related to achievement motivation. In that study it was suggested that middle age may be an important time for the arousal of achievement strivings in men. This age period seems to be a potential last ditch stand for a man's sense of accomplishment, both in retrospection of his youth and in anticipation of his old age. If he is not successful in his own eyes during this period he may conclude that he will live out the rest of the years disappointed. This interpretation was based on the fact that middle-aged men had high-achievement scores relative to younger and older age groups, particularly Catholic men who, it was argued, are perhaps most susceptible to external pressures for achievement during middle age. Although the results were interpreted as showing an increasing salience of achievement concerns for middle-aged men, they

65

can also be interpreted as reflections of differences in generations. Men who grew up at different time periods under different types of social influences might develop stronger or weaker achievement motivation. But no matter which interpretation is used, we encounter an important difference between different age groupings. In the present report we usually interpreted age differences in motive-role interaction as a function of life-cycle differences rather than as a function of generation differences. As Schaie (1965) has pointed out, however, the data from any cross-sectional study cannot unambiguously lead to either a generational or a life-cycle interpretation of psychological differences associated with the subjects' ages, unless some other relevant longitudinal data are available. We recognize our data are confounded.

OCCUPATION AS A BASIS FOR INFERRING JOB CHARACTERISTICS

Although age was one basis for inferring job characteristics, the primary source was the specific job the respondent held. We first distinguished ten relatively homogeneous occupational groupings for which we felt job demands, gratifications, and ambiguities could be described, such as self-employed businessmen, salesmen, farmers, and considered the relationships between motives and job reactions within each type of specific occupational grouping.

Besides isolating specific jobs, we looked for general characteristics of jobs from which we could infer certain role demands, gratifications, or ambiguities. The first characteristic that seemed relevant was the prestige accorded a person's job. We assume that a job's prestige connotes its responsibilities and status gratifications, and perhaps the ambiguity of specific role requirements. Generally speaking, more prestigeful jobs require considerable decision-making and result in financial and societal rewards. These characteristics increase the potential for achievement and power gratifications both within the job role and in other major life roles. The prestige of a job was based on ratings of the public obtained by the National Opinion Research Center (1953) in a 1947 survey. We will discuss this more fully in Chapter 5.

Another general job characteristic that interested us was its social demands. First we asked whether or not a person *is required* to react to another person or groups of other people in doing his work. Some jobs require men to react to, be responsive to, be in communication with, and coact with other people in many ways. Other jobs do not require this; they can be performed satisfactorily without attending to another person's responses. We used the specific occupations of the respondents to infer whether or not any social requirements were intrinsic to functioning in the job. For example, the job of teacher requires interpersonal activities, but that of accountant may not. The specific coding scheme used is described in Chapter 5.

Two further kinds of information about the social demands of a job were available for a portion of our respondents. On a random basis, approximately one-half of the men who were not self-employed had been asked whether they worked under anyone or whether anyone supervised their work, and if so, how much the supervisor had to do with them and their work. They were also asked whether or not they had any other person working under them. On the basis of these questions we distinguished respondents whose jobs required that they be supervised closely and whose jobs did not require them to submit to close supervision. We also distinguished those subjects whose jobs required that they supervise other persons and those subjects who did not supervise the work of other people. For each of these categories of subjects the relationships between motives and role reactions were separately computed since we assumed that these groups of subjects faced different role demands, gratifications, and ambiguities. We will look at each of these more closely in Chapter 5.

ANALYSIS DESIGN

The basic research question under investigation in this book is: what is the relationship between motivation and reactions to roles under different conditions of role demands, gratifications, and ambiguities? To answer this question within each of the three roles under investigation, we will consider the degree of association between a motive score and a given measure of role reaction for various subgroups of the subjects, the subgroupings being used to identify persons for whom the role of spouse (or parent, or worker) is comprised of somewhat different sets of expectations about the demands, gratifications, and ambiguities that are associated with that position. The data to be reported will consist of a series of indices of the degree of association between measures of a motive and of a role reaction.

In applying the congruence principle to these data, the relevant relationships will be those between motives and role reactions of an evaluative sort, those concerning levels of satisfaction or dissatisfaction, happiness or unhappiness, adequate or inadequate role performance, for subgroups of the subjects who are assumed to hold role expectations that are compatible or incompatible with their motivation. For example, we will assume that for men in jobs with high prestige there is congruence between role demands and achievement motivation. We will thus expect a higher positive correlation between achievement motivation and job satisfaction among men in jobs with high prestige than among men in jobs with less prestige. The latter correlation should be lower or even negative.

The relationships relevant to the sensitization principle will be those between motives and the role reactions concerning the kinds of demands, satisfactions, or dissatisfactions that exist in a role. For example, we expect there to be a higher correlation between affiliation motivation and mentioning relationship satisfactions in marriage than between achievement motivation and mentioning such satisfactions. Furthermore, since we expect motive sensitization to occur when the role is ambiguous in its gratification potential for that motive, the relationship between affiliative motive and mentioning relationship satisfaction in marriage should be greatest in marriages in which the demand for companionate activity between a husband and wife is most ambiguous.

In each chapter, we will present the relationships between each of the three motives and all measures of role reactions, even though we did not necessarily expect that each motive would be related to each role reaction. We did this for two reasons. First, the motives serve as controls for each other. That is, we can ask whether the relationship between a motive and a given role reaction is true of any of the three measured motives or of a particular motive. In the latter instance there is greater assurance that a particular characteristic of that motive should be used to account for the relationship. Second, the reader has available to him the same data that we did. He may have other hypotheses about how motives should relate to role reactions and we would like him to be able to check out his own hypotheses. Further, we view these data as providing a rich basis for generating hypotheses about the characteristics of marriage, parenthood, and work, as well as about the affiliation, achievement, and power motives and would like them to be readily available.

The basic tables for this study are those that present the relationships between motives and role reactions, within certain subgroups of the sample. These tables are presented in the relevant chapters. Supplementary tables, presenting the distributions on the various measures of role reactions and the interrelationships among these measures, are presented in Appendix B. References will be made to the Appendix B tables at appropriate points in each chapter.

The basic index of relationship used was the descriptive statistic, Gamma, a measure suggested by Goodman and Kruskal (1954). This measure describes how consistently you can reproduce the order of one variable (B) when the order of another variable (A) is given. Gamma predicts the direction of order of variable B and how consistently this order is reproduced when order of variable A is known. Gamma varies from -1 to $+1$, with perfect association occurring when the ordering of one variable reproduces the ordering on the second variable. The value of Gamma is not dependent upon the symmetry of the marginals. *Gamma essentially can be thought of as the percentage of increase in predicting the order of one variable from knowing the order of another variable.* The value of Gamma indicates how much more likely the rank order of a randomly selected observation on one variable will predict the same relative rank position on the second variable. Because of the lack of direct tests for the significance of Gamma,[10] and since high Gammas need not be important when skewed distributions of measures are obtained, we placed two types of limitations on their use in analyses. First, we did not report Gammas based on either a total $N < 10$, or on a variable with only two categories, where the less frequent category had $N < 5$, regardless of the total N. In the tables that follow in Chapters 3, 4, and 5, Gammas omitted for either of these reasons were indicated by a footnote stating "not reported due to inadequate distribution."

Secondly, we also computed Kendall's rank correlation statistic, Tau Beta (Kendall, 1955), and the significance of the Tau Beta associated with each of the relationships for which the Gammas were reported. In computing the significance of Tau we corrected for continuity and for the presence of tied observations in these categorical data. In the tables the value of Gamma was reported along with the significance level of the data based on Tau (two-tailed probability values are used). We chose to report the Gamma coefficients rather than the Taus because there appears to be no simple interpretation of the value of Tau when there are ties present in either ranking, as is the case here for data of ordered classes.[11]

The .10 significance level was adopted. This liberal level of significance was chosen because we assumed that in this type of research the errors of measurement are probably so numerous that obtaining a large number of significant relationships by chance would be extremely unlikely, whereas the errors of overlooking true departures from zero-order associations were more probable. We will also be on the lookout for consistency of Gammas across groups, even when the individual Gammas may not be at the significant level. Such consistency may indicate that more refined measurement would reveal more sizable relationships. In other words, we will not reject as uninteresting data, any *pattern of results* that presents a consistent picture that could be provocative for future research. This liberal use of statistical significance may be viewed as a fault. Since we see this book as being an impetus for other people to follow through on more intensive explorations of particular aspects of motive-role interaction, we justify the liberal use of statistics as a means of suggesting interesting leads for future refined work where more conservative estimates of significance would be appropriate.

[10]There have been two recent attempts to approximate a direct statistical test (Goodman and Kruskal, 1963; Rosenthal, 1966).

[11]Recent empirical investigations at the Survey Research Center (Robinson, John, Personal communication, 1966) point to the fact that the size of Gamma varies with number of classifications used in either of the variables. Therefore, the exact value of Gamma in one relationship is comparable to a value in another relationship only when the two relationships use the same number of classifications on both variables.

3

Motives
and
Marriage

In this chapter we begin our presentation of the data
interrelating roles and individual motivation. Our inquiry
begins with the marital role, a role that is essential to the functioning of
both the society and the individual. From the
societal point of view marriage is an institution that serves to insure
the continuation of the society: husbands and wives propagate and care for
children and become the agents of socialization of children into
the particular society. It is also one of the institutionalized
means of regulating the interpersonal and economic interactions between the members of the society. From
the individual point of view, the functions of the family have been
guarantees of assistance in the bearing and
raising of children, controls for the receipt and extension of affection
(Swanson, 1965), resources for economic
and protective care. In American society, the marital state is
an important symbol of the attainment of adulthood. Indeed,
marriage has sometimes been described as the final
stage in the socialization of the individual (Parsons and Bales, 1955), a
point in the development of the individual when he
assumes the obligations for his own future.

A casual glance at the American scene attests to the importance
of marriage. We will add only one bit of systematic
evidence from our current data to emphasize this point.

71

The one-third random subset of the national interview sample that did not receive the thematic apperceptive measures of motivation was asked to evaluate the status of the nonmarried adult as follows:

Suppose all you knew about a man (woman) was that he didn't want to get married. What would you guess he was like? Do you think he could live a happy life, or do you think he probably wouldn't be happy?

Only a minority of our respondents (9%) indicated that they felt that either the unmarried person or the unmarried state was a legitimate or positive condition. Furthermore, many of the respondents (40%) indicated that they felt that such a person would be unhappy.

Knowing that the role is very important, how would we describe it? Let us review the descriptions of the important role characteristics of marriage that were presented in Chapter 1. We described the primary marital role demands as involving economic provision by the husband, care of the home by the wife, sexual gratification of the partner, and the maintenance of emotional ties between the husband and wife. That the major function of marriage is currently seen as centered on the inter-personal relationship between the husband and wife is reflected in the responses given to a question in this national survey asking the respondents to describe how a man or a woman's life is changed by being married. The most frequent type of first-mentioned response to this question concerned emotional changes that resulted from, or involved, the relationship to spouse (24%). Also important were the economic or material aspects of the life changes accompanying marriage (14%), such as the economic security for the wife; the convenience for the husband of having a wife to take care of the house, the cooking, and other such chores; or the attainment of a house or home itself. Less salient was becoming a parent (2%). All of these responses are reflections of the primary role demands.

An interesting characteristic of marriage that encompasses all of these role demands is the formal commitment that men and women make to each other and to the world, the commitment to enter into an enduring relationship between husband and wife. This relationship involves the division of labor with its concomitant interlocking role expectations between husband and wife. The differentiation of function between husband and wife has been described in various ways, but for our purposes one of the most interesting is the distinction between the expressive functions of the wife and the instrumental role of the husband (Parsons and Bales, 1955). The instrumental functions of the husband involve social systems external to that of the family. They are largely concerned with the relation of the family to the outside world and with adapting to conditions necessary to the maintenance of the family. The expressive functions of the wife are mainly directed toward keeping the relations between family members integrated by regulating their patterns of interaction and tension levels.

This distinction helps us anticipate the nature of the relationship between personal motives and role demands, and in particular, the way in which it may differ for husbands and wives. Achievement motivation, because of its relationship to occupational aspirations and performances, should be particularly relevant to the adequacy with which husbands can cope with the instrumental role function. The requirements for assertive interactions with the social system outside the family also suggests that power motivation may facilitate the ability of the husband to satisfy the instrumental demands of his role. Both affiliation and power motivation, whose goals are certain types of interpersonal relationships, should be relevant to a wife's marital role, since her expressive functions concern the emotional relationships among persons. Dividing the functions of the family into instrumental or expressive functions, however, seems to neglect the importance of the quality of emotional relationship between the husband and wife that was characteristic of the family even prior to the modern so-called companionate family. The marriage vows with their emphasis on love and obedience serve to illustrate the importance of the personal relationship between husband and wife, without which a marriage cannot survive. Such an emphasis suggests that the interpersonal motives should be relevant to both husbands' and wives' reactions to their respective marital roles.

MOTIVES IN THE CONTEXT OF MARRIAGE

We now turn to more specific considerations of the ways in which affiliation, achievement, and power motivation may interact with the demands and potentials in the marital roles, not only from the standpoint of maintaining a family but also from the standpoint of maintaining the personal relationships between husband and wife.

INFERRING ROLE CHARACTERISTICS FROM EDUCATION, AGE, AND PARENTAL STATUS

In order to consider the interactive effects of an individual's motives and marital role requirements upon marital reactions, it was necessary first to determine the role requirements and expectations for both husband and wife, and then to look at the degree of flexibility and the limits on action that were available in enacting these roles.

A number of approaches were possible in describing the role of husband or wife. First, we could consider that the marital role offers common potentials and common hindrances to motive gratification for all American husbands and wives. This is obviously an oversimplified view of marriage in modern American life. We had already limited our consideration to a certain type of American marriage, because our sampling procedures only considered adults 21 years of age or older, who did not live in institutional settings. Furthermore, we decided to analyze the results only for white subjects who were currently married. However, even within this group we assumed that there were significant variations in the role demands and potentials for members of different social groups. In trying to determine what aspect of social-group membership we would use to define the kinds of role faced by respondents, two major possibilities were the age of the individual and his educational background. We had found (Gurin et al., 1960, Chapter 4) that both age and education were related to evaluations of level of marital role adjustment. (See Tables 3.c and 3.d, Appendix B.) However, educational background but not age was significantly related to the way in which persons defined their role when they were asked to discuss the sources of happiness and unhappiness in their marriage, the problems they have had, or the kinds of inadequacies they felt.

The major difference between persons of different educational levels in these results concerned the extent to which some aspect of the relationship with the spouse was seen as central to the marital role: the more-educated respondents were more likely to report that some aspect of the husband-wife interaction was important as a source of their marital happiness or unhappiness, their marriage problems, or their own feelings of inadequacy. Such an emphasis seemed to reflect the distinction between a traditional and a companionate marriage, with the traditional marital conceptions being characteristic of the less-educated. The clearly differentiated role functions for husbands and wives, where the husband is the provider and decision-maker in the household and the wife is the homemaker and mother, were more descriptive of the conceptions of marriage of husbands and wives who had little education. A different attitude toward homemaking is found among college-educated women. Komarovsky (1962) found that there is more expressed dissatisfaction with the domestic role of homemaker among college-trained females than among the working-class wives. This is not surprising. The college-trained wife defines her marital role with characteristics that are developed beyond the mere homemaking conception. Focusing only on the homemaking aspects of marriage makes her dissatisfied. To her, a marriage should be one in which the husband and wife share more or less equally in the decision-making and where the affectionate and companionate relationship between the husband and wife is central to them both.

We therefore decided to consider educational level as the basis for the most important social grouping of the respondents in this chapter and will present all the data analysis within the three major educational groups.

We distinguished three groups of married respondents according to the highest educational level attained: those with no more than a grade-school education; those with no more than a high-school education; those with some college education. We also recognize that a respondent's age reflects significant aspects of variation in role expectations. Certainly there are generational as well as life-cycle differences in the kinds of expectations, satisfactions, and dissatisfactions that may be experienced in the marital role. Lindner and Courtney (1953), for example, contrast the basic life styles at three age levels. They propose that most thirty-year-olds in our society adopt a family-centered view of life, that middle-aged people have more general social involvement with the world beyond the family, and that very old people seek a retrospective, moral, and ethical reaffirmation in the self.

To the extent that the different age groupings of our respondents reflect differences in marital role expectations for persons from different generations, we expected that the differentiation between younger and older subjects would coincide with the differentiation between traditional and companionate families and would be similar to the differentiation among the various educational groups. Since age of the respondents also reflects differences in the developmental life cycle, taking account of age provides further differentiation within educational subgroupings. It would be hard to specify all the changes in role characteristics that occur during the natural cycle of a marriage, but certainly different obligations, gratifications, and ambiguities exist in the marriages of young, middle-aged, and old people. Sexual intimacy in youth, the shared parental sense in middle age, and the mutual working out of a philosophy of existing in facing death are the most apparent role differences in these three age groups. In an attempt to specify those married respondents who were facing different role characteristics, three broad age groupings were formed: the young (21–34), the middle-aged (35–49), and the older (50 and above) married men and women.

In the early years of marriage the individual adapts to the marital role. This early period might be a time when, generally speaking, personality or motivational characteristics of the role occupants would be most evident in their adaptation to their marital roles. We would presume that a newly-wed who faces role expectations that are not totally compatible with his personality has not yet found the means of modifying either his own goals or the role demands and that role reactions would be most indicative of motive-role congruence at this point in the life cycle. Middle-aged husbands and wives may face different kinds of role situations than when they were younger, and new challenges to their marital role adjustment may arise. For men, middle-age is often a critical time in their job role. This is the period during which the success of their occupational efforts is often determined. Middle-aged men who are successful in their occupational aspirations may have to accommodate their marital role to job demands that limit their time at home. And middle-age may be a period of crisis for men who are not successful in their occupational aspirations. Women at this age period, whose husbands are in the midst of occupational crisis, may therefore face new problems in their marriage. In addition, middle-aged women are more likely to have children who are entering the larger social systems themselves. Their children are probably in schools a good part of the day. Therefore the parental focus of their marital role is probably changing. Women may be seeking new means of motivational satisfactions at this time.

By the time married couples reach the age of fifty or so, they are at a point in the life cycle where they will probably turn more towards one another as sources of gratification. Children are more likely to be grown and away from the home, and a man's career is more likely to have reached a stable point and to involve less challenge for him than in the past. Such a leveling off period might call into play new role expectations that might be especially relevant to the interpersonal motives. On the other hand, the marriage partners' patterns of interaction with one another are probably well established, and whatever adaptation they can make in themselves or their interpretations of their role has probably occurred. It might therefore be expected that the relationship between motivational characteristics and role reactions would be less clear because modifications may have been made in both individual goals and roles to increase congruence.

Another objective differentiation within the marital role that we considered in this chapter was whether or not the respondent currently had any living children. The behavior towards one another of husbands and wives who have children was expected to be different from those who are not parents. For the couple without children, the relationship between the husband and wife is the only interpersonal focus for their marriage. Individual motivation may therefore be closely associated with role expectations about the relationship between husband and wife not only because this relationship is usually the central aspect of a marriage but because the couple must compensate for absence of gratification through children in some way. Childless couples often face problems of an overinvestment in their relationship, expecting too much of it, or attaching too much importance to the inevitable frustrations of living together. Childless couples, however, may have more of an opportunity to obtain motivational gratification from social systems outside the family.

The couple with children, the typical family group, faces the full set of marital role demands that include parental role requirements for the emotional and physical care of the child. For most married couples, parental demands as well as parental gratification will have to be considered in trying to understand the interaction between motivation and marital role characteristics. For example, even in the traditional patriarchal family system where the husband and father has the dominant role in decision-making, the mother's role vis-à-vis her children has been a powerful one in American society. A woman may find opportunity for the gratification of power motivation in motherhood that is not found in the husband-wife interactions. With such gratification a wife can experience satisfaction with marriage that is not a direct reflection of her status with her husband but is an indirect reflection of her status with her children. Throughout this chapter we will thus be careful to keep in mind the potential impact of the parental role on the way motives relate to a variety of marital reactions. But we will be especially alerted to this possibility when contrasting husbands or wives who do have children with husbands or wives who do not.

AFFILIATION MOTIVATION AND MARITAL REACTIONS

Since the entrance into the marital status marks the formal, public acknowledgement of a person's commitment to an enduring relationship with another person in daily life until death do them part, we had expected that the role reactions to marriage would bear important relationships to the affiliation motive. However, this expected relationship between the affiliation motive and marital role reactions is a simple-minded view of motive-role interaction, both from the point of view of the meaning of affiliation motivation and the significance of interpersonal expectations and demands in marriage. As we indicated in Chapter 1, the affiliation motive, as measured here, included several elements; namely, the positive desire for affiliation, the desire to avoid aloneness, and the desire to avoid rejection. Finding out which ones are most strongly evoked by marriage would have important implications for expected relationships between affiliation motivation and marital reactions. Added to this ambiguity are others. These are listed below.

First, are the goals of affiliation most clearly established in marriage by "friendship" with one's spouse or by sexual love? This is a special question derived from the more general one, is affiliation more possible by contact with "similar" persons or with "complementary" persons? The marital relationship can be described both as a mutual sharing relationship based on similarity and as a complementary relationship that functions best when the differences between husbands and wives are accentuated.

Secondly, does marriage enhance or cut off affiliative gratification with friends? This is a special instance of the issue of whether affiliation motivation is more likely gratified by intimate contact or by more extensive contact. On the one hand marriage may take a person away from a wide circle of friends that existed before marriage, and the marital relationship may not compensate for this loss. On the other hand, marriage may even enhance contact with friends, especially if it was absent before marriage.

Thirdly, do marriages that explicitly demand companionate inter- action between husband and wife enhance or interfere with affiliative gratification? This raises the general question, if affiliation is obligatory, is gratification interfered with?

Answers to each of these questions would dramatically affect the way affiliation motivation interacts with different types of marital roles. We do not have answers to them, but in this section we will look at each of these ambiguities about affiliation motivation to see how they would affect the specific predictions we can make about affiliation motivation in this chapter.

Let us examine the first ambiguity about affiliation motivation: do affiliative strivings stem mainly from affiliative desires or from avoidant fears of isolation or rejection? We have no clear evidence of whether the approach or the avoidant aspects of affiliation motivation would be more central in consideration of the marital role. We have evidence that through marriage, men and women seek to avoid being alone. Although these results could be engendered by a positive affiliative motive, by a fear of isolation, or by a fear of rejection, these results do favor the interpretation that our measure of affiliation motivation strongly reflects a fear of isola- tion, or anxiety about acceptance.

What are these results? They emerge from the comparison of the strength of affiliation motivation found in groups differing in marital status. We realize that entrance into the married status may have implica- tions for affiliative possibilities aside from the conjugal relationship itself. The simple fact of being married is often viewed as evidence of one's popularity or ability to establish warm, affectionate relationships with another person. Thus, one could consider that the attainment of the married status would be related to the motivation for affiliation, regardless of the nature of the interpersonal relationship established with the spouse. In an effort to consider this proposition, we compared the affiliation moti- vation scores for varying marital status groupings of all the white subjects with motive scores.

Among those persons who were married at the time of the interview, we distinguished those for whom this was the first marriage and those whose current marriage was not their first one. Men who had some pre- viously disrupted marriage, but who had reentered the marital state, had higher affiliation motivation (62% above the median) than the first marriage group (47% above the median). What was of further interest was the lack of distinction between those whose previous marriage was dis- rupted by divorce and those whose previous marriage was disrupted by death. Contrary to what might be initially expected, the strength of affiliation motivation was not related to the source of disruption, but rather to the choice to reenter the married state. For women, there was less variation in affiliation motivation among those subgroups of the currently married women; the percentage of high affiliation motive scores was 55 in the remarried group and 51 in the first marriage group. It may be that the motivation to attain or reestablish the married state was more easily translated into the attainment of this goal for men, who in our society usually play a more active role in the initiation of marriage. It is also possible that affiliation motivation has more of the elements of the desire to avoid aloneness for men than for women.

One might further suppose that at least some persons who were single at the time of the interview (that is, who had never married) lacked this motivation to affiliate. We found, however, only slight evidence of this, and again, mainly for men: single men had somewhat lower affiliation motivation than currently married men.

Both men and women who were widowed at the time of the interview were the lowest in affiliation motivation. While affiliation motivation was somewhat related to age, with older persons manifesting less affiliation motivation, the apparently low affiliation motivation among the widowed group cannot be solely attributed to age, since the same trend occurred when comparing married and widowed persons with age controlled. What may be significant again here is that men and women in the widowed status have not reestablished their previous married status.

All these results tend to indicate that strong affiliation motivation is associated with seeking out and attaining the married status to avoid the discomfort of being alone. The evidence does not clearly substantiate this proposition, but it tends to support it. Therefore, we might be alerted to look for this avoidant aspect of affiliation motivation in relating this motive to marital reactions. It might be that being married itself removes this affiliative concern with regard to one's spouse. Once married, a person strongly motivated to affiliate may turn to other relationships to demonstrate his acceptance. But our best guess is that after marriage fears of isolation and rejection will continue to be central to the marital relationship itself.

Let us turn to the second ambiguity about affiliation motivation in the context of marriage: are the goals of affiliation most clearly established by friendship with one's spouse, or by sexual love? Again we cannot give any definitive answer to this question. We have no basis for knowing just how much sexual attraction to another would be part of the general affiliative incentive, or just how incompatible sexual attraction and affiliative attraction are. What we do know is that the expectations that a person be a companion to one's spouse is more pervasive among some social groups than others. In the more modern view of the marital relationship, the marriage partners should expect that they would find companionship, friendship, mutual sharing of interests with their marital partner. In the more traditional marriages, these expectations should not exist to as great an extent. In the traditional marital relationship a husband or wife expects support and assistance in carrying out quite a separate role. If affiliation motivation mostly reflects attraction to similar others, we would expect that persons whose social-group expectations included companionate marriages would be more able to satisfy a strong affiliation motive within the marital relationship than persons from social groups with a more traditional view of marriage. However, if affiliation motivation has a high component of sexual motivation, then we would perhaps expect affiliation motivation to relate to marital reactions in marriages where the sex role differentiation is greatest—in the traditional rather than the companionate marriages. The pattern of results in our study may elucidate these opposing hypotheses.

We turn now to the next ambiguity about the relationship of affiliation motivation to marriage: does marriage enhance or cut off affiliative gratification stemming from the extensive contact with friends?

Our efforts to investigate the leisure activities of the respondents provided some further insights into the extramarital implications of affiliation motivation. These data will be discussed in greater detail in Chapter 5. For our present purposes, it is only necessary to note that for men, affiliation motivation was related to the expressed feeling that the respondent does not have as many friends as he would like.

In addition, we found that men with high affiliation motivation were more likely to have described leisure activities that fell into the general affiliative category, such as visits with friends and family. Thus, it appears that our measure of affiliation for men is related to a positive reaching out for social contact and to the feeling that one's social contacts are not sufficient. A marital role that interferes with this reaching out might be incongruent with strong affiliation motivation.

One further point can be made about the effect of marriage on a person's affiliative potential outside the marital situation. Marriage can have both positive and negative implications for a person's extramarital affiliative activities. If we assume that individuals have a circle of friends prior to marriage, the marriage itself may interfere with the maintenance of these contacts due to the new obligations that the individual attains upon being married. In the popular folklore this conflict has traditionally been described as a problem for the man who still seeks to have his night out with his buddies and whose wife resents it. In the more traditional marriages it is possible that the man retains more freedom to maintain his contacts with his own peer group outside the marriage relationship. In the more companionate marriages, role expectations are more likely to involve social contacts where the husband and wife jointly engage in social activities with mutual friends. A logical follow-up question is whether joint social contacts with other married couples are as effective as same-sex peer-group contacts in satisfying the desires for affiliation that are tapped by the affiliation-motivation measures. Being aware, then, of the different kinds of social contact that may occur in companionate marriages as compared to traditional marriages may be important to our understanding of the interplay between affiliation motivation and marital reactions.

Finally, let us examine the last ambiguity about affiliation motivation and marriage: do marriages that explicitly demand affiliative behavior between husband and wife enhance or interfere with affiliative gratification? This same question will arise more dramatically within parenthood, a role where the nurturant function of parent to child is such an explicit expectation. In some marriages too, there are explicit demands that husband and wife accept each other, do things together, agree on beliefs and tastes. When such demands become obligations, do they change the character of gratification that a person might derive from such mutuality? Could a husband or a wife within such a marriage suspect that the spouse's affection is a response dictated by the role, and not by the special person that the husband or wife thinks he or she is? If this is so, we might entertain the hypothesis that men and women with high affiliation motivation in companionate marriages might experience more actual frustration than men and women with high motivation in more traditional marriages. Again, the pattern of results in our data may shed some light on this hypothesis.

ACHIEVEMENT MOTIVATION AND MARITAL REACTIONS

According to the general stereotype of a modern American marriage, there is little potential within the marital role of women for achievement gratification (Hoffman, 1963; Mead, 1946; Riesman, Glazer and Denny, 1953). Marriage prevents career aspirations, it is said; and furthermore, there are no clear standards of what constitutes competent performance as a wife. Therefore, the reward systems for achievement strivings would soon become out of reach for married women. This characterization of the marital role would lead to the hypothesis that women strong in achievement motivation should be more discontent with their marriages than women with weak achievement motivation. Since there has often been some beginning attempts at careers and a certain degree of professionalization among more-educated women, it was anticipated that interference with career aspirations would be more problematic for them than for women in the lower educational groups. Therefore, the relationship between the experience of difficulty with marriage and achievement motivation should be most evident among more-educated wives.

However, it is possible that certain of these women with strong achievement motivation can express their strivings in helping to foster the advancement of their husband's career. Numerous large business corporations have especially recognized this wifely role (Fortune, 1946).

We further recognize that the role of housewife itself may not be as devoid of the possibilities for achievement gratification as most social theorists assume. In our set of six pictures used to elicit stories that were scored for achievement motivation imagery, while the picture that elicited the most achievement-type imagery was of a work setting (Picture 1: Two women standing by a table and one woman is working with test tubes), two pictures usually interpreted as home scenes each elicited nearly as much achievement imagery (Picture 4: Woman kneeling and applying a cover to a chair; Picture 5: Two women preparing food in the kitchen). Thus, it is possible to view certain aspects of the wifely role as capable of providing achievement gratification.

For men, the relationship between achievement motivation and their marital functioning was expected to be quite different. It is usually assumed that a man satisfies his achievement strivings outside the marital situation, and that the gratifications and frustrations he experiences in his job role are the major basis for satisfying his achievement motivation. Therefore we expected that there would be little relationship between men's achievement motivation and their self-evaluations of their marital role-functioning. This should be particularly true of the more-educated men whose involvement in their job is much more achievement-oriented than that for less-educated men. (See Chapter 5.)

But it is impossible to ignore the indirect effects a man's marriage might have on his achievement even if he limits his goals to the occupational sphere. We were especially alerted to the possibility that more-educated men, who we assumed were engaged in more companionate marriages, might often experience demands from their wives for time and involvement with them and with their children. These men, if highly motivated for achievement, might regard such marital role demands as a hindrance to the devotion of time to the potentially greater achievement gratifications available in their job role. One might therefore suppose that highly achievement-oriented men at the more-educated levels would experience more dissatisfaction in their marital role because of the conflict they experience between the demands of their marital role and their job role. In the less-educated social groups where marriage is still more likely to be viewed traditionally, the husband's major role function is to provide; the highly achievement-oriented man who is willing to work hard and accomplish more on his job, may feel more satisfied in his marriage than a man with low achievement-orientation because the former more adequately fulfills the provider role that he sees essential to his marriage.

POWER MOTIVATION AND MARITAL REACTIONS

We assumed initially that the potential for gratification or frustration of the power motive in the marital role would be high, and therefore that level of power motivation would be an important dimension in understanding marital role reactions. Because of the complementary nature of power gratification in a two-person interaction, marital role demands that allow greater power expression and gratification for one spouse should automatically frustrate power expression and gratification of the other spouse. As is the case with the affiliation motive, however, it is not clear whether the measure of the power motive taps positive or avoidant motivation. Concern about the influence relationship vis-à-vis other persons can include positive strivings to assert one's own influence, or strivings to avoid either failing at one's own influence attempts or letting another person's influence attempts succeed. Our expectations about the specific ways that the power motive might influence marital role reactions are therefore contingent upon the interpretation of the power motive measure.

From one analysis it seems clear that the power motive measure reflects concern about, or involvement in, interpersonal relationships. We once again noted the level of motivation in varying marital status groupings. The results here were similar to those with our other measure of interpersonal motivation, the affiliation motive. Single men had lower power motive (and lower affiliation motive) than married men, and men who had remarried after a marriage previously disrupted by divorce were higher in power motive than men who were divorced at the time of the interview. These results suggest that an unmarried person maintains his unmarried status because he lacks a strong involvement in interpersonal relationships. This interpretation is consistent with a view that power motivation can propel a person into marriage and thus could be critical in understanding reactions to the married status. Once we accept that the measure of power motivation reflects an involvement with interpersonal interaction, we still need to specify whether this involvement is essentially power-assertive or weakness-avoidant. We will keep both interpretations in mind as we discuss further possible relationships between power motivation and marital reactions.

Let us first consider the traditional view of marriage, where the husband is the more influential figure, the decision-maker on major issues, or at least he is supposed to appear this way to his family and friends. We expected that for men who have a strong power motive with a positive, assertive goal, the traditional marital role would be congruent with their power motivation. For men low in this type of power motivation, the demands for influence assertion might either be irrelevant to their feelings about the role or might be associated with disquieting feelings about marriage because they find the demands onerous. But the role demands for assertion by the husband in marriage can be a potential threat to those men who feel anxious about the possibility of failure at attempts to be influential. On this basis we might make the reverse prediction: in traditional marriages, men who have a strong power motive with a failure-avoidant goal might often see their marriage as evidence of their own incapacity to influence.

For wives in a traditional marital relationship, assertive power motivation is assumed to be thwarted. Therefore the opposite types of relationships should occur: high power motivation should lead to unsatisfactory role adjustment while low power motivation should be compatible with satisfactory role reactions. But again, we must contrast this with the interpretation of the power motive as the concern over avoiding unsuccessful influence attempts. Women with high *avoidant* power motivation in traditional marriages, should be unthreatened because of the relative absence of role demands for power assertiveness.

The conception of the changing American family structure that we have discussed mainly as a change from a traditional (or institutional) to companionate family structure, also includes a change from a patriarchal to a more egalitarian family unit. Under such conditions, where more decision-making is a joint procedure and where the husband's decisions are not automatically presumed to be valid, we expected to find quite a different pattern of association between power motivation and marital role reactions. For women with strong assertive power motivation, this situation should be more compatible with their motivational requirement, but for men, it should be a more frustrating situation. Both men and women with strong avoidant power motivation would find their roles threatening and should evidence discontent or anxiety over their performance. We have assumed that such changes in the American family structure have already occurred to the greatest extent in the more-educated groups in our society. In these groups, both the ideal of the egalitarian family where there is joint decision-making by the husband and wife, and the implementation of this ideal, are more prevalent. So we expected that in the college-educated segment of society, women with strong assertive power motivation would be more satisfied with their marriages than their less-educated counterparts. On the other hand, college-educated men with either strong assertive or avoidant power motivation would be less satisfied with their marriages; they are in a situation where their own personal needs conflict with a commitment to the egalitarian family that arises partly out of group norms and out of their wives' expectations, and partly out of their own sense of rightness.

SUBJECTS

The men and women who are the subjects for this chapter constituted the entire subset of the national sample who were white, were married at the time of the interview, and had adequately completed the task used to measure motives. The maximum number of subjects who met these criteria were 514 wives and 464 husbands. The division of these subjects into subgroups based on education, age, and parental status maintained fairly sizable subsamples, except for the married persons who are not parents.[1]

MEASURES OF MARITAL REACTIONS

Six indices of marital reactions were used to infer evidences of role-functioning. They were based on a series of questions that attempted to uncover both the quantitative evaluation that the individual placed on the success of his or her marriage and the bases upon which the individual evaluated his marriage and his role-functioning.

We will first present the questions on which each index was based and indicate how replies were coded to yield the six indices. Then we will discuss each index in turn, indicating its significant relationships to other marital indices[2] or to previous factors isolated in our overall analysis of the dimensions of subjective adjustment (Veroff et al., 1962b), and its relative prevalence in certain subsamples as opposed to others.[3] Such discussion is intended to illuminate the meaning of each index.

The section in the interview dealing with marriage began with a question about the respondent's general conception of marriage without specific reference to his own marriage. Then followed a series of questions asking for descriptions of certain aspects of one's own marriage, and finally, overall evaluations of the levels of satisfaction and dissatisfaction

---

[1] The number of subjects in each subsample is presented in Appendix B, Table 3.a Missing data from some subjects on certain marital reactions slightly reduced these numbers for any given comparison. Subjects with missing data were eliminated from all tables, and any discrepancy in size of the subsamples from those reported in Table 3.a are attributable to this omission, unless noted otherwise.

[2] The interrelationships among these six measures of marital reactions are presented in Table 3.b of Appendix B for the entire sample of married men and women. These relationships were also calculated within each status subgrouping—for example, for grade-school-educated wives—and those results will be cited when appropriate.

[3] The relationship of each of the measures of marital reactions to education, age, and parental status are presented in Appendix B, Table 3.c for wives and Table 3.d for husbands. These tables show the percentage distributions on each variable, by subgroups, and thereby give the reader some perspective on the absolute levels of response to the questions about marriage. They also present the gamma indices of association between each role reaction and each status characteristic, thereby illustrating the levels of gammas that are associated with various contingency tables. It can be seen that relatively high gammas can occur in tables that do not yield statistically significant taus. This occurs when the marginal distribution is quite skewed, as for example, with the *Self-dissatisfaction* index in Table 3.c.

with different aspects of one's own marriage. (The entire series, questions 27 through 40, can be found in Appendix A.)

The *Marital Restrictiveness* index was based on the first question in the series:

Now I'd like to ask you some questions about marriage. First, thinking about a man's (woman's) life—how is a man's (woman's) life changed by being married?

Most subjects gave more than one response to this question. Each response was coded for whether or not it indicated that the respondent viewed the changes accompanying marriage as restricting one's life, or burdening a man or woman with new responsibilities—for example, "It makes you more responsible; You have to learn to think about someone else; You can't just do as you please anymore." The final index of *Marital Restrictiveness* was a three-point scale summarizing across all the responses: it indicated whether (1) no, (2) some, or (3) all responses indicated that the respondent saw marriage as restrictive.

The index of *Relationship Satisfaction* was derived from answers to the following question:

We've talked a little about marriage in general. Now thinking about your own marriage, what would you say were the nicest things about it?

The first response was coded as either (1) lacking in any relationship response, or (2) indicating that respondent's relationship with his or her spouse was one of the nicest things about one's marriage—for example, "We're happy being together; the companionship; my husband and I love each other." Only the first response was coded in order to avoid confounding the index with the effects of verbal productivity.

The index of *Self-dissatisfaction* was based on the next question in the marriage series:

Every marriage has its good and bad points. What things about your marriage are not quite as nice as you would like them to be?

The first response to this question was coded as either (1) lacking in any self-referent, or (2) indicating that anything about the respondent himself was not quite as nice as it could be—for example, "I haven't been able to earn enough; I'm not a good cook; I get angry too quickly." This index could be applied only when the respondents mentioned something about their marriages that was not satisfactory; about 36 percent of the sample were eliminated from this variable because they denied any marital dissatisfactions.

A four-point scale of *Marital Unhappiness* was built from the multiple choices permitted in the following question:

Taking things all together, how would you describe your marriage—would you say your marriage was *very happy, a little happier than average, just about average,* or *not too happy?*

The next question provided the basis for the index of *Marital Problems*:

Even in cases where married people are happy there have been times in the past when they weren't happy—when they had problems getting along with each other. Has this ever been true for you?

Replies were simply coded (1) No, or (2) Yes, to index admissions to a problem in a person's marriage. This question was not asked of those persons who said they were "not too happy" in reply to the previous question about marital happiness. It seemed inappropriate to ask persons who had just said that their marriage was not too happy, whether they ever had problems in their marriage. This reduced the maximum samples to 509 women and 447 men for analyses with this variable.

To derive the index of *Marital Inadequacy* we used the responses to the following questions:

Many men (women) feel that they're not as good husbands (wives) as they would like to be. Have you ever felt this way? (IF YES) Do you feel this way a lot of times, or only once in a while?

A five-point scale of the degree of felt inadequacy was derived: (1) never, (2) once, once or twice, (3) once in a while, sometimes, (4) often, and (5) a lot of times. The second and fourth points on the scale were added during the coding to take into account the spontaneous categories used by respondents who did not feel comfortable with the alternatives we gave them.

MARITAL RESTRICTIVENESS

The *Marital Restrictiveness* index was devised to infer the extent to which the individual saw marriage or the change from the single to the married status as being restricting or burdensome upon his or her life style. While most of the responses coded as restricting or burdensome were clearly negative in tone, this was not true of all the responses. For example, an individual might have said: "Marriage makes you more mature because you have more responsibilities." This might be considered a positive or neutral affective response, but it does have overtones of restricting the individual in new ways. Clearly negative responses that were coded as restrictive would be such statements as: "You have to work harder." "You have to take care of your husband, wash his clothes, do all the housework." "It prevents you from going out with the boys and having fun the way you used to." But not all negative responses were coded as burdensome; simple affective responses such as, "You probably get more unhappiness than happiness," were not coded as indicating that the life changes accompanying marriage were restrictive to the individual.

On the basis of a number of sets of data we viewed *Marital Restrictiveness* as a measure of the extent to which the role of husband or wife is seen as limiting the scope of activities, pleasures, potentialities, for the respondent. Its more subtle meaning, however, seems to be different for husband and wife. For women the *Marital Restrictiveness* index can reflect two different types of reactions. First, it can reflect a passive role reaction, a reaction to marriage as a role that *imposes* burdens on them. Second, it can reflect an active view of one's own part in the marital relationship, a view that suggests that marital burdens are self-imposed. For men, however, the *Marital Restrictiveness* index seems to reflect only the passive role reaction.

Our inference about the meaning of this measure was somewhat limited because it was not included in the previous factor analysis (Veroff et al., 1962b). Some other information suggests that the measure reflects an inability to cope with the demands of marriage, a kind of resignation to the tribulations of married life. Marriage was seen as significantly more restrictive among younger than older wives and among mothers as compared to wives without children. (See Table 3.c in Appendix B.) Less-educated wives also tended to report more *Marital Restrictiveness* than more-educated wives. Women tended to report it more than men. In each of these instances the more restrictive remarks come from the person with the fewer resources for coping *directly* with marriage. The younger wives are less experienced at handling the problems of marriage. The uneducated have fewer status symbols to compensate for marital burdens; and mothers have to attend to children, which takes time away from their marriage. With fewer resources they are more likely to find marriage an imposition. Women were generally higher on the *Marital Restrictiveness* index than men, perhaps because by comparison they lack independent resources to shift the salience of the role. If a man is burdened by marital difficulties, he can easily shift his investment to his job role and make this or other extramarital roles the most salient parts of his experience. A woman is generally more trapped in her family roles. These are the pivotal roles for her experience and she must resign herself to making the best of family roles, for there are no others that can easily assume their importance. The interpretation of this index as a resignation to marriage is further supported by another result. For women, viewing the entrance into marriage as restricting was significantly positively related to *Marital Unhappiness*, which we will see can be clearly interpreted as a passive type of marital reaction.

To complicate the picture, however, we found that *Marital Restrictiveness* was positively associated with *Marital Problems* and *Marital Inadequacy*, both of which we will interpret as rather *active* distress signals from women who attempt to cope with their difficulties. Thus for women, *Marital Restrictiveness* seems both a positive and a negative reaction.

The results differ for men, for whom *Marital Restrictiveness* was not significantly related to any other marital reaction. (See Table 3.b in Appendix B.) Thus, for men this index seems to be a reaction distinctive from the other measures of marital reactions. However, when we considered the subgroup of married men who had children, there were two significant relationships: *Marital Restrictiveness* was significantly *negatively* related to *Marital Inadequacy* and to *Relationship Satisfaction*. We will view both feelings of inadequacy and satisfaction with one's relationship with one's wife as reflections of an active self-involvement in the marital role. Thus, these correlations seem to imply that for married men with children the view of marriage as restrictive does not imply this type of active involvement of one's self in the marital role. For married men with children the *Marital Restrictiveness* index seems to reflect reactions to what *happens* to a man as a result of the marital role; it especially reflects his desire to avoid the difficulties or burdens that marriage imposes upon him.

A further corroboration of this interpretation is that single men in all age and education groups viewed marriage as more restrictive than married men. Single men seem to be avoiding the burdens of marriage and most likely they are also avoiding the responsibilities to children that marriage usually brings. Thus, for men, seeing marriage as restrictive seems to reflect the view that marriage imposes obligations that limit your freedom, obligations over which you have little control. *Marital Restrictiveness* seems to reflect a passive desire to avoid the difficulties of marital obligations.

Other evidence from the demographic analysis confirms the interpretation. Less-educated men reported significantly more marital restrictions than the more-educated. Like women, men who were younger were more likely to view marriage as restricting than older men. (See Table 3.d in Appendix B.) Again we would see the distress reaction arising in these groups because they have fewer resources for coping with marriage. They are passively avoiding difficulty.

MARITAL UNHAPPINESS

Whereas *Marital Restrictiveness* implies a passive avoidance of burdens, *Marital Unhappiness* implies a passive open distress. For both men and women *Marital Unhappiness*, as well as reports of general unhappiness with one's life, were highly correlated with the *Unhappiness Factor* in the previously reported factor analysis. However, the other indices with high correlations with this factor were different for men and women. For men, the report of having problems with children and perceiving some shortcomings in oneself were also highly correlated with this factor. Neither of these two indices had high correlations with this factor for women, but for them *Marital Problems* did have a high correlation. We concluded that among women, the *Unhappiness Factor* seems more exclusively tied to marriage than it is for men.

In the present samples, *Marital Unhappiness* and *Marital Problems* were positively related for both men and women, but this relationship was more consistent across subgroups for women. (See Table 3.b in Appendix B.) And for women, *Marital Restrictiveness* was also positively associated with *Marital Unhappiness*, while *Relationship Satisfaction* was negatively associated with it in the total group and certain subgroups. Thus, for a woman, the *Marital Unhappiness* index seems to reflect a variety of reactions to her marriage specifically, while for a man *Marital Unhappiness* seems to reflect discontent about his general life situation.

For both men and women we continue to assume, as we did in the earliest evaluation of these measures (Gurin et al., 1960), that questions dealing with unhappiness ask for a passive evaluation of one's life-functioning, rather than how much active investment or commitment the person has to the role.

This conclusion is supported by the relative prevalence of *Marital Unhappiness* in certain groups. (See Tables 3.c and 3.d in Appendix B.) Feelings of marital unhappiness were significantly less prevalent among younger than older women. More-educated men and women reported significantly less marital unhappiness than less-educated men and women. *Marital Unhappiness* was not significantly related to parental status for either men or women, although there was a tendency for childless respondents to report happier marriages. Thus, we found the passive distress expressed in *Marital Unhappiness* prevalent in groups who are in a sense caught by the role—the less-educated who have few marital options, the older men and women who may feel too committed to their spouse to see any possibility for change, and parents who may feel required to keep up a poor marital relationship "for the children."

MARITAL PROBLEMS

It seems that *Marital Problems* can have a dual meaning. For some men and women it can reflect a complaint about a spouse or situation to which they attribute some difficulty. For others, it can reflect an awareness of one's own shortcomings in a marriage. Thus both extrapunitive and intropunitive reactions can be involved in seeing one's marriage as a problem.

In earlier analyses (Gurin et al., 1960) we found that women were much more likely to blame their marital problems upon their spouses than were men; men tended to blame themselves more than women. These findings are further reflected in the fact that *Marital Problems* correlated more highly with the *Unhappiness Factor*, a passive, non-self-involved dimension of distress, for women than it did for men.

Although its extrapunitive quality seems primarily found in women, and its intropunitive quality is primarily found in men, both sexes show some evidence for the duality of meaning in the index of *Marital Problems*. In the present samples of both men and women, the *Marital Problems* index was significantly positively related to both *Marital Unhappiness* and *Marital Inadequacy*, even though *Marital Inadequacy* and *Marital Unhappiness* were unrelated to each other. (See Table 3.b in Appendix B.) The fact that the measure has this dual significance does not explain its differential distribution in various groups of married men and women. The report of problems in their marriages was significantly higher among younger than older men and women, and among persons who were parents rather than childless. (See Tables 3.c and 3.d in Appendix B.) Younger couples more often face problems of adaptation, whether they externalize them or blame themselves for them. Children in a family also force certain problems of adaptation for couples that childless couples never have to face. And so we conclude that a person who admits having marital problems recognizes some real tension in interpersonal adaptation. This tension can be either extrapunitive or intropunitive.

MARITAL INADEQUACY

Although the index of *Marital Inadequacy* is, by definition, a self-questioning reaction, there are empirical bases for such an interpretation as well. In the factor analyses for both men and women we found this index highly related to the *Social Inadequacy Factor* which, as we have already indicated, we viewed as representing the self-questioning that an individual engages in when he considers himself in relation to the social world about him. The subgroups who were high on this index were those whom we view as being more self-questioning. (See Tables 3.c and 3.d in Appendix B.) Younger men and women reported more *Marital Inadequacy* than older ones. More frequent feelings of inadequacy were also characteristic of wives with higher education.[4]

The hypothesis that men assume greater self-responsibility for their marriage was also evidenced in some of the results with the *Marital Inadequacy* measure. Women tended to report unhappier marriages and marriages with more problems, both of which were indices that we viewed

[4]Feelings of inadequacy were also more frequently reported by men who had children than by men without children. The reason for this is not immediately apparent.

as not involving self-blame for the women. But on the *Marital Inadequacy* index, which clearly asked about self-blame, we found that husbands and wives reported feelings of their own role inadequacy with equal frequency.

Among the total groups of both men and women used in this chapter, *Marital Inadequacy* was significantly positively associated with *Marital Problems*. (See Table 3.b in Appendix B.) This relationship was also found in all subgroups except the college-educated. For college-educated men, *Marital Problems* and *Marital Inadequacy* were unrelated (gamma = .00), and for women the gamma was the lowest in any subgroup of women (gamma = .17). To help explain this result, we recall that these subgroups of college men and women reported primarily interpersonal rather than situational bases of inadequacy. They mentioned their own lack of adequate affection rather than not earning enough money or not being a good cook. We viewed these results as indicating that especially strong feelings of self-questioning were reflected in college-educated persons' responses of inadequacy. Could it be that the type of active involvement reflected in reporting inadequacy in role function for college-educated men and women is a reflection, not of problematic distress with one's marriage, but an indication of very high standards of excellence for the marital relationship? College men and women may feel that they are not as good spouses as they would like to be, but do not associate these feelings with problems in their marriage. At other educational levels, self-questioning may coincide with the perception of problems rather than with high aspiration for one's own role performance.

RELATIONSHIP SATISFACTION

The index of *Relationship Satisfaction* had not been included in the earlier factor analysis. Our present analyses showed that it was significantly positively related to the *Marital Inadequacy* index for both sexes. (See Table 3.b in Appendix B.) Is this because both of these measures imply some amount of self-involvement in role-functioning? Perhaps people who stress the importance of marital interaction in responses about their marriage are those people who set standards of marital adjustment that are especially difficult to meet. Relationship satisfactions were mentioned significantly more often by the more-educated respondents. (See Tables 3.c and 3.d in Appendix B.) These are people who set very high standards for personal interaction in marriage. Self-imposed criteria for being a good husband or wife may be harder to master than externally imposed ones.

Relationship Satisfaction was significantly negatively related to *Marital Unhappiness* and *Marital Problems* for women only. Thus, wives who see their relationship with their spouses as highly statisfying also view their marriages as happy and lacking in marital problems, but feel inadequate;

that is, women with an active self-involvement in the marital relationship and in their own role-functioning also react favorably to their life situation. For women then, we view this index as a reflection of both self-questioning and satisfaction with the marital situation. For men, however, in this index self-questioning is not necessarily accompanied by satisfactions.

This index was viewed as potentially relevant to the affiliative gratifications that are possible in marriage. It had previously been found that evaluation of marital happiness was positively related to mentioning the husband-wife relationship as a source of marital satisfaction (Gurin et al., 1960). In contrast, mentioning one's spouse as the nicest thing about marriage was unrelated to the evaluation of a person's own marital happiness, and mentioning situational factors as the nicest thing about marriage was negatively related to a person's own evaluation of marital happiness.

SELF-DISSATISFACTION

We constructed the *Self-dissatisfaction* index in order to distinguish between the passive experience of satisfaction and dissatisfaction in marriage, and the involved, active evaluation of one's own role-functioning. We viewed *Self-dissatisfaction* as being indicative of taking responsibility for the course of one's marriage. Its differentiation from a more passive response to marital difficulty is seen in the finding that those persons who evaluated their marriage as least happy did not report self-dissatisfaction.

We must, however, be cautious in our interpretation of the measure of *Self-dissatisfaction*, since it was available only for the select group of married men ($N = 368$) and women ($N = 249$) who indicated that there were some things about their marriage that were not as nice as they would like them to be. It is perhaps surprising to realize that 25 percent of the married women and 45 percent of the married men indicated that there was nothing about their marriage that was not as nice as they would have liked. This finding would imply that if a respondent is willing to describe some negative feature in his marriage, he is likely to have a self-questioning attitude towards his marriage. Thus we very likely have an attenuated distribution of responses about *Self-dissatisfaction*. Probably those persons *least* likely to doubt themselves are omitted from this index altogether.

There were no significant relationships overall between *Self-dissatisfaction* and any of the other marital reaction measures. (See Table 3.b in Appendix B.) Nor was this index significantly associated with any of the status groupings. (See Tables 3.c and 3.d in Appendix B.) This is probably due in part to the small percentage of subjects who reported any type of self-dissatisfaction. Perhaps more important is that those persons least likely to mention self-dissatisfaction, those who denied any difficulty with their marriage at all, were excluded from this index. However, it is interesting to note that the largest gammas for the entire samples of husbands and wives were found for the association between *Marital Inadequacy* and *Self-dissatisfaction*. The positive relationship between these two variables that were intended to tap self-questioning is as expected. Among the college-educated men this positive relationship between their feelings of self-dissatisfaction and inadequacy was significant (gamma = .62, $p < .05$ for tau beta). Both these measures seem to be tapping an active view of the marital role where one's own performance is seen as central to the success of the marriage. It is also interesting that men more frequently reported *Self-dissatisfaction* than did women, since we have seen throughout our discussion of these measures that men seem to feel a more self-directed responsibility for marital difficulties than women.

ROLE REACTIONS IN RELATION TO EDUCATION, AGE, AND PARENTAL STATUS

In the examination of the meaning of the six indices of marital reaction, among other things we have described how these indices differentially distributed themselves in the various subpopulations that we used to infer role characteristics. In so doing, we obtained some further clues about the definition of the marital role in these different groups.

First, what can we infer about marriage patterns at different educational levels? The general picture that emerges from these results is that the more educated a person is, the more likely he is to have an unrestrictive, happy view of his marriage. This view emphasizes his relationship to his spouse and is accompanied by self-questioning. Although the picture is in general clearer for women than for men, the more-educated spouses seem to be reporting both active self-involvement and a generally satisfactory response to the marital situation.

The younger spouses seem also to be actively involved in their marriages, but more concerned about possible difficulties. Young men and women are more apt to take a restrictive view of marriage. Although younger women are especially happy in their marriages, both younger wives and husbands are more likely to report marriage problems and to question their own role-functioning than are older spouses. Perhaps these results reflect the problems of newlyweds in adapting to a changed life situation, and especially to another person's needs.

While both childless husbands and wives report fewer marital problems than parents do, only childless wives feel less restricted by marriage, and only childless husbands are less self-questioning of their adequacy. These reports could reflect the fact that compared to married men and women with children, childless spouses are less involved in their marriages. But it could also mean that it is easier in general to adjust to a spouse role that does not also include parental functions.

RESULTS: MOTIVE-ROLE INTERACTIONS IN MARRIAGE

In the sections to follow we will discuss the relationships between each of the three motives and the six dimensions of marital role reactions. The results are discussed separately for each of these three major educational subgroups: grade-school-educated wives and husbands, high-school-educated wives and husbands, and college-educated wives and husbands. In the beginning of each of these sections we will present an overall capsule summary of the significant results for that educational level. The casual reader can get an overall picture of the results emerging from the exploration of motive-role interaction from reading the summaries only. We have attempted to maintain a general continuity in the presentation of the summaries. For readers who would like to examine the details of the results that were the sources for the overall portrayal of each educational group, following each summary we have also presented a more complete description of the results concerning each motive. On occasion we do draw some tenuous inferences, and we would like them readily apparent to any reader seriously concerned with research strategies in this area of social psychology.

The data for each educational level are presented in a separate table, which includes the results for both husbands and wives (Tables 3.1–3.3). Each table includes three subtables, showing the relationship of each of the six indices of marital role reactions to: (1) the affiliation motive, (2) the achievement motive, and (3) the power motive. As we indicated previously, the motives serve as the controls for each other; that is, we can ask whether the relationship obtained between a motive and a reaction to marriage is true of all the motives we have measured or is only true of a particular motive. In the latter instance there is greater assurance that a particular characteristic of that motive should be used to account for the relationship. Within each subtable, the relationships are presented separately for subjects at each of the three age levels and for all subjects at this educational level, disregarding age. The table entries are the gamma coefficient between a given motive and role reaction. The probability levels reported are for the significance of the tau beta rank order correlations computed for the same data; all probability values are for two-tailed tests.

After we present the capsule summaries and detailed analyses for each educational level, we will then present some results comparing the motive-role interactions found for married persons with children to those found for married persons without children. Parental status was the only other major subgroup membership position that we used to describe role distinctions.

After considering the results concerning motive-role interaction, we will then reassess our views of how each motive interacts with the marital role. And then we will reassess our views of the marital role in general.

Chapters 4 and 5 will follow the same format: presentation of summary and detailed analyses of motive-role interaction within certain role distinctions, presentation of our revised conception of the motives in the context of the role, and finally, presentation of our revised assessment of the role characteristics.

MARRIED MEN AND WOMEN WITH A GRADE-SCHOOL EDUCATION

We anticipated that for persons with a grade-school education, the traditional marital relationship would be most prevalent. Such a relationship would imply clear differentiation of the husband's and wife's roles, with the husband's role primarily centering on the demand that he provide sufficiently for his family and also on the privilege of being the major decision-maker in the home, and with the wife's role centering on demands and privileges associated with home-making and child-rearing. We recognized that the actual power of women in these traditional marriages in American society may be greater than their husbands'. Indeed, much empirical study of power in the family suggests this is so (Zelditch, 1964). Nevertheless we have assumed that the ideal control of power remains in the hands of the husbands in these marriages. This recognition of the different covert and overt demands and gratifications helps to clarify some of the results about motive-role interaction in the least-educated groups.

The traditional marital role of grade-school-educated women seems congruent with strong power motivation. These women felt significantly more adequate as wives and also were more likely to be satisfied with their relationship to their husbands than women with weak power motivation. Thus these women with high power motivation were satisfied with their marriages. In contrast, grade-school-educated men with high power motivation did not consistently differ in their overall reactions to the marital role from men with low power motivation. Only among middle-aged and older men did we find any indication that the traditional marriage role of these subjects is satisfying to men with high power motivation. These older men with high power motivation were significantly more likely to describe their relationship with their spouse as satisfying than were comparable men with low power motivation. The covert power given to women in a traditional marriage evidently can gratify women's sense of adequacy, while the overt power can gratify men's feelings of satisfaction with marriage. The covert weakness attendant to the role for men, however, can often counteract the satisfying effect that the power motive might have on their reactions to marriage.

Both affiliation and achievement motivation seem to facilitate the adjustment of grade-school-educated wives to marriage. Women with strong affiliation motivation had positive views of their own marriages, especially as revealed through their thoughts about their happiness and satisfaction with the husband-wife relationship, but also in their unrestrictive, problem-free views of marriage. Marital happiness was also prevalent among grade-school-educated women with strong achievement motivation. There is some evidence that for the young, uneducated housewives, high achievement motivation may be disruptive, since these women showed strong feelings of inadequacy.

Grade-school-educated men with strong achievement motivation do not seem to be very involved in their marital role. They were unlikely to describe the change from the single to the married status as restrictive, or to hold themselves responsible for marital difficulties. We interpret these descriptions to mean that these men have very little personal commitment to marriage as an arena of self-evaluation.

The results relating affiliation motivation to marital reactions suggest that marriage may be incongruent with the maintenance of a man's ongoing affiliative satisfactions. There is self-involvement in marriage for men with strong affiliation motivation, an inference we draw from their comparatively high levels of self-dissatisfaction. And young grade-school-educated men with strong affiliation motivation were unhappier with their marriages than men with weak affiliation motivation. Perhaps they were unhappier because marriage interferes with their affiliative gratifications outside the marriage. This interpretation is consistent with the earlier finding that grade-school-educated men in general felt most restricted by the transition from single to married status.

The data for grade-school-educated men and women are presented in Table 3.1. Due to the small numbers of subjects or few reports of *Self-dissatisfaction* among grade-school-educated persons, the criteria for reporting the gamma index was not met for any of the grade-school-educated women and for only certain subgroupings of grade-school-educated men. This effectively eliminated this index from systematic consideration in this section.

Affiliation For women, strong affiliation motivation was significantly associated with marital happiness, when age was disregarded. This relationship was similar within all age groups and also was significant for the youngest group of wives. Compatible with this relationship was the significant overall association between affiliation motivation and *Relationship Satisfaction*. This association seems to be clear evidence for the sensitization principle. The direction of the relationships with restrictiveness, problems, and inadequacy, showed a similar tendency for affiliation motivation to be associated with positive views of one's own marriage, although perhaps this tendency should be interpreted as a passive rather than active sense of satisfaction.

For men we found a rather different set of relationships. Among young, grade-school-educated men, affiliation motivation was significantly related to the expression of marital unhappiness. There was a similar tendency, although not significant, for reports of more problems among these young men with high affiliation motivation. Quite in contrast was the finding that for middle-aged men affiliation motivation was significantly associated with the absence of feelings of marital inadequacy. The relationship between *Self-dissatisfaction* and affiliation motivation was positive in all age groups and was significant for the entire group of grade-school-educated men.

We interpreted these results to imply that for grade-school-educated women, who were assumed to be participants in traditional marriages,

TABLE 3-1 THE RELATIONSHIP (γ) OF MOTIVES TO MARITAL REACTIONS FOR GRADE-SCHOOL-EDUCATED SUBJECTS (WITHIN SEX AND AGE)

Marital Reaction	Type of Motive												Number of Subjects at Each Age Level			
	Affiliation				Achievement				Power							
	young	middle	old	all ages	young	middle	old	all ages	young	middle	old	all ages	young	middle	old	all ages
Wives																
Restrictiveness	−.16	.17	−.14	−.02	−.06	−.10	.12	.00	.16	−.04	−.24	−.11	(20)	(42)	(56)	(118)
Unhappiness	−.53*	−.18	−.11	−.22*	.13	−.31	−.23	−.22*	.14	−.15	−.24	−.14	(20)	(42)	(56)	(118)
Problems	−.27	−.13	−.07	−.11	.08	−.06	−.03	−.04	.43	−.31	−.34	−.21	(17)	(40)	(48)	(105)
Inadequacy	−.10	−.36	.18	−.08	.54*	−.26	.24	.12	−.60†	−.16	−.44†	−.35‡	(20)	(39)	(55)	(114)
Relationship satisfaction	.05	.30	.41	.28*	−.10	−.01	.41	.14	.08	.11	.14	.12	(20)	(41)	(55)	(116)
Self-dissatisfaction	—a	—a	—a	—a	—a	—a	—a	—a	—a	—a	—a	—a	(14)	(27)	(41)	(82)
Husbands																
Restrictiveness	.25	.27	.06	.06	−.36	−.17	−.19	−.22*	.25	−.14	.07	.07	(23)	(30)	(68)	(121)
Unhappiness	.62†	−.09	−.03	.05	−.13	.24	.07	.06	.09	.07	−.06	.02	(23)	(32)	(71)	(126)
Problems	.52	−.38	−.14	−.11	.20	.10	−.05	.04	.05	−.31	−.15	−.15	(22)	(32)	(69)	(123)
Inadequacy	.08	−.60†	.03	−.14	−.04	−.21	−.16	−.14	.18	.04	−.05	.05	(23)	(30)	(68)	(121)
Relationship satisfaction	.20	.34	−.21	.01	.56	−.64†	.11	.02	−.39	.40	.43†	.28*	(23)	(32)	(70)	(125)
Self-dissatisfaction	—a	—a	.57	.61†	—a	—a	−.51	−.27	—a	—a	.09	.18	(9)	(14)	(32)	(55)

Note: In this and subsequent tables in this Chapter entries are the gamma indexes of association between a given motive and marital reaction for the specified subgroup of wives or husbands. Probability levels are reported for tau beta rank-order correlation coefficients computed for the same relationships. For example, in this table, the gamma for the relationship between the affiliation motive and **Restrictiveness** is −.16 for the young wives and −.02 for all wives, disregarding age.

aNot reported because of inadequate distribution.

*p < .10.

†p < .05.

‡p < .01.

affiliation motivation facilitates marital satisfaction. These findings have two reasonable interpretations. The marital relationship itself is more likely to be satisfying for women with strong rather than weak affiliation motive in this social group. Or, for this social group, the attainment of the married status is sufficiently important to the affiliation-motivated women, so that the married state itself is positively evaluated. Because of the association between affiliation motivation and the mention of the relationship with the spouse as the nicest thing about one's marriage, the day-to-day marital interactions themselves seem to be the salient characteristic of marriages to which these women with high affiliation motivation are reacting.

If we interpreted the results for young, grade-school-educated men in a similar fashion to those for women, we would infer that when these men seek affiliative gratifications within their marriage they are not satisfied, or that marriage in some way interferes with affiliative gratification outside of marriage. The latter interpretation seems most appropriate. A grade-school-educated man, "caught" in a traditional marriage, may find that the demands placed upon him by his new family "eat into" his usual social behavior. These men, more so than the more-educated men, are probably seeking affiliative contracts with their "buddies," while the upper-status groups are more likely to socialize as couples. Marriage will initially be more disruptive of the social behavior of lower-status men than it will of the more-educated groups. This result makes us recall the fact that grade-school-educated men feel especially restricted by the changes that occur in a man's life when he gets married.

It is interesting to note that age appears to be a more important conditioner of the relationship between affiliation motivation and marital reaction for men than for women. By middle age, affiliation motivation seems to have similar implications for men and women. Our guess is that the transition from single to married status affects the affiliative satisfactions and frustrations most dramatically. New and more idiosyncratic adaptations to affiliative motivation can occur as men and women get older, and they can cut down on the apparent motive-role interaction.

Achievement   The data presented in Table 3.1 for women show little clear evidence for the proposition that achievement orientation interferes with marital role functioning. In contrast to what might be expected from the view that marriage interferes with achievement aspirations of a woman, there was no relationship between viewing marriage as restrictive and level of achievement motivation at any age level. And high achievement motivation was significantly associated with feelings of marital happiness when all grade-school-educated age groups were combined. This general finding is inconsistent with the congruence principle if our interpretation of the lack of achievement potential in marriage was correct. However, the relationship between achievement motivation and *Marital Unhappiness* for young, grade-school-educated wives tended to be in the opposite direction. For this young group, *Marital Inadequacy*, an index that we viewed as indicative of both involvement and self-evaluation, was significantly positively associated with high achievement motivation. This finding could either reflect the high level of aspiration set by women with strong achievement motivation or the lack of outlets for gratifying achievement goals within the traditional marriage. Thus, only among the young group is there any evidence that might be consistent with our congruence principle.

While there were no significant relationships between achievement motivation and the report of *Relationship Satisfaction* at any age level, there was a tendency for achievement-oriented older women to report more *Relationship Satisfaction* in their marriage. This tendency suggested that within traditional marriage patterns, older women may not be in conflict about making marriage the arena for achievement.

On the whole, the directions of the relationships for men were reversed from those for women, although the relationships were not always significant. Compared to men low in achievement motivation, highly motivated men viewed marriage as significantly less restrictive and tended to feel less inadequate in their role-functioning. There were also consistent tendencies among men at all ages for achievement motivation to be associated with the lack of *Self-dissatisfaction* in marriage. For middle-aged, grade-school-educated men, achievement motivation had a significant negative association with *Relationship Satisfaction*, although in the other age groups this association was in the reverse direction.

Our general impression from these data for men is that there does not appear to be a great deal of involvement in the marital role for men with high achievement motivation if they are in a social status group that has traditional marital role definitions. High achievement motivation was associated with not seeing marriage as restrictive and with not being satisfied with the conjugal relationship. High achievement motivation tended to be associated with feeling *adequate* in marriage and with the lack of feelings of self-dissatisfaction. There is no direct emphasis on marital performance for this group of men. Holding a job and being around home to make certain decisions may be the uppermost demands. Men with high achievement motivation may be those husbands who can most adequately fulfill these obligations without major psychological commitment.

Power The clearest relationship with the power motive for the grade-school-educated wives was the significant negative association with *Marital Inadequacy* among the entire group, as well as for the youngest and oldest women. For the middle-aged and old groups there was also a general trend for the other role reactions to show that women with high power motivation were satisfied with their marriages (lack of *Marital Restrictiveness*, *Marital Unhappiness*, and *Marital Problems*), and with their relationship to their husbands. The only hint that power-motivated women are frustrated in their marital relationship occurred for the young, grade-school-educated wives, where there were tendencies for power motivation to be associated with the presence of *Marital Restrictiveness*, *Marital Unhappiness*, and *Marital Problems*.

Two interpretations can be made of these results with respect to the congruence principle. One social observer might say that traditional marriages evidently provide women with few overt demands for power assertion, but many possibilities for covert power assertion. Interpreting a strong power motive as a high fear of weakness, we could further say that facing minimal influence demands, but maximal opportunities, women with high power motivation might feel especially adequate. This would be meshing a role with a motivational orientation. In fact, a woman with such a motivational orientation might feel especially integrated into her marriage in general. This might be less true for younger women because they may be in greater conflict about accepting the traditional marital demands.

Another view of these results suggests that the potential for power gratification in marriage is minimal for grade-school-educated women. If feelings of adequacy imply lack of active role involvement, these power-motivated women would not be engaged actively in their marriages. This may be a defensive reaction to the lack of opportunity for motive satisfaction, perhaps especially in younger women. Again this would be in keeping with a congruence principle—but in an opposite manner.

The relationships between power motivation and marital role reactions for grade-school-educated husbands were on the whole smaller than those for wives. The one exception was the significant positive association between the power motive and mentioning interpersonal satisfactions involving the spouse as one of the nicest things about marriage. This relationship was significant both for the total group of grade-school-educated husbands and also for the older grade-school-educated husbands; the direction of relationship was reversed for the young, grade-school-educated husbands.

Generally speaking, the power motive does not seem relevant to the overall evaluations of marital satisfaction and dissatisfaction for grade-school-educated husbands, perhaps because of the fact that they are expected to wield power in the family, but in fact, do not. The one significant relationship confirms the view that in a traditional family situation, power-motivated men can find interpersonal relations satisfying.

101

MARRIED MEN AND WOMEN WITH A HIGH-SCHOOL EDUCATION

It is hard to say whether men and women with a high-school education are expected to be engaged in typically traditional or companionate marriages. Their intermediate social status could mean that there is a high level of differentiation within the group, and/or that there is a high incidence of group members with intermediate or conflicting role expectations. This transitional status, between the traditional and the companionate norms for the marital relationship, may explain why there were no overall relationships between power motivation and marital role reactions for either sex. What we may have here is a more heterogeneous group of respondents than is true either for the grade-school-educated or college-educated groups. It may be a group that includes some families where overt power clearly resides in the husband's role and other families where overt power does not clearly reside in either spouse's role.

As in the grade-school-educated group, for high-school-educated subjects affiliation motivation seems to enhance positive reactive responses to the marital role for women but to be largely irrelevant to the marital reactions of men. For women in this group, the clearest relationships were found among the middle-aged and older wives, who felt happier and less self-dissatisfied if they had strong affiliation motivation. In contrast, for the less-educated group the strongest results occurred with the youngest age group. This suggests that the mere fact of being married, which might have enhanced the affiliative gratification in a less-educated woman, is insufficient for affiliative satisfaction in a more-educated woman. As a woman begins to expect a more companionate relationship with her husband, she perhaps requires some years of contact before affiliative gratification is possible. Indeed, it is only after many years in a relationship that some people can feel accepted. Young wives, perhaps most oriented toward the sexual aspect of the marital relationship, may not reap affiliative gratification until there is some other well-established basis of companionship with their husbands. These results suggest that as marriages become desexualized they have greater potential for affiliative gratification. Perhaps sexual and affiliative goals are incompatible.

Contrary to our original hypothesis about incongruence between achievement motivation and marriage for women, women with high achievement motivation are not disgruntled. Quite the contrary. They were unlikely to report marital problems and were satisfied with their relationship to their spouse. Thus, high achievement motivation seems to be congruent with the marital role of high-school-educated women and seems to sensitize them to successful interpersonal relations.

We had expected that achievement motivation would not be central to the marital adjustment of men, and there were in fact no overall relationships between achievement motivation and marital reactions for men. An exception was found in the case of the young high-school-educated husbands. They and the comparable group of wives clearly differ in the way their achievement motivation affects the perception of problems in marriage. These young wives, who may be beginning to assume the companionate approach to marriage, are evidently seeking and creating achievement possibilities in their marriages. These young men, however, more frequently reported marriage problems if they had high achievement motivation. Perhaps the combination of being high in achievement motivation and finding that their high-school educations bring limited rewards on the vocational front leads these men into an unusually strong push to success at work. This involvement might interfere with any attempts to devote themselves to the companionate demands of marriage.

In Table 3.2 are presented the relationships between the three motives and the marital reactions for men and women who had at least some high-school education, but who did not attend college.

Affiliation We can see in Table 3.2 that the relationships between the affiliation motive and marital reactions among high-school-educated wives showed generally similar tendencies to those for the grade-school-educated wives. Strong affiliation motivation was associated with a relatively passive, but satisfied orientation to marriage. Once again there was a significant negative relationship between *Marital Unhappiness* and affiliation motivation for the total group, and also for the oldest group. But in contrast to the less-educated group, there was no significant association between affiliation motivation and the *Relationship Satisfaction* index. There were insufficient numbers of grade-school-educated wives who described *Self-dissatisfaction*, to have used the variable in that analysis. For the high-school-educated wives there were significant negative relationships between *Self-dissatisfaction* and affiliation motivation for the total group and the middle-aged women: wives who were highly motivated for affiliation were less likely to describe some aspect of themselves as a source of difficulty in their marriage.

High-school-educated husbands show similar tendencies with the *Self-dissatisfaction* index, although not significant in this instance. The only significant relationship with affiliation motivation among high-school-educated husbands was a negative one with *Relationship Satisfaction*: young men with strong affiliation motivation were less likely to mention their relationships with their spouse as the nicest thing about their marriage; similar trends occurred for the middle-aged men, but the relationship was reversed for the older age group. These results parallel the general trends for women, but there is an indication that affiliation motivation affects marital reactions more for women than for men.

Achievement There was a significant relationship between achievement motivation and the absence of reported *Marital Problems* for the wives with a high-school education. It was significant both for the young women and for the total group of high-school women. For each age group, and significantly so in the total group, the report of *Relationship Satisfaction* was positively associated with achievement motivation. There were no other significant relationships between achievement motivation and any of the other marital role reactions for these women. Generally speaking the results for women with a high-school education tended to be different from those for the women with only a grade-school education. However, once again, we found no clear evidence that achievement-oriented women viewed their marriages as more difficult than women with low achievement motivation. If anything, achievement motivation enhances the assessment

TABLE 3-2 THE RELATIONSHIP (γ) OF MOTIVES TO MARITAL REACTIONS FOR HIGH-SCHOOL-EDUCATED SUBJECTS (WITHIN SEX AND AGE)

Marital Reaction	Type of Motive												Number of Subjects at Each Age Level			
	Affiliation				Achievement				Power							
	young	middle	old	all ages	young	middle	old	all ages	young	middle	old	all ages	young	middle	old	all ages
Wives																
Restrictiveness	.10	.03	−.03	.06	.00	.06	−.11	.01	−.03	−.03	−.02	−.02	(136)	(114)	(47)	(299)
Unhappiness	−.02	−.18	−.31*	−.12*	−.08	.08	.30	.03	.05	.05	−.00	.05	(137)	(117)	(48)	(304)
Problems	.15	−.20	.15	.03	−.26*	−.22	.15	−.16*	−.01	−.12	.00	−.05	(134)	(115)	(48)	(299)
Inadequacy	.10	.02	.12	.10	−.03	.06	.02	.04	−.07	.22*	−.28	.02	(130)	(115)	(46)	(293)
Relationship satisfaction	−.16	−.21	.16	−.12	.16	.19	.06	.16*	.03	.06	−.31	−.00	(130)	(111)	(47)	(290)
Self-dissatisfaction	—a	−.53*	—a	−.40*	—a	.05	—a	.19	—a	−.30	—a	−.24	(98)	(90)	(29)	(219)
Husbands																
Restrictiveness	−.04	.04	.04	.00	.13	.02	.12	.08	−.10	−.24	−.14	−.14	(92)	(76)	(52)	(220)
Unhappiness	.02	.14	−.11	.03	.04	−.04	−.30	−.08	−.10	.16	.12	.05	(93)	(77)	(51)	(221)
Problems	.20	−.07	−.06	.04	.30*	.18	−.19	.15	.00	−.05	.48†	.10	(93)	(76)	(49)	(218)
Inadequacy	.06	.20	−.16	.06	.08	−.29*	.17	−.03	−.13	.04	−.30	−.10	(92)	(76)	(51)	(219)
Relationship satisfaction	−.29*	−.13	.26	−.11	−.12	.07	.29	.04	.05	.04	−.14	−.01	(92)	(75)	(52)	(219)
Self-dissatisfaction	−.08	—a	—a	−.32	−.19	—a	—a	.11	−.03	—a	—a	−.04	(62)	(45)	(20)	(127)

aNot reported because of inadequate distribution.
*p < .10.
†p < .05.

104

of the interpersonal satisfactions in marriage for women with high-school backgrounds.

The relationships between achievement motivation and marital reactions for high-school-educated men were somewhat different than those for grade-school-educated men. There were no significant relationships when age was disregarded. Among the young men with a high-school education there was a significant positive relationship between achievement motivation and the report of *Marital Problems*. And for the middle-aged men with a high-school education, achievement motivation was significantly associated with the lack of feelings of *Marital Inadequacy* as a husband.

These results suggest that for young men who are members of social groups that are beginning to assume the companionate values of marriage, there is a beginning involvement of achievement motivation in marital role reactions. It is interesting to note that within this social group the clearest differentiation between men and women occurs in the youngest age group. For these women, achievement motivation was significantly negatively associated with *Marital Problems*, while for these men, achievement motivation was significantly positively associated with *Marital Problems*. For these two groups, the overall direction of the relationships also differ for *Marital Unhappiness, Marital Inadequacy, Relationship Satisfaction,* and *Self-dissatisfaction*. These men may be very involved in getting started in their jobs, and with their limited education their marriage responsibilities may be difficult to meet. The middle-aged and especially the oldest men showed less association between achievement motivation and marital difficulties. Perhaps these men face less conflict between ideologies about the compationate obligations of marriage and their achievement strivings in the world of work than younger men do.

Power On the whole, the power motivation of high-school-educated wives seems unrelated to their marital role reactions. The one exception occurred for the middle-aged, high-school-educated wives who reported significantly more feelings of *Marital Inadequacy* if highly motivated for power. This relationship was opposite to that found for the grade-school-educated wives.

The data for high-school-educated husbands also reflect the relative lack of relevance of power motivation for marital role reactions. There was, however, a significant positive relationship between *Marital Problems* and power motivation for the oldest, high-school-educated husbands.

MARRIED MEN AND WOMEN WITH A COLLEGE EDUCATION

We turn now to the college-educated groups. For these subjects we had expected that a consistently companionate, egalitarian view of marriage would prevail, and that achievement strivings would most likely interfere with marital role-functioning.

We were greatly surprised to find that for these highly educated subjects affiliation motivation was not related to marital reactions. These results suggest that, contrary to our expectation, the companionate quality to marriages of the avant garde does not consistently interfere with, or aid, the adjustment of people with strong affiliation motivation who presumably are concerned about companionship.

In contrast, the power motive is very salient to the felt adjustment of college-educated men and women. Power motivation is associated with a sense of contentment among college-educated women and a sense of distress among college-educated men. It appears that in a marital relationship where the role definition permits either party to attempt to influence the other, the woman's general feminine role does not permit her to be distressed by unsuccessful influence attempts. Therefore, the possibilities of power assertion in an egalitarian marriage are congruent with strong power motivation in women; they felt unrestricted, happy, and free of problems. But even for men who presumably accept the egalitarian marital role, this role poses a threat to the masculine self-image of men with strong power motivation; they felt restricted and had marital problems. For them there is a lack of congruence between their motivation and the role demands.

The demands of marriage seem to be incongruent with the achievement motivation of older college-educated men, but congruent with the achievement motivation of younger men in this educational status. The older men with strong achievement motivation felt that marriage was restricting and yet were happier with their marriage than those with weak motivation to achieve. We interpret this to mean that older men can feel that marriage impedes a highly successful career—or at least impedes their attempts to reach even higher goals—if they have high achievement motivation, even though their marriage itself is satisfactory. But young men with strong achievement motivation felt less restricted by marriage than those with weak motivation to achieve. These young, college-educated men who are also achievement-motivated have only a prospective view of the achievement opportunities open to them; they may view their entrance into the marital status as syntonic with their long-range achievement goals.

The achievement motivation of college-educated women, contrary to our expectations, seemed neither congruent nor incongruent with marital adjustment. Since we were greatly surprised by these findings, we looked more closely at some further data, which we will report in the section on the Reassessment of Achievement Motivation in the Context of Marriage, later in this chapter.

The number of women in the oldest age group was too small to meet the criterion for reporting the gamma index and therefore the age comparisons are somewhat limited for the college-educated women. The data for the college-educated men and women are presented in Table 3.3.

Affiliation We had expected that college-educated husbands and wives, who are participants in more companionate marriages, would show clearer relationships between affiliation motivation and role reactions than any other group. The data in Table 3.3 indicate that this was not the case. The only significant relationship that occurred was that middle-aged, college-educated men were significantly less likely to feel inadequate as husbands if they had high affiliation motivation than if they had low affiliation motivation. The paucity of strong relationships in this group

TABLE 3-3 THE RELATIONSHIP (γ) OF MOTIVES TO MARITAL REACTIONS FOR COLLEGE-EDUCATED SUBJECTS (WITHIN SEX AND AGE)

Marital Reaction	Affiliation				Achievement				Power				Number of Subjects at Each Age Level			
	young	middle	old	all ages	young	middle	old	all ages	young	middle	old	all ages	young	middle	old	all ages
Wives																
Restrictiveness	−.00	−.25	—a	−.12	.20	.07	—a	.02	−.46†	−.20	—a	−.21	(41)	(42)	(9)	(92)
Unhappiness	.01	−.13	—a	−.01	−.19	.06	—a	.02	−.40*	−.09	—a	−.22	(41)	(42)	(9)	(92)
Problems	.18	−.15	—a	−.06	−.22	−.13	—a	−.11	−.67‡	−.42*	—a	−.53‡	(41)	(42)	(9)	(92)
Inadequacy	−.10	−.07	—a	.03	.24	.28	—a	.08	.15	−.23	—a	.04	(41)	(39)	(8)	(88)
Relationship satisfaction	.16	−.22	—a	−.04	.23	−.05	—a	.19	.07	−.33	—a	−.12	(40)	(35)	(9)	(91)
Self-dissatisfaction	—a	—a	—a	.33	—a	—a	—a	−.41	—a	—a	—a	−.02	(35)	(30)	(3)	(68)
Husbands																
Restrictiveness	.02	.15	.12	.12	−.35*	.13	.43*	−.06	.14	.16	.49*	.19	(43)	(38)	(29)	(110)
Unhappiness	−.08	.17	.28	.10	−.18	.10	−.65†	−.21	.31	.08	.19	.20	(43)	(37)	(31)	(111)
Problems	−.26	−.42	.12	−.18	−.09	.21	−.33	−.02	.27	.12	.36	.26*	(43)	(37)	(30)	(110)
Inadequacy	.13	−.40*	.06	−.06	−.02	−.12	.19	.02	−.12	−.02	−.02	.03	(42)	(38)	(30)	(110)
Relationship satisfaction	−.20	−.10	.27	−.01	.08	−.07	−.14	−.04	.27	−.02	−.10	.04	(43)	(38)	(30)	(111)
Self-dissatisfaction	—a	−.11	—a	−.04	—a	−.10	—a	.09	—a	−.23	—a	−.01	(26)	(25)	(16)	(67)

aNot reported because of inadequate distribution.
*p < .10.
†p < .05.
‡p < .01.

107

suggested the desirability of a reappraisal of the significance of marriage for affiliative gratification. We will make this reappraisal in a succeeding summarizing section on affiliation motivation.

Achievement There were no significant relationships between achievement motivation and marital responses for women. This, too, was in contrast to our findings for less-educated women. There was clearly no support for our initial view that highly-educated women who were achievement motivated would have more difficulties in marriage. It may be that these women are participants in the changing American family structure and that there is greater diversity in their marital roles than is true for less-educated women. Some college-educated women in new versions of the companionate marriage may find opportunities to combine careers with raising a family. Other college-educated women may still find their extrafamilial achievement orientations severely limited by the companionate role. Therefore, some women in this educational group may have sufficient opportunity to satisfy achievement strivings while others are frustrated. In looking at all marriages in this group, there may thus be little overall relationship to individual motivation.

The results for college-educated men did reveal some interesting relationships. There was a significant negative relationship between *Marital Unhappiness* and achievement motivation for the older, college-educated men and this also tended to be true for the youngest men. Thus achievement motivation seems to enhance marital happiness. There was an interesting differentiation between the view of entrance into marriage for youngest and oldest college-educated men with high achievement motivation. For young men, achievement motivation was significantly negatively associated with *Marital Restrictiveness*. Just the opposite was true for older men, who, if they were highly achievement-motivated, were more likely to have viewed the life changes accompanying marriage as restricting a man. It may be that the achievement motivation of young, college-educated men enhances an active energetic orientation to life which delays their encounter with the full force of possible conflict between the demands of their work and of their marriage.

The more puzzling set of results are those for older, college-educated men. It seems reasonable to interpret the significant positive relationship between *Marital Restrictiveness* and achievement motivation as supportive of our original view that achievement-motivated men retrospectively might have felt impeded by marital demands in their career aspirations. But then it is difficult to understand why they also reported happier marriages. Perhaps college-educated men with high achievement motivation view marriage as a performance to be evaluated, and hence produce successful "happy" marriages.

Power The relevance of power motivation for marital role reactions is quite strong for the young, college-educated wives. These women consistently indicated more satisfaction with their marriage when they were highly motivated for power than when they had weak power motives. There were significant negative relationships between power motivation and *Marital Restrictiveness*, *Marital Unhappiness*, and *Marital Problems*, for the young, college-educated wives. The relationship between power motivation and the lack of reported marital problems was similar in the other age groups and was significant both for the middle-aged group and for the total group of college-educated wives. Thus, it does appear that these data are compatible with the view that college-educated wives are engaged in more egalitarian marital relationships that are therefore more potentially satisfying to those women who are highly motivated to seek power. The role fits; there is congruence.

College-educated men who were highly motivated for power, on the other hand, generally reported more marital dissatisfaction on various indices than those who were low in power motivation. There was a significant positive relationship across all age groups between the report of *Marital Problems* and power motivation. This was opposite to the relationship for college-educated wives. In addition, for older college-educated men, there was a significant positive relationship between *Marital Restrictiveness* and power motivation; the same trends occurred in the other age groups.

These data are on the whole consistent with our view that in egalitarian marriages, which are assumed to occur more frequently among college-educated persons, strong power motivation will be more congruent with the marital role for women than for men. The complementary nature of the possibilities for power gratification in the marital relationship are most clearly seen in this group, where wives with power motivation are generally pleased with their marriages and report the absence of difficulties, while the opposite is true for college-educated husbands. We emerge with a view of the egalitarian marriage as one which gives a woman considerable opportunity for influence without stimulating a fear of weakness. While egalitarian marriages give a man some opportunity for power assertion, it evokes his fear of weakness or frustrates his assertion of power.

MEN AND WOMEN WITH AND WITHOUT CHILDREN

The definition of the marital role generally includes having and raising children. We have considered whether the marital reactions of persons without children relate to their own motivational characteristics in ways distinctive from such motive-role interaction in married persons with children. In order to exert some control on whether or not childless spouses were permanently in this status, either by reasons of choice or of sterility, we used the age of the respondent as a further control, assuming that older persons without children are likely never to have children. However, since close to 90 percent of all the respondents who were married at the time of the interview did have children, the group of childless husbands and wives was quite small. Therefore we were able to use only two gross age groupings, those under 45 and those 45 and above, and were forced to eliminate the use of education as a further control. Within each sex and parental status, we computed the relationships between each of the three motives and the six marital role reactions, both within and across the two gross age groupings.

Our overall conclusion from these detailed analyses was that the presence or absence of children had little effect upon the relationship between motivation and role reactions. There were, however, some interesting exceptions to this overall pattern, and we will discuss them now. (Table 3.e in Appendix B presents those relationships between motives and marital reactions that distinguish persons with and without children.)

The relationship of motive level to the index of *Marital Restrictiveness* seemed to depend to some degree on the presence or absence of children. It will be recalled that for the entire sample of married women the reaction of *Marital Restrictiveness* showed no significant overall relationships with any of the motives. But for those wives who were childless, strong affiliation motivation was consistently associated with the absence of a restrictive view of the life changes that accompany marriage, significantly so for both the younger women (gamma $= -.34$, $p < .10$ for tau beta) and the total group (gamma $= -.31$, $p < .05$ for tau beta). The overall relationship between not having children and viewing marriage as relatively unrestrictive was previously reported. (See Table 3.c, Appendix B.) The present result suggests that the relatively unrestrictive view of marriage among childless wives stems largely from those childless women who have high affiliation motivation. The fact that affiliation motivation facilitates an unrestrictive view of the marital status for childless wives suggests that for those women the absence of children does not interfere with affiliative satisfactions, either those directly obtained in the husband-wife relationship or those available to married women outside the marital relationship itself.

Affiliation motivation was also somewhat differently related to *Marital Unhappiness* for wives with and without children. Wives who were also mothers were consistently more likely to be happy in their marriages if they were high in affiliation motivation than if they had low affiliation motivation, significantly so for younger women (gamma $= -.13$, $p < .10$ for tau beta) and for the entire group of mothers (gamma $= -.15$, $p < .05$ for tau beta). In contrast, for childless wives, there was no significant relationship between these variables, and in the younger group the relationship was slightly in the opposite direction (gamma = .03). *Marital Unhappiness* had been similarly negatively related to the affiliation motive for grade-school and high-school-educated wives when parental status was disregarded. Since the group of wives with children was by far the major portion of our general sample of wives, the absence of this relationship in childless women then is perhaps the more interesting result. We had suggested that affiliation motivation can be satisfied by the mere status of being married. But beyond that, these results suggest it is the status of being married and having children that is important for the satisfaction of wives with high affiliation motivation. Children can become a means of establishing affiliative satisfaction not only within the marriage relationship itself, especially in a traditional marriage, but also with other women who are mothers. A child can become the basis for closer inter-action between husband and wife. Without a child, a marriage can become unfocused. However, childless couples can more easily seek affiliative satisfactions outside the marriage and perhaps it is for this reason that their affiliation motivation is irrelevant to their marital happiness. This latter interpretation would be consistent with the previous finding that a less restrictive view of marriage was found among childless women with strong affiliation motivation. Those women presumably are concerned with establishing and maintaining social contacts and do not see marriage as interfering with these efforts.

For husbands, as for wives, we once again found that *Marital Restrictiveness* is a reaction that is differentially related to motivation for spouses with and without children. However, for husbands it is not affiliation motivation, but rather both achievement and power motivation that are relevant. Younger men who were fathers were less likely to view their marriages as restrictive if they had high achievement motivation than if they had low achievement motivation (gamma = $-.15$, $p < .10$ for tau beta). This negative relationship between *Marital Restrictiveness* and the achievement motive suggests that the demand of being a provider to wife and children may be more compatible with the career involvement of men with strong achievement motivation than it is for men with weak achievement motivation. That this relationship was near zero for young childless husbands raised an interesting possibility. A man with strong career aspirations may be allowed greater leeway in striving to meet his ambitions when he has children, compared to when his marriage is childless. In the latter instance a wife does not have the extra responsibility of childrearing to fill her time and so she may make greater demands upon her husband for companionship.

The centrality of the husband-wife relationship in childless marriages may also be the key to interpreting the positive relationship between the power motive and *Marital Restrictiveness* for older childless husbands (gamma = .48, $p < .10$ for tau beta). In the absence of children the contention for the influential role in the husband and wife interaction may be stronger. Therefore those men who are high in power motivation might feel more restricted by their marital role when their wives' attention cannot be turned to influencing their children rather than their husbands. Wives without children can have more time to "henpeck" their husbands; their husbands might feel that marriage is constraining.

REASSESSMENT OF MOTIVES IN THE CONTEXT OF MARRIAGE

Let us integrate the disparate findings that we have reported about the three motives and their relationships to marital reactions. We have gained some new insights about the significance of each of the motives.

AFFILIATION MOTIVATION AND MARITAL REACTIONS

Our initial view that affiliation motivation would be a central personality variable contributing to the analysis of reactions of men and women in the marital role has been modified by our results. It is not a major correlate of marital adjustment among either college-educated men or women, or for men generally. Affiliation motivation is important in the marital role on three counts: first, for the entrance into the marital relationship; second, for the husband-wife interaction itself; and third, for interactions with persons other than the marital partner, which can indirectly affect marital adjustment. Affiliation motivation, as a tendency to avoid aloneness and to seek out companionship can affect each of these facets of marriage. Let us look at each in turn.

The relevance of affiliation motivation to the entrance into the married status seems to be a positive one for both men and women. We found that those persons who had experienced some past marital disruption and had remarried by the time of the interview were highest in affiliation motivation. A strong impetus toward remarriage seems to exist among those persons with strong affiliation motivation, especially for men. Many people assume that with the switch from unmarried to married status, companionship will ensue. These expectations appear to underlie the selection into the married status of persons with strong affiliation motivation.

At lower-status levels women strongly motivated to affiliate seem to experience more interpersonal satisfactions within the marital role. For grade-school-educated women, affiliation motivation was related to reporting that the relationship with one's spouse was the nicest thing about one's marriage. For both grade-school and high-school women, as well as the entire group of women with children, marital happiness was associated with strong affiliation motivation. Whether or not these results mean that full-fledged companionate activity is more often found by these women with high affiliation motivation is an open question. We doubt it. It could be that the mere status of being married, or of being married and having children, allows them to have sufficient contact with their husbands to feel taken care of, economically secure, and satisfied with their marriage. In the more-educated groups, where more modern marital-role relationships are assumed to be valued, there was no association between affiliation motivation and relationship satisfaction or any other marital reaction. We suspect that what women with high affiliation motivation in the traditional marriage are finding especially gratifying is their dependent security in the marital arrangement; marriage is a bridge to other social ties and to the world at large. In the marriages of the more-educated, in spite of the demand for companionate interaction between husband and wife, affiliation motivation seems irrelevant to marital reaction. It begins to look as if companionship in marriage might also breed distress as well as contentment. Perhaps sexual and affiliative love are not as easy to amalgamate as marriage manuals would have us believe. For men and women who are able to interweave their sexual and friendly feelings to their spouse, affiliation motivation should enhance adjustment. For those who cannot, affiliation motivation could lead to some anxiety about the sexual side of marriage. These are speculations but they aid us to understand the paucity of findings when we related affiliation motivation to marital reactions in the college-educated groups. Of course, this sort of interpretation remains open to question.

We have also interpreted some of our results as consistent with the view that women highly motivated to affiliate can gratify their longings outside the marital relationship itself. We suggested this interpretation when we found that the group of wives who had high motivation and also reported feeling less restricted by the entrance into the married status were those wives without children. We viewed the absence of children as increasing the possibility for interactions with persons other than the spouse. We would guess that these interactions are with other women who are also married, although there remains the possibility that these interactions may be with other men as well.

In general, we find less indication that affiliation motivation is relevant to postmarital role reactions for men. The few significant results that did occur mainly suggest that affiliation motivation for men is associated with dissatisfaction with one's marriage, but it is not at all clear from these results whether the marital relationship is unsatisfying or whether marriage thwarts other social satisfactions. The findings in Chapter 5 will suggest that men with high affiliation motivation are more likely to be engaged in social activities with friends than are men with low affiliation motivation. This result suggests that men with high affiliation motivation who feel distressed in marriage may be reacting to the interference with affiliative behavior with friends that marriage can cause. The intimacy of marriage evidently does not compensate for curtailed social behavior with other men.

ACHIEVEMENT MOTIVATION AND MARITAL REACTIONS

We had assumed that achievement motivation would not be an important variable in predicting men's marital role reactions, and the results generally support this view. Those results that did occur suggested that achievement-oriented men with minimal education experience less involvement in the role than men who are less motivated to achieve. While the young, college-educated men with strong achievement motivation might also be considered uninvolved by virtue of their view of marriage as less restrictive, their older counterparts' retrospective view of entry into the married status is especially restrictive, even though they evaluate their marriages as happy.

Our initial expectations were that achievement motivation in women would be related to marital dissatisfaction, because women probably find it hard to find achievement gratification within the marital role itself, and because the marital role interferes with finding achievement gratification in job roles. Clearly the data we have presented do not support this proposition. The relationships that do occur between achievement motivation and marital reactions for women generally support the view that achievement-oriented women are more satisfied rather than less satisfied with their marriages. However, these results occur only for the women with grade-school and high-school educations and not for the college-educated women. If we assume that there is some validity to the general congruence principle, then we must consider the possibility that despite the apparent consensus among observers of the American scene, the women's marital role is not low in achievement potential. However, it seems more reasonable to conclude that the wife role actually is ambiguous or flexible with regard to its achievement potential rather than in fact generally high in achievement potential. The wife role could then offer possibilities for achievement gratification if the appropriate effort is made by the role occupants. Presumably, achievement-motivated women would be quick to perceive achievement gratification possibilities in the role. However, the direct questions about how a woman's life is changed by being married, or about the nicest things about marriage, included too few responses that fell into the achievement gratification category to yield useful variables to check the sensitization principle. So instead we turned to a more indirect assessment of role expectations based on the different types of pictures employed to tap achievement motivation in the thematic apperceptive method. We will present the analysis of this differentiation at this point.

Career and home-oriented achievement motivation in women In keeping with our previous work (Veroff et al., 1966), we assumed that the motivation score obtained by an individual in response to a picture depicting a particular situation was a function of both an enduring disposition for gratification from that type of activity and the expectation that gratification was indeed possible. Discussions of the absence of achievement potential in the marital role have often contrasted it with the achievement gratification potential available to women in a job or career. Therefore, we were interested in considering whether women who obtained high achievement motivation scores for stories told about pictures with a job or career setting reacted differently to their marriages than did women who obtained high achievement motivation scores for stories told about pictures with a home setting. The assumptions behind this approach and the details of the procedures are presented in Veroff et al. (1966).

Three of the six pictures used in the assessment of motivation elicited sufficient achievement scores to warrant their use in this analysis. One picture concerned a job or career setting. It was Picture 1, described as: Two women standing by a table and one woman is working with test tubes. Two pictures elicited stories of achievement motivation in home situations. They were: Picture 4—Woman kneeling and applying a cover to a chair; Picture 5—Two women preparing food in the kitchen. For this analysis, we developed an index of career achievement motivation and home achievement motivation from the stories told about these three pictures. The index of career achievement motivation was a dichotomized variable, scored (1) if there was a total absence of achievement imagery in the story told about the career picture (Picture 1), and (2) if there was any achievement imagery in that story. The index of home achievement motivation was also a dichotomy, scored (1) if there was an absence of achievement imagery to stories told about *both* home pictures (Pictures 4 and 5), and (2) if stories with achievement imagery were told about *either* of the two home pictures.

Each of these dichotomous achievement motivation subscores was related to the six measures of marital role reactions, controlling for both age and education of the respondents. These data are summarized in Table 3.4. In the summary table, we have noted relationships in which women with different types of achievement motivation showed different patterns of correlation with the marital role reactions. For comparative purposes, the relationship based on the total achievement motivation score for the six pictures is also included.

We are now in a somewhat better position to clarify our interpretation of the opportunities and implications for achievement gratification in the

TABLE 3-4 RELATIONSHIPS (γ) FOR WIVES IN WHICH DIFFERENT TYPES OF ACHIEVEMENT MOTIVATION SHOWED DIFFERENT PATTERNS OF ASSOCIATION WITH MARITAL REACTIONS (WITHIN EDUCATION AND AGE)

Education and Age	Marital Reaction	Type of Achievement Motive			N
		Career	Home	Total	
Grade school	Unhappiness	.21	−.31†	−.22*	(118)
Grade school: Young	Inadequacy	.89†	.10	.54*	(20)
Grade school: Middle-aged	Unhappiness	.23	−.48*	−.31	(42)
High school	Problems	−.07	−.10	−.16*	(299)
High school	Relationship satisfaction	.01	.14	.16*	(290)
High school: Young	Problems	−.10	−.16	−.26*	(134)
College	Restrictiveness	.30*	−.15	.02	(92)
College: Middle-aged	Restrictiveness	.44*	−.20	.07	(42)
All wives	Inadequacy	.20†	−.03	.08	(493)

*p < .10.
†p < .05.

wife role. Home-achievement motivation and career-achievement motivation were related to different marital role reactions. In practically all instances where the overall achievement motivation score had been found to be significantly related to one of the marital role reaction variables, *either* career-achievement motivation or home-achievement motivation was also found to be related to this marital reaction, but usually not both.

So we see in Table 3.4 that the overall negative relationships between achievement motivation and *Marital Unhappiness* that had been found in the grade-school-educated women stems from the relationship between *home*-achievement motivation and *Marital Unhappiness*. Grade-school-educated women who expressed achievement motivation in relation to home activities felt happier about their marriages than those who did not. The relationship for career-achievement-motivation scores was in the opposite direction; women with high career-achievement motivation tended to be unhappier in their marriages than those lacking in such motivation.

It had also been found that *Marital Inadequacy* was positively related to the total achievement motivation scores among young, grade-school-educated women. In this subscore analysis we found that this relationship stemmed mainly from those women who were high in *career*-achievement motivation. Furthermore, the relationship between *Marital Inadequacy* and career-achievement motivation was significant for the entire sample of married women. Women who expressed achievement motivation in relation to a job felt more inadequate about their marital role-functioning than those who did not. The college-educated women who evidenced career-achievement motivation, and especially those in the middle-age range, saw marriage as more restrictive than those who did not. The total achievement-motivation score had not been related to *Marital Restrictiveness*, and the home-achievement-motivation score tended to be negatively related to *Marital Restrictiveness* for the college-educated women.

For the *Marital Problems* and *Relationship Satisfaction* indices of marital reactions the differentiation between the career-achievement motivation and home-achievement motivation is not as clear. However, in both instances there is a suggestion that the home-achievement-motivation score is contributing more to the overall relationships than the career-achievement-motivation score.

If, for the moment, we ignore the age and education subgrouping in which these differential relationships were found, it appears as if home-achievement motivation is related to reports of satisfaction with marriage, especially to marital happiness. Since we view the index of *Marital Unhappiness* as measuring a passive reaction to marriage rather than a self-involved reaction to the marital role, it appears that women with home-oriented-achievement motivation show a passive acceptance of their marital role. In contrast, career-achievement motivation is related to a view that marriage is restricting and that one's own performance in the marital role is not totally adequate. Thus, the picture that emerges with career-achievement motivation scores is more compatible with our initial suppositions about the conflicts between the marital role and achievement aspirations. The woman who describes achievement-oriented behavior in a career setting is more likely to feel that marriage restricts her life and to have doubts about the adequacy of her functioning in the marital role. The adequacy dimension seems to tap a self-questioning, self-involved view of one's own role-functioning, and some dissatisfaction with that role-functioning.

If we now consider these data within the various subgroups, we find that grade-school-educated women with high home-achievement motivation apparently find the marital role satisfying. We might suppose that they can find means of gratifying their achievement desires within the home situation and that careers are not a realistic alternative to the housewife and mother role. For these women, having a job is also unlikely to increase the possibility for achievement gratification because of the limited type of jobs available to them. When women from this social group perceive achievement possibilities in the career setting, we find that they are likely to question the adequacy of their role-functioning within marriage. High-school-educated women with high home-achievement motivation also react positively to their marital role, as reflected in the absence of problems and presence of relationship satisfactions. But these

117

relationships were not as clear as those for the grade-school-educated women, nor was the differentiation between the two types of achievement motivation as clear as it was for the less-educated women. In contrast, college-educated women with high career-achievement motivation seem to view marriage as restrictive. This association is precisely what we had expected to be true for this social group, as well as more generally. However, we did also assume that there would be other indications of dissatisfaction with the marital role for this group besides feelings that marriage was restrictive or burdensome.

POWER MOTIVATION AND MARITAL REACTION

Because of the relatively new status of the power-motivation measure and the consequent lack of previous research with this measure, we had fewer preconceived notions about its significance for marital role reactions. We had made the general assumption that because of the complementary nature of the power gratification in a two-person interaction, the relationships between power motivation and marital role reactions would be of opposite sorts for husbands and wives.

We found particularly interesting educational group variations in the results with power motivation. For grade-school-educated men and women, power motivation seemed to be related to feelings of satisfaction in the role for both men and women. Grade-school-educated women with strong power motivation felt less inadequate than those with weak power motivation, and grade-school-educated men with high power motivation described their relationship with their spouse as the nicest thing about their marriage more frequently than men with low power motivation. The assertive role of the husband in the grade-school-educated social group seemed to be accompanied by a view that the relationship with the spouse was a satisfactory and important aspect of the marriage. There were only few relationships for the high-school-educated group and they were not very illuminating ones. In the college-educated group, however, we found the kind of contrasting relationships for husbands and wives that we had speculated might be a consequence of the complementary nature of the influential position in a two-person interaction. One particularly interesting result was that the college-educated husbands with high power motivation reported problems with their marriage. This measure largely concerned interpersonal difficulties in marriage. These men also reported that marriage was restrictive. In contrast, college-educated women who were power motivated, and especially the youngest of these, felt less restricted by their marriage and reported fewer marriage problems and more marital happiness than those with low power motivation. The college-educated women seem to be more able to assert themselves in their marital relationship and obtain satisfaction from this assertive role. This power assertion by women seems most possible with the more egalitarian norm for the husband-wife relationship that exists in this social group. This norm, however, appears to create difficulties for the college-educated man who has high power motivation; egalitarian marriage threatens his position of power, opens up the possibility of his weakness.

One further comment on the apparent "plight" of the married man with strong power motivation can be made on the basis of comparison of married and unmarried men (widowed, single, or divorced men). Early in the interview, prior to questioning about marriage, the respondents were asked: "Taking all things together, how would you say things are these days—would you say you are very happy, pretty happy, or not too happy these days?" For men who were married at the time of the interview, this evaluation of their general happiness was inversely related to the strength of their power motivation; men with strong power motivation were less happy than men with weak power motivation (Chi square = 4.40, 1 d.f., $p < .05$). For unmarried men, on the other hand, there was no relationship between power motivation and general happiness. Once again then, we see the potential frustration of the power strivings of men within the marital relationship.

REASSESSMENT OF THE MARITAL ROLE

Now that we have presented the results, suggested possible interpretations of them, and reviewed the motivational consistencies, it seems appropriate to see what conceptions we now hold of the marital role. Our original conception emphasized the variations in role characteristics of traditional and modern marriages, and we attempted to crudely approximate these variations by use of the educational level of the respondent. This orientation proved to be a useful one even though the results seem to require revisions of certain specific assumptions.

ROLE DEMANDS

The primary role demand for husbands to support their family, and therefore to be competent to deal with the outside world, seems to be essentially similar in all social groups. However, the impact of this demand seems to vary, depending on the kinds of interpersonal demands of the marriage partnership that are also accepted. Being competent as a provider can interfere with the affiliative interpersonal requirements stressed in higher status groups. The most crucial aspect of variations in interpersonal marital demands in different social strata, however, seems to center on the regulation of appropriate influence over one another. It is the structure of the power relationships between spouses rather than their affiliative relationships that seems to be critical in distinguishing traditional from "companionate" marriages. The necessity for the husbands from more-educated backgrounds to acknowledge openly their wives' opinions and to accept their privileges in the decision-making arena is a critical difference from the more traditional demands accepted by our least-educated respondents. Companionate marriages do seem to demand greater "friendship" in the sexual relationship, but our results do not present clear-cut evidence for the importance of this distinction.

ROLE GRATIFICATIONS

The attainment of the marital state itself is an important source of gratification of affiliative goals for both men and women. For women who have little education and who are participants in traditional marriages, this attainment by itself continues to satisfy affiliative needs. But for women who are more-educated and whose marriages include more complex interpersonal demands, the marital state itself is not sufficient to satisfy affiliative goals. Nor does the husband-wife relationship among the more-educated husbands and wives appear to develop or be maintained in a way that is a substitute for, or a complement to, peer-group friendships. The expectations for companionship that characterize the modern marital role are not easily translated into gratification.

The most striking aspect of the variations of social-status groups in marital role gratifications occurs for the power motive. The marital relationship of persons with a grade-school education allows both men and women to avoid weakness and to attain satisfactory power relationships. What seems especially striking is that the covert power relegated to the less-educated woman in her marriage may be gratifying because it is covert. But a sharp distinction must be made in the power gratification potential of well-educated men and women. These women can enjoy their egalitarian relationship to their husbands, apparently in spite of how much this relationship might threaten their husbands' own power needs.

ROLE AMBIGUITIES

The transition that is occurring in marital demands is most evident in those persons with moderate amounts of education. Especially for men with a high-school education, there appears to be a lack of consensus or a diffuseness about the role demands and gratifications. This aggregation of men, therefore, provides the least homogeneous social grouping of any we used.

Among our least-educated subjects, there appears to be another kind of role ambiguity in evidence, which we had not considered in our theoretical discussion of this topic. Although the husband may clearly be acknowledged to be the wielder of influence, women are covertly accorded much power. This discrepancy between overt and covert power is a special kind of ambiguity that may underlie a grade-school-educated women's potential gratification of power needs in the marital relationship.

The effects of other ambiguities in marital role demands are seen among the most-educated men. They appear to have accepted conflicting role demands—to be successful in the provider aspects of the marital role, which usually requires great expenditure of time and effort in the job role—and to be successful husbands by spending considerable time with their wives and family. This appears to be a kind of role overload. Added to this is the direct conflict that may exist between expectations for their behavior in their job and marital roles: they must be successful influence agents at work but permit their wives to be influential on home territory.

There seems to be some ambiguity about how much potential the marital role has for gratifying the achievement strivings of some women. This ambiguity, however, appears to stem from a diffuseness of role expectations. For women with little education, for whom the job world offers little possibility for achievement gratification, it seems to provide a flexibility that permits achievement gratification within the marital role. The possibilities for successful mastery within the wife and mother role can be emphasized under these circumstances. But this flexibility does not seem to be an advantage for more-educated women, for whom marriage seems to interfere with the otherwise attainable achievement gratification possibilities in more prestigeful jobs. We suspect that this ambiguity will become less functional for more women as more women become better trained for good jobs.

4
Motives
and
Parenthood

A man or woman begins parenthood already equipped
with a varied and complex set of motives that have influenced
his behavior and his responses to the world up until this time. These
motives continue to influence him when he becomes
a parent, and affect in many ways his reaction to being a parent.
We are often dramatically aware of the more pathological instances where
parents act out their own motives in their dealing with their
children: the vain mother who dresses her child as she
would a doll in the latest pretty-girl fashion; the father who
belittles his son to maintain his own status in his
wife's eyes; the mother who finds sexually-tinged fulfillment by
being seductive with her young son. In each
of these cases the parent has imposed his own needs on the parent-
child situation and has found an avenue
for satisfying these needs. Similarly, the motives of a parent
can play a less pathological part in fashioning the parent's interaction with his child and his view of himself as a parent.
In the first pages of this chapter we will introduce some speculations
about the ways that parenthood can affect the nature
of fulfillment and frustration of affiliation,
achievement, and power motivations.

123

MOTIVES IN THE CONTEXT OF PARENTHOOD

In addition to looking at the direct relationships between motives and reactions to parenthood, we should like to focus some attention on relationships that can arise from essentially unconscious patterns of needs in parents. Obviously, in this analysis of a nationwide sample survey we will not be able to deal with subtleties in great detail nor make very specific speculations. Our data do not include unique descriptions of the individual. We do not have at our disposal the subtle variations in family structure and social settings that give the clinical psychologist a better perspective on the motive-role interaction of a particular individual. In this analysis we are looking for general linkages between motives and the parental role. We hope this chapter will set the stage for more intensive and subtle exploration of motive interactions with aspects of parenthood.

The role of parenthood entails a set of demands that vary as the role is differently defined in different educational groups and at different stages in the life cycle of parenthood. We assume that these demands can have greater or lesser attraction to people with different motivational patterns. As we indicated in the first chapter, parents find gratification or frustration not only in the process of fulfilling certain requirements of role performance, but also from the mere fact of being a parent. In this chapter we will try to see how the three motives we have measured relate to role reactions as a result of: fulfilling or not fulfilling role demands; finding or not finding gratification from being a parent, either in the day-to-day activities of parenthood or in the mere ascription of the role to the person; reacting one way or another to the ambiguities that exist in the role.

Motives may be related to parental reactions not only because they directly affect these role reactions, but because motives can affect the kinds of skills acquired by a person in the course of his life, and some of these skills are required of parents. For example, some people may have learned to be nurturing throughout their motivational history. Having already developed nurturing skills, they should find the demands of taking care of a young child easy to fulfill and gratifying. Another example of indirect motive-parenthood interaction is seen in the way that other roles can affect the parenthood of men with high achievement motivation. Such men probably perform well in the business world. Thus they can provide the kind of financial support to their family that would make them feel that they are performing their parental role adequately. In either example, people with certain motivational patterns may be especially skilled in activities that are important for parental role-functioning and will, therefore, react to the role in a different way from those who are not so skilled.

Let us begin by taking a closer look at the parental role demands, listed in Chapter 1, in order to get a clearer picture of both potential gratifications in parenthood and the potential ambiguities in the role. Among the major demands of parenthood for all parents in our society, two types of functions stand out: nurturing and influencing. In a recent review of studies of parental behaviors in relationship to children, W. Becker and Krug (1964) attempted to induce common dimensions that seem to underlie parental role performance in general. They posited three dimensions that can be used to categorize all parental behaviors. These dimensions reflect three types of parental reactions: warmth, control, and involvement. Warmth and control correspond to what we have listed as the major functions for parenthood—nurturing and influencing. Becker and Krug presented less support for the involvement dimension than for the other two, and from our perspective, it would be easier to categorize it as a role reaction than as a role demand. Brim (1957) discusses the contrast between adaptive-instrumental roles and integrative-expressive roles, particularly with respect to the Parsons-Bales hypothesis that the former is the father's role in the family, while the latter is the mother's role. Again the distinction between instrumental and expressive roles seems to parallel our categories of influencing and nurturing. Kohn and Carrol (1960) have reported results suggesting that this formulation about sex-role family differentiation may be overly simple. Mothers of fifth graders were more likely than fathers to be the influencers as well as the emotional supporters, especially in the working class. Therefore we will be aware of the possibility that both functions are potential demands for mothers and fathers.

Rossi (1968) also notes that some sociologists have been over-simplifying the dimensions of parenthood by suggesting that the influencing function belongs to the rational instrumental role of father while the nurturing function belongs to the emotional expressive role of mother. She takes social theorists to task for such oversimplification in the face of clearly changing patterns in the daily experiences of mothers and fathers in American society today. Rossi further notes that this oversimplification distorts any guidelines that a couple might use in trying to negotiate the transition to parenthood successfully, a change in life style that is in many ways more abrupt than the change from single to married status. With a realistic appraisal of the dual demands in becoming either a mother or a father, a young wife or husband might well be better prepared to cope with the difficulties of this transition, to which Rossi so astutely alludes.

INFERRING ROLE CHARACTERISTICS FROM EDUCATION AND PARENTAL STAGE

We expect that the role demands of nurturing and influencing, and the gratifications associated with them, vary depending on the educational level of the parents and also on the stage they are at in the life cycle of parenthood. A good deal of study has been devoted to differences in the parental role that depend on social class. These findings are relevant to the role demands of influencing and nurturing. Miller and Swanson, in *The Changing American Parent* (1958), point to the different types of disciplines that are required of parents who want to socialize their children in preparation for life in a bureaucratic status as opposed to a more individually directed entrepreneurial status. Parents from bureaucratic social settings are more likely to see that their function is to train children to be socially approved in society, while this concern is less dominant for parents from an entrepreneurial setting. More important to our concerns is their finding that paternal involvement in both nurturing and socializing functions increases with the educational level of the parent. Bowerman and Elder (1964) found that fathers were less frequently perceived as the authority figure in child-rearing among lower status groups, perhaps reflecting the difference in involvement of fathers from lower and middle or upper status groups. They also observed that fathers who were not seen as assuming leadership functions in family affairs were also not seen as assuming major nurturing functions by their adolescent children. Another relevant finding, from the present national sample, was reported earlier in *Americans View Their Mental Health* (Gurin et al., 1960). These data clearly indicate that the more highly educated the parent, the more likely he is to view the psychological aspects of his parental role as central requirements. Highly educated mothers were more likely to include being intolerant with their children as part of their feelings of inadequacy. Highly educated fathers were more likely to include "not seeing his children enough" as part of their feelings of inadequacy. When grade-school-educated fathers were asked about things that made them feel inadequate, they were more likely to mention feeling unable to supply enough physical security or affluence. The less-educated fathers thus focus more heavily on the basic primary nurturing demand of fatherhood —to materially provide for their children.

These research data and our own attempts to integrate them suggest that some differences in the role demands of influencing and nurturing may appear for parents from the three different educational levels represented here (grade school, high school, and college). The cultural shift away from a traditional authoritarian role for fathers seems to start with the "avant-garde," the more highly educated parents. Although this shift is already filtering through the entire society, the cultural lag is sufficient to suggest a difference between the more and the less highly educated parents. Fathers and mothers of upper status groups are responding to this shift in paternal role by equally sharing parental functions; there is an apparent increase in the involvement of fathers with the family and its affairs. By virtue of greater involvement we would expect the more highly educated fathers to be more actively engaged in both the nurturing and influencing demands of the parental role. This engagement should occur not only in a sheerly physical sense of spending more time in the home and thus being asked more frequently to nurture and to influence, but also, we would expect, in their feeling more day-to-day responsibility to nurture and to influence, to discipline, to diaper, to comfort, to entertain, and to instruct. These shifts should have occurred most frequently among college-educated fathers, most infrequently among the grade-school-educated fathers, and with moderate frequency among the high-school-educated fathers.

The shift in family structure noted above is probably not unrelated to another change in the parental role that again is currently more character-istic of more highly educated parents. In this view, which has gradually become more widely accepted, parents play a part in determining the psychological health of their offspring. We would expect that in highly educated groups the definitions of nurturing and influencing functions in parenthood would include *psychological* nurturing and *psychological* in-fluencing. Highly educated parents may feel that the quality of the love they give their children may be as important as the quality of the physical care they administer. To the extent that highly educated people see themselves as holding some responsibility for leadership and activity in society for the good of society, we would expect that they would feel that they should not only teach their children to conform to the rules of society but also to assume social obligations for contributions in the world at large. Therefore, the more-educated parents, and especially those with a college education, would be attempting to teach their children different and perhaps more complex orientations toward life than the less-educated parents.

There are other studies that demonstrate that different parental role demands and gratifications are associated with different stages in the parental life cycle. Bowerman and Elder (1964) found as children got older they were more likely to see the parent of the same sex as being dominant. These results suggest that the role demands that are central to the maternal role in early child-rearing may branch out into the paternal role as children reach adolescence. These results further suggest that helping the adolescent choose a proper adult identity may be handled in different ways by fathers and by mothers depending on whether their child is a son or a daughter.

Our own data suggest that parents find most satisfaction during the stage of parenthood when children are young and least satisfaction in the stages when their children are adolescent and adult. Parents were asked which of five times would be the happiest for a parent:

1. When the children are very little;
2. When the children are about three or four years old, and haven't started school yet;
3. When the children are going to grade school, around the ages of eight or nine;

4. When the children are teenagers, around high-school age;
5. When the children are grown up and ready to go out on their own.

The preschool era was selected as the happiest time by 35 percent of the mothers and fathers. Teenagers and grown children were each selected by 7 percent of the parents as the ages with which they would be happiest. These results may be interpreted in terms of the difference in role demands, gratifications, and ambiguities at different stages in the life cycle of parenthood.

We turn now to consider specifically how the nurturing and influencing functions may vary at different stages of the life cycle of parenthood. We had suggested that what is necessary and expected in the care and rearing of a very young child, for example, may be quite different from what is necessary and expected for an older child or an adolescent. For the present chapter, we divided the parental life cycle into four stages identified by the age range of the children: parents of preschool children only (0–4 years old); parents whose oldest child was of elementary school age (5–12 years old); parents whose oldest child was an adolescent who was living at home (13–20 years old); parents whose children were all adults (21 years of age or older) and who were not living with the parent. Not included in these groupings were parents who had both grown children living away from home and younger children living at home, or parents who had grown children living at home. The role demands for these conditions seemed too complex to include in our analysis of a parental life cycle.

First, let us examine the nurturing function for these four stages. The nurturing function—physical care by mothers and material provision by fathers—should be most salient for parents of preschool children. Children of this age are both most attached to the parent and most dependent on him for support. This nurturing function should diminish considerably for parents when children go to school. Although the nurturing function generally diminishes as the child grows older, it may, in a peculiar way, become stronger again when the parent is confronted with an adolescent. During adolescence the child is attempting to work out a separation from his parent, and there is presumably a resurgence of the child's concern about his attachments to the parent and an increase in the child's anxieties. Furthermore, the child and the parent are both confronted with the child's budding sexuality in overt physical manifestations. With these psychological and physical changes and the attendant strains that they bring, the child needs reassurance about his validity as a person. The child at this stage is asking his parent to accept his sexuality and his general integrity as a separate adult. Thus, we propose that parents are inevitably faced with at least some demand for the nurturing function during this time, to which they may or may not accede.

The nurturing function is virtually at an end for parents whose children are adults. In our society once a child is grown up and has moved out on his own, a parent need no longer be nurturant and certainly is not expected to encourage his child to continue to be dependent. The nurturing relationship ideally changes into an affectionate attachment between adults. The family of origin is no longer expected to nurture; instead, presumably, nurturing becomes the function of the family of procreation. A wife no longer turns to her mother but to her husband; the husband no longer turns to his mother but to his wife for nurturing support. We have posited this transition as the ideal development in parent-child relationships. There is no doubt that some parents will continue to encourage dependence in their children and will demand that their children continue to accept nurturance. Likewise, children may continue to demand that their parents be nurturing. But we would argue that *all* parents must at least react to the role demand of terminate nurturing when their children grow up. Thus, regardless of individual variations in the enactment of the relationship between parents and adult children, the role itself no longer requires the parent to be nurturing.

Let us turn to the influencing function and examine what changes it undergoes as a parent is faced with different types of demands during his life cycle as a parent. The responsibility of parents of preschool children is to socialize very primitive reactions in children, to train the child to be "good" in the immediate situation, and to begin to teach a more general morality. Most of what the preschool child is taught has moral implications to him: for example, he is taught not to destroy, to be toilet-trained, and to share. We could expand this list indefinitely. The responsibility to teach the child these types of behavior is clearly a role demand for the parent to influence the child.

The quality of teaching demanded of the parent of an elementary-school child is somewhat different. Society, assuming that the child has already learned basic moral values in early childhood, now asks the parent to teach the child how to perform and behave with competence and grace. The parent of an elementary-school child is thus required to transmit to the child any skills he possesses in dealing with the world. Most parents relegate a large part of this responsibility to the schools; nevertheless parents take on this responsibility as part of their overall functioning. The parent also continues to teach moral attitudes to the elementary-school child, but not as explicitly as he did when the child was younger. At this stage parents face problems of relinquishing parental control to another authority, but there is still no question of the child's dependency on the parent and the parent's ultimate responsibility for the child. Furthermore, during the elementary-school years peer socialization can become dominant and can present certain unique problems for the parent. A parent has to come to grips with possible conflicts between his own and peer norms. Such conflict occurs in adolescence too, but the first confrontation with this conflict is during middle childhood, usually when the child goes to school and comes into consistent contact with potentially conflicting norms.

Just as we have postulated a resurgence of demands for nurturing on parents of adolescents, a similar recapitulation can be seen with regard to the role of influencing. When the child is very young, the parent must teach him at least the minimum of civilized behavior to allow the child to negotiate in social situations. When the child reaches adolescence, the parent's responsibility is to teach the child enough about the norms of society to allow the adolescent to enter into and deal with the adult world. The parent is again actively engaged in the teaching of morality. The child must learn societal roles about sexual behavior, marriage, and general adult conduct. The influence demand for parents is different in adolescence than in early childhood. The parent must teach the very young child basic moral values—ideas that separate man from savagery; the parent must teach the adolescent the more specific and refined values that constitute the societal rules for adulthood. The adolescent may resist, but the parent is legally and morally expected to influence him. Some of the responsibility of the parent of an adolescent is shared by various institutions of the society; some of the learning grows rather spontaneously out of the early moral learning without conscious and constant parental vigilance.

There is another major shift when children reach adulthood. The influencing function of a parent of an adult is that of counseling. By "counseling" we mean advice given only when it is *sought out*. When adults speak of "interfering parents" they usually mean parents who offer advice *when not asked*. Parents of adults can assume the position of a wise man or a counselor. In our society this role can be enacted only when and if the child asks. As with the nurturing function, many parents may not give up the influence role demand when children mature, and many children may not want them to give it up. But this social rule is a role demand that both parents and children are undoubtedly cognizant of. Perhaps few children do ask advice spontaneously. Perhaps we have few institutionalized mechanisms for this role enactment. Nevertheless, the minimization of the influence function for parents of grown children is probably a critical role demand. Reactions of parents to adult children are determined to a considerable extent by the fact that the parents are required to face up to the fact that children have lives of their own to lead. The way a parent relates to a grown child's autonomy, however, presents certain problems that are distinct from the problems created when a parent relates to an adolescent's autonomy. Parents must still discreetly guide adolescents. Grown children have their decisions to make, more or less completely on their own.

In describing possible relationships between motives and role reactions in the next section, we will thus be cognizant of the fact that the two major role demands, nurturing and influencing, may be different, not only at different educational levels of parents, but also at different stages of the parental life cycle. There are many permutations and combinations to be considered in determining the possible interactions and interrelationships among the three motives and the changing demands for parents of different educational levels and at different stages of the life cycle. Although there is a potential for affiliation and power gratification in the enactment of the nurturing and influencing demands of parenthood, this potential does vary. The potential relationship between achievement motivation and the achievement gratifications possible in assuming and maintaining the parental role also varies. Furthermore, although we have presented these role demands as if they were sharply defined, in reality they are not. There is a lack of clarity and a lack of consensus among parents due to conflicting ideologies, especially in certain groups. For example, adolescence is a time when the parental role is particularly ambiguous. So is adulthood. We suspect that for most parents it would be highly probable that the sensitization hypothesis would operate at these times in the parental life cycle, but we are also aware that the ambiguity of the role at these times may also vary for groups with different social status.

We will not examine each of these possible interrelationships within each social group in this introductory section. Rather we will examine some of the most significant expectations we have about the general effect that each of the motives might have in determining parental reactions. Sometimes our speculations may be most relevant to particular educational levels or particular stages, but our focus will not be on subcultural differences.

Let us turn then to our ideas about the relationships of the motives to role reactions. As in the previous chapter, we will discuss each motive separately.

AFFILIATION MOTIVATION AND THE PARENTAL ROLE

In the last chapter we went into considerable detail about the ambiguities of the affiliation motive that bear on understanding the marital role. Much of the same discussion applies to the parental role. In order to anticipate the affiliative potential of parenthood, it is particularly important to be able to analyze the characteristics of children that make them appropriate or inappropriate as objects of affiliative goals. It is also necessary for our present discussion of parenthood to be able to specify qualities in the parent-child relationship that may be conducive to affiliative relationships, both in and outside of the parent-child relationship. At the outset we were alerted to the following problems about affiliation in the context of parenthood: (1) the extent to which the parent-child relationship is governed by obligatory role demands; (2) the degree of similarity or dissimilarity between parent and child; and (3) the degree to which parenthood affects both affiliative and sexual goals with other adults. To make our discussion of the affiliative potential of parenthood coherent, we took certain positions on these problems.

Parent-child interaction *is* obligatory. Therefore we are cautious about anticipating that a parent's interaction with a child would have the same significance for affiliation gratification as interactions between friends or lovers. The type of interpersonal response that a parent receives from a child is qualitatively different from the kind of response he receives from a friend because of several qualities inherent in the reciprocal role relationship between parent and child. A child's dependence on his parents may compel him to respond with unqualified love and acceptance. Children do not choose their parents. Children may feel obliged to demonstrate some signs of familial loyalty. That the child cannot choose another family, cannot choose to be elsewhere, cannot choose to love or not to love may in effect define the child's response to the parent as something different from a general affiliative response. The child can be seen as always responding to the parent as a parent and rarely responding to him as a person in his own right. A parent may feel that his child is obliged to love him because he is dependent upon him. "Genuine" affiliative gratification may come about only when a person likes another for what he is *in toto* and not because the other person is obliged to help him in some way, such as is required of parents in nurturing.

There is another sense in which the parent-child relationship may depart from the kind of relationship in which individuals ordinarily experience gratification of affiliative needs. Most parents in American society expect a child not only to love his parents but also to exhibit respect and deference toward them. However, because respect and deference may interfere with an exchange of fully loving responses between parent and child, some parents do not feel comfortable in the role of the one who must be respected. Indeed, some parents try very hard to establish a "buddy-buddy" relationship with their children. Such efforts may be attempts to minimize the obligatory aspects of their interactions with their children and to accentuate the affiliative potential in the parent-child relationship.

To sum up this point, parents undoubtedly get some affiliative gratification from their children, but we are suggesting that there may be some limitation in the nature and extent of this gratification. The inherent nature of the parent-child relationship may work against the establishment of a very strong "pure" affiliative tie. As a result, some people with high affiliation motivation may not even consider the parent-child relationship as suitable for affiliative gratification. Therefore, we did not anticipate a strong relationship between high affiliation motivation and obtaining gratification from parenthood, despite the fact that nurturing, one of the primary demands of parenthood, is essentially an affiliatively-oriented demand.

It is appropriate at this point to consider the affiliative impact of parenthood in terms of its potential hindrance or enhancement of affiliative relationships with persons other than the child. For a woman, motherhood implies a curtailment of some affiliative contacts, especially when her children are very young. Her time for involvement with her husband and with other family members and friends is by necessity curtailed. Parenthood has a similar impact for men, but to a much lesser extent.

If we assume, however, that similarity between persons increases their affiliative attractiveness to one another, parenthood would be likely to increase the possibilities for affiliative contacts by providing a new source of communality with other parents. A father's comments about his children can become an excellent vehicle for interpersonal contact both with his spouse and with people he encounters outside the home, and can lead to new areas of shared interests with other people. Furthermore, parenthood can be a symbol of adulthood and social adequacy that may enhance one's desirability in a variety of social situations. Both of these potential assets of parenthood could be true for both men and women, but the mother's early enforced seclusion may interfere with her taking advantage of them as readily as the father.

To the extent that direct sexual interests facilitate affiliative gratification, parenthood can affect the affiliative relationship between husband and wife. The proof of masculinity or femininity implicit in parenthood might increase sexual attractiveness. On the other hand, parenthood could act to decrease the marital partner's sexual attractiveness by changing his or her status from that of carefree lover to that of a responsible parent whose primary concern is for a child. While it is impossible for us to assess the relative likelihood of these two possibilities, we tend to think that the latter effect, coupled with the mother's increased time and psychological commitment to the child decreases the sexual attraction between parents. Similarly, confinement and involvement in the home makes a women less mobile in her contacts with other men. A man also may find he has fewer contacts with other women once he has become a father. The effect of parenthood on reducing social contact in general and

133

potential sexual contact specifically would, of course, be most notable in the early years of parenthood. A more enduring effect might be the intensification of taboos against adultery. Parenthood generally strengthens such taboos not only because the individual feels bound by his internal values to exercise more restraint, but because the world also is less tolerant of adultery among parents. Increased immobility and intensified taboos against adultery can therefore *lessen* a person's sexual potential. Considering these aspects alone, and assuming that affiliative and sexual goals for each spouse have been clarified and coordinated, we would anticipate that individuals with high affiliation motivation may perceive parenthood as less gratifying than those with low affiliation motivation because of its interference with potential sexual interests that may be a part of their affiliative needs. Since both the confinement and taboos apply more strongly to mothers, this interfering effect of parenthood should be more likely to be experienced by mothers with strong affiliation motivation than by fathers, if it is correct to assume that sexual attractiveness enhances affiliative gratification.

On the other hand, if affiliative goals are not related to sexual goals at all, then parenthood could facilitate certain kinds of "friendly" relationships. Marriage partners may interact with one another on friendship terms. Furthermore, by apparently eliminating the sexual implications of a relationship, parenthood can make a man a safe object of interest for a woman, and a woman a safe object of interest for a man. And within the framework of such a safe "Platonic" relationship, a well-delimited covert sexual flavor to the friendship may, in fact, enhance its pleasure. In these instances, parenthood may actually facilitate heterosexual contacts.

A somewhat different line of reasoning would also reinforce the prediction that people with strong affiliative needs might find heterosexual friendships enhanced by the state of parenthood. Let us assume that the measure of affiliation motivation indicates the strength of a person's attraction to other people who are similar to oneself rather than to people who are distinctly different. People with high affiliation motivation may desexualize heterosexual friendships to make it possible to perceive someone of the opposite sex as being more like oneself. Heterosexual contacts after parenthood are very compatible with this reaction. Hence, we might guess that parenthood in this respect may gratify affiliation motivation rather than frustrate it.

In conclusion, these considerations would lead us to predict that if similarity between persons is an important basis for establishing affiliative relationships, then parenthood should be congruent with high affiliation motivation. However, this congruence should be somewhat limited for women with young children because of their decreased opportunities for affiliative contacts. If sexual attraction facilitates affiliative relationships, parenthood should generally be dissatisfying to persons with a strong affiliation motive.

ACHIEVEMENT MOTIVATION AND THE PARENTAL ROLE

Three aspects of parenthood seem to be most clearly related to achievement strivings. First, having children in and of itself may be an achievement goal. Secondly, rearing children may present many opportunities for obtaining achievement goals. And finally, vicarious achievement—accomplishments through one's children—may represent very potent achievement goals for some individuals. We still consider each of these facets of parental gratifications in turn.

Having children is a major accomplishment for a woman, an act which by its very essence can gratify her achievement strivings. In fact, it may be the most unconflicted achievement she can experience in our society. For a man, having a child can be a sign of his potency, a symbol to the world of his sexual excellence. These gratifications may be most intensely felt in the early moments of parenthood, but for some parents the mere status of parenthood can continue to be a long-term manifestation of their accomplishment. While bearing a child may be a uniquely fulfilling creative experience, it is an experience available to nearly everyone and its value as an achievement goal generally is not too high, since unusual accomplishments or excellence are usually assumed to be most valued (Atkinson, 1958a). Furthermore, the existential potential for achievement gratification in bearing a child is countered for some individuals by the possibility that having children may hinder creative performance in realms that most men and women perceive as more relevant for achievement evaluations. In fact, the demands of parenthood may use up energy that might otherwise be devoted to a career or to other achievement endeavors outside the family. This possibility can be true for men as well as women.

Childrearing is the second aspect of parenthood potentially relevant to achievement strivings. Within certain social groups the criteria for successful childrearing are explicit. These criteria may include provision of material goods, especially for working-class men; they may include being permissive or even playing with children for certain other groups of men. Or, among the most avant-garde families, any behavior that is directed toward establishing "creativity" in the child would be deemed excellent. Providing materials for individual expression, taking children to various types of instruction classes, and encouraging rather than thwarting their imagination are examples of the kind of behavior that can be considered excellent achievement performance for mothers in highly educated groups. In each of these cases the parental activity is, at least in part, stimulated by a desire to do a good job of rearing children. Such achievement motivation can prime a person's perception of parenthood as a role that allows for an achievement orientation. As such, many men and women with high achievement motivation should be quite involved with the role.

However, childrearing may be severely limited in its potential for actually gratifying achievement motivation because the feedback that is needed to evaluate performance is often unclear. Feedback is thought to be an important characteristic of the conditions that allow for achievement satisfaction (McClelland, 1961). The individual presumably does not experience achievement satisfaction if he cannot determine how well he has performed a certain act. It is obvious that when the criteria for success as a parent are unclear, feedback about performance will be impaired. Because the standards for childrearing in our society have undergone several radical changes in the last few decades, there may be a particularly important limit upon the achievement gratifications in parenthood. In addition, even when the criteria for success are clear, feedback may be delayed. A parent may not know that he is actually performing appropriately until the child behaves in a way that gains approval in the parent's reference group. Since many goals of childrearing refer to long-range effects upon the child, it may not be until the child reaches adolescence or early adulthood, when certain performances and certain abilities become apparent, that the success or failure of a parent's efforts can be assessed. For the avant-garde group discussed above, the mother may not know whether she has elicited creativity in her child until some public recognition of the child's creativity occurs. Indeed, some of the childrearing activities that are thought to nurture creativity often also produce unsocial, unruly behavior in children (Baldwin, 1949), and a woman may feel her performance as a mother is questionable until she knows for sure whether she has helped establish a creative soul or a destructive misfit. Public recognition for achievement can occur early in a child's development, but it still is usually tempered by the kind of philosophy reflected in the saying, "the proof of the pudding is in the eating." Ultimately, most parents may not be able to be sure that they have done a good job until their job is finished. During the long period of early childhood, the person who is highly motivated for successful achievement as a parent may find his role very unsatisfying.

As the child becomes recognized as an accomplisher in the social world, the parent can experience a new kind of gratification—vicarious satisfaction with the child's accomplishment. This route to achievement gratification represents the third way that motivation can be related to role performance. A mother can identify with a child's success; a father can see a son's accomplishment as a means of fulfilling his own frustrated ambitions. Willie Loman's grand illusion that his son was very well-liked and would be among the great poignantly reflects his own sense of failure.

This kind of gratification also relies on public recognition. To the extent that it does, such gratification should occur most potently when the child reaches adolescence or young adulthood.

In summary, the relationship between achievement motivation and the gratification of being a parent seems clearest when the child is grown because of the greater clarity in evaluating the outcome of the parent's efforts by referring to the child's accomplishments and characteristics. We do not doubt that parental achievement motivation can be gratified while children are still young. For some mothers and fathers with strong achievement motivation, the criteria for being good parents may be clear even in the early stages of development. The ambiguity of the role permits idiosyncratic standards of excellence for parental performance to develop, and here the sensitization principle should be applicable. We are suggesting, however, that generally high parental achievement motivation is most congruent to the demands and gratifications available in the parental role when children are most ripe for evaluation from the outside world.

POWER MOTIVATION AND THE PARENTAL ROLE

In thinking about the behavioral correlates of power motivation, such as influencing others and being argumentative, we were naturally led to the hypothesis that the demands involved in the influence function of parenthood may have clear implications for power gratifications. The degree to which the parental role demand of influencing the child provides power gratification or frustration may be a function of how resistant the child is to socialization efforts by the parent. Therefore, the parental stage of the life cycle is an important conditioning variable to consider. During parental stages when the influence demand is strong and there is little resistance, persons with strong motivation to assert power should potentially be able to find power gratification. But at these same stages persons motivated to avoid evidence of power weakness might be particularly threatened, since their failure to influence their children at these stages would be difficult to rationalize. Early childhood and adolescence may be the times when resistance to parental authority is most dominant. The prominence of parent-child conflicts during these times in our society is documented by the superabundance of popular and scientific literature devoted to these stages of the life cycle of parenthood. The sheer quantity of printed material advising parents about how to toilet-train the young child and how to regulate the social contacts of the adolescent would attest to how critical are the power conflicts that occur at these periods. Persons with strong power motivation, with either power assertive or weakness-avoidant goals, should find the parental role threatening during these stages.

During middle childhood parental teaching primarily shifts to skill teaching and there should be less resistance than there was to moral teaching. Our general hypothesis would be that power motivation will have less relevance for role reactions during this period. When children are grown the parental rights to influence are in jeopardy, according to our view of the role obligations of parents of grown children. We would anticipate that parents with high power motivation would find it very difficult to relinquish their control when their children reach adulthood. The interruption of earlier power gratifications arising from the parental role might, in fact, produce intense frustration at this time for the highly power-motivated person and might exacerbate his feeling of growing impotence with encroaching old age.

These considerations point out the potential importance of the parental role for both power gratifications and frustrations. Because of this we were interested in whether or not the entrance into the parental status was related to power motivation. Using the sample examined in the last chapter, all married men and women who did and did not have children were compared on the three motive scores. Married men and women who did not have children had higher power motive scores than married men and women who did have children. This result was consistent for both older and younger spouses. No consistent relationships were found between parental status and the other two motives. One possible interpretation of these findings is that men and women who are concerned about their power might anticipate difficulties as socializing agents for children. Perhaps they do not like to be in positions where their influence is potentially called into question either by the child himself in resisting parental persuasions, or by society in evaluating their parental effectiveness. This interpretation would lead to the conclusion that the parental role is generally perceived as a troublesome one by men and women with high power motivation.

SUBJECTS

The men and women who are the subjects for this chapter comprise the entire subset of the national sample who were white, had a living child at the time of the interview, and who gave adequate responses to the motive measures. The maximum sample size was 433 fathers and 564 mothers.[1] We included parents without spouses, although we recognized that the parental roles of a married person and of someone who is not currently married are considerably different.

[1]The number of subjects available at each educational and parental stage is reported in Appendix B, Table 4.a, page 379. While each of these major subgroups is of substantial size, it should be noted that these are the maximum numbers of subjects. Missing data from some subjects on certain role reactions slightly reduces the sample size for any given motive-role reaction comparison. Subjects with missing data were eliminated from all subsequent tables, and any discrepancy in size of these subsamples from those reported in Table 4.a. are attributable to this omission, unless noted otherwise.

MEASURES OF PARENTAL REACTIONS

Seven indices were constructed from three series of the questions about parenthood that were asked in the interview. These questions directly followed those about marriage. As was the case with the marital role, the questions were designed to develop information about both the bases on which parents evaluate their role functioning and their overall evaluation of that functioning. (See Appendix A, Section III, questions 41 through 51.)

Again we will first present the questions on which each index was based and indicate how replies were coded to yield the seven indices. Then we will discuss each index in turn, indicating our conclusions about its interpretation.

The first question about parenthood was a general one; it did not specifically ask about one's own children:

Thinking about a man's (woman's) life, how is a man's (woman's) life changed by having children?

Two indices were constructed from the replies to this question. The index of *Parental Negative Orientation* to children was based on coders' ratings of the affective quality of replies.[2] Most respondents gave more than one answer to this question. Each response was coded to determine whether or not it indicated that the changes brought about by parenthood were satisfying (positive) or frustrating (negative). Examples of positive responses were: "Children bring you much happiness," "Children are a way to a woman's fulfillment," "You learn many new things." Negative responses included: "It's a lot of hard work," "You can't do the things you want to do," "There is new responsibility that takes your time," "It causes you to worry." Neutral responses included: "You have more responsibility," "You settle down." In addition, a further coding judgment was made of the affective tone of the entire reply; this was a six-point rating scale: very positive, positive, ambivalent, negative, very negative, and neutral. These two sets of ratings were then combined to yield the eight categories of the *Parental Negative Orientation* index, which accounted for both the frequency of occurrence of positive or negative responses and the overall affective tone of the reply. The index is reproduced below:

1. All positive responses and rated very positive
2. All positive responses and rated positive or neutral
3. Both positive and negative responses and rated very positive or positive

---

[2]To assess overall parental satisfaction, we used this general indirect question about parenthood rather than one specifically asking about one's own children, because pretests indicated that respondents uniformly said they were happy or satisfied with their parenthood when directly queried on this subject.

4. Both positive and negative responses and rated ambivalent
5. Both positive and negative responses and rated neutral
6. Both positive and negative responses and rated negative or very negative
7. All neutral responses and rated neutral
8. All negative responses and rated neutral, negative, or very negative

The index of *Parental Restrictiveness* was derived from replies to the same question used to code *Parental Negative Orientation*. Each reply to that question was also rated by a coder for whether or not the parent mentioned any restrictions or burdens accompanying being a parent. These ratings of each response were summarized in a three-point index: (1) no responses included anything about the restrictions of being a parent; (2) some responses concerned restrictions and others did not; (3) all responses implied that parenthood is restrictive to the person.

The next questions also did not specifically refer to the respondents' own children. We first asked about the joys of parenthood in an effort to dispel any defensiveness:

What would you say is the nicest thing about having children?
What other kinds of things do you think of?

The index of *Parental Distancing* was developed from replies to this question. Each reply was coded for whether the satisfaction described showed the parent as actively involved in the obligations of the parental role or distancing himself from the role. Whereas some parents responded to this question in terms of the things *they* did in relationship to their children, others answered in terms of the characteristics of their children that they thought of as gratifying. We viewed parents in the first category as being actively involved in their own role performance; we viewed parents in the second category as distancing themselves from the role. Examples of active involvement with role performance were: "playing with children," "teaching children about the world." Examples of distancing from the role would be "watching the children grow," "seeing them develop." The *Parental Distancing* index was a three-point scale based on the frequency of distancing versus actively involved replies: (1) none of the satisfactions were coded as indicating distancing from the parental role; (2) the satisfactions mentioned included both distancing and self-involved role behaviors; (3) all satisfactions were coded as indicating distancing from the parental role.

The subsequent questions concerned the respondent's own children. The question designed to assess the recognition of the difficulties in raising children was the basis for the *Parental Problems* index:

Most parents have had some problems in raising their children.
What are the main problems you've had in raising your children?

The replies to this question were simply coded into two categories: (1) no problems, and (2) some problem was acknowledged.[3]

The next series of questions were used to construct the other three indices of parental reactions used in this chapter.[4] These questions were:

Many men (women) feel they're not as good fathers (mothers) as they would like to be. Have you ever felt this way?
(IF YES) What kinds of things have made you feel this way? Have you felt this way a lot of times, or only once in a while?

The index of *Parental Inadequacy* indicated the frequency with which parents reported feeling inadequate, using five categories: (1) never; (2) once or twice; (3) once in a while; (4) often; (5) a lot of times. The second and fourth categories were added in coding to handle responses from parents who used alternatives other than the original three presented to them.

We also coded the kinds of things that made the subject feel inadequate in order to assess role demands that the respondents said they felt bad about not meeting. The first type of inadequacy mentioned was coded into one of three categories: (a) *tolerance*—feeling inadequate about control of one's temper, being impatient, unkind, or not being understanding of one's children; (b) *affiliation*—not spending as much time with one's children as one would like to; (c) all others. The two indices derived from this coding of the first kind of inadequacy mentioned were *Tolerance Inadequacy* and *Affiliative Inadequacy*. Each was a two-point index scored: (1) no mention, or (2) mention of that type of inadequacy. Both of these indices could be applied only when the respondent reported some feelings of inadequacy. Therefore, these variables were scored for only a subsample of the total sample of parents, those 52 percent of the parents who reported some feelings of inadequacy. Since only the first response was considered in order to avoid confounding the number and type of inadequacies, a respondent who was coded as high on *Tolerance Inadequacy* automatically was low on *Affiliative Inadequacy*, and vice versa. A subject could, however, be low on both indices if he mentioned another source of inadequacy. With this scoring, however, these two indices had a built-in very high negative relationship.

As in the marriage chapter, our interpretations of the measures of role reactions were based on three sources of information, beyond their

[3]Previous work (Gurin et al., 1960) had indicated that the specific problems listed by the respondents were not particularly diagnostic of different groups; therefore, we did not use a qualitative analysis of the parents' experience of problems in the present study.

[4]Unfortunately for our present purposes, this series was only asked on two of the three forms of the interview schedule, and only one of these forms also included the motive measures. Therefore, the number of subjects available for these three indices is reduced by approximately half.

face validity: (1) the previous factor analysis of dimensions of subjective adjustment (Veroff et al., 1962b); (2) the associations among these measures for the present samples;[5] and (3) the distribution of these indices among various social groups—among the same three educational levels assessed in the marriage chapter, and among mothers and fathers at four different points in the parental life cycle.[6] In the succeeding sections, we will discuss our interpretation of each of these indices.

PARENTAL NEGATIVE ORIENTATION

The index of *Parental Negative Orientation* had been included in the factor analysis study, but it was found to share little common variance with the other measures of subjective adjustment. Its correlations with both the *Unhappiness Factor* and the *Social Inadequacy Factor* were low for men and women. This would imply that it is not simply measuring either a person's passive experiential discomfort with what is happening to him, or his active concern about coping with the demands of life. The other information we had about this index was also equivocal, and a review of those data led us to the tentative conclusion that this measure reflects distinctly different reactions in men and women at the earlier stages of parenthood than in the later stages of parenthood.

We were especially influenced in this conclusion by the intercorrelations of this measure and the other measures of parental reactions for parents at different stages of the life cycle.[7] For mothers with young children *Parental Negative Orientation* tended to be positively related to *Parental Problems* and *Parental Inadequacy* while these relationships were negative for the mothers with older children (significantly negative in the case of mothers of adults). For fathers, the opposite pattern occurred. Among fathers with young children there were negative correlations describing

[5]The interrelationships among these seven measures of parental reactions are presented in Table 4.b. of Appendix B. Two sets of gamma coefficients are presented, one based on all mothers and the other on all fathers. The various indices also have been intercorrelated separately for mothers and fathers at different stages of the parental life cycle. In general, the relationships within the separate subgroups of mothers and fathers paralleled the results that were obtained for the total groups. In certain instances there were significant associations within one or two subgroups that were reversed from these associations in other groups or that were not in evidence for the total sample of mothers and fathers. We will indicate these distinctive patterns when they seem to be important.

[6]The relationship of each of the measures of parental reactions to educational and parental stage are presented in Appendix B, Table 4.c for mothers and Table 4.d for fathers. These tables show the percentage distributions on each variable, by subgroups, and thereby give the reader some perspective on the absolute levels of response to the questions about parenthood. They also present the gamma indices of association between each role reaction and each status characteristic.

[7]The relationships between *Parental Negative Orientation* and each of the other measures of parental reactions are presented in Appendix B, Table 4.e. The gamma coefficients are presented separately for mothers and fathers at each of the four parental stages.

the relationship of *Parental Negative Orientation* to both *Parental Problems* and *Parental Inadequacy*, the correlation to the latter being significantly negative for fathers of school-age children; these relationships were positive for fathers at later parental stages, the correlation to *Parental Problems* being significantly positive for fathers of adults. In addition, for fathers of school-age children, there was a significant negative association between *Parental Negative Orientation* and *Affiliative Inadequacy*, while that relationship was significantly positive for fathers of adults.

What does this pattern of correlations signify? We will be interpreting the *Parental Problems* and the *Parental Inadequacy* measures in the next section to mean different things for fathers and mothers. In particular we will conclude that these measures usually reflect passive reactions to parenthood in men, while they reflect active concerns about role-functioning in women. Such being the case, we would conclude from the foregoing pattern of results that *Parental Negative Orientation* in younger men and women measures an active engagement with the difficulties of parenthood, a symptom of attempts to cope with parenthood. On the other hand, *Parental Negative Orientation* in older men and women most likely reflects *passive* reactions to parental difficulties. It is as if people at the later stages of the parental life cycle who say negative things about parenthood are expressing their retrospective bitterness about being parents, about how much it *has* cost them in the way of unhappiness and distress. In contrast the younger parents who describe negative feelings about their children are ones who are actively attempting to manage their current role. This interpretation also could describe the way that the measure reverses its relationship to *Affiliative Inadequacy* in fathers. The younger group of fathers who felt negative about having children did not mention that they felt they spent too little time with their children. It is as if these fathers are actively engaged in raising their children, so that it does not occur to them to think of affiliative shortcomings in their own performance. In the older group of fathers, feeling negative about children is associated with feelings that they had not seen their children enough, as if feeling negative about children reflects an absence of a relationship rather than an actively engaging one.

Thus, *Parental Negative Orientation* is an index to which it is difficult to give an unequivocal interpretation. On the one hand, it seems to reflect active engagement with life for parents at early stages of the parental life cycle; on the other hand, it seems to reflect passive experiences of distress in response to life difficulties for persons at later parental stages.

How does this conclusion affect our interpretation of the patterns of relationships between *Parental Negative Orientation* and either parental stage or education? For fathers this index did not vary directly with increased age of children nor the fathers' educational level. (See Table 4.d in Appendix B.) But for mothers this index did vary according to the mothers' parental stage and their educational level. (See Appendix B, Table 4.c.) If we accept the validity of our interpretation of *Parental Negative Orientation*, how do we explain these differences for women?

We are led to say that there is more active distress in young mothers than passive distress in older mothers, since the level of *Parental Negative Orientation* varied significantly with parental life stage for mothers, with its being lowest in mothers whose children were adults. Women with older children may look back upon their motherhood with nostalgia and forget any earlier negative reactions to having children. They therefore appear to be the group of women most positive about parenthood. Women with younger children are most likely to be currently experiencing the crises and burdens of parenthood, and they therefore appear to have more negative attitudes toward parenthood.

Education of mothers was also significantly related to *Parental Negative Orientation*. The less-educated group of mothers, and especially those with only a grade-school education, were higher on the index of *Parental Negative Orientation*. The grade-school-educated woman less often plans her maternity—she is often by herself, without a husband, and often has more children than she can manage. This may explain why this group of mothers might be particularly negative towards motherhood, either in the active or passive sense of the early or late stages of the parental cycle.

PARENTAL RESTRICTIVENESS

Since both *Parental Restrictiveness* and *Parental Negative Orientation* were derived from replies to the same question, it was anticipated that these indices would be positively correlated, and this was true in all subgroups. Logically, however, there would not be a perfect overlap. First, some parents could mention a restrictive aspect of parenthood, while the majority of their responses concerned positive joys. Second, all responses stated in the imperative were coded as restrictive. In some cases this included positive responses—for example, "You have to set an example for good behavior" and "It makes you a better person because you must think of someone else"; some affectively neutral responses were also coded as restrictive—for example, "You have more responsibility." Finally, while most negative responses were coded as restrictive, this was not always true. In instances where only general affect was conveyed—for example, "It leads to unhappiness" and "You think it's wonderful and then they turn on you"— these responses were not coded as restrictive.

The index of *Parental Restrictiveness* was constructed to assess a *specific* negative orientation to parenthood—the extent to which a person perceived the life changes accompanying parenthood as requiring new restrictions on his life style or adding new burdens to his responsibilities.

Because it had not been included in the previous factor analysis, we must rely on its relationship with the other measures of parental reactions and its distribution among the educational groups and at different parental stages to determine its empirical interpretation. The only consistent relationship with the other parental reactions across sex was with *Parental Negative Orientation*. (See Table 4.b in Appendix B.) For the total group of mothers it was also significantly negatively associated with *Affiliative Inadequacy*, as was *Parental Negative Orientation*. There were no other significant associations with *Parental Restrictiveness* in the total groups of mothers or fathers. Its distinction from the *Parental Negative Orientation* is thus not clear. For both sexes it varied at different parental stages in the same way that *Parental Negative Orientation* did, and it was higher among grade-school-educated mothers than those with more education. (See Tables 4.c and 4.d in Appendix B.) Women tended to describe children in a more retrictive way than did men, just as they had been more generally negative about parenthood. Thus, other than their different face validities, which suggest that *Parental Negative Orientation* is a very general negative reaction while *Parental Restriction* is a more specific negative reaction describing felt restriction by parenthood, we would assume that our conclusions about *Parental Negative Orientation* are appropriate to *Parental Restrictiveness* as well—that it can reflect both active coping with parenthood and passive distress about the role.

PARENTAL PROBLEMS

For fathers the *Parental Problems* index had a high correlation with the *Unhappiness Factor* in the previous factor analysis. Following our previous line of reasoning about the *Unhappiness Factor*, we concluded that reporting problems in raising one's children is a passive reaction to the responsibilities of parenthood for a man. This index seems to be more ambiguous for a woman; it was not strongly associated with any one factor for women, although it did have a moderate correlation with the *Social Inadequacy Factor*. The *Parental Problems* index, thus, seems to reflect a somewhat more active concern for mothers than for fathers.

We get no further clues about the subtle meaning of the *Parental Problems* index from its distribution in various groups. The experience of *Parental Problems* did not differ by education of parent and was not simply related to parental stage. (See Tables 4.c and 4.d in Appendix B.) Parents seem least engaged with problems in raising their children during the beginning and especially the final stage of parenthood; mothers and fathers of preschoolers and adults were less likely to report having had problems in raising their children than were parents of school-age children or adolescents. Mothers were more likely to report *Parental Problems* than fathers. Perhaps this is related to the more active concern that is reflected

145

in the women's reports of problems in raising their children. We will comment further on the index after the discussion of *Parental Inadequacy*.

PARENTAL INADEQUACY

Admission of feelings of inadequacy as a parent seems to have very different psychological meaning for a mother or a father. When a man reports not having been as good a father as he would like to be, he is probably reacting either to his own deficiencies as a provider, or to his having too little contact with his child, perhaps because of his job pressures. These two types of responses account for 62 percent of all sources of men's feelings of inadequacies as fathers. Both providing too little money and having too little contact are sources of felt inadequacy that stem from circumstances external to the father's relationship with his children, and furthermore may be seen as things that happen to him rather than things he voluntarily initiates. These kinds of felt inadequacies in a man can thus be seen as more passive distress reactions imposed on him by the demands of his parental role than are the sources of a woman's distress about the adequacy of her role-functioning.

By contrast, a mother is likely to be more psychologically invested in her parental role than is a father. When she recognizes a deficiency in her role as a mother, it is likely she will consider it to be due to some failing in her relationship to her children and to be under her own control, rather than caused by external circumstances. Her reports of inadequacies, thus, are likely to reflect an active concern about her own personal interpretation of her role as a mother. Although both paternal and maternal feelings of inadequacies were equally correlated with the *Social Inadequacy Factor*, a man's feelings of adequacy are viewed as determined more by accomplishments external to fatherhood than those of a woman, who relies on social interaction with her children as a demonstration of her skill as a mother. Since women more frequently felt inadequate than did men, the above interpretation would also imply that women's active concerns about their role functioning are more prevalent than men's passive concerns.

For both fathers and mothers, however, the expression of self-doubt about role functioning does seem to reflect a personal commitment to the role, perhaps more so than merely admitting to having had a problem in raising children. The evidence for this interpretation is seen in both the relationship of this index to the educational level of the parent and to the parental stage.

Parental Inadequacy had a significant positive relationship to education for both sexes. Grade-school-educated men and women were least likely to feel *Parental Inadequacy*; they were the most likely to reply "No" to the question of whether they have ever felt they were not as good parents as they would like to be. (See Tables 4.c and 4.d in Appendix B.) In contrast to the more-educated groups, their perception of role demands may be so limited that it is easy for them to fulfill those demands that make them feel competent. Or, their orientation to life in general may not require as much self-responsibility for the outcome of their role performances, as that of more-educated parents.

Parental Inadequacy was also related to parental stage for fathers. Fathers of preschoolers had felt inadequate least often and fathers at later parental stages did not differ much from one another. This may simply stem from the fact that men at the earliest stage of the parental life cycle have not had much exposure to role demands, or it may mean that the role demands at later parental stages, being of a different order, are more likely to elicit feelings of inadequacy. There was a similar, slight trend for mothers.

We have already suggested that *Parental Inadequacy* may reflect a deeper personal commitment to the causes of admitted distress than does *Parental Problems*. But there seems to be a further difference between these measures. This we discover in the different degree of positive correlation between the two for men and women. (See Table 4.b in Appendix B.) They are more highly related among men than women. Thus, we interpret both the index of *Parental Problems* and the index of *Parental Inadequacy* as indicating a passive involvement with parenthood for a father. The man who admits that he has had problems in raising his children and who also feels inadequate in his role as a father is likely to be reacting passively to the responsibilities of parenthood. For a mother, on the other hand, admitting having problems with her children can reflect either active or passive concerns, while feelings of inadequacy represent an active, self-involved distress in not meeting role obligations.

TOLERANCE INADEQUACY AND AFFILIATIVE INADEQUACY

Mentioning either tolerance or affiliative inadequacies suggests that the person is involved in the psychological impact he has on his children. As was noted in previous work with the total national sample (Gurin et al., 1960), these types of admissions of inadequacy were more frequent among parents with higher educational backgrounds. In the present subsamples, more-educated men reported affiliative inadequacies significantly more often than less-educated men and more-educated women reported tolerance inadequacies significantly more often than less-educated women. (See Tables 4.c and 4.d in Appendix B.) With more education a parent becomes more psychologically oriented towards his role and more frequently mentions interpersonal inadequacies. This seems to reflect the

147

twentieth-century psychological revolution in theories about parents and children, most notably evident in child development literature, mental-hygiene clinics, and advanced educational institutions.

Therefore, if a parent reported either affiliative or tolerance inadequacies, we assumed that the interpersonal aspects of parenthood were important to him. However, the implications of these two types of inadequacies seem to be different. Mothers were generally more concerned than fathers about their intolerance for their children, while fathers were more concerned than mothers about not spending enough time with their children. *Affiliative Inadequacy* probably signifies less self-responsibility and involvement than *Tolerance Inadequacy*. Not spending enough time with children can often be attributed to some other kind of role requirement. Being impatient with a child, however, suggests that the person is more directly at fault with what is happening. *Affiliative Inadequacy* may then reflect a less active involvement with the parental role than reporting *Tolerance Inadequacy*, although both of these admissions are likely to emanate from a highly involved parent.

We get further confirmation for these ideas about *Tolerance Inadequacy* and *Affiliative Inadequacy* by examining how these measures vary at different times in the parental cycle. Mothers' concern about *Affiliative Inadequacy* seems to increase as their children get older, when they are required to spend less time with them. This concern is especially strong for both mothers and fathers when their children are adolescents. In contrast, *Tolerance Inadequacy* decreases for mothers as their children mature. Thus, there seems to be a shift in the bases for maternal concern about the parent-child relationship. The focus is on concern about maternal impatience and anger when mothers are forced to spend a great deal of time with their children and it shifts to concern over not spending enough time with the children at a period when the compulsory time demands of the mother-child relationship are lessened. The parental stage seems less relevant to the father's concerns. Only at adolescence does there seem to be a major shift, away from concern about tolerance in interpersonal relations and toward concern about the amount of time spent with one's children.

The patterns of interrelationships with these indices were complex. *Tolerance Inadequacy* among fathers was significantly related to the *absence* of *Parental Problems* in raising children and the *absence* of *Parental Distancing* from the role. Thus, a father who is concerned about losing his temper with his child tends to have personal (not distant) involvement in the joys of parenthood, but also tends to deny having had any problems in raising his child. For women, *Affiliative Inadequacy* was significantly negatively related to the two parallel indices—*Parental Negative Orientation* and *Parental Restrictiveness*. These relationships were mostly due to the older women—mothers of adolescents and adults. Thus, a mother of older children who is concerned about not having spent enough time with her children is likely to feel positive about having children and unrestricted by parenthood. Again we have an instance of mentioning certain inadequacies being associated with an *absence* of distress.

How would we interpret this whole pattern of findings about women's admission to affiliative inadequacies and men's admission to tolerance inadequacies? They seem to be not only reflections of a salient involvement in parenthood, but also reflections of an overly sensitive, somewhat defensive stance to the role. They are associated with denial of certain distress. Let us try to outline a basis for such a defensive involvement.

A woman who has a less active involvement with her role of mother (revealed in *Affiliative Inadequacy*), and a man who has a very active involvement with the role of father (revealed in *Tolerance Inadequacy*), are each in some way deviating from normative expectations about what mothers and fathers do. On this basis we suspect that these parents might be very sensitive about their roles as parents and be quick to overlook difficulties their children might be having. These are parents who are involved in parenthood, but who have taken a stance toward parenthood which is perhaps different from what they think they should be doing as mothers and fathers. Any defensiveness resulting from their deviant stance is probably not great enough to allow them to say that everything about being a parent is fine, but they may exaggerate or distort their parental situation in some way. We will be alert to highly sensitive reactions from mothers who admit to affiliative inadequacies as a parent and from fathers who admit to tolerance inadequacies as a parent even though generally we will interpret these measures at face value for both sexes.

PARENTAL DISTANCING

We assumed that *Parental Distancing* was an important qualitative aspect of parental reactions, that this measure would reflect whether a parent's own active involvement is important for obtaining the gratifications of parenthood. Those parents who are able to distance themselves from children are perhaps not very involved with their own roles as parents, even though they may be quite involved with their children. This variable did not appear in the factor analysis. We suspect that it is similar to those measures that loaded on the *Unhappiness Factor*, except that it concerns satisfaction rather than distress. Although it did not relate significantly to any other index of distress, as we noted, fathers high on *Parental Distancing* did not mention *Tolerance Inadequacy* as often as fathers low on *Parental Distancing*. (See Table 4.b in Appendix B.) This is consistent with interpreting *Parental Distancing* as evidence of lack of active involvement and *Tolerance Inadequacy* as evidence of very active involvement for fathers. We would use this relationship as evidence that fathers who do not distance themselves from parenthood are involved with the same interpersonal difficulties in parenthood that women find. Fathers who do not maintain their distance, who become personally invested in the role soon find difficulty in controlling their anger—and begin to feel that they should be more tolerant.

Parental Distancing varied only slightly with sex, education, or parental stage, although it was somewhat more likely to occur at adolescence. (See Tables 4.c and 4.d in Appendix B.) This is a time when the child is attempting to set up a new identity. It is indeed curious that a parent's reaction to his role should parallel so well the child's need at that time.

ROLE REACTIONS IN RELATION TO PARENTAL STAGE AND EDUCATIONAL LEVEL

In the previous discussion of the interpretation of the measures of parental reactions, we described the differential distribution of these measures among the various subgroups that were used to infer role characteristics. If we now focus on these differences, they may help us to understand further the significance of parenthood for persons at different stages of the parental life cycle and at different educational levels.

As children get older, the reactions of mothers shift from negative to positive. *Parental Negative Orientation* and *Parental Restrictiveness* varied significantly with parental life stage for mothers; these reactions were lowest when their children were adults. Women with older children may look back upon their motherhood with nostalgia and forget any earlier negative reactions to raising children. They therefore appear to be the group of women most positive about parenthood.

By contrast, women with younger children are more likely to be currently experiencing restrictions upon their lives, and they therefore appear to have more negative attitudes about parenthood. Younger mothers tend to report more tolerance inadequacies. Thus it seems that the role demands at this stage force mothers to spend a great deal of time with their children, and a focus of concern might center on parental impatience and rage. During adolescence there is an increased distancing from active involvement in the maternal role, and complaints about affiliative inadequacies reach their maximum when children are adults and living away from the parental home. At these parental stages the role no longer requires that the mother spend a lot of time with her children.

For fathers, the indices do not vary directly with the increasing age of their children. Instead, the earlier and the later stages seem less problematic to them than do the two middle periods, when they have school-age and adolescent children. These two latter periods may be times when the demands of being a good provider are most difficult to meet; it is during these stages that fathers are most prone to see children as restrictive and to mention problems in raising their children. During their children's adolescence fathers also tend to take a more distant attitude towards their children at the same time that they feel that they do not spend as much time with their children as they should. This pattern suggests that the demands of fatherhood are most difficult to meet in a gratifying way when children are adolescents.

Educational differences in parents seem mostly to be reflected in different perceptions of parental inadequacies. Grade-school-educated fathers and mothers are more likely to deny feelings of inadequacy as parents. A man or woman without the orientation of a higher education may have such limited perceptions of his role demands that he feels competent more easily than parents with more education. Their lower educational status may also orient them to denial of any self-responsibility for the outcome of their lives. Hence, any difficulties they perceive in raising their children can be easily attributed to things outside them- selves—housing difficulties, in-law problems, poor schools, or just bad luck in not having financial security. By contrast, college-educated fathers tend to exaggerate their affiliative inadequacies and college-educated mothers tend to exaggerate their tolerance inadequacy. As previously, we interpreted these results to signify that higher social status groups were more likely to define satisfactory interpersonal relationship with their children as one of the demands of the role of parenthood (see Gurin et al., 1960, p. 120 ff.).

RESULTS: MOTIVE-ROLE INTERACTION FOR MOTHERS

Because the parental role differentiations for mothers and fathers are so major, we will present the results of our analyses of motive-role inter- actions separately for mothers and fathers. In this section we will present the results for mothers concerning the relationships between each of the motives of affiliation, achievement, and power, and the seven indices of parental reactions. Since the parental stage of the life cycle was the major basis we used to infer distinctions in role characteristics among parents, we will present the results for mothers (or fathers) at one stage of the parental life cycle at a time. The data in this section were thus considered in four major units: mothers of preschool-age children, mothers of school- age children, mothers of adolescents, mothers of adults. Four parallel units will be used in presenting the results for fathers. Further distinction into the three educational levels was made within each parental stage. As in the previous chapter, in this chapter we will present capsule summaries of each major analysis section. In this case, the summaries will concern each parental stage. Detailed discussions of the results then follow these summaries for those readers who are interested.

The data for each stage are presented in a separate table (Tables 4.1–4.4 for mothers and 4.6–4.9 for fathers). Each table includes three subtables, showing the relationship of each of the seven indices of parental role reactions to: (1) the affiliation motive, (2) the achievement motive, and (3) the power motive. This presentation parallels the general plan adopted in Chapter 3. Within each subtable, the relationships are presented separately for subjects at each of the three educational levels and for all subjects at this parental stage, disregarding educational level. The table entries are the gamma coefficient between a given motive and role reaction. The probability levels reported are for the significance of the tau beta rank order correlations computed for the same data; all probability values are for two-tailed tests.

After we examine the results for mothers within each stage, we will then present a reanalysis of the data in which the patterns of motive-role interactions for mothers who hold full-time jobs are compared to those for mothers who are full-time housewives. In that section we will be interested in seeing whether women who must meet the obligations of the job role as well as the maternal role exhibit different relationships between motives and maternal role reactions than women who fully occupy themselves with the maternal role.

MOTHERS OF PRESCHOOL-AGE CHILDREN

The earliest phase of the maternal life cycle—taking care of infants and toddlers—sets off positive challenges to the ongoing lives of some mothers but seems to induce interfering blocks to the ongoing lives of other mothers. Which of these patterns gets engaged seems to depend on a woman's motives, but is further conditioned by her social status.

Women with high affiliation motivation generally react to this first stage of motherhood in a defensive way: they significantly more often denied any problems in raising their children but they also tended to see motherhood negatively and the role as restrictive. College-educated mothers with high affiliation motivation tended to distance themselves from their preschool-age children, which we interpret to mean that affiliation satisfactions are not easily forthcoming, perhaps because the requirement to nurture one's child interferes with other social relationships.

Women with high achievement motivation tend to react to the initial stage of motherhood in a way that sensitizes them to possible achievement goals within motherhood, but these goals seem to differ for mothers at different educational levels. Raising children seems to be an achievement goal for a college-educated woman with high achievement motivation. Hence at this stage of maternity, where the initial parental influences on the child occur, her parental satisfactions were significantly more often focused on her own active involvement with her children rather than on impersonal sources of joy. Having children seems to be an achievement goal for a woman with a high-school education. In contrast to the college-educated women, the high-school educated women with high achievement motivation felt especially uninvolved or distant from this stage of maternity; her parental satisfactions arise from the existence of her children and from passively watching them grow and develop.

This difference in basic goals for high-school and college-educated mothers also seems to underlie the differential reaction to early motherhood for those women with high power motivation. The role seems congruent for the college-educated women with high power motivation and incongruent for power-oriented women with a high-school education; college-educated women were significantly less likely to have felt inadequate as mothers if they have high rather than low power motivation, while the opposite was true for mothers with a high-school education.

The maternal role reactions of women whose oldest children were of preschool age (4 years or younger) are presented in Table 4.1. There were an insufficient number of mothers with preschool-age children who had only a grade-school education, to present data for them. Mothers at this educational level were therefore eliminated from our discussion of this stage of the parental life cycle. It should be noted, however, that these subjects were included in the relationships reported in Table 4.1 based on the total group of mothers at this parental stage. The number of mothers of preschoolers who reported any type of inadequacy was too low to permit any gamma coefficients to be reported for either the *Tolerance Inadequacy* or *Affiliative Inadequacy* index. Therefore, our discussion of the qualitative aspects of the parental role reactions at this stage is limited to the index of *Parental Distancing*.

Affiliation Common to both high-school and college-educated mothers was a negative relationship between the affiliation motive and *Parental Problems*. This relationship was significant for the college-educated mothers and total group of mothers; women with strong affiliation motivation were significantly less likely to see any problems in raising children than mothers with weak affiliation motivation. By itself, this suggested that mothers with a high affiliation motive might be finding gratification in the nurturing demands during this early preschool time and, hence, that they were finding the maternal role unproblematic.

The total pattern of results suggested something different. On the one hand, a mother may feel that affiliative contacts are restricted by the new arrival; on the other hand, her new status as mother makes her a more valid social being in many types of social relationships. From previous analyses we knew that feeling restricted and negative was characteristic of mothers at this stage in their maternal cycle. (See Table 4.5, Appendix B.) These consequences seem especially true for those women with a high affiliation motive. There were consistent, although not statistically significant, trends for mothers with a high affiliation motive at this parental stage to view having children negatively or to feel restricted by having children. These trends may reflect concern about interference with

TABLE 4-1 THE RELATIONSHIP (γ) OF MOTIVES TO PARENTAL REACTIONS FOR MOTHERS WHOSE CHILDREN WERE PRESCHOOL AGE (WITHIN AND ACROSS EDUCATIONAL LEVEL)

Parental Reaction	Affiliation Motive				Achievement Motive				Power Motive				Number of Subjects at Each Educational Level			
	Grade school	High school	College	All	Grade school	High school	College	All	Grade school	High school	College	All	Grade school	High school	College	All
Negative orientation	—[a]	.15	.11	.10	—[a]	−.23	−.07	−.16	—[a]	−.02	−.27	−.09	(11)	(41)	(14)	(57)
Restrictiveness	—[a]	.19	.24	.18	—[a]	−.28	−.10	−.25	—[a]	−.07	−.06	−.07	(2)	(41)	(14)	(57)
Inadequacy	—[a]	−.06	—[a]	−.14	—[a]	−.26	—[a]	.17	—[a]	.84†	—[a]	.30	(2)	(12)	(8)	(22)
Problems	—[a]	−.27	−1.00‡	−.52†	—[a]	.08	.16	.13	—[a]	.18	−.53	−.06	(2)	(40)	(14)	(56)
Tolerance inadequacy	—[a]	—[a]	—[a]	—[a]	—[a]	—[a]	—[a]	—[a]	—[a]	—[a]	—[a]	—[a]	(0)	(6)	(2)	(8)
Affiliative inadequacy	—[a]	—[a]	—[a]	—[a]	—[a]	—[a]	—[a]	—[a]	—[a]	—[a]	—[a]	—[a]	(0)	(6)	(2)	(8)
Distancing	—[a]	−.16	.73	.02	—[a]	.43*	−.71*	.10	—[a]	.20	.03	.16	(1)	(38)	(12)	(51)

Note: In this and subsequent tables in this chapter, entries are gamma indices of association between a given motive and parental reaction for the specified subgroup. Probability levels are reported for tau beta rank-order correlation coefficients computed for the same relationship. For example, in this table the gamma for the relationship between the affiliation motive and Negative Orientation is .15 for the high-school educated mothers of preschoolers and .10 for all mothers of preschoolers, disregarding educational level.

[a]Not reported because of inadequate distribution.
*p $<$ .10.
†p $<$ .05.
‡p $<$ .01.

154

affiliative contacts caused by a young child. But, on the other hand, a mother has a new status that makes her a more valid social being in many types of social relationships. This new validity and acceptance by others might also especially affect a woman with a high affiliation motive. This new status might be threatened by an admission of having already had problems with raising one's children. Thus we have a picture of a woman at this parental stage so upset by parental problems if they interfere with her perception of herself as an acceptable human being that she denies having them. Therefore, we view the association between affiliation motivation and the absence of *Parental Problems* as a defensive response by women at this earliest stage of the parental life cycle.

Achievement There was an interesting differentiation in the relationship of the achievement motive to role reactions for women with high-school and college backgrounds. The relationship between the achievement motive and *Parental Inadequacy* was significantly positive for college-educated women, although based on a small number of subjects,[8] and negative, although insignificant, for high-school-educated mothers. The relationship between the achievement motive and *Parental Distancing* was significantly negative for college-educated mothers, and was significantly positive for high-school-educated mothers. These correlations suggest that the meaning of raising young children is perhaps different at the two educational levels.

The college-educated woman with a high achievement motive is actively engaged in raising her children. She sees the process of child-rearing at this early age as a possible achievement goal. In her college classrooms she has learned that the preschool era is a time when she can play a strong role in shaping her child's personality, and a high achievement motive sensitizes her to those aspects of childrearing that can be evaluated for accomplishment. This helps explain why college-educated women with a high achievement motive distance themselves less from the childrearing process. They throw themselves into the role, so to speak, because they are sensitive to the possible achievements in mothering—especially during the early years of children's lives. These mothers could become as much involved with their own performance as a mother as in their child's performance. This sort of active involvement is epitomized by the low end in the measure of distancing. This also helps explain why college-educated mothers with high achievement motivation should be quick to report inadequacies. At this parental stage, there is minimal feedback on evaluations of childrearing success. These women should therefore wonder what they are doing, whether it is appropriate, whether

[8]Although the number of subjects ($N = 8$) did not meet the criteria for tabulation, the gamma coefficient for the relationship between achievement motive and *Parental Inadequacy* was 1.00, and $p < .10$, for the tau beta correlation.

it is the best method of raising children, and whether they are as good mothers as they would like to be. There is a lack of congruence between their motives and the role possibilities, and they are actively distressed.

An opposite pattern of results existed between the achievement motive and both the *Parental Distancing* and *Parental Inadequacy* indices for the mothers with high-school education. These women seem clearly to have a different motivational investment in early childrearing than do the college-educated women. There seems to be a disengagement from parenthood for women with strong achievement motive and a high-school education. For these women, the process of successfully socializing a young child may be irrelevant to gaining achievement satisfaction. Instead, having children may be a sufficient condition for achievement gratification and, hence, for being an adequate mother. One could further speculate that, if having children itself satisfies strong achievement needs for high-school-educated women, they may then be willing to sit back and enjoy the fruits of their labors. The sensitization principle may be operating for these women. Their achievement motivation sensitizes them to enjoying children as objects that give them status. It is this attitude that is revealed in a distancing orientation toward their children.

The distinction between having children and raising children as types of accomplishment is an important one to keep in mind in discussing the obligations and potentials that exist in the parental role for women in our culture in general. As the whole culture moves toward assuming the psychological framework of the college classroom and superimposes this framework on the maternal role, then the process of raising children should become an important accomplishment rather than a perfunctory consequence of the once important act of having children. We should find then that women with high achievement motivation would be more actually invested in childbearing and childrearing and would question their role performance. Such results should become more commonplace twenty-five years hence.

Power A similar interpretation of the differential meaning of the parental role for mothers with high-school and college backgrounds was also applied to the differences found in the relationship of parental reactions with the power motive. For high-school-educated women, the power motive was significantly positively related to *Parental Inadequacy*, whereas for women with college backgrounds, the power motive was significantly negatively related to *Parental Inadequacy*.[9] These results again may be explained in terms of the active involvement in childrearing that may exist for a college graduate but not for the high-school graduate.

[9]Again the number of subjects was too small for presentation of the gamma in the table, but the gamma for these 8 women was -1.00 and $p < .05$ for the tau beta correlation.

The college-educated mother may be eager to take on the central influencing demand of the early parental stage because she sees that the main function of her role is socialization. For women with strong power motivation this challenge should be central to power gratification. We have interpreted the power motive as signifying the interest in avoiding weakness or being influenced. It is the very young child who most primitively resists the impact of the mother and who struggles valiantly to establish his own sphere of control. But the mandate to the parents to exercise their influence is clear. And they, being psychologically and physically more powerful than children at this early age, can and do overcome the primitive resistance to being influenced typical of very young children. Thus, influencing a preschooler could be very gratifying to the power needs of a woman. We suggest that this is the case for a college-educated woman. Being able to see herself as effective, she may be less disconcerted by the problems of her role-functioning, and may be less likely to feel inadequate. Thus, at this parental stage the congruence between the power motive and the demands of parenthood may account for the finding that college-educated women with high power motive less frequently reported feelings of inadequacy. They are not actively distressed because they are effectively finding the role gratifying.

If we assume that in general the high-school-educated woman does not see her own role as socializer of preschool children as an important and meaningful part of parenthood, she may be less interested in the day-to-day influence she has on her children. But if she is also high in the power motive she is sensitized to the fact that having children requires influence behaviors from her. We suggest that among high-school-educated women with preschool children, those with high power motivation are propelled into relatively greater involvement with the enactment of the parental role. Being generally not as attuned to, or prepared for, the socializing functions of the maternal role as are the college-educated mothers, high-school-educated women with high power motivation may find the initial stages of motherhood frustrating to their general orientation to motherhood. There is a lack of congruence between motherhood and power motivation for these women, and this is reflected in their own doubts about how they are enacting the maternal role. They are actively distressed by the incongruence between their power motive and the potential for its gratification in role enactment.

MOTHERS OF SCHOOL-AGE CHILDREN

Although the affiliation motive was not significantly related to any of the measures of parental role reactions, the trend found at the initial parental stage for women with high affiliation motivation to feel negative about restrictions brought on by motherhood continued for mothers whose older children were of school age.

The implication emerges that when children are young they are disappointing affiliative objects, who either interfere with gratifying affiliative relationships or are irrelevant to obtaining such gratifications.

For college-educated women, a high achievement motive was significantly associated with feelings of adequacy in the parental role when the oldest child was of school age. This is an especially important result since it was opposite to one found for college-educated women whose children were preschoolers. The doubts that the college-educated mother felt when her children were very young, in the absence of any external confirmation of her success as a parent, can shift to a sense of competence and gratification as the children mature and as the mother can see the outcome of her efforts. This shift should be especially striking for college-educated mothers with a high achievement motive.

The power motivation of women with school-aged children was not significantly related to any of the measures of parental role reactions. This suggests that when children leave the home and turn to teachers and peers for guidance, they are no longer relevant objects of gratification or frustration of maternal power motivation. There were trends to suggest that such relinquishment of power elicits defensive reactions in mothers with high power motivation; they tended to deny having problems with their children or feeling inadequate in their own role functioning, and to derive satisfaction in motherhood mainly from distancing themselves from their children.

One further observation is warranted at this point—about grade-school-educated mothers. Neither at this nor at subsequent stages was there any statistically significant relationship between the maternal reactions of grade-school-educated mothers and their motives. Furthermore, at this parental stage, we noted that in most cases the direction of the relationships between motives and parental reactions for grade-school-educated mothers was opposite to that for the other two educational groups. These results suggest that the parental role does not interact with personality characteristics for women from this social status in the same way it does for other social status groups. We will discuss this further in our reassessment of the parental role.

Table 4.2 presents the relationships between each of the motives and the role reactions of mothers whose oldest children were of school age (5–12 years old). Although the distribution of scores on the index of *Affiliative Inadequacy* did not permit reporting the gammas for any single education level, relationships with this index are reported for the total group of mothers of school-age children.

Affiliation There were no statistically significant relationships between the affiliation motive and parental role reactions for mothers with school-age children. This apparent lack of relevance of affiliation motivation to parental reactions may reflect the fact that children are turning to their peers for their own affiliative gratifications. It may also mean that school-age children are not as convenient a means for mothers to establish social contacts with other adults as were younger children. One trend seemed noteworthy in these data: there was a positive relationship between affiliation motive and feelings of *Tolerance Inadequacy* for college-educated mothers. Having already argued that this reaction on the part of a mother reflects not only involvement but also a highly psychological orientation

TABLE 4-2 THE RELATIONSHIP (γ) OF MOTIVES TO PARENTAL REACTIONS FOR MOTHERS WHOSE OLDEST CHILDREN WERE SCHOOL AGE (WITHIN AND ACROSS EDUCATIONAL LEVEL)

Parental Reaction	Affiliation Motive				Achievement Motive				Power Motive				Number of Subjects at Each Educational Level			
	Grade school	High school	College	All	Grade school	High school	College	All	Grade school	High school	College	All	Grade school	High school	College	All
Negative orientation	.14	.08	.11	.09	.29	−.22	−.08	−.14	−.20	−.04	−.01	−.05	(19)	(102)	(33)	(154)
Restrictiveness	−.39	.18	.08	.09	.39	−.12	−.22	−.08	.15	−.09	−.24	−.09	(18)	(101)	(32)	(151)
Inadequacy	.16	.07	−.16	.05	.14	−.16	−.62*	−.15	.09	−.15	−.41	−.14	(13)	(49)	(13)	(75)
Problems	—ᵃ	−.16	—ᵃ	.01	—ᵃ	.05	—ᵃ	.04	—ᵃ	−.25	—ᵃ	−.26	(19)	(102)	(32)	(153)
Tolerance inadequacy	—ᵃ	.15	.67	.09	—ᵃ	.30	.48	.26	—ᵃ	−.25	.20	−.08	(7)	(40)	(11)	(58)
Affiliative inadequacy	—ᵃ	—ᵃ	—ᵃ	−.22	—ᵃ	—ᵃ	—ᵃ	−.39	—ᵃ	—ᵃ	—ᵃ	.36	(7)	(40)	(11)	(58)
Distancing	.22	−.02	−.01	.02	−.01	.07	.29	.10	−.01	.18	.17	.16	(18)	(90)	(30)	(138)

ᵃNot reported because of inadequate distribution.
*p < .10.

159

to parenthood, we can suggest that college-educated mothers with high affiliation motive were especially psychologically involved in motherhood at this stage of their life cycle. Perhaps this is another instance where the sensitization principle is useful. As children grow older there is more possibility for a parent to have affiliative relationships with a child. But this stage may be a particularly ambiguous time for mothers since it is not clear whether school-age children, with their burgeoning independence and movement into peer-oriented relationships, are suitable targets for an affiliative relationship. Highly affiliative mothers who are involved with parenthood might be most likely to desire and seek out affiliative relationships with their children and might consequently be most prone to feel upset about any disruption in the relationship apparently produced by their own lack of tolerance.

Achievement In comparison to college-educated mothers with preschool children, college-educated mothers with school-age children showed an interesting reversal in the direction of the relationship between achievement motivation and *Parental Inadequacy*: among mothers with preschool-age children, achievement motivation was associated with feelings of inadequacy, but among those with school-age children, achievement motivation was significantly associated with feelings of adequacy. Why should this reversal occur? Two shifts in the parental role seem relevant. Some of the obligations attendant to raising children are removed for college-educated women as children move from the confines of the home to the school. Responsibility for skill training is shifted to the school. Thus some of the burden is removed from women who feel that skill training is important, and it seems clear that college-educated women *do* feel that such training is important. But even more important for a mother's own achievement motivation is the fact that in school the child's accomplishments are evaluated and the mother gets feedback about this performance from the school and from the child's peer group. As college-educated mothers find that their children are performing well in school and are adequately coping with the world around them, their own maternal performance in rearing the children during preschool days is justified. At this parental stage, then, it seems that the achievement motive is congruent with both the role demands and the role gratifications of parenthood for the college-educated woman intent on making the rearing of children an achievement goal.

There was also a trend for high-school and college women at this parental stage to show a negative association between achievement motive and *Parental Negative Orientation;* that is, the stronger the motive, the more positive the attitude towards parenthood. This trend was most marked for those with a high-school background. We point this out because a parallel trend emerged for high-school-educated mothers of preschool children as well. This relationship was consistent, though insignificant at other stages of parenthood for this group. This pattern of results may reflect the fact that a mother who gets achievement gratification out of merely being a parent (high-school group) can have the least frustration to this gratification when the children are younger, when she can look at her emotional entanglement with her children more matter-of-factly and can more easily resist personalizing conflicts than is possible in later stages of parenthood. The joys of having children can slowly be replaced by the distress that a mother feels in conflicts with them, especially when they are old enough to separate themselves from parents both physically and psychologically.

Power Just a few trends emerged in relating power motivation to maternal reactions at this second stage of the parental cycle. By and large, we can suggest that the influencing function for mothers slackens in the early school years and is taken up by school teachers and peers. Thus, threats to apparent weakness are minimal. Some mothers with high power motivation, however, could easily be threatened by the encroachment of society on their domain. The relationships of power motivation to role reactions that did emerge seem to reflect a defensive posture for those women high in power motivation. High-school- and college-educated women with high power motivation tended to take a distant position toward the satisfactions stemming from their children, to deny having problems in raising them, and to deny having self-doubts about how good a mother they were.

We would expect this defensiveness to be characteristic of mothers of adolescents, but its possible emergence at this earlier point may reflect the fact that women with high power motivation are more alerted to possible threats to their relationship to their children as children grow up, than are women with low power motivation. For those who are sensitive to power relationships, even the limited autonomy accorded to school-age children would become important.

This is a period when children are supposed to be encouraged to grow up, to become more independent, and to learn many new skills from nonfamilial sources. The movement toward independence at school age is ostensibly desirable, especially for the more-educated groups. But if we interpret the strength of power motivation to represent the degree to which the parent is involved in overcoming any feelings of weakness in relationship to people, then children's contact with the outside world can, in fact, offer serious threats to parents with high need for power. This may account for the trends for mothers with high power motivation to be defensive about their role at this point in their children's development.

MOTHERS OF ADOLESCENT CHILDREN

Although there were no significant relationships between affiliation motivation and parental reactions at this stage, there were a number of noteworthy trends that were also present at previous periods in the life cycle.

The sensitization principle seems useful in understanding the continued trends for affiliation motivation to be positively correlated with a mother's feeling of tolerance inadequacy. As a child reaches more mature status and therefore becomes a clearer affiliative object, the parent with strong affiliation motivation appears to maintain her concern about any disruptions in the relationship, particularly disruptions resulting from the parent's lack of tolerance for the child.

Despite the increasing interest in adolescent children as objects of affiliation goals, children do not gratify affiliative strivings for women. If anything, adolescent children are still likely to interfere with other affiliative strivings of the mother. This conclusion is suggested by the continued trends for a positive relationship between the affiliation motive and a negative orientation to children. Only for the final group to be considered, the mothers of adults, was this result not obtained.

We see this set of findings as a possible instance of a lack of congruence between motive and role demands that produces distress feelings. While there appear to be possibilities for affiliation gratification in the maternal role, they are not realized when a child becomes adolescent, perhaps because of an earlier history of not finding a child appropriate for fulfilling affiliative needs, perhaps because of the inequality in power between the mother and child, perhaps because of the continued obligatory role demand for the mother to nurture the child and for the child to return love.

There were no significant associations between the achievement motive and maternal reactions for mothers of adolescents. In the earlier stages we did find some significant correlations. Perhaps this difference stems from changes in standards of good maternal performance. Mothers who invest maternity with achievement standards have vague standards for preschoolers, clear ones for school-age children, but both vague ones and clear ones when children are adolescent. On the one hand, mothers may be getting good feedback about their adolescent children and their competences, but, on the other hand, they are confronted with new ambiguities about what they should be doing as mothers of adolescents. Thus some mothers' achievement strivings may be particularly gratified at this time, while others may be newly frustrated. This may account for the minimal relationship between achievement motivation and parental reactions for mothers of adolescents.

While power issues remained dormant for mothers of school-age children, they evidently are salient for mothers of adolescents. For all three educational groups, women with high power motive were more likely to feel adequate as parents than women with low power motive. One could argue that adolescence is a time so rampant with unsuccessful influence attempts on the part of parents, that parents with high power motivation who report feeling adequate during this time are reacting defensively. And we would suggest that this reaction is prevalent for this group of mothers.

Table 4.3 presents the relationships between each of the motives and the role reactions of mothers whose oldest children were adolescents (age 13–20).

Affiliation In the last section we discussed the possibility that

TABLE 4-3 THE RELATIONSHIP (γ) OF MOTIVES TO PARENTAL REACTIONS FOR MOTHERS WHOSE OLDEST CHILDREN WERE ADOLESCENTS (WITHIN AND ACROSS EDUCATIONAL LEVEL)

Parental Reaction	Affiliation Motive				Achievement Motive				Power Motive				Number of Subjects at Each Educational Level			
	Grade school	High school	College	All	Grade school	High school	College	All	Grade school	High school	College	All	Grade school	High school	College	All
Negative orientation	.06	.14	.13	.12	−.10	−.04	.01	−.06	−.07	.01	−.26	−.04	(18)	(71)	(21)	(110)
Restrictiveness	−.16	.01	−.12	−.03	−.22	−.15	.18	−.12	.09	.09	−.20	.02	(18)	(71)	(21)	(110)
Inadequacy	—[a]	−.02	−.39	−.21	—[a]	.15	−.19	.20	—[a]	−.48†	−.49	−.40†	(8)	(33)	(11)	(52)
Problems	—[a]	−.14	—[a]	−.14	—[a]	.03	—[a]	−.06	—[a]	.04	—[a]	−.01	(18)	(71)	(20)	(109)
Tolerance inadequacy	—[a]	—[a]	—[a]	—[a]	—[a]	—[a]	—[a]	—[a]	—[a]	—[a]	—[a]	—[a]	(5)	(18)	(9)	(32)
Affiliative inadequacy	—[a]	−.26	—[a]	.00	—[a]	.03	—[a]	−.19	—[a]	−.23	—[a]	−.14	(5)	(18)	(9)	(32)
Distancing	−.13	−.17	.39	−.04	.08	.20	.09	.12	.05	.17	.35	.18	(18)	(63)	(21)	(102)

[a]Not reported because of inadequate distribution.
†p < .05.

163

parents may begin to see their school-age children as affiliative objects, as possible participants in a truly affiliative relationship, in contrast to their more nurturing relationship with the younger child. If affiliative goals require some equality in status, the potential for arousing the parent's interests in children as affiliative objects should become even greater during adolescence. As children get even closer to adult status, they become more similar to their parents and more appropriate affiliative objects for them. There were trends in the data to support this assumption, but surprisingly, affiliation motivation was not significantly related to any parental reactions at this stage.

The trend for a positive relationship between affiliation motivation and mothers' feelings of *Tolerance Inadequacy*, found for the school-age stage, was continued here. The number of cases was too small to have been presented in the table, but the gammas describing the relationship between the affiliation motive and *Tolerance Inadequacy* were .25 and .83 for high-school- and college-educated mothers, respectively. We would again argue that the sensitization hypothesis is useful here, but the increasing possibility for the child to be an affiliative object for the mother as he reaches more mature status sensitizes her to her own anger and her own intolerance.

Although the positive relationships between the affiliation motive and *Parental Negative Orientation* were small at all educational levels, they are important because they replicate parallel findings at the earlier stages of development for all educational levels. We expected this relationship to diminish for parents with older children—and indeed it did for mothers with children who are adult (see pages 166f). But we thought there could be a new affiliative freedom found when adolescents emerge on the scene. Whereas younger children might have interfered with other affiliative goals, adolescents are fairly self-sufficient and can even be called upon to take care of younger siblings.

Perhaps the new type of parental involvement with adolescents interferes with affiliation, with seeing adolescents as suitable targets for affiliation. In particular, psychologically-demanding parental conecrns about socialization are awakened by the adolescent child's marginal status between childhood and adulthood. Parents must begin again to take steps to guarantee the transmission of the moral order of their society—especially in the context of complex social relationships. The child's assertion of his own motivations, of his own sense of what is right and wrong, disturbs many parents, perhaps even more than the feeding, diapering, and tantrum problems of very young children. The discrepancy between the status of parent and child must still be apparent. An affiliative relationship may thus be a difficult state for the parent to achieve with his child at adolescence.

Achievement   Although there were no significant associations between the achievement motive and maternal reactions for mothers of adolescents, there was a continued trend for a negative association between achievement motivation and *Parental Inadequacy* for the college-educated group. But unlike the relationship for mothers of school-age children, it was not significant for mothers of adolescents. For high-school-educated women, the relationship was reversed from the earlier trend: mothers in this group with strong achievement motivation tended to feel more inadequate than those with weak achievement motivation. Undoubtedly the new demands put upon mothers for guiding children in the socialization process during adolescence add new standards for evaluating one's adequacy as a mother. Thus there may be a resurgence of doubts about whether or not the mother has reared a good human being as the child approaches the final testing ground of their upbringing just prior to adulthood. Although mothers have outside standards with which to judge their own performance and their children's performance, there are these new ambiguities and doubts about parental role demands. These new standards seemed to affect the sense of adequacy of high-school-educated women with high achievement motivation, but not of the college-educated women, and this may indicate that college-educated mothers are less disturbed than the high-school group by the challenge of an adolescent child. (Or else the feedback the college-educated mothers receive about the children's performance continues to be satisfactory.) College-educated women are also more likely to have turned to other arenas for achievement striving at this time and, as a result, no longer infuse the maternal role with such intense achievement needs.

Power   The power motive was significantly negatively related to *Parental Inadequacy* in the high-school-educated group of mothers, and in the group formed when all educational levels were considered together. The direction was the same at the other educational levels; women with high power motivation felt adequate as mothers. These results, combined with the fact that at all educational levels mothers with a high power motive tended to distance themselves from their children in thinking about the joys of parenthood, suggested that we were confronting a defensive pattern.

We had expected that the adolescent stage of the parental life cycle would be particularly threatening for persons with strong power motivation, whether it be of the power assertive or weakness-avoidant type. Then why should mothers with high power motivation feel *more* adequate in dealing with adolescents than mothers with low power motivation? We have previously noted the new set of socialization demands put on parents when their children are adolescent. Adolescence in these terms could be seen as a fresh, new battlefield full of potential for gratifying power needs.

However, the legendary free-floating rebelliousness of the adolescent child makes the power battle a particularly bitterly fought and often doomed endeavor for parents during this stage. Whereas the little child finally does capitulate to socialization, is toilet trained, does not wreak primitive destruction, the adolescent child is often notably successful in resisting parental training. That such a state of affairs should confer a sense of adequacy on any parent with high power motivation seems improbable. Thus these feelings of adequacy seem defensive. These women also tend to distance themselves from the joys of parenthood, which is a kind of defensive style in itself. This kind of psychological removal combined with feelings of adequacy in the face of obvious difficulty does not seem to be the response of a person whose power needs are gratified.

Why should distancing from the parental role be a part of the defensive style of the power-motivated mothers of adolescents? Distancing as a defensive technique often means treating one's own children merely as instances of the general class of people called children; it often means taking a universalistic approach to one's own children instead of examining them as particular individuals with particular attributes and problems. This technique might easily be employed by a woman who is concerned with her lack of power. She can view her unsuccessful attempts to influence her adolescent children as instances of "adolescent rebellion." She has the perfect excuse when her child resists her—"teenagers are that way." Thus a mother who is power-motivated may be quick to view her own power failures as within the bounds of the trying circumstances faced by any mother of an adolescent. She may begin to take a distant perspective toward her children.

MOTHERS OF ADULTS

There continued to be what we view as a remarkable lack of association between the affiliation motive and reactions to the role of mother. Thus, for mothers whose children were adults, as for mothers of school-age and adolescent children, affiliation motivation appeared to be generally irrelevant to maternal satisfactions and dissatisfactions. We had thought that the affiliation motive would be positively related to adjustment at this particular stage because adult children can appropriately be affiliative objects. One interpretation of the lack of relationship between affiliation motivation and feelings about being a parent is that, perhaps for mothers, children never become independent adults. The reciprocal nurture-love relationship may continue to govern mother-child interaction. Furthermore, mothers may always perceive their offspring as children to be socialized and influenced.

Indeed, the power motive is the motive that appears to be most related to parental adjustment at this stage, especially for high-school-educated mothers. For these women, the power motive was significantly associated with having a positive attitude toward children, not feeling restricted by having children, and having a distancing reaction to children. These responses, coming from women whose children are now grown and living away from the parental home all seem to reflect an uninvolved, but comfortable relationship with one's children.

For the other groups, the grade-school- and college-educated mothers, we found some evidence that mothers feel defensive about their role if they have high power motivation. Grade-school-educated women with high power motivation were significantly more likely to mention affiliative inadequacy than those with low power motivation. College-educated women with high power motivation tended to have a negative and restrictive orientation toward children. These college-educated mothers, who have been strongly involved in the childrearing process, now see their children functioning independently of them and emphasize the trials and tribulations accompanying parenthood.

We interpret all these results about the power motive as indicating that women with high power motivation experience some difficulty when faced with adult children whom they can no longer greatly influence. The women with different educational backgrounds expressed their frustrations in different ways: the grade-school-educated women showed defensive involvement in not feeling adequate about their contact with their children; the college-educated women expressed open negative feelings about the role of motherhood and the demands it made upon them; the high-school-educated women, for whom this parental stage may be less problematic, take a passive but positive reflective view of parenthood.

The latter group of women also were the only ones for whom achievement motivation continues to be significantly associated with feeling inadequate as a parent. From other information we know that high-school-educated women have more social contact with their families than women at different educational levels. Perhaps this fact underlies the correlation between achievement motivation and feelings of parental inadequacy for the high-school-educated group. Even when they are mature their children can evoke questions of parental competence, because their children have never been granted independence.

There was a significant positive relationship between the achievement motive and affiliative inadequacy for the total group of mothers of adult children. We offer two interpretations of this result. First we would suggest that women with high achievement motivation in fact are involved in activities away from the children and feel bad about the inroads such activities make on their maternal relationship. A second interpretation would be that women with high achievement motivation may avoid seeing their children because they are alerted to failure in their children, and then feel guilty about such avoidance.

The results for that group of mothers whose children were adults and were living away from the parental home are reported in Table 4.4. For these mothers we looked for parental reactions that reflected the role shifts occurring when children emerge from the protection of the family to the adult role. At this time children are recognized as adults by the outside world. And when they marry, our society generally underscores their potential to be decisionmakers in their own right within their own families of procreation. What havoc does this play with relationships to their families of origin? New kinds of maternal role obligations, role gratifications, or role ambiguities occur at this point, which may elicit very different reactions from mothers with different motives.

Affiliation As we have indicated, there was a general trend at this parental stage for affiliation motive to be unrelated to maternal reactions. One notable difference at this parental stage was the absence of prior

TABLE 4-4 THE RELATIONSHIP(γ) OF MOTIVES TO PARENTAL REACTIONS FOR MOTHERS WHOSE CHILDREN WERE ADULTS (WITHIN AND ACROSS EDUCATIONAL LEVEL)

Parental Reaction	Affiliation Motive				Achievement Motive				Power Motive				Number of Subjects at Each Educational Level			
	Grade school	High school	College	All	Grade school	High school	College	All	Grade school	High school	College	All	Grade school	High school	College	All
Negative orientation	−.00	−.04	−.08	−.02	.08	−.17	−.11	−.04	−.11	−.44‡	.33	−.19*	(67)	(66)	(13)	(146)
Restrictiveness	.07	.23	.30	.15	.10	.15	−.62	.09	−.01	−.29*	.11	−.13	(67)	(66)	(13)	(146)
Inadequacy	−.29	−.05	—a	−.12	−.34	.53†	—a	.25	−.04	.21	—a	.06	(30)	(40)	(5)	(75)
Problems	−.08	−.12	—a	−.09	.02	−.22	—a	−.06	−.26	.05	—a	−.13	(66)	(68)	(13)	(147)
Tolerance inadequacy	—a	−.25	—a	.17	—a	−.39	—a	−.23	—a	−.26	—a	−.29	(11)	(19)	(4)	(34)
Affiliative inadequacy	—a	.07	—a	.02	—a	.58	—a	.50*	—a	.56	—a	.72†	(11)	(19)	(4)	(34)
Distancing	−.07	−.05	−.19	−.08	.09	.16	−.23	.10	−.15	.51‡	.02	.14	(62)	(56)	(13)	(131)

aNot reported because of inadequate distribution.
*p < .10.
†p < .05.
‡p < .01.

168

trends for affiliation motivation to be positively associated with a mother's negative orientation to the role. Evidently enough mothers with high affiliation motivation now feel more affiliative to their children or at least they do not feel so involved with them that they interfere with other affiliative relationships.

Achievement There was an interesting differentiation in the relationship between achievement motivation and *Parental Inadequacy* at the various educational levels: for grade-school-educated mothers, achievement motivation was associated with feelings of adequacy; for the other two groups the mothers with high achievement motivation doubted their adequacy more than those with low achievement motivation, and this relationship was significant among the high-school group. Perhaps the limited goals set by grade-school-educated mothers enable those among them with a high achievement motive to feel satisfied with their efforts at childrearing when the children reach independent adult status. But the women with higher educational backgrounds probably expect greater success from their grown children. Thus, when they assess their own and their children's accomplishments, the mothers with high achievement strivings may feel that they could have done more for their children. This "never satisfied" quality to achievement motivation in women with respect to their childrearing will have its counterpart in a "never satisfied" quality to men's achievement strivings at work, as we will see in Chapter 5.

There may be another related explanation of why the high-school-educated mother with high achievement motivation may continue to feel inadequate as a mother, although her children have reached adulthood. There are data to suggest that mothers at this educational level are the ones most likely to have extended contact with their children when their children establish homes of their own. Axelrod (1956, p. 17) plotted the type of informal groups with which a population of urban men and women had frequent association by selected characteristics. One of these characteristics was education. Sixty-nine percent of high-school-educated men and women reported frequent association with relatives compared to 57 percent of those with less than high-school education and 50 percent of those with a college education. With such extended family contact the high-school-educated woman, if she has high achievement motivation, may continue to evaluate her maternal performance in relationship to her children. She may continue in her old patterns of assuming major responsibilities in decision-making vis-à-vis her children. She may continue to ask herself whether she is doing a good job of taking care of them. This continued reign over her children also will help explain some of the results we find relating the power motive to the maternal reactions of high-school-educated mothers at this stage in the parental cycle.

Despite this differentiation in the relationship of achievement motivation to overall feelings of parental adequacy among the different educational groups, there was a trend at *each* educational level for high achievement motivation to be associated with *Affiliative Inadequacy*, and this relationship was significant for the total group. We have already noted that a mother who reports not spending enough time with her children should be viewed as indicating defensive involvement in her role. The relationship between achievement motivation and such defensiveness seemed to have two possible explanations. One explanation assumes that women who have a high achievement motive are likely to turn to activities outside of the home at this time, thereby reducing contacts with their children. If their new found achievement activities are quite satisfying and are eagerly undertaken when their childrearing duties are over, they may become defensive about them since they were originally very involved with their children. Hence, these women may be especially prone to report "not spending enough time with their children" as an inadequacy. Their own achievement strivings outside the home may make them defensive about their maternal performance.

Another possibility is that women with high achievement motivation at this point of the life cycle may be particularly disappointed in their expectations for vicarious achievement satisfactions from their children. Some children fail; some children succeed, but the reflected glory may not be as gratifying as the glory expected. As a result, these women may indeed cut down affiliative contact—a reaction that may make them feel guilty and thus report affiliative inadequacies. The first explanation is more in keeping with the general trend of results from other role comparisons, but the latter cannot be discounted.

Power The most important results that emerged were the strong relationships that existed between the power motive and parental reactions for high-school-educated mothers whose children were adults. Power-motivated women in this group were positive about parenthood, and did not feel restricted by it on the one hand, but were also more distant about its joys. These were all significant relationships. Throughout the discussion of these data we have interpreted the results from mothers in the high-school group as reflecting a lack of involvement in the child-rearing, socializing process itself. These mothers, especially in contrast to the college-educated mothers who are assumed to be very invested in their own roles as socializers, teachers, and influencers of their children, may not experience a major shift in their influence role vis-à-vis their children at this life stage. Could it be that for this social group with moderate educational background, control exerted by the mothers remains relatively intact when the children emerge from the home of origin to family of procreation? Could it be that for this social group the control of extended family activity remains in the hands of these women, and so they remain in relatively peaceful harmony with children's autonomy when their children grow up?

The previously discussed data from Axelrod's (1956) comparison of informal familial contact at different educational levels can be used to support these ideas. The relatively high level of familial contact in the high-school-educated group is consistent with our suggestion for that group that the role of being a parent to grown children could provide a sufficient potential for influence to make the role congruent with a high power motive. On the one hand, then, these women with a high power motive may feel more gratification and less burden from the role. On the other hand, by virtue of their less self-involved attitude toward motherhood, they may be able to enjoy passively the fruits of their labor while taking a distancing position toward the satisfactions of motherhood.

Although the number of grade-school-educated women who responded with affiliative inadequacies was too small to report the relevant correlation in Table 4.4, there was a significant association (gamma = .81, $p < .10$ for the tau beta correlation) between the power motive and *Affiliative Inadequacy*. The same trends occurred for the other two groups, but they were not significant. However, when all women with adult children were considered, this same relationship was significant. It is this type of reaction that we view as defensive in women who are involved in parenthood. Thus it appears that at this parental stage, when parent-child contact has diminished, there is general regret among power-motivated women that they did not spend enough time with their children. As an explanation of their current diminution of influence over their children, they perhaps think that if they had spent more time with their children at earlier stages, their influence would have been better maintained. That this is especially true of grade-school-educated women is not surprising. These mothers were likely to have maintained the least influence over their children, who probably left the parental home at an early age. Furthermore, these mothers probably had spent less time with their children because of large families or outside employment.

A curious finding was that, although power motivation was associated with a positive orientation towards parenthood for mothers at the two lower educational levels, there was an opposite trend in the most-educated group. It might be that college-educated women are most aware of the need for psychic separation between mothers and adults. If they have a high power motivation they thus may feel especially upset when their children reach adulthood.

MOTHERS WHO ARE EMPLOYED

For the present section we reanalyzed the data just discussed, by comparing the relationships between motives and role reactions for mothers who were full-time housewives and those who were employed full-time outside the home, while maintaining the separation into different stages of the parental life cycle.[10] We were interested in whether there were any conspicuous differences between the pattern of results that were obtained for housewives and the results for women who were working full-time. Generally speaking, the results for these two groups paralleled the results we have already reported, with a few exceptions. The exceptions are noted in Table 4.5 and we will discuss them in this section in order to accentuate the effect the role of working may have on maternal reactions.

There were no instances where working and nonworking mothers showed different patterns of association between the affiliation motive and role reactions. However, in view of the minimal nature of these associations in the total sample of mothers of school-age and older children, this lack of differentiation must be viewed with caution. It is still interesting that working full-time outside the home does not affect these relationships, since it might be presumed that one reason for such work would be to satisfy affiliative goals (Hoffman, 1963).[11]

In contrast, the associations between both achievement and power motivations and the role reactions do show differentiation for working and nonworking mothers of either school-age or adolescent children. Working mothers whose children were of school age and who had high achievement motive were significantly more likely than comparable mothers with low achievement motive to have a positive attitude toward parenthood. While the housewives showed a similar negative relationship between achievement motivation and *Parental Negative Orientation*, it was smaller and not significant. One could assume that the development of achievement gratifications outside the home is a condition that allows these women to find the parental role satisfying.

This result stands in striking contrast to the results comparing working and nonworking mothers of adolescents. Here, there was a significant negative relationship between the achievement motive and *Parental Negative Orientation* for housewives while for working mothers of adolescents, the relationship was positive. Although the latter relationship was not significant, the unique shift in direction is noteworthy. It requires that we modify our previous speculation that the development of achievement gratifications outside the home allows women with high achievement

[10]In fact, however, there were too few working mothers of preschool children for that stage to be used in the comparisons. Because of the limited sample size, the additional educational level control was not utilized.

[11]Unfortunately, we could not make any comparisons for working and nonworking mothers using the content of inadequacies (Tolerance or Affiliative) measures because of inadequate distributions for working mothers.

TABLE 4-5 RELATIONSHIPS BETWEEN MOTIVES AND PARENTAL REACTIONS FOR FULL-TIME HOUSEWIVES AND EMPLOYED MOTHERS

Parental Stage	Motive	Parental Reaction	Work Status			
			Full-time Housewives		Full-time Employed	
			γ	(N)	γ	(N)
School age children	Achievement	Negative orientation	−.13	(114)	−.41*	(27)
	Power	Inadequacy	−.28*	(61)	1.00	(10)
Adolescent children	Achievement	Negative orientation	−.23*	(68)	.36	(26)
	Power	Inadequacy	−.68†	(31)	.25	(11)

*p < .10.
†p < .05.

motive to find the parental role satisfying. If we view adolescence as the time when parents are likely to get the most feedback about their children's performance in the world and also as a time when the parent-child relationship again requires active socialization efforts on the part of the parent, we can perhaps cast some light on this finding. The mother who spends all her time at home is again confronted with an active demand for socialization in contrast to the relative plateau of such demands when her child was of school age. She may be able to relate the feedback she receives about her adolescent child directly to her own efforts and interactions with him. It could be a time of maximum satisfaction of achievement strivings with respect to raising her child and thus could be a time when she feels particularly positive about being a parent. In contrast, the working mother at this time may feel that she is not meeting the increased demands for socialization of her child because she is out of the home. She may attribute any difficulties she has in relationship with her child at this time to the fact of her working. The relatively unconflicted achievement gratifications she may have experienced from her work when her child was of school age may become, during her child's adolescence, much more conflicted and, in some instances, a source of guilt.

In summary, the pattern of these results suggests that when the achievement gratifications from work are relatively unconflicted for a woman, she can feel particularly positive not only about her work *but about the parental role;* however, when her work can be seen as interfering with her functioning as a mother and meeting the demands of the maternal role, she may be very likely to view the maternal role negatively.

Employment status seemed to interact with power motivation in a manner that was not dependent on parental stage. For working women there tended to be a positive relationship between power motivation and *Parental Inadequacy* whereas significant negative relationships were obtained for full-time housewives. Full-time employed women tended to feel more inadequate if they had high power motivation than if they had low power motivation, while full-time housewives felt particularly adequate if they had high power motivation (either when they had school-age children or when they had children who were adolescents). This suggests that working does not allow a mother to feel that she has satisfactorily met the influence demands of parenthood. That the working mother with high power motivation openly reported these self-doubts is an interesting finding. She can rationalize her lack of influence by realistically thinking that time at work interferes with time for direct influence at home. But the full-time housewife does not have this excuse. In contrast, a full-time housewife has ample opportunity to meet the influence demands of parenthood. Thus her parental role, unencumbered by other roles, is an opportunity to act in a manner congruent with her power motivation. But we have already noted that children at adolescence are typically resistant to their parents' attempts to influence them. Such a situation should make women with high power motivation defensive and cause under-reporting of feelings of inadequacy.

There were no relationships significantly differentiating full-time employed mothers and full-time housewives when their children were adults. This would suggest that for this older group the role of work does not have much bearing on the role of motherhood. It seems obvious that only in special instances would a job for a mother of an adult present any interferences or difficulties in the functions that are required of her as a mother.

RESULTS: MOTIVE-ROLE INTERACTION FOR FATHERS

In the next four sections we will present results about fathers in a parallel fashion to those we have just presented for mothers, proceeding through the parental stages from fathers of preschool-age children through fathers of adults.

FATHERS OF PRESCHOOL-AGE CHILDREN

In its earliest stage fatherhood seems to trigger many motivationally relevant reactions. Fatherhood seems to enhance affiliative and power gratifications, but it seems to block achievement gratifications.

Fathers with high affiliation motivation were generally less likely to describe parenthood as burdensome than those with low motivation, and this relationship was significant for fathers with a grade-school education. We suggest that new affiliative possibilities are opened up to men when they become fathers. We had suggested that the advent of motherhood had the opposite effect on women's affiliative gratifications.

Fathers with high achievement motivation compared to those with low motivation were significantly more likely to feel inadequate as fathers and tended to have a negative orientation to children. We suggest that the new competences demanded of fathers of young children are incongruent with the usual achievement demands. A man's ability to meet these new paternal demands seems to be somewhat affected by his educational level. There was a significant relationship between having a negative orientation toward children and high achievement motivation for men with a high-school education, but there was little evidence to support this relationship among college-educated men. Furthermore, college-educated fathers were significantly more likely to feel that fatherhood was unproblematic if they had high, rather than low achievement motivation. This suggests that achievement in the extrafamilial aspects of the role—providing financial support through one's work—can compensate for difficulties in meeting the achievement demands in the intrafamilial role—socializing and nurturing children.

There seems to be a congruence of power motivation and the socializing functions that fathers are expected to assume in the earliest stage of parenthood. All fathers with high power motivation tended to feel more positive about this stage of parenthood than men with low power motivation, but this relationship was significant only for college-educated fathers.

At the initial stage of fatherhood, when children are of preschool age, fathers at all educational levels seem to react in similar ways to parenthood. The motives of fathers at different educational levels related to role reactions in the same general direction, although sometimes a given trend was especially clear at only one level of education. This pattern may reflect the fact that all fathers of very young children in our society have similar contact with their children. Thus, fathers of young children, regardless of social strata, are probably reacting to the general fact of being a father, rather than to the day-to-day responsibilities of child care.

Let us now look at the separate motives and their relationship to the parental reactions for fathers of preschool-age children. The data for this section are presented in Table 4.6.

Affiliation For all social strata the affiliation motive was negatively related to feeling restricted by children. The relationship was significant for fathers with a grade-school education. Perhaps fathers who are high in affiliation motivation do not feel restricted by having children because of the potential enhancement of affiliative relationships that may result from being a father. We have discussed previously the possibility that becoming a father may increase a man's potential interaction with other people, may add to his masculine validity in the eyes of other people, and may enhance his affiliative gratification from the world at large. It may be that men with high affiliation motivation are most likely to recognize this possibility. Their sensitivity to the possibilities for affiliative gratification via the parental role is greater than that of fathers low in affiliation motivation; the latter group, instead, reacts to the added responsibilities and burdens of parenthood. This effect may be particularly true for a

TABLE 4-6 THE RELATIONSHIP (γ) OF MOTIVES TO PARENTAL REACTIONS FOR FATHERS WHOSE CHILDREN WERE PRESCHOOL AGE (WITHIN AND ACROSS EDUCATIONAL LEVEL)

Parental Reaction	Affiliation Motive				Achievement Motive				Power Motive				Number of Subjects at Each Educational Level			
	Grade school	High school	College	All	Grade school	High school	College	All	Grade school	High school	College	All	Grade school	High school	College	All
Negative orientation	-.60	-.00	.28	-.04	.52	.27*	.08	.26	-.79	-.08	-.63*	-.25	(10)	(42)	(19)	(71)
Restrictiveness	-.92†	-.12	-.14	-.24	.22	-.09	.16	-.01	-.65	-.04	-.22	-.14	(10)	(42)	(19)	(71)
Inadequacy	—a	-.25	—a	-.41	—a	.29	—a	.64*	—a	-.40	—a	-.17	(5)	(20)	(9)	(34)
Problems	—a	.23	.24	.16	—a	-.27	-.67*	-.30	—a	-.03	-.59	-.08	(9)	(41)	(18)	(68)
Tolerance inadequacy	—a	—a	—a	—a	—a	—a	—a	—a	—a	—a	—a	—a	(1)	(4)	(2)	(7)
Affiliative inadequacy	—a	—a	—a	—a	—a	—a	—a	—a	—a	—a	—a	—a	(1)	(4)	(2)	(7)
Distancing	—a	-.14	.38	-.04	—a	-.03	-.25	-.17	—a	-.29	-.01	-.20	(9)	(39)	(17)	(65)

aNot reported because of inadequate distribution.
*p < .05.
†p < .10.

176

grade-school-educated man for whom formal events or overt characteristics of people may be necessary for cementing or establishing relationships. It may operate less strikingly for more-educated men because it
seems likely that they would establish friendships and interpersonal
relationships that are based on more complex and varied psychological
characteristics. The grade-school-educated men may also be more likely
to be seeking affiliative gratification from the parent-child relationship
itself. Kornhauser and Reid (1965) point out that workers in repetitive
jobs—those likely to come from low educational background—tend to
be socially withdrawn. It is interesting to look ahead at this point, for we
will find that for grade-school-educated fathers this trend for a negative
association between the affiliation motive and *Parental Restrictiveness* continues at the next two stages, but reverses, and is significant in the opposite
direction when their children are adult. Perhaps a father who has little in
the way of social status in the community no longer sees parenthood as
satisfying when he has lost his close ties to the child by virtue of the
child's becoming adult.

Achievement For fathers of preschool-age children at each educational
level, there was a positive relationship between *Parental Inadequacy* and
achievement motivation; this association was significant in the total
group.[12] We interpret this result to mean that the new role demands for
performance as a father of an infant are alien to the assertive behavior
usually required of masculine achievement performance. The young
father has no previous experience to teach him how to perform the duties
that may be asked of him as a father; the duties themselves are incongruent
with what he has previously learned is good masculine performance; and
in many cases the father is relegated to a position of very little responsibility
in the care of the child, with only a few duties to perform even if he were
skilled or knowledgeable about them. The images of the young father
struggling to change a diaper or feeling like a fifth wheel with the advent of
a new baby in his household come immediately to mind. The general
uneasiness young fathers feel toward their young children should be
especially marked for those with high achievement aspirations. In this
instance there is high motivation but few opportunities to perform
adequately in the achievement activities of the father role. The consequence of such incongruity is a sense of inadequacy. While men with low
achievement motivation are no better equipped to fulfill the duties of
fatherhood, they would be less likely to evaluate their role according to its
possibilities for achievement, and thus would be less likely to be concerned
about being skilled in the role. It is noteworthy that this relationship

[12]Although the number of college-educated fathers of preschoolers did not reach our
criterion, the gamma between the achievement motive and *Parental Inadequacy* in this
group was 1.00, and $p < .10$ for tau beta.

between achievement motivation and feelings of inadequacy is reversed for fathers of school-age children, suggesting that either fathers come to be more comfortable or habituated to performance in the paternal role or that there are new characteristics demanded of fathers of older children that are more compatible with the capacities that accompany strong achievement motivation. The role appears then to shift from being incongruent to being congruent to a man's high achievement goals.

There was also a consistent positive relationship between the achievement motive and *Parental Negative Orientation*, which was significant among the fathers with a high-school education. We interpret this as another reflection of the difficulties that a man with strong achievement motivation might have in satisfying these strivings in fulfilling the role of parent of a very young child.

Parental Problems was consistently negatively related to the achievement motive, and this relationship was significant for the college-educated group. College-educated fathers with high achievement motivation were less likely to mention problems in raising children than were their counterparts with low achievement motivation. Fathers with high achievement motivation have probably been doing relatively well in their achievements outside the home. This should be especially true for college-educated fathers. They are less likely to be besieged by financial insecurity or low status at work. In *Americans View Their Mental Health* (Gurin et al., 1960) we noted that young parents and particularly young fathers, are more likely to mention physical or material problems than psychological problems, such as disobedience. Thus, the fathers who are more relatively free of these problems—as college-educated fathers with high achievement motivation are likely to be—would be less likely to give too much notice to problems with their very young children.

The overall picture that emerges of a highly achievement-oriented father with preschool-age children is of someone trying to master his parental role as he has mastered other life roles, but who is thwarted by the characteristics of his small children. The consistently negative, although nonsignificant, relationships between high achievement motivation and *Parental Distancing* further support this picture.

Power The negative relationship between power motivation and *Parental Negative Orientation* was consistent for all fathers and was significant for college-educated fathers: men with strong power motives had more positive orientations to parenthood than men with low power motivation. We would interpret this result to be an instance where there was congruence between motivation and the demands of the role. The father is called upon to influence his child at any age, but perhaps particularly at the age of general socialization—the preschool age—and perhaps again later during adolescence. At this early age the father is expected to teach his child how to separate right from wrong and how to be an obedient child. So much opportunity for influence activity undoubtedly makes the role attractive to those with high power motivation. Furthermore, the child at this age, although often resistant, ultimately complies with the demands put upon him. Parents, if they persist long enough, will be able to see the effectiveness of their influence attempts in the capitulation of the child. Both the many opportunities for influence and the ultimate success of influence attempts are features of this stage in the parental life cycle that make this preschool period particularly gratifying for those with high power motives.

The above relationship between power motivation and positive attitude towards children was especially striking among college-educated men. Perhaps of all groups of fathers this group takes the socialization of children most seriously as part of their role demand. (This attitude did not appear to be true for the college-educated mothers at this stage in the parental life cycle.) We should remind ourselves here that for college-educated men there was a positive relationship between achievement and power motivation. Since achievement motivation was not significantly related to *Parental Negative Orientation* for college-educated men, we might speculate that for power-motivated men it is the exercise and subsequent effect of influence that makes this stage in the life cycle gratifying, rather than perceiving influence as part of the achievement demand of raising a child. Indeed, we have suggested that there is a *lack of congruence* between being a father of a pre-schooler and achievement motivation. Evidently a man with high achievement motivation does not see *influencing* as an achievement gratification. Perhaps feedback about "good performance as a father" is not available to a father of very young children. There is little social comparison made in our society about how obedient very young children are. The bases for comparison are usually in their physical and social attractiveness, rather than physical and social competence, and the former dimensions are probably not relevant to fathers' achievement concerns.

While there was a tendency for a similar relationship between power motivation and a positive orientation towards children for mothers with preschool-age children, it was not significant. This pattern of results suggests that the influence potential of parenthood is a more salient characteristic of the role for men than for women when children are young. Obviously, mothers as well as fathers discipline, direct, and influence young children. However, it may be that the influence function is more central for fathers of young children than for mothers for whom the dominant demand is that of nurturing the child. Again, of course, fathers *do* nurture little children, but at this age the major responsibility for this function probably belongs to mothers. This separation of role functions into loving for women and controlling for men is a common pattern in other societies as well. (See Parsons and Bales, 1955.) Aside from its utility for maintaining the social organization of the family, this separation of role functioning may provide appropriate types of gratification for each of the sexes. The nurturing function most important for a man to perform to maintain society is to care for his wife. If he attaches too much of his concern about nurturing his family to his children, he may generate tensions within the family structure. Such tensions could result both from his failure to provide sufficient nuturing to his wife and also from her resentment toward his usurping of her function. The nurturing function is appropriate for the mother not only biologically but also because of the amount of time she spends with the children and the types of functions she performs. Similarly, since in our society the father is the major contact with the outside world, it is most appropriate for him to convey social norms and values and to provide the appropriate contacts for the child's integration into the family as well as into the larger society.

FATHERS OF SCHOOL-AGE CHILDREN

The trend for men with high affiliation motivation to find parenthood less burdensome than men with low affiliation motivation continued into the second stage of parenthood when children are of school age. A new finding, however, was the significant positive relationship between the affiliation motive and feelings of inadequacy as a parent among college-educated men. There are other data available to suggest that the reason for this relationship is that college-educated men concerned about affiliation are sensitive to the amount of time their jobs demand. At this point in the life cycle, work represents their attempt to solidify their career for the sake of their family's security. They are torn between their desire to establish a close relationship with their children and their desire to establish financial security for their family.

From the standpoint of achievement and power motivation, however, it is not college-educated fathers but the two other groups whose motives seem to be most entangled in this stage of childrearing. High-school-educated fathers with high rather than low achievement motivation were significantly more likely to distance themselves from their children. This result in combination with other trends suggests that these men are getting vicarious achievement gratification from their school-age children.

Grade-school-educated fathers with high power motivation were significantly more likely to distance themselves from the satisfactions in having children. We suggest that this orientation is a defensive pattern, adopted because the status of these fathers is increasingly challenged as their children come into contact with people who have more status than they themselves have.

Table 4.7 presents the data from that point in the life cycle for fathers when their children are of school age. At this stage we begin to see differential motive-role interaction for men with different educational backgrounds.

Affiliation The same pattern of negative association between

TABLE 4-7 THE RELATIONSHIP (γ) OF MOTIVES TO PARENTAL REACTIONS FOR FATHERS WHOSE OLDEST CHILDREN WERE SCHOOL AGE (WITHIN AND ACROSS EDUCATIONAL LEVEL)

Parental Reaction	Affiliation Motive				Achievement Motive				Power Motive				Number of Subjects at Each Educational Level			
	Grade school	High school	College	All	Grade school	High school	College	All	Grade school	High school	College	All	Grade school	High school	College	All
Negative orientation	−.21	−.10	.06	−.08	.46	.07	−.19	.06	−.15	−.11	−.05	−.10	(19)	(63)	(34)	(116)
Restrictiveness	−.32	−.16	−.03	−.14	.52	.17	−.21	.10	−.17	.04	−.04	−.01	(19)	(63)	(34)	(116)
Inadequacy	—ᵃ	.10	.65†	.18	—ᵃ	−.32	−.24	−.27	—ᵃ	.23	.06	.09	(11)	(28)	(18)	(57)
Problems	−.54	−.27	.06	.08	−.28	.11	.37	.12	−.20	.18	.10	.08	(19)	(63)	(35)	(117)
Tolerance inadequacy	—ᵃ	−.61	—ᵃ	−.54	—ᵃ	.35	—ᵃ	.07	—ᵃ	.44	—ᵃ	.17	(1)	(14)	(11)	(26)
Affiliative inadequacy	—ᵃ	—ᵃ	—ᵃ	.24	—ᵃ	—ᵃ	—ᵃ	−.31	—ᵃ	—ᵃ	—ᵃ	.17	(1)	(14)	(11)	(26)
Distancing	.14	.12	−.23	.04	.05	.48‡	−.25	.18	.72†	.04	−.02	.16	(17)	(59)	(34)	(110)

ᵃNot reported because of inadequate distribution.
†$p < .05$.
‡$p < .01$.

181

affiliation motive and *Parental Restrictiveness* found among fathers of preschool children was maintained for fathers in the second stage of the parental life cycle: the higher the affiliation motive, the less the father tended to feel restricted by parenthood. Our previous discussion is also appropriate here; fatherhood increases the potential for social interaction in general, and men with a high-affiliation motive should be more sensitive to this possibility than men with a low affiliation motive. In addition, as children grow up, they themselves can be the objects of affiliative relationships, especially in lower educational groups where the family's social world may be limited.

There were consistently positive relationships between *Parental Inadequacy* and the affiliation motive for fathers of school-age children. However, this relationship was significant only for college-educated men. Although the obtained relationship between *Affiliative Inadequacy* and affiliation motive did not reach significance, it was positive in direction in all groups, while at all educational levels high-affiliation motivation was associated with fewer mentions of *Tolerance Inadequacy*. Thus, the father who has a high level of affiliation motive probably is concerned with *seeing* his children, not *arguing with them*. He may feel that if only he were able to spend more time with his child, as he may have been able to do when the child was younger, he would be able to compete more successfully with the child's peers for the child's affection. His doubts about whether he is as good a father as he would like to be may reflect the decreased time he spends with his child in conjunction with his child's turning away from the home in search of peers for friendship.

There are some reasons why a college-educated father with a high affiliation motive might especially feel himself inadequate in his role of father. First, we would think of the college-educated father as likely to be an involved father, one who is concerned about his psychological impact on his child. Particularly if he has strong affiliative needs, we would expect him to want to spend time with his child and to feel that it is psychologically important to do so. And we note that it is only for the college-trained man that affiliation motive implies an active rather than a distancing orientation to the joys of parenthood. However, the stage of his career that probably requires the most diligent attention and the greatest amount of time is likely to coincide with the time when his children are of school age. He may feel realistically frustrated in his affiliative relationship with his school-age child because of the special time and energy he must devote to his work. Since this is also a stage where most children move from a family-oriented life to one of greater interaction with peers, affiliative contact between the father and children may be even further reduced.

Achievement At each of the educational levels there was a negative relationship between *Parental Inadequacy* and achievement motivation for fathers whose children were of school age. None of these relationships was significant but each represents a reversal in direction from the results obtained for fathers of preschoolers. Why this reversal? Let us follow the line of thinking we developed for the previous groups of fathers. We argued that the role functioning demanded of fathers when their children are very young do not provide adequate feedback about their own performance and are not compatible with the assertive performances that are usually required of men. We have seen that fathers with high achievement motivation who have very young children are more subject to feeling inadequate in their role of father. Now we see that when children are of school age, fathers with a high achievement motive are less likely than fathers with a low achievement motive to report feeling inadequate in their role. This reversal implies that the behaviors required of a father of a school-age child are more compatible with the general achievement behavior of men. Middle childhood is a time for learning many new motor skills and facts about the world. The example we cited previously of the inept father struggling to change a diaper stands in marked contrast to the image of the father teaching his son how to bat a ball or helping his son or daughter with a difficult arithmetic problem. We can assume that the father is usually much better equipped to perform the latter functions and consequently feels more competent in his own skill and knowledge. These new rewards for competence in teaching children are probably at the root of the reversal of the relationship between achievement motivation and felt inadequacy at this age period. Achievement-motivated men perhaps feel most adequate and most interested in teaching their children; their motivations are most congruent with the role. Generally, these people are successful, and have the greatest contact with decision-making in the world at large. Furthermore, this is the time when parents begin to get feedback about their children's performance, and by inference, their own performance. As a result of all these factors, we would assume that fathers with high achievement motivation are most sensitized to the potential of role performance and achievement in parenthood.

The only significant association between achievement motive and parental reactions at this stage highlights an interesting differentiation among men from the three educational backgrounds. For high-school-educated men, there was a significant positive relationship between *Parental Distancing* and the achievement motive; for this group achievement motivation was accompanied by a passive enjoyment of the satisfactions of having children. At the earlier stage this relationship was negative for all groups, and we interpreted it to imply an active self-involvement in parenthood for men with high achievement motives. At the school-age stage, only college-educated men appeared to retain this active involvement. In order to understand these results, it seemed necessary to consider the entire pattern of results for the three educational groups.

Let us look first at the college-educated men with school-age children. Those among them who had high achievement motivation tended to have a positive, unrestrictive view of parenthood, in which active participation with their children was important for their enjoyment of parenthood, in which they performed according to their expectations of what it meant to be a good father, but in which they recognized the problems of raising children. This gives us a picture of a group for whom feeling adequate seems to stem from both involvement and competence in new role requirements. This interpretation is similar to the one we gave to the same relationship for college-educated mothers at this parental stage.

In sharp contrast, the grade-school-educated fathers with a high achievement motive tended to have negative and restrictive views about parenthood, although they saw it as a role they carried out adequately and which presented them with no problems. Their achievement motivation was irrelevant to the kinds of satisfaction parenthood brings. This set of relationships suggested that fathers with little education but strong achievement strivings are not engaged by parenthood. They may find the responsibilities of parenthood burdensome, because they are struggling with their work and find little energy for parenthood. In so doing, however, they could feel they are good providers. And if they set economic provision for children as the major aspect of their obligation to nurture, they can feel especially adequate as fathers and experience fewer problems than their fellow grade-school-educated fathers who do not direct strong achievement strivings toward their jobs.

The pattern of results for the high-school-educated fathers shared some similarity to the pattern for grade-school-educated fathers. High-school-educated fathers with high achievement motivation also tended to have a negative, restrictive view of parenthood and to feel adequate as fathers. But there was an additional relationship with achievement motivation for them. High-school-educated fathers with high achievement motivation were significantly more likely to distance themselves from parental satisfactions, in contrast to their counterparts with low achievement motivation. When asked about satisfactions, they mentioned such things as watching one's child grow and develop. Because of the general similarity in results for the two lower status groups, it seems reasonable to interpret the feelings of adequacy of high-school-educated fathers' like their counterparts with a grade-school education. That is, their feelings of adequacy stem not from their interpersonal interactions that are designed to teach their children, as they probably do for the college-educated men with high achievement motivation, but rather from their presumably successful efforts to meet the requirements of being a good provider.

There was an important difference, however, between the grade-school and high-school-educated groups. The high achievement motivation of high-school-educated fathers directs them to certain other types of parental satisfactions as well, those we have identified as distant sources of satisfaction. We suggest that *Parental Distancing* can represent *vicarious achievement gratification*. This is a new way of looking at the *Parental Distancing* measure, but it is consistent with this and subsequent results. To enjoy a child at a distance often is to admire him for his growth and accomplishments. Such a view puts a new perspective on the positive relationship between *Parental Distancing* and achievement motivation for high-school-educated fathers at this stage of the life cycle. These men may get particularly strong vicarious achievement pleasures from their school-aged children's acquisition of new skills and knowledge. At this time children are involved with their school or peer groups, and the central focus of this involvement is on the new cognitive, motor, or social talents they can develop. High-school-educated men with high achievement motivation seem to be particularly attuned to these changes, and we suggest that they derive vicarious pleasure from them.

This interpretation might help also to account for trends indicating a positive relationship between achievement motivation and *Parental Distancing* during other stages in the parental life cycle. We will see in the next sections that when children are adolescents and adults, achievement motivation in the college-educated father tends to be positively related to *Parental Distancing*, while at these points *Parental Distancing* is no longer related to achievement motivation for the high-school-educated father. One might differentiate the kinds of achievement behaviors typical for school-age children and for older children. Whereas achievements for school-age children are focused on the acquisition of skills (for example, excellence on the Little League baseball team), achievements for adolescents or adults begin to approximate or are identical with adult achievements in whatever realm they occur, be it sports, intellectual activity, or work. This difference suggests that the high-school-educated father is most vicariously gratified and least threatened by the achievements of the school-age child, while the college-educated father may be vicariously satisfied by more typically adult achievements.

Power For fathers whose children were of school age there was one significant association with the power motive. There was a positive relationship between power motivation and *Parental Distancing* among grade-school-educated men. We found a similar tendency for women with children at this age. In explaining that result, we suggested that most women may feel as if their influence is called into question when the child's contact with the outside world expands. Women with high power motivation, we suggested, should be most sensitive to this threat and should defensively withdraw from their active involvement with children. The same kind of reasoning can be used to explain the relationship found for the grade-school-educated father with high power motivation. He may fear that the child's contact with the world outside may alert him to the father's lack of status. He may fear that he will become less of a pillar of strength for the child, less of a source of information or values. The fear of dethronement from a position of influence may make a father with high power motivation retreat from parental involvement. Thus, among the low social-status group, where we might expect that the child's entering school could constitute the greatest challenge to the father's authority, we found a positive relationship between power motivation and a *Parental Distancing* reaction to children. Again we view this result as support for the sensitization principle. For a lower-status father there is some ambiguity about his own status vis-à-vis his child. For the high-school and college-educated groups there should be no such dramatic challenge to the father's status when the children move on to school. Indeed, we found no relationship between power motive and *Parental Distancing* in those groups.

FATHERS OF ADOLESCENTS

Whereas the grade-school-educated father with high power motivation seems to be concerned about his status when his children are of school age, the high-school-educated father's moderate status seems to become problematic when his children get to be adolescent. We see this in three significant relationships, in the high-school-educated father's sensitivity to problems with children if he has high affiliation motivation, in what seems to us his defensive denial of inadequacy if he has high achievement motivation, and in his defensive denial of problems if he has high power motivation.

We picture these men with high affiliation motivation upset by the threat to their affiliative relationship with their children posed by the adolescents' growing rebelliousness, independence, and demands; they cannot provide the financial resources that a teenager respects and desires. We picture these men concerned about their own sense of inadequacy if they have high achievement motivation. Their moderate success in life pales by comparison to the more-educated fathers, who by this stage of the parental cycle have orbited into positions of high professional and business prestige. We picture these men denying problems of influence raised by adolescent rebellion if they have high power motivation; it is at this stage in the life cycle that these men might feel especially threatened by questions of their own power. The grade-school-educated men experience these threats at an earlier stage in the parental life cycle. The high-school-trained men experience them at this juncture in the parental cycle. The college-educated fathers with high power motivation appear to be less seriously threatened by their children's adolescent rebelliousness—they can openly acknowledge various difficulties with their parenthood. In particular, they are significantly more likely to feel restricted by children than college-educated men with low power motivation.

As children move on into adolescence, parents more and more relate to them and feel resistance from them as they become adults. For fathers this period may involve an additional characteristic, since by this time they are often at the peak of their productivity in their career. Veroff et al.

(1960) have noted that middle age is particularly critical for men's achievement motivation. A crisis in their own achievement at work undoubtedly has ramifications in their relationships with their children. With this general orientation let us review the data in Table 4.8 in more detail, considering each motive in relationship to parental reactions during this stage in the life cycle.

Affiliation There was a significant positive relationship between affiliation motivation and *Parental Problems* among high-school-educated fathers of adolescents. Consistent with this result were trends towards a positive relationship between affiliation motivation and *Parental Negative Orientation*, and a negative relationship between this motive and *Affiliative Inadequacy*.[13] For both the grade-school-educated and the college-educated fathers there were no significant relationships between the affiliation motive and the parental reactions, although in the case of the grade-school sample, its small size may have contributed to these negative findings.

The pattern of findings raises two questions. First, why should any father with high affiliation motive react in a distressed way to his adolescent children? Second, why when children are adolescents should the affiliation motive of fathers with a high-school education be more activated by the enactment of the paternal role than it is for fathers of our other groups?

It will be recalled that for parents with school-age children, upper-status men with high affiliation motive seemed sensitized to the affiliative potential of the parental role, felt concerned about their adequacy as fathers, and wanted to spend more time with their children. Why then should any fathers with high affiliation motive be disappointed by the changes in the parent-child relationship that may accompany adolescence? There are several reasons. Adolescents seem far less willing to share activities with their parents; they are more likely to be at odds with them interpersonally; and they may become involved in activities that are not acceptable to their fathers. The adolescents' disobedience could loom as a major problem for fathers—especially for those concerned about their affiliative ties to their children—because while adolescents disobey, they also do require adult support. They do require implicit approval for their experimentation. This dilemma can put a father with high affiliation motivation into a bind.

There is another problem at adolescence that could particularly affect a father with high affiliation motivation. An adolescent often makes new financial demands upon parents in order to keep up his new found status: it is important to dress properly, have a record player, a car, etc., in order to be a successful teenager. Men with strong affiliation motive

[13]Although the sample size did not meet the criterion for inclusion in the table, the gamma was −.75 for these 7 subjects.

TABLE 4-8 THE RELATIONSHIP (γ) OF MOTIVES TO PARENTAL REACTIONS FOR FATHERS WHOSE OLDEST CHILDREN WERE ADOLESCENTS (WITHIN AND ACROSS EDUCATIONAL LEVELS)

Parental Reaction	Affiliation Motive				Achievement Motive				Power Motive				Number of Subjects at Each Educational Level			
	Grade school	High school	Col- lege	All	Grade school	High school	Col- lege	All	Grade school	High school	Col- lege	All	Grade school	High school	Col- lege	All
Negative orientation	.05	.31	.13	.20	−.30	.13	.30	.12	−.37	−.21	.39	−.06	(14)	(36)	(25)	(75)
Restrictiveness	−.05	.19	−.14	.04	.07	−.12	.06	−.04	.00	−.31	.58†	.04	(14)	(36)	(25)	(75)
Inadequacy	—a	.11	−.26	.02	—a	−.73‡	−.33	−.28	—a	−.17	.66	.32	(5)	(13)	(13)	(31)
Problems	—a	.67*	.14	.30	—a	−.38	−.31	−.29	—a	−.74‡	.20	−.12	(14)	(35)	(25)	(74)
Tolerance inadequacy	—a	—a	—a	—a	—a	—a	—a	—a	—a	—a	—a	—a	(1)	(7)	(7)	(15)
Affiliative inadequacy	—a	—a	—a	—a	—a	—a	—a	—a	—a	—a	—a	—a	(1)	(7)	(7)	(15)
Distancing	.33	−.08	.35	.09	−.63	−.19	.25	−.11	−.65	.01	−.16	−.12	(14)	(32)	(23)	(69)

aNot reported because of inadequate distribution.
*p < .10.
†p < .05.
‡p < .01.

would be concerned about denying these requests, for fear of threatening their relationship with their children.

It is interesting that men apparently do not perceive the amount of time spent with their children as relevant to the affiliative threat that arises at adolescence. For while this is the parental stage when fathers are most likely to report *Affiliative Inadequacy* (see Table 4.d in Appendix B), its report is negatively associated with affiliation motive.[14] Instead of feeling personal responsibility for this adolescent crisis, men with strong affiliation motive, and especially those with a high-school education, apparently perceive *Parental Problems*. We viewed this measure as a fairly passive reaction to the responsibilities of fatherhood. The content of problems generally mentioned emphasized the difficulties in making adequate material provision for children and in getting children to obey, both of which we have just suggested are problems to which men with high affiliation motivation might be particularly sensitive during their children's adolescence.

While the relationship between affiliation motive and *Parental Problems* was positive for both high-school and college-educated fathers, it was significant only for the former group. Why is it especially strong for the high-school-educated group? The grade-school-educated fathers' relationships with his child is in jeopardy at a younger age—when the child first confronts the overall social system in his contacts at school, and discovers his father's low status. For college-educated fathers, the threat to their relationship posed by the adolescent's disobedience can be tempered by the father's high social status in the community; the adolescent's demands for material support can be handled by the father's adequate bank account. But the high-school-educated father can appeal neither to his high social status nor his bank account to help him maintain his relationship with his children. He should be the one most disrupted by adolescent problems, and if he has high affiliation motivation, he should be especially sensitive to these problems.

Achievement There was a significant negative relationship between *Parental Inadequacy* and the achievement motive for fathers with a high-school education, and the results were in the same direction for fathers at other educational levels. The same general trend had appeared at the previous parental stage. Thus, high achievement motivation is associated with feeling adequate as a father. Although we suggested in the introduction to this section that the time when children are adolescent may coincide with the time men are most affected by crises in their work, we also noted that this is the time when they are at the peak of their productivity

---

[14]For the entire sample at this parental stage gamma $= -.89, p < .10$ for the tau beta correlation, with skewed distribution.

in their career setting. As a result, this relationship can have both a defensive and a more positive interpretation.

First, the more positive interpretation. Despite any problems that may exist, this may be the time when most men feel particularly adequate in fulfilling their achievement strivings. Perhaps the feeling of maximum adequacy is most marked for high-school-educated men with high achievement motive, who may neither set such high goals or be so future-oriented in career terms as the college-educated man, nor be as frustrated in total fulfillment of achievement needs as the grade-school-educated man. Thus, for all men with strong achievement motivation, this point in their life may be a time when they are relatively unharrassed by feelings of inadequacy, and this may be particularly true for high-school-educated men.

An interpretation of these results as suggestive of a defensive reaction seems more in keeping with the other results. Compared to more-educated men, a high-school-educated man's achievements are likely to look pale, not only in terms of prestige but also in terms of take-home pay. Being especially interested in successful accomplishments, a man with high achievement motivation thus would be threatened by a sense of inadequacy about his status as a parent. Thus he may deny feelings of inadequacy. This interpretation is in keeping with the result we will discuss in the next section on power motivation.

Power The most noteworthy finding concerning power motivation was the marked contrast between the pattern of relationships for the high-school and college-educated fathers of adolescents. All the quantitative measures of distress were negatively related to power motivation in the high-school-educated group (although significantly so only in the case of the *Parental Problems* index): the high-school-educated fathers with high power motivation reported less parental distress than those with low power motivation. In contrast, all these measures were positively related to power motivation in the college-educated group (although significantly so only in the case of *Parental Restrictiveness* measure): for college-educated men, high power motivation was associated with parental difficulties. How do we account for such a different pattern in the two groups of fathers?

All adolescents attempt to move away into their own spheres away from parents and to establish their own social roles. This phenomenon can be more or less threatening to the father, depending on his general social position in the community, how involved he is in socializing his child, and the extent to which his personal needs are satisfied through his parental authority. We have already suggested that the grade-school-educated father may feel threatened by his school-age child's contact with his authority; adolescence may be time for the father to detach himself from the socialization process. But we suspect that the high-school-educated and college-educated fathers do not treat their adolescent children with detachment, and probably take their responsibilities for upholding the standards of the social community very seriously. Unfortunately for the high-school-educated father, his social status is not sufficient for him to feel that his prerogatives to be the standard bearer are unthreatened. We have already suggested that the high-school-educated father's disappointment in his affiliative relationship with his adolescent child is in part a reaction to a growing threat to his status as an authority. And the high-school-educated father with high power motivation would be very threatened by recognition of his loss of control over his teenage children. Thus we would interpret the parental reactions that distinguish high-school-educated fathers with high power motivation from their counterparts with low power motivation as a highly defensive pattern. They do not want to admit to problems or harbor any resentments about their fate as parents. They are defensive because they want to influence their children, but feel they cannot do it very well because of their lack of status. Our interpretation here is similar to that offered for mothers at this stage, when feelings of adequacy were associated with power motive.

We would interpret the parental reactions that distinguish the college-educated fathers of high power motivation from their counterparts with low power motivation, as a pattern showing their genuine negative feeling about the difficulties of socializing their children at this point in the parental life cycle. They need not react defensively because they feel they have a right to such influence and may eventually assert it, even if it is difficult to exert at this time. College-educated men with a high power motive probably do find adolescence very trying. They dislike losing their influence, and they are often confronted with defiant adolescents.

Adolescents often express their defiance by spending time away from home. Men who are concerned with influence at this time may feel frustrated by not having contact with their children. For this reason we expected and found consistent trends in both this and in the next phase of the parental life cycle for fathers with high power motives to mention *Affiliative Inadequacy.* [15]

FATHERS OF ADULTS

When children are grown and out of the psychological life space of their fathers, the pattern of results for each of the motives was more distinctive for grade-school-educated men than it was for fathers at the other educational levels. Parenthood is a role that is perhaps minimally rewarding for the lower-status father when he is old; yet he may have no other important role satisfactions to fill the gaps

---

[15]Although the distribution was too skewed to allow for an adequate statistical test, gamma = .73 between the power motive and *Affiliative Inadequacy* for all fathers at this stage of the life cycle. Similar trends were found in the next stage of the parental life cycle.

created when his children leave home; his motivational goals therefore are not easily disengaged from the parental role. A grade-school-educated father reacts particularly negatively to his parenthood at this stage if he has any strong motivation. In contrast fathers from higher-status backgrounds, having less at stake emotionally in parenthood, end up feeling more gratified with what parenthood has brought them. At this point in the life cycle, grade-school-educated fathers with high achievement motivation, felt significantly more negative about parenthood than those with low achievement motivation; those with high power motivation, were significantly more likely to view raising children as problematic than fathers with low power motivation; and men with high affiliation motivation felt significantly more restricted by what parenthood had wrought in their lives than those with low affiliation motivation.

The men with higher educational status, those with high-school and college training, evidently are in better positions to defend their status with their children and to work out a more compatible relationship with them. The strong relationship between achievement motivation and feeling adequate as a parent, which was found in the prior period in the parental life cycle for high-school-educated men, continues for these men when their children are adult. Again we can offer a dual interpretation to this result. It can be an example of the congruence principle: at this point in the life cycle, men high in achievement motivation can look back with satisfaction at their ability to meet the parental demand to provide financial security for their children. It can also reflect a defensive unwillingness to engage in any self-questioning of parental adequacy by men with high achievement motivation who have set high standards of accomplishment for themselves, which they may not have met.

The relationships between motives and parental reactions for our last group of fathers, those whose children were all adults no longer residing in the parental home, are presented in Table 4.9. Unfortunately, for most measures of parental reactions, the sample size or skewed distributions prevented the statistical reporting of the results for college-educated men.

Affiliation When their children were mature, grade-school-educated men with a high affiliation motive were significantly more likely to feel restricted by parenthood than men with a low affiliation motive. Here we have come full circle: for grade-school-educated men with pre-school children, affiliation motivation was significantly associated with *not feeling restricted* by parenthood. The entire set of results, from this and the previous stages of the life cycle, suggests that men who have high affiliative investments in their children and who are at the lower social strata in our society, are bitterly disappointed in parenthood as their children grow up and leave home. These men probably expected much from their children and did not invest themselves socially in other spheres of life—their community, church, or other social organizations.[16] Because

---

[16]We will find, in Chapter 5, that older men with high affiliation motivation in the low prestige jobs are less likely to belong to formal social groups than those with a low affiliation motive.

TABLE 4-9 THE RELATIONSHIP (γ) OF MOTIVES TO PARENTAL REACTIONS FOR FATHERS WHOSE CHILDREN WERE ADULTS (WITHIN AND ACROSS EDUCATIONAL LEVEL)

Parental Reaction	Affiliation Motive				Achievement Motive				Power Motive				Number of Subjects at Each Educational Level			
	Grade school	High school	College	All	Grade school	High school	College	All	Grade school	High school	College	All	Grade school	High school	College	All
Negative orientation	.08	−.12	−.22	−.02	.32*	−.30	−.56	−.01	.22	.17	.49	.19	(50)	(40)	(15)	(105)
Restrictiveness	.34*	.05	−.16	.19	−.07	−.12	−.26	−.12	.25	.10	−.09	.12	(50)	(40)	(15)	(105)
Inadequacy	.17	−.14	—a	.02	.10	−.61†	—a	−.12	−.34	.39	—a	−.04	(27)	(19)	(9)	(55)
Problems	−.08	−.20	—a	−.12	.13	.08	—a	.06	.45†	−.13	—a	.16	(53)	(38)	(15)	(106)
Tolerance inadequacy	—a	—a	—a	—a	—a	—a	—a	—a	—a	—a	—a	—a	(8)	(14)	(6)	(28)
Affiliative inadequacy	—a	.27	—a	.07	—a	−.76	—a	−.44	—a	.41	—a	.33	(8)	(14)	(6)	(28)
Distancing	.29	−.16	−.13	.02	.08	.10	.26	.12	−.11	−.15	.02	−.07	(43)	(38)	(16)	(97)

aNot reported because of inadequate distribution.
*p < .10.
†p < .05.

193

grade-school-educated fathers have used their parenthood as a means of forming their central affiliative relationships, they are left with an affiliative void when their children leave home. They then look back upon the advent of children as a time fraught with new responsibilities and burdens that, perhaps, can be the rationalization for their present lack of affiliative ties. Men at other statuses have other resources that temper their reaction to their children's departure from home.

Achievement For grade-school-educated men with mature children, men who have been low in the status hierarchy for years, there was a significant positive relationship between achievement motivation and *Parental Negative Orientation.* At the two other educational levels the comparable relationships were in the reverse direction, but neither was significant. These data suggest that men with a high achievement motive who are disappointed with their own lack of achievement and who perhaps are further disappointed by their children's assessment of them as unsuccessful, defend against these disappointments by rejecting their children.

For high-school-educated men, achievement motivation was significantly negatively associated with *Parental Inadequacy;* that is, when men in this group had a high achievement motive they were likely to feel that they had done a good job as fathers. This result parallels the one obtained for high-school-educated men with adolescent children and we assume that it reflects the same phenomena. Again two alternative explanations are possible, but as before, we prefer the interpretation that reports of adequacy are a defensive maneuver. The direct interpretation would assume that high-school-educated men with high achievement motive have probably come closer to their achievement goals than comparable men with low achievement motivation, or with only grade-school education. They may view their accomplishments on their jobs as having met the crux of their parental role—to provide for the material needs of their children. In such a case, the demands of parenthood would be congruent with their achievement motivation. However, their financial achievements are probably below those of more-educated men, and we feel that these men with high achievement motivation perceive their financial status as relatively deprived. And this relative deprivation leads them to focus much of their energy on financial achievement, to become defensive about their own adequacy, and to suppress any feelings of inadequacy as a provider.

While college-educated men with a high achievement motive would presumably be relatively successful, we have suggested that they might be more concerned with the interpersonal aspects of parenthood and therefore not accrue feelings of self-satisfaction from their accomplishments as breadwinners. We cannot adequately check this comparison with college-educated fathers of mature children, however, because of our very small sample.

Power   Grade-school-educated fathers with high power motivation reported significantly more *Parental Problems* than men with low power motivation. There were no significant relationships for men at the other educational levels, perhaps indicating that fathers at the higher educational levels are less likely to use adult children as vehicles for fulfillment of their power goals. As men age, they can turn to other spheres—to social organizations, and to their work—as arenas of influence. Such possibilities are open less often to lower-status men. With children gone, their potential, albeit fragile, realm of influence disappears. Men with low social-status and high power motivation feel such a loss particularly hard. Hence they are likely to feel that raising their children was problematic for them.

Finally, we should note the trends for power-motivated fathers to mention *Affiliative Inadequacy*, among high-school and college-educated men. Such trends existed at the previous parental stage as well. Affiliative contact is a means by which men do maintain some sense of strength with their children. When there is insufficient control, men with high power motivation should be particularly upset and perhaps seek to explain it in their not having spent enough time with their children.

REASSESSMENT OF MOTIVES IN THE CONTEXT OF PARENTHOOD

We will now review the main body of results and attempt to integrate the findings concerning the relationships of each of the motives to the parental role reactions. This reassessment will highlight the motivational significance of parenthood across the different educational levels and the different periods in the life cycle of parents. We will then be in a position to reevaluate some of our initial ideas about motive-role interaction, presented earlier in this chapter.

AFFILIATION MOTIVATION AND PARENTAL REACTIONS

We had considered that parenthood could have two types of affiliative consequences. First, it could affect affiliative gratifications through the relationship between the parent and the child. Secondly, it could affect affiliative gratifications through changes in the parent's relationships with other adults, including the spouse, that stem from attaining the new adult status of parenthood.

On the whole, we had presupposed that the relationship between the parent and the child, despite its great intimacy and its status as a love relationship, would not be a suitable relationship in which the affiliation motive could be satisfied or frustrated. We were led to this hypothesis by reasoning that both the obligatory nature of the love relationship between the parent and child and also the authoritative position of the parent can interfere with affiliative goals. This supposition seemed most warranted when we examined the relationships between affiliation motivation and maternal role reactions. The major conclusion from a review of our data is that there is little interaction between affiliation motivation and reactions to the maternal role. We view this as an indication that parents, and especially mothers, relate to their children mainly in ways that uphold their higher parental status and fulfill their nurturing obligations, but that do not establish personal affiliative relationships. We suggested in the section on mothers whose children were adults, that even with grown children, mothers never lose a sense of their children as their children. Most mothers probably do not consider even their grown children as independent adults with whom friendship relationships can or should be established. It was only for the college-educated mothers with preschool children that we found it useful to consider the idea that the mother seeks affiliative gratification directly in her relationship with her children.

The possibility that parenthood could be important for affiliative gratification because of its enhancement or interference with other potential sources of affiliation did seem to be somewhat more useful in understanding the results for the mothers. When we reexamined the results for mothers at the four different points in the life cycle, we noted that affiliation motivation had a consistent though low relationship to either feeling negative about, or restricted by, the role, although these trends were not significant at any point in the life cycle. This consistency may imply that motherhood is in some sense an interference with the ongoing affiliative concerns of women, and as a result women with high affiliation motivation are more likely to find motherhood restrictive. This type of interpretation is in keeping with the idea that affiliation motivation is primarily directed towards people who are similar to the self, and that children are not satisfying objects for affiliation. Therefore, women who are highly motivated to seek out affiliative relationships are the ones whom we would expect to be quick to perceive the ways in which the demands of parenthood limit contacts with the social world.

The negative impact that motherhood can have on the affiliative interests of women perhaps takes its greatest toll in women whose greatest contacts with the outside world are generally minimal. For mothers of preschool-age children, there was some tendency for affiliation motivation to be accompanied by what were interpreted as defensive reactions to being a mother. These women denied having any problems in raising their children, but felt restricted by and negative about motherhood.

We had also considered the idea that parenthood provides new bases for relating to other adults, new dimensions of perceived similarity to other parents, and therefore might enhance affiliative gratifications. This consideration did not seem useful in understanding our present data from mothers, but it did aid in our interpretations of the data from fathers. Fathers of young children—of preschool or school age—seem sensitized to the potential affiliative satisfactions attendant to the adult status of parenthood rather than to the responsibilities and restrictions of parenthood. The absence of a restrictive view of parenthood among men with high affiliation motivation was clearest for grade-school-educated fathers when their children were preschoolers. The initial favorable reactions to parenthood by a grade-school-educated man with high affiliation motive, in our view, rests on the assumption that being a parent enhances his potential interaction with others.

The affiliation motive also seems to bear on a father's reaction to the parent-child relationship itself, as well as to the effect the role has on other adult relationships. Fathers with high affiliation motive show an active concern with their affiliative relationships with their own children when they are of school age and then feel disappointment when this affiliative relationship is no longer continued in later years with the same tempo or impact. This disappointment is clearly expressed in the restrictive view of parenthood voiced by grade-school-educated men with high affiliation motivation when their children are adults. Our interpretation of this switch for grade-school-educated men rests on the supposition that their other sources of affiliative gratifications were somewhat limited in contrast to fathers at the other educational levels and hence they maintain their concern about affiliating with their children. Support for this view comes from Axelrod (1956), who reports that grade-school-educated men and women report less frequent associations with friends, neighbors, and coworkers, than do upper-status men and women. Our idea is specific to men; it can be examined in future research on affiliative behavior of men from different educational backgrounds.

Involvement in the parent-child relationship itself is also true of high-school and college-educated men. For the college-educated fathers it is most clearly seen at the school-age parental stage. At this period fathers with high affiliation motive exhibit parental distress. Their relationship with their child is apparently disrupted as the child moves into the peer culture at school; they doubt their own adequacy as fathers, and especially do not see themselves as fulfilling their obligations of spending time with their children. This is probably an instance where the sensitization principle is useful. It is not surprising that it is the college-educated men who exemplify this principle most strongly since they are probably the most involved in the psychological demands of parenthood and yet most subject to career pressures that take them away from their homes. However, college-educated fathers with a high affiliation motive do not seem to feel the affiliative frustrations that are ultimately in store for people who invest themselves in the parent-child relationship as a potentially mature, intimate relationship any more than fathers with a low affiliation motive feel such frustrations. These results suggest that affiliation in the social world is so automatic for higher status men, through their jobs and their inevitable social relationships requiring interpersonal intimacy, that they do not continue to invest the parent-child relationship with as much personal significance as men from the other status groups do, and especially not as much as the grade-school-educated fathers.

The high-school-educated father with high affiliation motivation maintains his investment in the affiliative aspects of the parent-child relationship through the adolescent stage. But this stage seems particularly problematic. Adolescence is a time when his children, previously untroubling to him during latency, begin to question his validity. The basis for a mature affiliative relationship is disrupted. Because the high-school-educated father, along with the college-educated father, can find affiliative fulfillment in activities outside the family—at work, or in organizations—he can be initially disappointed by this disruption; but it doesn't persist as children mature further, as it does for the fathers with lower educational status and fewer outside channels for affiliative gratification.

In summary, our results suggest that parenthood has different motivational significance for mothers and fathers, although high affiliation motivation is not easily satisfied in either the role of mother or father. Fathers appear to *attempt* to use the parent-child relationship itself as a source of affiliative satisfaction, more so than mothers. Perhaps the earlier greater intimacy of mother and child, or the more obligatory nature of the love relationship between mother and child, precludes this possibility. For mothers with high affiliation motivation, the impact of parenthood is mainly upon its interference with other affiliative contacts. Parenthood does not severely restrict other affiliative contacts for men, and in fact may enhance such contact. The total impact that fatherhood may have on the affiliative gratification for a man thus may depend on the availability of *other* sources of affiliative gratification. The more affiliative relationships are available, the greater the possible enhancement through parenthood. Furthermore, the more affiliative relationships are available, the greater chance there is to turn to these relationships when he finds his affiliative relationships with his children disappointing. We argue that such disappointment seems inevitable.

ACHIEVEMENT MOTIVATION AND PARENTAL REACTIONS

Earlier we suggested that parenthood could be relevant to parental achievement strivings in three ways: (1) achieving parenthood could be an accomplishment; (2) childrearing could be evaluated; (3) the child's achievements could be vicariously satisfying. The data suggest that all three possibilities do operate.

When children are very young, maternal achievement motivation seems to be important both in determining the mother's reactions to becoming a mother and to the process of childrearing itself. High-school-educated women seem to be most involved in the achievement goal of becoming mothers, while college-educated women seem to be most involved in the childrearing process as an achievement goal. Because her involvement is in the childrearing process itself, the maternal achievement satisfactions of college-educated women are dependent upon the varying socialization demands and gratifications at the different stages of the parental life cycle. In particular, her satisfaction about achievement seems to be dependent on how much feedback she can get from the rest of the world about her childrearing excellence. Thus at middle childhood there is a sense of adequacy with her own achievement as the feedback from the world increases with the child's entry into school.

The possibilities for vicarious achievement satisfactions through children's accomplishments may be relevant to mothers when children are adults, although mainly in their negative impact. The disappointment a mother feels about her child's failure to achieve her grand expectations for his accomplishments may be the reason why women with high achievement motivation are more likely to mention feeling inadequate about not spending enough time with her children. She may want to avoid contacts that remind her of her own disappointments. But on the whole, men are more likely to be striving for vicarious achievement satisfaction through their children than are women.

Work outside the home as a way to satisfy high achievement strivings can enhance positive feelings about motherhood when children are school age, but can lead to negative feelings about parenthood when children are adolescent. Thus, various groups of women attempt to satisfy their achievement strivings in different ways—in *being* a mother, in *doing* the kinds of things mothers are supposed to do, in *vicarious enjoyment* of their children's success, or in *working* outside the home. These various paths are accompanied by somewhat different reactions to parenthood. No one summary statement about maternal achievement motivation and parenthood is appropriate, since differentiation of roles according to social strata and life cycle seems very important in determining role reactions.

The attainment of the status of father, unlike that of mother, did not seem to be differentially related to parental role reactions for parents with high and low achievement motivation. However, in the early phases of fatherhood, achievement motivation seems to be related to the reactions fathers have to their enactment of the paternal roles, and to the reactions fathers have to meeting or not meeting the standards of excellence required in this role. Probably because at this stage of parenthood these standards are extremely ambiguous and because the fathers are not yet skilled at paternal behaviors, early experiences of fatherhood hold special problems for fathers with high achievement motivation. This seems to reflect the incongruence between their traditional achievement skills and the demands of fatherhood. Although fathers of preschoolers are the least likely of any age group to report parental inadequacy, those with high achievement motivation among the fathers of preschoolers do feel this way more often than those with low achievement motivation. The opposite occurs in later age cycles: feelings of adequacy are associated with a high achievement motive, as children mature. Men with a high achievement motive are more likely to be successful providers. Men who are successful providers may feel more adequate as fathers. At these stages there seems to be congruence between achievement motivation and paternal role demands.

The interaction between the satisfaction of achievement strivings as a worker and as a father is a central aspect of parental role reactions. This interaction can have positive as well as negative consequences. The negative effect can be seen for grade-school-educated fathers of adult children. Those men with high achievement motivation viewed parenthood significantly more negatively than their counterparts with low achievement motivation and tended to feel more inadequate as fathers. We interpreted this finding as reflecting their sensitivity to their own lack of attainment in the occupational world and their defensive reaction to not being successful models for their children. As men get older, they can also feel that their children have interfered with the possibility for career-achievement satisfactions, or children can be sources of financial obligations that necessitate achievement beyond their attainments.

Achievement-motivated men from a high-school background may also react defensively to their occupational accomplishments in the context of the parental role. In the latter part of the parental cycle the achievement motivation of these men was associated with feelings of parental adequacy. We suggested that these results may reflect some parental defensiveness. Compared to fathers who came from higher educational backgrounds, fathers who, by and large, held jobs that provided better for their families, these men of moderate status may feel relatively unsuccessful and hence inadequate as parental caretakers. Those men among them with high achievement motivation may be provoked into denying their shortcomings, into denying their feelings of parental inadequacy.

Vicarious achievement satisfactions seem more relevant for fathers than for mothers. At the school-age period, high-school-educated fathers with high achievement motivation seem to feel adequate about their enactment of the paternal role, probably reflecting successful efforts to meet the requirements of being a good provider, and also seem to enjoy the accomplishments of their children with a distancing orientation. At this age it seems easy for these fathers to enjoy their children's acquisition of skills and knowledge without feeling that their adequacy is threatened. Such vicarious pleasure through a distant orientation to the satisfactions of parenthood is more typical of the college-educated fathers when their children are adolescents and adults, when accomplishments are judged by more adult standards. These results suggest that perhaps grade-school-educated fathers rarely get to enjoy their children's accomplishments vicariously; the high-school-educated father does so only when his children are young, and the college-educated father only when his children are mature. There is little evidence of such vicarious achievement striving among women. Thus, our original idea, that as children grow older, they present more complete feedback for vicarious achievement or for looking at what a *parent* accomplishes, should be modified. Instead, there is variation in the period at which feedback about one's own effects on children and on children's accomplishments is important for parents' achievement gratification. This variation seems to be a function of the values of the particular social group to which a parent belongs.

POWER MOTIVATION AND PARENTAL REACTIONS

We started this chapter with the assumption that the influence function was one of the central parental role demands and that therefore parental power motivation would be an important determinant of parental role reactions. The results for both mothers and fathers clearly support this assumption and indeed for mothers, the power motive appears to be the most relevant motive for understanding reactions to the role of motherhood. The significance of power motivation for parental role reactions was expected to be strongly linked to the particular stage of the life cycle, with the relevance being high during the preschool stage, low at school age, and high again, though with more negative implications, at adolescence and adulthood. While these expectations were generally consistent with the data, there were some interesting deviations from them as well as some interesting variations for the several educational groupings. We will consider some of these variations now.

Power motivation seemed especially important for high-school-educated women, who perhaps more than any other group, feel that controlling children is an important potential source of gratification, and lack of control a potential source of difficulty. It was especially interesting to note that for high-school-educated women power motivation still played a particularly strong part in the reaction to parenthood when all their children were grown and living away from the parental home. In contrast, power motivation was no longer strongly predictive of reactions to parenthood for grade-school and college-educated women with mature children, although college- and grade-school-educated women with older children seemed to be defensive about their lack of influence with their grown children, if they had a high power motive. It was suggested that there was some retreat from efforts at control for the latter two groups as the children moved away from home, while for high-school-educated women, such control perhaps remained more intact as the children grew up. Power motivation was related to great feelings of affiliative inadequacies for older women in general, as it was for older men, indicating that interpersonal contacts with adult children may be perceived as means by which parents can maintain certain controls. We feel the data suggest that this contact is more the pattern of living for high-school-educated women than it is for the other two groups. There are other data to support this position.

The relationship between power motivation and a distancing orientation to children at certain periods in the life cycle was interpreted to mean that parents could experience fears of weakness in relationship to their children if they had high power motivation. We have noted that married men and women with high power motivation may avoid having children, perhaps out of an anticipated sense of weakness. They may be right. A sense of weakness does seem to develop from contact with the role per se. This sense of weakness may cause some disengagement from the role. Thus, a lack of congruence between power motivation and parenthood can produce a distancing orientation to the satisfactions of parenthood.

Working women who had high power motivation felt particularly inadequate as parents. Why should this be? Working removes attention from the socialization of children. Working women with high power motivation should be particularly sensitive to the influence demands of parenthood, and this sensitivity may cause self-doubt about the adequacy with which they are fulfilling the parental role. At the same time absence from the home because of work may prevent them from feeling *extremely* inadequate in the interpersonal struggle with children. A situational requirement—working—can be used as an excuse for lack of control. An employed woman might feel that she could have controlled her child had she been home. This realization might make her feel guilty about working but less defensive about her lack of influence. She thus might be freely expressing her own doubts about her adequacy at influence during a parental stage when it is difficult for most other parents to acknowledge their limited success at influencing their children.

Power motivation seems salient to the father's adjustment to the parental cycle also, but its relevance is heavily dependent on what stage of the parental cycle is considered. Power motivation seems to elicit feelings toward the parental role that are negative when children are mature. We have already mentioned the fact that affiliative inadequacies seem to be elicited by power motivation in fathers with older children. Although at the adult parental stage there were no significant relationships between having a negative orientation to children and power motivation, there were consistent trends in that direction. These trends were noteworthy because in the earlier stages power motivation tended to be related to positive attitude toward children. It would seem, therefore, that the role of father is much more compatible with power motivation when children are young than when the children become older. It appears that when children grow older they become a threat to the father's power and status and create feelings of paternal inadequacy and feelings of weakness in general. Perhaps fears of such feelings influence the decision to have children.

However, during the early years, children do seem to be sources of power gratification. At that point the father has social sanctions for influencing them, and this assertion of power may perhaps relieve frustrations to power he may experience in his major sphere of concern—his occupation. When children grow up, they can no longer be an easy target of influence for their father. This shift from children being easily influenced, to being resistant, occurs early in the life cycle for the least-educated fathers, at adolescence for those at moderate educational levels, and may even be prolonged to adulthood for the most-educated fathers.

REASSESSMENT OF THE PARENTAL ROLE

We had begun with the hypothesis that the two major functions of parenthood, nurturing and influencing, would be differentially elicited at different points in the parental life cycle. This general hypothesis seems to be well substantiated in the data. That is, depending upon different situations confronted by parents when their children are at different ages, there are variations in the relationships between parental role reactions and motives; the psychological significance of the role demands dramatically shifts. Let us now look at each of the major role characteristics in order to see what amplification we need to make in our description as a result of the findings in this chapter.

ROLE DEMANDS

The pattern of associations obtained between motives and role reactions in this study suggests that middle childhood is a time in our society when parents withdraw from some of the major role demands, nurturing and influencing, and replace them with a more specific role demand—skill teaching. Nurturing seems to be a very important demand for young mothers and fathers in their affiliative relationships with their adolescent children. Influencing seems to be most important as a demand for all fathers when the children are very young, but is important for all mothers for a much longer time—both when the children are very young and when they emerge from the home into school. It is as if the role demands shift for the two parents as their children grow up. The influence function initially starts out as the important demand for a father, but this diminishes at school age for the least-educated men, at adolescence for those with moderate education, and later for men at the highest educational level. However, for a father, the nurturing function increases as children mature, possibly as a revised route to influence. For women, the initial role demand of nurturing slowly diminishes and is replaced by the demand for influence and socialization. In passing, it could be pointed out that this pattern reflects an interesting interchange of parental demands which, if properly regulated, can lead to family stability. If there is any disproportionate use of these functions by either the mother or father at the wrong time, perhaps one can predict there would be family difficulties, both for the child and the parents.

ROLE GRATIFICATIONS

It is clear that direct achievement gratifications from the activities of parenthood seem primarily possible for women with higher educational status. Expectations of vicarious achievement gratifications from children seem more likely to be attained for men than for women. High-school-educated fathers seem particularly keyed to attain vicarious enjoyment of their children's achievements when their children are of school age, while college-educated fathers seem more keyed to attain such achievement satisfactions when their children are at least adolescent. The mere fact of being a parent seems to be an important source of gratification of achievement strivings at the early stages of parenthood for women of moderate educational status, but this source of achievement satisfaction does not appear important to women from other educational statuses, or to fathers.

Affiliative gratifications from parenthood seem to be clearest for fathers at the lowest educational status when their children are young. This may be as much a reflection of an enhanced social integration into the larger society that stems from their attainment of parenthood, as it is a reflection of any close feeling about the new found relationships with children. Generally speaking, however, affiliative gratifications are not easily attained from parenthood. Parents are more likely to be frustrated than gratified if they approach the parent-child relationship with expectations about an enduring intimate, friendship-like relationship. The loving bond between parent and child has obligations and complications.

Parents and children are rarely "friends." The initial dependence of children on their parents, and their gradual movement away from this dependence often prevents a mature affiliative relationship from developing between mother and child, or father and child.

Power gratification comes from very early influence functions that all mothers and fathers are required to fulfill, but such gratification is especially available to those parents who are psychologically involved in the meaning of parenthood. Continued power gratification from parenthood seems possible only among mothers who have some awareness that there will be a continuing close contact between the parent and child when the child is grown up and on his own. Such a situation seems to exist for mothers who are with moderate educational status. If anything, the opposite is true for mothers of the other social strata, and for fathers in general. As children mature, most parents feel that they will lose control. A sense of power weakness can mushroom either at adolescence or when children leave home—especially among fathers. The later stages of fatherhood in modern America are more likely to be sources of increased power frustrations than of increased power gratification, in contrast to what changes must occur in societies where there is veneration of the old and the wise.

ROLE AMBIGUITIES

A number of major role ambiguities about parenthood in the United States have been suggested by the present study. Such ambiguities are clearly present in motive-role interactions to which the sensitization principle can be effectively applied. Sometimes we expected ambiguities in this role and there did not seem to be any. We would suggest that such circumstances occurred when the sensitization principle did not apply at all, indeed, when motive-role interaction was minimal.

For the least-educated mothers we appear to be dealing with a version of the maternal role with little ambiguity, a role that is so narrowly defined that the possibility for variations in role reactions to be related to motives is minimal. There was a total lack of relationships between parental reactions and motives for grade-school-educated women. We would argue that there is little ambiguity in this role. What is expected of mothers from the social group is so specific, that the sensitization principle did not apply, nor is it likely to in further study of motive-role interaction in parenthood.

From our overview of the instances of motive-role interaction to which the sensitization principle could be applied, we find that three ambiguities about parenthood seemed to stand out. Let us discuss each.

First, *during school age and adolescence, should children be appropriate affiliative objects for a father or mother?* As we anticipated in Chapter 1, there is an overriding ambiguity for parents in America. Are they *authorities* who assert influence? Or are they *permissive friends* who indirectly promote socialization? Women especially are unsure about whether they should react to children as close associates, potential friends and companions, although men seem to suffer from this ambiguity about the role, too.

Second, *at what point does the influence that a parent has over his child effectively cease?* There is no legal ambiguity. All fathers and mothers are responsible for the children's unsocialized behavior until the child is legally responsible for his own action in society. In our country we might take the age at which the states charge a child with a crime, rather than his parents, as the legal age when parental influence should cease. Psychologically, however, it is not so easy to pinpoint this shift in influence potential for a parent. High-school-educated mothers seem to act as if this potential never ceases. Mothers at the other two educational levels act as if adolescence was the last period in a child's life wherein they, as mothers, could exert influence. These confusions in expectations for mothers make it difficult for them to respond without conflict. A similar conflict exists for fathers, but perhaps they even extend this ambiguity downward to earlier ages. Some men at lower educational levels act as if their influence over their children ceases when the children enter school. And the college-educated fathers seem to have expectations that they can extend their influence into their children's adulthood.

A final ambiguity about parenthood is: *how much achievement gratification can there be in the day-to-day necessities for the care of small children?* Both mothers and fathers seem to suffer from this ambiguity. Parents at upper educational levels structured the role of parent of preschoolers with the same achievement orientation that they approached other tasks, as if children were products to be fashioned to certain standards of excellence. This view of the parental role in early childhood has been bred in the college classroom and is gradually seeping into less-educated circles. Unless the society as a whole adopts this psychological framework to parenthood, there will always remain the more traditional attitude to childrearing that will compete with the more psychological one; these competing orientations serve to make the requirements and gratifications of parenthood very ambiguous.

5

Motives and Work

Turning from parenthood to work, we are turning from
the role that is traditionally the major domain for women to the
role that is traditionally the prime domain for men. As a woman may feel
that bearing and caring for children may be the
way she can demonstrate to herself and others that she is a valid
individual and truly deserving of the title of adult, so a man finds his adult
validity in work, in providing for a family and in performing
activities prescribed to him from society's unwritten law
that men must labor to keep the society in operation. Very few
men will accept the opportunity to avoid work as a
possible way of life. In this connection a very interesting result has
emerged from examinations of the job role in
repeated national surveys done by the Survey Research Center.
Most employed American men say
that they would continue working even if there was no
economic necessity for them to do so (see, for example, Morse and
Weiss, 1955); only about 20 percent would stop
working. Men's activities in work evidently provide for them the sense
that they are doing what they are supposed to do.
When society does not permit a man to work, or when a man is
incapacitated, severe problems arise. In a society
like ours, where men are likely both to enjoy a decreasing
work week and to survive past retirement age, a new psychological question has emerged for investigation: what

happens to a man's psychic economy when he is given a sanctioned opportunity for leisure?

This is not to say that men will work no matter what the obstacles. Many men cannot hold jobs for very long because their motivations or expectations interfere with their performance at work or prevent them from coming to work. It has been suggested that many men in our society are unmotivated to perform their jobs, not because they dislike work but because their jobs give them little personal dignity (Goodman, 1960). Many of the unemployed can only locate jobs that promise no security and that offer little in the way of psychological returns and little assurance that they are performing an important task.

In spite of instances where men clearly are their own obstacles to performing well at work, we generally will assume that for men to be alive is to work and to be a man is to work. But what are a man's expectations about what "work" should be like? Obviously, answers to this question will vary according to the cultural context the man exists in, his particular subcultural reference group, his educational background, and work attitudes in his family of origin and in his family of procreation. We would like to examine some of these problems in this chapter.

Expectations about work in American society reflect a strong Calvinistic ideology; we have inherited a view that it is good to work hard and if you do not work hard, somehow you are an inadequate individual. Not all societies or cultures harbor such an exaggerated attitude towards industriousness, some are more nonchalant about it. The Sunday neurosis, men fidgeting and not knowing what to do with themselves in leisure, would be an anomaly in some of the countries around the Mediterranean and certainly in Bali. With enforced leisure on the increase, perhaps this country will have to shift to a more benign attitude towards leisure. Perhaps at that point in our society we will find ourselves in a transition from a severe Calvinistic attitude toward work to a less moral stance.

Many American men raised to believe in the morality of work, and raised to believe that their acceptance of themselves and their acceptance by others depends on how well they perform at a job, often have to "prove themselves" at work. They do not treat their failures lightly; anxieties about performance pervade the job setting. Perhaps our society is moving to a less moral approach to work. If so, work may cause fewer of these anxieties, and men can be free to express more positive motives in work. Without anxiety about performance, men may be free to enjoy mastery experiences or affiliative possibilities at work. In either case, whether men are experiencing anxiety or finding ways of meeting positive goals, we would expect that men's motives influence their selection and adjustment in work. This will be the central focus of this chapter.

MOTIVES IN THE GENERAL CONTEXT OF
WORK AND LEISURE

How do motives interact with major demands of the job role to influence job selection and adjustment? In listing the major characteristics of the job role in Chapter 1, the only common primary role demand we cited was that some type of activity within certain definitions of accomplishment was required of all working men. This activity can take quite different forms; men can socially interact with others at work or can work with some inanimate object; men can solve new problems at work, or be rather automatic in their responses. Although many different types of activity are required in different jobs, they are all *performances* of certain kinds that *can be evaluated*. Work is a performance potentially evaluated by oneself or by others. Thus, a man's job, his job role, is in potential interaction with his achievement motivation. A job can be more or less demanding with regard to a person's achievement capacities; a job can be more or less difficult; a job can be more or less of a stimulant to a man's evaluation of his own achievement capacities.

In the course of trying to meet job requirements, a man can also come in contact with social demands to influence others or to be influenced, or to engage in affiliative relationships. Although these activities may not be necessary aspects of job performance or may not be evaluated, the social requirements of jobs can interact with social motives to determine job reactions or to determine whether the job is initially attractive to the individual. Thus, work can affect the gratification of men's affiliation and power motivations, as well as their achievement motivation.

Work, being both a requirement for men to achieve adult recognition and an activity where performance interacts with men's motives, can potentially affect men's gratifications in two ways: work in its *universal* role significance, and work as defined by the *particular* activity required in the performance of the specific job. Merely having a job, any type of job, can be gratifying for a man with a certain motive, or can lead to certain problems for a man with another type of motive. Furthermore, having a *particular* job, with the particular kinds of activities that it requires, can lead to different reactions in a man, depending on his motivation. We will be interested in this chapter in both types of explanations of motive-role interaction in the job role. We will be interested in ways in which affiliation, achievement, and power motivation may determine reactions to being a "worker," and we will be interested in ways in which affiliation, achievement, and power motivation determine feelings of adjustment on particular types of jobs. The interpretations we will give to results in this chapter will depend on viewing men with high or low motive levels sometimes as reacting to being employed, and sometimes as reacting to the particular characteristics of their jobs. These dual interpretations parallel the two interpretations of goal conditions we saw as underlying interactions between parental role and motives: *being* a parent and what that represents; and *reacting* to the activities that are specifically required in that role. The general distinction is between *being* in a certain position and *doing* the specific activity that the role requires. Our interest in this distinction is how each of these relates to motivational reactions.

The presentation of results in this chapter will be organized around two main aspects of motive-work interaction: *job selection* and *job reactions*. In the next section of this chapter we will describe the motives that were found to typify men in certain positions, and we will interpret these findings as indicating the impact that motives have on job selection. And in the following section, the major focus of this chapter, we will examine the relationship of motives to reactions in the job itself.

In the third section of this chapter, we will examine the relationships between men's motives and certain aspects of their use of leisure time. We have anticipated that the relative diminution of the importance of the job role in American society has increased the value of leisure activities for men. Therefore, some of the results concerning motive-job role interactions may be clarified by examining some of the relationships between motives and leisure activities.

Before considering these three aspects of the job role and leisure activities, we will first discuss the bases we used to infer variations in job-role characteristics and the subjects used in the analyses.

INFERRING ROLE CHARACTERISTICS FROM SPECIFIC OCCUPATIONS, GENERAL OCCUPATIONAL CHARACTERISTICS, AND AGE

In the analysis of the job role, unlike the marital and parental roles, the primary basis for inferring job characteristics was the specific job the respondent held rather than the general status characteristics of the respondents. Five such job-related distinctions were used, in addition to the age of the subject. Here we will mainly describe the classification schemes we utilized for these job-related distinctions, and in the succeeding sections on job selection and job reactions, we will describe the relationships that we expected to find when we used these job qualities to analyze motive-role interaction. Then in the section on job selection, we present the relationships of the three motives to each of these job characteristics in order to determine whether men with different types of motives select jobs with these different characteristics. In the section on job reactions, we present the relationships of the three motives to each of the job reactions, separately for subjects differing in these job characteristics.

SPECIFIC OCCUPATIONS

The most obvious source of role variations occurs when we specify the class of job an individual holds. Because sociologists have concentrated on this type of analysis for many years, we have a clearer view of what role characteristics will potentially interact with the motivational dispositions of affiliation, achievement, and power in the occupational role than in the marital and parental roles. There has been more attention in the empirical literature to occupational roles than to either the marital or parental roles. We did not have enough subjects in any particular occupation to analyze our data within very specific occupational groups. Therefore, we limited ourselves to ten relatively homogeneous occupational groupings that could be distinguished by grouping respondents on the three-digit occupational classification as specified by the United States Bureau of the Census (1950). These groupings are listed below:

1. *Professional advisers:* teachers, lawyers, judges, recreation leaders, clergymen, social workers. The common characteristic of this group is that each job in some way demands influence skills.
2. *Self-employed businessmen and managers* who are owners or part-owners of industries or businesses. Self-employed artisans and craftsmen are excluded.
3. *Non-self-employed managers and officials* in industry.
4. *Salesmen* who are not self-employed: advertising agents or salesmen; auctioneers; demonstrators; insurance agents and brokers; real estate agents and brokers; stock and bond salesmen. This category excludes lower status sales workers such as retail store clerks.
5. *Clerical workers.* This category excludes attendants and tellers and other clerical workers dealing primarily with people.
6. *Foremen* in industry.
7. *Skilled workers* in industry (other than foremen), as well as other craftsmen.
8. *Semiskilled workers* in factories, mines, mills, or in the transportation industries.
9. *Unskilled workers.* This category excludes farm laborers and private household or other such service workers.
10. *Farmers:* farm operators or tenant farmers. This category excludes sharecroppers and farm managers.

We expected that each of these occupational groupings would be characterized by different specific role demands, gratifications and ambiguities, and will discuss some of these differences in succeeding sections. Furthermore, with the exception of the farmer, these occupations are listed in a rough prestige hierarchy. At times we will be using two different groups of these occupations—the white collar and the blue collar. The white collar occupations include the first five and the blue collar the next four. Each of these groups in turn has its own prestige hierarchy, from highest to lowest, in the order we have listed the specific occupations.

GENERAL OCCUPATIONAL CHARACTERISTICS

Regardless of the specific work activities involved in a job, there are other important characteristics that help specify job demands and gratifications. One of these general job characteristics is found in the public prestige accorded a job. The above listing of the ten specific job categories, with the exception of the place given the farmers, could be viewed as a crude status hierarchy of jobs. In turn, it could be interpreted as reflecting the prestige of the job as experienced by the occupants of the jobs and by the public. However, we had available more specific ratings of the public's evaluation of the prestige of various jobs, done by Crockett (1962) in a specific analysis of achievement motivation in men for this sample. We decided to use this measure of prestige as the definition of the social-status characteristic of the job role. The ratings used by Crockett were based on the National Opinion Research Center's (1953) survey in 1947 of the prestige accorded various occupations by the general public. Not all occupations that occurred in our sample were included in that study. Therefore, a number of occupations had to be individually rated, with prestige ratings assigned by criteria of education and income. Crockett's procedure (1961) generally results in a status hierarchy that overlaps that produced by the census classification, but there are some exceptions. We used Crockett's groupings of subjects into those with high and low *Prestige*, which were based on these prestige ratings. This two-way categorization was an a priori grouping based to some extent on the empirical distribution obtained with his sample. However, the distribution was not evenly split; there were many more respondents in the *Low Prestige* group than in the *High Prestige* group.

It was possible to classify all subjects into these two groups, those in jobs with *High Prestige* and those in jobs with *Low Prestige*. In the analysis of job selection, we considered whether men with different levels and types of motives were more or less likely to hold jobs with *High Prestige*. In the analysis of job reactions, we considered the relationship between motives and job reactions separately for men in jobs with *High Prestige* and *Low Prestige*.

We had suggested in Chapter 1 that one of the general secondary role demands of the job role concerned the nature of the social interaction—the extent to which social interaction was required by the work activity itself. Asking whether social interaction is a requirement of a job is different than asking how much contact there is with people on the job.

A man working in a machine shop is not required to interact with other people in order to do his job, but he may have considerable contact with others on the job. We regard the social stimulation of work associates as being different from the social requirements of the job. It would have been useful for our purposes to have a measure of social stimulation over and above the measure of social requirements of the job, but this measure was not available in the data. To determine the *Social Requirements* of jobs we first reviewed the 47 job classifications into which the subjects' jobs had originally been classified.[1] We noted that the jobs in which the work activities required social interaction were prevalent only in prestigeful jobs. Therefore, the assessment of social requirements of the job was made only for those jobs with *High Prestige*, described previously, and when analyses are reported using this role characteristic, only respondents holding *High Prestige* jobs are included. We divided all jobs in the *High Prestige* group into those low or high in *Social Requirements* on the basis of our judgments of whether or not social interaction with other persons was required for successful completion of the work activities of the job. For this task, we relied upon our general knowledge of the work activities of various jobs, supplemented by the *Dictionary of Occupational Titles* (U.S. Bureau of Employment Security, 1949). Examples of how occupations were coded for *Social Requirements* appear in Table 5.1.

Information on two other kinds of social demands were available to us; they concerned the supervisory relations experienced by the specific occupants of different jobs. This information was based on the respondents'

TABLE 5-1 EXAMPLES OF JOBS CODED HIGH AND LOW IN SOCIAL REQUIREMENTS

Jobs High in Social Requirements	Jobs Low in Social Requirements
Doctors	Engineers
Lawyers	Physical scientists
Teachers	Accountants
Clergymen	Airplane pilots
Social workers	Self-employed artisans
Self-employed businessmen	Plumbers
Real estate men	Contractors
Investment broker	Jewelers
Retail store managers	Farmers
Foremen	

[1]These 47 job categories resulted from a two-digit classification which was, in turn, based on the three-digit occupational classification scheme of the U.S. Bureau of the Census (1950). All respondents' jobs were coded into the two-digit classification scheme as part of the original coding of the interview schedules for the larger study.

own descriptions of the supervisory relationship in their jobs. Unlike *Prestige* and *Social Requirements*, therefore, these distinctions are based on responses of individuals rather than assumptions about jobs. We distinguished subjects whose jobs were high and low in *Supervision* and those whose jobs were high and low in *Supervisory Potential*.[2]

The dichotomy on *Supervision* was based on the replies of the men who were not self-employed to the following series of questions:

Do you work under anyone—supervisor or anyone in charge of your work?
(IF YES) Just how much does he (she) have to do with you and your work?

Respondents who indicated that no one supervised their work or that the person who supervised them had "little or nothing" to do with their work were coded as in jobs with *Low Supervision;* the remaining subjects were coded as holding jobs with *High Supervision.*

We also asked the same sample of subjects, who were not self-employed:

Do you have any people working under you? (IF YES) How many?

We grouped the respondents according to whether or not they had any other person working under them. Those who supervised at least one other person were considered as having a job of *High Supervisory Potential* and those who did not supervise anyone were considered to be in a job of *Low Supervisory Potential.*

In reporting the results concerning both motives and job selection and motives and job reactions, the four general occupational classifications and the ten specific occupations are used to define different types of job roles. Because of our limited number of subjects, the occupational classifications can be used only singly rather than simultaneously. In this section, therefore, we would like to consider their possible interrelationships, for with such knowledge we will be better prepared to know when results using one of these occupational classifications is independent, or dependent on a parallel result using another occupational classification.

We first considered whether any of the specific occupations were distinctively represented in any of the general occupational categories. (See Appendix B, Table 5.a for the data relevant to this question.) Several noteworthy instances of this sort were found.

1. The occupations that were high in measured *Prestige* were the professional advisers, managers, foremen, and farmers; all other specific

---

[2]The series of questions on which these categorizations were based were asked on only one form of the interview schedule. Therefore, the number of subjects available for these distinctions is approximately half the total sample for this chapter.

occupations were coded low in *Prestige*. Such relationships between the gross prestige grouping and the classes of specific occupations were expected in view of the occupational bases of the *Prestige* ratings. However, two aspects of these results should be highlighted. The first is the fact that most farmers were high in *Prestige*. This is mainly the result of the fact that our definition of this category excluded tenant farmers and share-croppers. The fact that we are dealing with the more entrepreneurial, independent farmer should be kept in mind in future speculation about the nature of the farmer role. The second relationship requiring comment is that the salesmen were all low in *Prestige*, despite the fact that the lowest status sales jobs, such as in the retail trades, were excluded from this category. It should be pointed out that the prestige rank of many jobs in this occupation, such as insurance salesman, stock and bond salesman, fell just below the cutting point developed by Crockett to divide the low from the high *Prestige* categories.

2.   The *Social Requirements* characterizing the specific occupational groups were uniformly high for the professional advisers, managers who were not self-employed, and foremen, were generally high for the self-employed managers as well, and were uniformly low only for the farmers.[3]

3.   The *Supervision* and *Supervisory Potential* ratings did not as sharply differentiate the ten specific occupational groups as did those of *Prestige* or *Social Requirements*.[4] Those occupations that were most highly supervised among the blue-collar jobs were the semi-skilled workers and unskilled workers, and among the white-collar jobs, the clerical workers. Those jobs with generally high *Supervisory Potential* were the managers and foremen.

We also considered the relationships among the four general occupational characteristics. (See Appendix B, Table 5.b.) The relationships obtained were all within our expectations about these job characteristics. *Prestige* was negatively related to *Supervision* and positively related to *Supervisory Potential*. Furthermore, among the high *Prestige* subjects whose jobs were classified for *Social Requirements*, those whose jobs required social

---

[3]The remaining five specific occupational groups were low in *Prestige*, and therefore were not rated for *Social Requirements*. Many persons with *High Prestige* jobs did not have jobs that were included in the ten specific occupational groups—for example, accountants, engineers, and a large proportion of these subjects were in jobs classified as low in *Social Requirements*.

[4]It should be noted that the more dramatic distinctions among the specific occupational groups along the *Prestige* and *Social Requirements* criteria were partly due to our method of classifying subjects on the general occupational characteristics. *Prestige* and *Social Requirements* were coded using the U.S. Census Bureau's detailed occupational classification scheme, and it was from this same source that the *Specific Occupations* were accumulated. The other general occupational classifications were coded on the basis of the respondents' replies to questions about supervisory structure in their specific job situation.

interaction, received less supervision in their jobs than those in jobs that did not require social interaction. The relationship between *Social Requirements* and *Supervisory Potential* tended to be in the opposite direction, but this association was not significant. And the amount of *Supervision* in a job was negatively related to its *Supervisory Potential*. These interrelations suggest that we need to be cautious in interpreting parallel findings for two different job characteristics that in turn are interrelated.

AGE

As in our analysis of marriage and parenthood, we had every reason to believe that in the analysis of the job role age differences would lead to important inferences about role characteristics that affect motive-role interactions. In *Americans View Their Mental Health* we concluded that age plays an important part in determining how men feel about their work. In particular, we noted that as men grow older they begin to consolidate their attitudes and feelings about their work. Perhaps most important, older men seem to view their work in a way that would tend to guarantee fulfillment of their earlier expectations about their work: "... age seems to bring both an increase in satisfaction and a diminution of problems in the work area. This relationship between age and problems ... suggests that age brings a growing adaptation to a role, a minimization of aspiration and accomplishment" (Gurin et al., 1960, p. 169). Thus, older men may tend to be defensive about their feelings of failure or their lack of fulfillment from working.

We would thus propose that different problems in their work confront men of different ages. The demands, gratifications, and ambiguities of a job may be similar for younger or older men in the same position, but these role characteristics take on new meanings when approached by men of different ages. In the early period of work most men approach their jobs with some awareness that there is the possibility of changing their place of employment and even changing the kind of job they hold. A major problem they face as young men, therefore, is job selection. As men become older they become less mobile both in the occupational hierarchy and in their actual job location. They react to the characteristics of their job with this knowledge. Thus, middle-aged men begin to think of their particular job as a relatively permanent position. Investment in *particular* jobs can occur. The major work problems men of middle age face are found in the job itself, in the ease with which they can fill the job demands, in the degree of motive satisfaction or dissatisfaction they can obtain, and in the ambiguities about the job demands or gratification potentials. In old age the possibility arises that one's changed physical status or lack of new knowledge may interfere with meeting the continued or changing role demands. Loss of the job or decreased proficiency at job performance becomes an issue. The major work problem of old men is maintaining a sense of adequacy at the job for fear of losing one's work status or respect from family or colleagues.

Two findings reported earlier illustrate these differences:

[There was] . . . a very strong relationship between age and the response to the question on whether or not one would rather be doing some other kind of work. Whereas 52 percent of the youngest group, twenty-one to thirty-four years of age, express a desire for some other kind of work, this desire is expressed by only 25 percent of the oldest group (fifty-five years and over). The second finding relates to the differences in the nature of the work problems discussed by the several age groups . . . . The younger men more often mention problems indicative of the unsettled nature of their work choice—problems in vocational choice, dissatisfaction with a job that is not need-satisfying, problems in meeting the demands of a job. The older workers, on the other hand, more often refer to problems that do not reflect on the work itself or on the particular choice they have made. Thus, they speak in terms of such things as failures in health, dissatisfaction with certain extrinsic aspects of a job, problems that arose because of external factors (such as losing a job when the company closed) [Gurin et al., 1960, pp. 170-171].

We found further corroboration for this latter conclusion for the men in the sample used in this chapter. For these men the following additional information is relevant: (1) older men mentioned achievement dissatisfactions (for example, "There's no chance to show my ability.") less often than the younger men (gamma = $-.23$, $p < .05$ for tau beta); (2) older men mentioned economic dissatisfactions ("The pay is low.") more often than younger men (gamma = $.28$, $p < .05$ for tau beta); (3) older men were less likely to say that they were very satisfied with the people they worked with than younger men (gamma = $-.24$, $p < .05$ for tau beta). All of these reactions reflect the greater direct emotional investment that younger men have in their work when compared to older men. The younger men are more committed to the actual ongoing psychological life at work, including achievement activities and affiliative relationships, while the older men are more concerned with the extrinsic aspects of the job role.

Thus we have good evidence that in the sample we will be exploring in this chapter, age will be an important variable that reflects the psychological commitments that men have both to having a job and to doing the work required in their job. A man's age will be a very important conditioning variable in describing motive-role interactions. One expectation is that older men, being less committed to the activity in work per se and being more committed to the fact of holding a job, might show fewer instances where their motivations directly influence their role reactions. The younger men, being more invested in their work, perhaps will evidence more consistent and meaningful patterns of results in the analysis of motive-work interaction. Thus, where the sample size is sufficient, we will look at the relationships between motives and job reactions separately for different age groups.

Where we can, we will also control for age in motive-job selection analyses. When we look at what motives are associated with different types of jobs, we may get some insights into the relationships that motives might have to job selection. In order to infer such relationships, however, we have to assume that the measure of the motives is a relatively constant, stable measure. We have made this assumption for this research effort, but we wish to underscore that we assume that the measures are *relatively* stable measures of motives. A long period of socialization in a job may indeed affect a man's motives. We admit this possibility, although we have generally taken the stand that we are looking at motives as stable dispositions over the life span. If we assume that there is some socialization of motives in the job itself, it is only when we look at the results for younger age groups that we will be in a good position to infer how motives determine job selection. Presumably the older age groups will represent men who have experienced greater socialization into their jobs than the younger age groups. In older groups where motives mesh with certain jobs, the congruence may not only be the result of selection by the role occupant but the result of socialization of the role occupant while he has been in the job.

SUBJECTS

Throughout this chapter we will be examining the responses of a maximum of 466 men.[5] This was the entire subset of white males who held full-time jobs and who gave adequate responses to the thematic apperceptive measures of motives. As we noted in Chapter 2, the criterion of an adequate protocol to measure motivation yielded a sample that was somewhat biased due to the overrepresentation of men in higher occupational status positions. This sample does, however, approximate a representative sample of full-time employed men in our society at the time of the interview in 1957.

In the tables to follow, there will be variations in the total number of subjects for whom the results are reported. These discrepancies could result from two sources. First, a small number of subjects did not give adequate responses to each question used to measure job reactions or job

[5]The number of subjects available within each type of job classification and at each age level is reported in Appendix B, Table 5.c page 387. Except for the specific occupations, the number of subjects available within each job classification was of substantial size.

characteristics. Second, certain of the occupational classifications did not apply to all subjects, either because the measure did not pertain to them or because there were insufficient data available. These limitations were described in the previous section.

In the next section we consider what relationship motives might have to job selection. In subsequent sections, we will analyze the relationship of motives to job reactions, and finally, motives to leisure. In each one of these contexts we will first try to clarify our theoretical expectations about each of the motives, describe special procedures of assessment in each section, and finally, present the relevant results. As in the two preceding chapters, we will present a synopsis of the major results of each section before giving detailed accounts of the results. We hope that by examining these different aspects of motive-role interaction we can gain a better understanding of the effects that affiliation, achievement, and power motivations may have on adjustment to work.

MOTIVES AND JOB SELECTION

Men obviously differ greatly in the ways they approach the problem of initially finding a suitable occupation for themselves. Some young men are forced into the job market long before they finish high school or before they have the amount of education they might consider necessary for the work of their choice. Others apparently stumble into the job market unconcerned about their educational preparation, either because they may inaccurately judge the educational requirements of the job market or because they may consider it as irrelevant to success in life. Still others plan their careers very carefully and, acknowledging the vital importance of education, persist even in the face of economic hardships and other obstacles to get the appropriate training for the type of career that they have staked out for themselves. These different approaches to job selection are probably highly correlated with the positions of social status that young men find themselves in as they grow up. The higher the status, the more planning is likely to occur for a career choice. Even though there may be a high correlation between social status and the amount of planning young men do about job selection, we still should find within various social strata many factors that also influence job selection. It is easy to enumerate a number of circumstantial factors that might underlie different approaches to job selection. A young man may be so absorbed in alleviating his state of financial deprivation that the major basis for his job selection is to find the shortest route to money. Or another might consistently seek jobs that give him a chance to move ahead in order to satisfy the demands of a nagging wife. Still another might select a ready-made route to success—to do what his father does, to join his father's firm, or to continue an inherited business. However, it is the assumption of the present investigation that in addition to factors of social background and to circumstantial factors of the sort just enumerated, initial selection and resulting achievement of job goals are likely to be influenced by qualitative differences in the motives that characterize individuals and that define for them the kinds of satisfactions they are predisposed to seek in their work. This assumption stems from each of the guiding principles we have been operating under. According to the sensitization principle persons with high motive levels are likely to perceive features of jobs that are relevant to their motives, providing there is some ambiguity in job characteristics. The congruence principle implies that men seek out and remain in job-role situations that are congruent with their motives and, conversely, that they are more likely to leave jobs that are not congruent with their motives.

A substantial fund of past research about affiliation, achievement, and power motivations provides a useful basis for our hypotheses concerning how these motives might be related to the individual's choice of an occupation, his efforts to climb to a position of higher status, or his desire to seek a certain quality of satisfaction from work. What, then, are the attributes of occupations that might be motivationally relevant to selecting or maintaining a certain type of job? What are the dimensions of jobs to consider when we relate affiliation, achievement, and power motives to job selection? Let us examine these questions for each motive separately. In an examination we should keep in mind that there may be different conceptions of role characteristics as perceived by men who are *not yet in the role* and by those who are already *in* the role, or as viewed by social scientists and by role occupants. The former contrast can be seen in the disparity between the initial role perceptions of entering medical students who choose to specialize in psychiatry and the later role perceptions of these men as they begin to gain actual clinical experience. Perhaps they initially choose psychiatry because they perceive that it offers many social potentials, but later they probably find that the therapeutic demands in the role preclude the social gratifications they anticipated, a phenomenon Wheelis (1958) so well dramatizes in *The Quest for Identity*. We will be thinking of the motive-relevant characteristics of roles as if men not yet in the role saw the role *accurately*. In certain cases this assumption will be in error.

THEORETICAL BACKGROUND

Affiliation motivation and job selection   There are a number of ways to look at the affiliation potential a job has. We have previously discussed affiliation motivation as the desire to avoid aloneness. On this basis we might expect that men with a high affiliation motive would avoid jobs where they worked alone, classic examples of which are being a fire watcher or a lighthouse keeper. If we assumed that mere contact with other people can be an affiliative satisfaction, we could determine whether other people are present or whether contact is possible. Except for a few jobs, contact with people in some form or other occurs in most job settings. How much contact the person has with another person on the job sometimes depends on his own interest in establishing or maintaining a social relationship. Therefore, perhaps we should focus on another series of questions to determine the affiliation potential in a job: Is contact with other people a usual but optional part of the job? Does the person's work *require* that he come in contact with people? And if contact is required, what is the nature of this contact? The distinction that is important here is illustrated by the contrast between the assembly line operator and the retail store salesman. The former job may place the individual in the same room with hundreds of other people, and may permit him to talk with the operators adjacent to him, but the job does not require contact with other persons for its successful completion. The job of the salesman, on the other hand, cannot be carried out adequately unless he talks with, establishes rapport with, and tries to influence another person. His job depends on his social skill. Our examination of the research on affiliation motivation suggested that the kind of relationship required with other people at work should be an important aspect of its affiliative attraction. The quality and kind of supervision that one receives on the job, the quality and kinds of supervising that may have to be done as part of one's job, the quality of the interactions with others who have reciprocal roles, each is also an aspect of a job that can establish whether or not a man with high affiliation motivation will be attracted to it.

We assume that a person with high affiliation motivation would not be attracted to jobs where the job requirements could easily result in his being disliked, since the fear of rejection is probably a strong component of affiliation motivation. Thus, supervising the work of others may not be an attractive characteristic of a job for men with high affiliation motivation. Another social requirement of jobs that could deter persons with high affiliation motivation would be the necessity of trying to influence other persons, especially from a position of authority. On this basis we would assume that an advising profession could be unattractive to men with high affiliation motivation if it did not also require considerable display of nurturance. Teaching may be a good illustration of an advising profession that amalgamates nurturance and the use of authority. Students often like teachers because teachers nurture them, but they often dislike teachers because teachers continually try to influence them from their position of authority. Therefore, we may in general think that although high affiliation-motivated men would be attracted to occupations that require social activity on the job, they would be wary of those jobs, like being a teacher or foreman, where there is a possibility that they may be rejected by the people they are in contact with.

Jobs in which there is close supervision, however, may provide affiliative gratification. Prior research has shown that approval-seeking is a characteristic of men with high affiliation motivation and ingratiating oneself with the supervisor may be a vehicle for obtaining approval. The kinds of supervision received should be important in this regard. Jobs in which supervision is accomplished by subtle means, by establishing friendly relationships with the supervisee and jobs in which there is some mutuality experienced in the supervisor-supervisee relationship, might attract men with high affiliation motivation. Supervision by assertion of authority, or jobs where there is a wide social distance between supervisor and worker, may not permit a man with high affiliation motivation to view the approval of his supervisor as an affiliative response.

In another sense, however, both parties to supervisory relationships might find this contact an unsatisfactory means of attaining affiliative goals. It has been suggested that the aim of the affiliation motive is the warm acceptance by a person who is *similar to the affiliation seeker*—by a peer. This would suggest that the presence of colleagues or coworkers *at the same status level* would be a critical dimension for describing jobs with high affiliation potential. Men in a higher status position would in this sense be an irrelevant target of affiliative strivings. Although we do not have any direct measures of the "colleague potential" of a job for our respondents, certain kinds of occupations typically occur in settings where this potential is obvious and upon occasion we will point to such a characteristic of jobs in interpreting our results.

Another possible prediction about men with high affiliation motivation is that they may be interested in jobs where the requirements for work are clear and unconflicted. Some of Schachter's (1959) findings, and other more recent ones (Zimbardo and Formica, 1963), suggest that the affiliative syndrome is based on moving toward others who lend emotional support for feelings of anxiety. If a job is characterized by conflicting information about what is expected of the job holder, if too many people put demands on him, demands that may in fact be in conflict with one another, then a person with high affiliation motivation should be less attracted to this kind of job.

In summary, we have suggested that there are a number of relevant characteristics of jobs that may attract or repel men with high affiliation motivation. Perhaps the most important job characteristic is how much option for social interaction the role occupant is allowed. We can see, however, that the mere presence of others, the status relationships with others, and the clarity of the work demands are also relevant. However, as was the case in our theoretical discussions of affiliation motivation and marriage or parenthood, our predictions are not clear-cut.

Achievement motivation and job selection Particularly important in a job's attractiveness for a person with high achievement motivation is its generally recognized status or prestige. Although the status of an occupation is not a direct measure of the achievement potential of a job, it encompasses other attributes that are very clearly associated with a job's achievement potential. The prestige normally accorded different occupations is visible to all members of the society. Thus, achievement rewards are readily available through public recognition. But perhaps more important, the status of a man's job is highly correlated with its difficulty and the degree of risk associated with it (see Atkinson, 1964, pp. 250–251). Both the difficulty and prestige of a job, McClelland (1961) and others have cogently argued, are basic features of an occupation that can engage a man's achievement motivation in the job requirements themselves.

To the degree that the prestige of a job reflects the difficulty of the work, we have firm expectations that men with higher achievement motivation should be more attracted to jobs of relatively high status. Using Atkinson's (1958a) theory about risk-taking, we would not suggest that men with high achievement motivation would always aim for the highest rung of the occupational ladder or set the highest level of aspiration, but rather we would suggest that their aspirations are well at the upper end. We say this because we assume that men with high achievement motivation, generally speaking, have been more successful than men with low achievement motivation. If superimposed on that assumption, we recognize that men with high achievement motivation take more calculated risks, we are led to the prediction that men with high achievement motivation are more likely than men with low achievement motivation to be aiming for jobs that are relatively high in prestige. Indeed, Crockett (1962) has shown that men with high achievement motivation are likely to be more upwardly mobile in the job hierarchy than men with low achievement motivation. Mahone (1960) has also found that male college students with high achievement motivation have realistic occupational aspirations, while the occupational choices of students with low achievement motivation are either too low or too high relative to their ability. Burnstein, Moulton, and Liberty (1963) present some evidence that men with high achievement motive, and, in particular, men with high achievement values, are aiming for higher status positions in the occupational hierarchy. The fact that these results are most striking for college men with high achievement *values* rather than with high achievement *motive* suggests that a job choice based on its societal prestige is much more an expression of social values than it is basic reflection of motive intensity. Therefore, we might look for characteristics of a job other than its prestige that might be the bases for job selection among those men high in achievement motivation.

One possible criterion that a highly achievement-motivated man might implicitly use in job selection would be the extent of a sense of individual accomplishment that can be attained in the job. To the degree that one can ascribe problem-solving at work to *individual* effort, then perhaps one can get more achievement satisfaction than if the ascription of achievement is to group effort. *Individual* accomplishment, therefore, may be an important quality of a job that a high achievement-motivated man seeks in work. On this basis, the relative autonomy in decision-making at work may be an important aspect of the achievement potential of jobs. Thus, a man with high achievement motive may be less attracted to jobs where they would be highly supervised by another person. Furthermore, one might expect that a man with high achievement motivation might be less interested in jobs where he has the responsibility for other people's decisions than he would be in jobs where he takes upon himself all the problems of job performance. Perhaps, therefore, he would not be attracted to jobs that entail considerable supervision of others.

Because the achievement motive is an asocial motive, men with a high achievement motive may be attracted to jobs where the social requirements of the job are not the major requirement for work. Social requirements could be detrimental to feelings of accomplishment. Although a person with high achievement motivation has to have clear feedback from the world that what he has done is excellent, there is evidence from the research literature that men with high achievement motivation will not respond to pressures for conformity (McClelland et al., 1953). Thus, high achievement motivation does not necessarily imply high social-approval motivation. We would expect that the social requirements of a job might be irrelevant to the job choices of men with high achievement motivation, but we are also alerted to the possibility that in jobs that constantly demand social performance, there may be less chance for men with high achievement motivation to perform as an individual.

In summary, the sorts of jobs that would be attractive to men with high achievement motivation are: jobs high in prestige; jobs that permit relative autonomy both from being supervised and from supervising others; and jobs that do not require constant social interaction. Implicitly, we also have taken the position that men with a high achievement motive will be attracted to jobs where there are possibilities for clear feedback about excellent performance.

Power motivation and job selection In another context we have already discussed power motivation as being a tendency to approach activities that lessen the likelihood that a person's influence is going to appear feeble. The results of a study by Lindman (1958) suggest that high power motivation should influence men to be attracted either to jobs with high potential for power in the work setting itself or to jobs with low power potential. We were led to this conclusion by Lindman's finding that high school boys with high power motivation ranked high those jobs that they perceived as being very high or very low in potential for influence in the work setting. This suggests that a man with high power motivation, if he is very strongly oriented to avoiding weakness, would be attracted to jobs that do not present any threat to his power. For quite different reasons, then, jobs with very high power requirements and jobs with very low power requirements would be attractive to men with high power motivation.

The best indication of the direct power potential of a job is how it fits into the hierarchical structure of an organization: how many people work under the man in question, how many people hold superior positions to him, and how much supervision does he receive? Supervising and being supervised, therefore, were the job conditions that we considered would foster or hinder the satisfaction of power motivation.

A man's job also gives him the trademark for potential influence in the community. A man with a prestigious job is more likely to hold sway in a social community than a man with an unskilled job. Such being the case, the highly power-motivated individual might be attracted to jobs that offer great potential for influence in the community at large—jobs with high prestige. We recognize then that both on-the-job power and the broader power potential reflected in the prestige of the job have potential relevance to job selection for men high in power motivation.

Specific jobs require men to exert power as their major job function. Therefore we separated out several groups of jobs with such "influence" requirements. From the professional setting, we isolated the judges, lawyers, teachers, clergymen, recreational workers, social workers, and others as a group of men who in their job performance need to influence other people (the "advising professions"). Salesmen, also, in a more subtle way influence decisions in people's lives. A foreman, by definition, also has a job high in power assertion. The advising professions, salesmen, and foremen, then, are three job classifications in which men could potentially get considerable power gratification from their work. Thus, we predict that these groups will include a high proportion of men with high power motivation. But we should keep Lindman's results in mind. These so-called high power jobs may be the very jobs that men with high power motive may avoid. These jobs can easily stimulate fear of weakness since the essential job function demands influence, and therefore the influence of the job occupant is frequently being tested. A highly power-motivated man may be especially anxious if he thinks he will not be influential on the job. Highly power-motivated men may thus deliberately avoid jobs where their influence potential is publicly evident and where perceptual distortion about their own power is not possible.

RESULTS CONCERNING MOTIVES AND JOB SELECTION

As we expected, the congruence principle seems to be a useful key to understanding the significant associations between motives and job selection. Men with certain motives seem to be in certain jobs because their motives "fit" the jobs.

Men with high affiliation motivation tended to be prevalent in jobs with high social requirements and were distinctly absent from farming. Thus jobs that make it possible to be with people, but more important, jobs that require social interaction, seem to have attractive demands for men with high affiliation motivation. Not all jobs that require social interaction seem to lead to a prevalence of people with high affiliation, however. Older men with high affiliation motivation were significantly less likely to be in jobs with high supervisory potential than men with low affiliation motivation. To supervise someone else evidently runs counter to the concerns of a person with a high affiliation motive.

The congruence principle seems applicable also to some of the findings that relate achievement motivation to job selection. Unskilled workers, men in jobs in which there is little chance for achievement evaluation, did not characteristically have high achievement motivation. This finding occurred in a more general form as well. There was a positive relationship between achievement motivation and being in jobs of high prestige in each age group. This relationship was significant only among older men. If we assume that the prestige of a job is highly correlated with perceived skill required by that job, then we could say that men with high achievement motivation are attracted to jobs where their skills can be highly evaluated.

Some of the other results about the prevalence of men with high achievement motivation in certain jobs are not so clearly related to the congruence principle. Although managers who were not self-employed were characteristically high in achievement motivation, in general men with high achievement motivation were significantly less likely to be in jobs of high supervisory potential than were men with low achievement motivation. The curious thing about this set of findings was that the job of the self-employed manager was not distinctively attractive to those scoring high in achievement motivation. We suspect that for self-employed managers, the supervisory functions in their job are particularly salient because they have individual responsibility for this function. Thus we suggest that certain kinds of interaction at work, especially supervising others, may actually interfere with achievement possibilities in jobs.

The congruence principle seems applicable to the association of power motivation and job selection only if we assume that the measure of power motivation predominately reflects an active avoidance of displays of weakness. Men with high power motivation were not common in the occupational categories of foremen or salesmen, and were significantly unlikely to be in jobs that required supervising others. But at the same time, young men with high power motivation were significantly more likely to be in jobs in which they were highly supervised than those with low power motivation. These data suggest that compared to men with low power motivation, men with high power motivation avoid jobs that can attest to their vulnerability if they are unsuccessful, even if successful execution of the job would provide a clear opportunity to demonstrate the extent of their influence.

TABLE 5-2 PERCENTAGE OF MEN WITH HIGH MOTIVE SCORES WITHIN 10 SPECIFIC OCCUPATIONS

Specific Occupation	Affiliation Motive	Achievement Motive	Power Motive	(N)
Professional advisers	59[a]	47	53	(17)
Managers: self-employed	51	54	51	(33)
Managers: not self-employed	56	69	53	(32)
Salesmen	44	56	38	(29)
Clerical workers	51	51	42	(31)
Foremen	49	51	24	(33)
Skilled workers	61	44	54	(83)
Semiskilled workers	42	53	52	(81)
Unskilled workers	47	35	47	(17)
Farmers	25	53	47	(32)

[a]Percentage of occupational group scoring above the median motive score for the entire distribution of all males in the total national sample.

We will now present the data on motives and job selection in more detail, first describing the relationships concerning the ten specific occupational groups, and then those concerning the four general occupational characteristics.

Specific occupational groups In Table 5.2 we present the percentage of men with high affiliation, achievement, and power motivation scores within each of the specific occupational groups.[6] Five of the specific occupational groups showed distinctive levels[7] of motivation on one of the three measured motives:

1. Farmers were low in affiliation motivation:
2. Managers who were not self-employed were high in achievement motivation:
3. Unskilled workers were low in power motivation:
4. Salesmen were low in power motivation:
5. Foremen were low in power motivation.

Thus it appears that men with certain motivational characteristics either seek out or avoid certain occupations. Let us examine each of these provocative results in turn.

That *farmers were low in affiliation motive* is in keeping with the conclusions reached in the chapters on marriage and parenthood that men with a high affiliation motive seek social contacts and avoid being alone.

[6]Since the available samples for most of the groups were small, the age control has unfortunately been disregarded.

[7]Although tests of statistical significance were not applied to these percentages, we are presenting results that stand out in the array of percentages. See Appendix A, Section II for sampling errors of percentages required in estimating statistical significance in the context of this survey.

The role of the farmer often calls for him to work alone, to concentrate his attention upon the reactions of natural forces to his activities rather than those of other persons. If our earlier conclusions about the goal of the affiliation motive are correct, then men with high affiliation motivation would not seek out the role of farmer. We would assume that a man with high affiliation motive would be likely to reject the role and migrate to more urban centers when he enters the labor force. It seems likely that a man who has a high affiliation motive may try farming for a while, find the job particularly difficult, and eventually drift into another occupation. A man who grows up in a rural area and has low affiliation motivation may be content to remain in the asocial activity of farming.

We were somewhat surprised that *managers who were not self-employed were particularly high in achievement motivation*. We had anticipated that men with high achievement motivation would be most attracted to the *self-employed* managerial jobs. Although this latter group of subjects was moderately high in achievement motivation, the group of managers who were not independent businessmen tended to have more men with high achievement motivation within its ranks than did the managers who were self-employed. This requires some explanation. Let us examine the roles of each, the self-employed managers and the non-self-employed managers, to see what might account for our surprising findings.

First, let us assume that we can divide any manager's role demands into two major kinds of functions: supervisory and non-supervisory requirements. We would assume the non-supervisory functions—decision-making about changes in production, buying, selling plans—provide the major sources of achievement gratification among managers. As we asserted earlier, the supervisory function can interfere with a sense of personal accomplishment. Both types of managers—self-employed and non-self-employed—are likely to supervise. The salience of the supervisory function, however, would be much stronger in general among the self-employed managers than the non-self-employed because the latter operate within a bureaucracy. The greater salience of supervision of others among the self-employed, we would assume, might detract from the achievement potential of their work.

The second important consideration involves how much personal day-to-day feedback about performance occurs within jobs with and without a supervisor. A self-employed manager is on his own; he must rely on his own daily estimate of his performance or wait for long-term outcomes of his business ventures; a manager who is employed in someone else's business, whether that of another individual or a corporation, is likely to get organizational feedback from a supervisor either directly or indirectly through the written or unwritten regulations of the organization. We anticipated that because his role is often noted for its demands for independence of action and involvement in calculated risk-taking, the self-employed businessman would epitomize the entrepreneurial role that has been considered attractive to those with high achievement motivation. We would now modify this view and assert that it is the decision-maker's role with *clear organizational feedback about performance* that is especially attractive to someone with high achievement motivation.

A third interpretation of the especially high achievement motivation among non-self-employed managers is possible. In an advanced capitalistic economic system like ours, financial success—the symbol of achievement—is often hastened if a businessman makes himself a part of a well-functioning large organization. Credit is easier to obtain and many other problems are simplified if a man is willing to make his business a subsidiary of a larger one. It may be easier to make a "grand success" as an executive in the Xerox Corporation than as an owner of a smaller company competing with Xerox.

The fact that *unskilled workers were particularly low in achievement motivation* hardly needs any comment. But perhaps it is instructive to note the result since it does enhance the apparent validity of the achievement motive measure in the survey setting.

By contrast, the reasons why *both salesmen and foremen were low in power motivation* are less self-evident. Our earlier speculations suggested that the capacity for influence in a job might be the major job characteristic that would be attractive to a man high in power motivation. However, we made this prediction cautiously because of the possibility that the measure of power motive indicates fear of weakness. If a man with a high power motive score has a strong fear of weakness, he would deliberately avoid those jobs that call his capacity to influence into question. Success as a salesman or a foreman particularly depends on the influence capacity of the person. Therefore, if a person is unable to exert influence on these jobs or anticipates any difficulty in being influential, he may become extremely anxious about work. This anticipatory anxiety about weakness in these jobs is perhaps what makes the job of a salesman and a foreman particularly unattractive for a man high in power motivation.

If this interpretation is correct, why did the managers not also have particularly low power motive scores? Two possible sources of difference between managers on the one hand and foremen or salesmen on the other hand may explain this difference: (1) the characteristics of men who become managers; (2) the characteristics of the influence demands of these jobs.

It might be that there is a sufficiently high positive power orientation among managers, or among those who are attracted to the managerial job, to compensate for the fear of weakness that seems to underlie the power motivation scores. Such positive power orientations can develop in an individual when he is granted *automatic* influence. When does this occur? When a person has obvious social status in society. Men coming from high social status families might learn positive power orientation more easily than men from lower status background. Probably managers are men with higher social-status backgrounds than foremen or salesmen, and are more likely to have a positive power orientation. These speculations suggest that the use of Uleman's (1966) or Winter's (1967) new measure of power, which presumably reflect a positive concern for power, would show that managers are high in positive power need while foremen and salesmen are low in this positive power need.

The kinds of influence demanded by these jobs may also differ. The success of a salesman is directly dependent upon his powers of persuasion. Each customer is a potential threat. The foreman's job is not so solely dependent upon persuasion as is the salesman's, but his authority may be limited. His primary job requirement is to supervise the production work of other employees.[8] The foreman is typically familiar with the procedures of the actual production work and often has previously been one of the production workers himself. He is often in a marginal position of identification, between labor and management (Lieberman, 1950). For these reasons we would expect that his influence over the men he supervises may be subject to question. The manager, by contrast, whether he be a self-employed businessman or not, is more clearly identified with the management and as such has a clear authority position. Furthermore, his duties usually include administrative or management functions in addition to direct supervision, and thus his job requires the exercise of other skills besides influence. For these reasons the job of manager may be less frequently perceived as primarily demanding influence assertion and as having threatening influence requirements, than that of either foreman or salesman.

General occupational characteristics　In Table 5.3 we report the relationship of motive scores to the four general occupational characteristics, both within and across the three age ranges. Here we are interested in seeing whether men with high levels of a given motive are more or less likely than men with low levels of that motive to be found in jobs with certain general occupational characteristics. The data show that there were associations between men's motives and these four general characteristics of their jobs.

There was a consistent positive association between affiliation motivation and being in a job that has high *Social Requirements*. None of these relationships was significant, but they were consistent across the age

---

[8]The category of foremen used here excluded craft foremen—for example, "foreman electrician"; it is equivalent to the U.S. Bureau of the Census (1950) occupational code category "523."

TABLE 5-3	THE RELATIONSHIP(γ) OF MOTIVES TO GENERAL OCCUPATIONAL CHARACTERISTICS (WITHIN AGE)				
Occupational Characteristic	Age	Affiliation Motive	Achievement Motive	Power Motive	(N)
Prestige	Young	−.01	.08	−.02	(166)
	Middle	.10‡	.07	.02	(159)
	Old	.02	.20†	−.15	(141)
	All ages	.05	.10	−.04	(466)
Social requirements	Young	.15	.14	−.05	(57)
	Middle	.01	−.06	−.01	(72)
	Old	.32	.11	−.21	(61)
	All ages	.15	.08	−.07	(190)
Supervision	Young	−.19	.19	.35†	(68)
	Middle	.03	.07	−.22	(63)
	Old	.37	.29	.06	(47)
	All ages	.04	.18	.07	(178)
Supervisory potential	Young	.27	−.24	−.41†	(73)
	Middle	.00	−.14	−.29	(66)
	Old	−.37*	−.25	.03	(50)
	All ages	.00	−.20*	−.20*	(189)

*p < .10.
†p < .05.
‡p < .01.

groups. These tendencies are in keeping with a plug-socket model of job choice. In addition, affiliation motivation was significantly negatively associated with *Supervisory Potential* among older men. This age-specific relationship may also be interpreted as an instance of the congruence principle. The fact that older men with high affiliation motivation were unlikely to supervise the work of others is consistent with the suggestion that high affiliation motivation is, in part, a desire to avoid rejection by others. As we mentioned before, a supervisor may be disliked. The occurrence of this association only for older men may imply that this characteristic of jobs may not be readily apparent to younger men in their initial job selection. It may be that only with years of experience does a man learn that to supervise others can block his affiliation with them. Only then can he select himself out of such work, voluntarily, or by his lack of success as a supervisor. For middle-aged men, affiliation motivation also was significantly positively associated with being in jobs with high *Prestige*. This relationship puzzles us and we frankly cannot offer any explanation.

Achievement motivation showed a consistent positive relationship, significant for older men, to being in jobs that were high in *Prestige*. This relationship also fits the idea that job selection is affected by the congruence principle. A man with a high achievement motive should be attracted to prestigious jobs because they are challenging. The fact that this relationship was significant for older men perhaps reflects the long-term persistence of older men with high achievement motivation that enables them to attain these desirable jobs.

There was also a consistently negative relationship, significant for all men, between achievement motivation and *Supervisory Potential*, and a consistently positive relationship, but not at significant levels, between achievement motivation and being in jobs that involved *Supervision* of the respondent. Because of the significant negative relationship between *Supervision* and *Supervisory Potential*, we cannot be sure that these are independent relationships with achievement motivation. Why do men with high achievement motive seem to be attracted to jobs that require them to do little supervising but in which they receive some supervision? Might it be that men with high achievement motivation are distracted by the supervisor's role, as we suggested earlier, and are attracted to jobs with supervisory feedback? A supervisor must rely on another person's ability to perform rather than on his own individual accomplishment. Such reliance upon others could be frustrating to a man with strong achievement goals. The other part of this result, the fact that men with high achievement motivation were more often in jobs that involved some supervision of their work by someone else, is more baffling. We tentatively interpret this finding as reflecting the importance of feedback about adequacy of performance for satisfying achievement goals. Earlier, we distinguished between the achievement gratifications possible among self-employed and non-self-employed managers on a similar basis. For a clear sense of pride in accomplishment a person may need either clear organizational requirements or someone in a higher status position than he, who provides standards of excellence and who evaluates his performance. In jobs where a person is his own interpreter of performance, where he must decide how well he is doing in his work, then perhaps achievement interests are not easily gratified. This interpretation implies that there must be some social basis for understanding what excellence is and when it occurs. It may also explain why farming, which is traditionally considered to be a job that enables a person to fulfill goals of individual enterprise, may not be very attractive to those with high achievement motivation. A farmer typically operates without knowing the reactions of others to his job performance. He must depend on the quality and quantity of crops to attest to his job performance. But perhaps a person needs day-to-day evaluations or explicit organizational standards of evaluation to reap genuine achievement gratifications from his job. These results may also help to explain why we did not get a set of high correlations between achievement motivation and *Prestige*. *Prestige* is positively related to

Supervisory Potential and negatively related to *Supervision*. Since the achievement motive is negatively related to *Supervisory Potential* and positively related to *Supervision*, the correlation of the achievement motive to *Prestige* would be higher if these effects with the *Supervision* variables were partialed out. This suggests that we are getting underestimates of the interests of highly achievement-oriented men in prestigious jobs, but it also suggests that the day-to-day feedbacks about achievement within the organizational setting are perhaps of primary concern for those with high achievement aspirations. Over and above the prestige of an occupation, a man with high achievement motivation will seek out specialized work that will minimize supervisory responsibility and maximize evaluative feedback on the job. What occupational groups have jobs that meet these criteria? Scientists, engineers, business administrators, and architects come to mind. These men are in jobs that are prestigious and can involve day-to-day evaluation of their performance, but which may well have minimal requirements to supervise others.

Finally we found that for young men the power motive was significantly related to being in jobs that were low in *Supervisory Potential* and high in *Supervision*. The negative relationship between the power motive and *Supervisory Potential* was also significant for all men, despite the contrary trend for old men. The finding that in the youngest age group the power motive was related to both being supervised and not supervising fits into our previous interpretation of the power motive measure as a measure of fear of weakness. If a person is fearful of being weak, he might be less attracted to jobs that require him to supervise others and to exert influence. Because of a desire to avoid situations that could threaten or test his own potential for influence, it would be less threatening to hold a job that does not require supervising others. Jobs in which there is close supervision also can be thought of as low in threat to one's power. The lack of opportunity for potential influence could be a safeguard against feelings of weakness. In fact, the person with high fear of weakness may seek out jobs where he will be influenced, where he can offer some resistance to the influence attempts being made on him, but where his failure to successfully resist is not disturbing or threatening. This interpretation assumes that the measure of the power motive we are using assesses a person's tendencies to avoid power and his concern about protecting himself from being influenced and from appearing weak, rather than his tendencies to approach and use power or his desire to influence others.

MOTIVES AND JOB REACTIONS

THEORETICAL BACKGROUND

The effect that a man's work has on his feelings of well-being or his feelings of disequilibrium can be influenced by his general personality characteristics only if the job is seen as part of man's basic psychic economy. Early in this chapter we assumed that a man's job still does engage important aspects of his identity even though this society is undoubtedly moving away from an emphasis on work. Although the working day has become shorter and there is an increasing emphasis on leisure, we do assume that a man's personality would still help determine his reactions to work—whether he feels satisfied or committed to his work and the kinds of satisfactions and dissatisfactions he finds in his job. Kornhauser and Reid (1965), from their analysis of the working population in Detroit, contend that it is hard to find a substitute for work that would provide a man with an equal sense of justification for his life. In this section we will be examining motive-role interactions to discover how the personality characteristics we have outlined can affect various kinds of job reactions.

For men who no longer view their work with great personal attachment, factors other than personality patterns may become more influential in accounting for behavior at work. These might include salary, hours, fringe benefits, effort required, particular organizational characteristics of the company (its size, the chain of communication, the friendliness of supervisor, and the employee's voice in decision-making). We did not have much information about such job or organizational characteristics. If these are sufficient bases for understanding job reactions, we can only anticipate that there will be little relationship between the three motives—affiliation, achievement, and power—and men's reactions to jobs, especially in those men who separate themselves from their work and invest other aspects of their lives with the energy that they once directed to work. The expected relationships in these groups of men, between job reactions and certain job or organizational characteristics, cannot be tested directly.

The assumption that a man's personal investment in his work will influence the pattern of motive-role interaction will be used to interpret certain findings about older men to be presented in the following sections. What we found in relating affiliation, achievement, and power motives to different aspects of job adjustment was that some relationships were confined to younger-aged or middle-aged groups. It could be that the motive measures are inappropriate for older groups. But another interpretation of this general finding is that the job role is just not an appropriate role in which to investigate motive-role interaction for most older men.

We have speculated that as men grow older, they shift their energies from work to other areas of life. An older man's level of achievement at work is probably at some stable point: he does not anticipate much further advancement in a job or up the status hierarchy. A job for an older man becomes psychologically less demanding, less open to personal challenge,

and less fulfilling to most personal needs. Consolidating his home, maintaining his interpersonal life and health, preparing for retirement are the
goals that become salient in later years. This shift away from work as a
major concern in old age may help explain why motivations seem to show
little or no relationships to job reactions for the older-aged groups.

Having foreshadowed the results of this section, noting where relationships between motives and job reactions may be minimal, we now
turn to the implications of the guiding principles of this research for our
expectations about job reactions, discussing each motive separately. As
the reader will recall, when applied to the job role these principles state
that: (a) where men's motives are congruent with their work roles, there
should be job satisfaction and commitment; and (b) motives will tend to
influence the kinds of satisfactions and dissatisfactions men find in their
jobs when there is some ambiguity about what is gratifying or frustrating
at work. Since, in general, similar considerations presented as determining
job selection are assumed to determine congruence between motives and
the job role, our discussion here will be brief.

Affiliation motivation and job reactions   Our initial hypothesis was that
jobs that require social interaction as part of the work activity should yield
the greatest affiliation satisfaction. If so, these jobs would be congruent
with the affiliation motive, and men with high affiliation motivation in
these jobs should be especially satisfied. Furthermore, men with high
affiliation motivation in jobs that do not require social activity should be
most dissatisfied. But we also recognized that affiliation gratification often
can come from peers at work, independent of the requirements of the job
itself. Kornhauser and Reid (1965) point out that many workers speak of
their personal relations as a principal source of pleasure on their job. This
additional possible source of congruence of the affiliation motive with a
job raises two related questions. First, is there a relationship between the
social requirements of a job and the opportunity for peer group affiliative
contacts? And second, can satisfying friendships arise out of social interaction that is *required*?

It seems possible that if a job requires much in the way of social
responsibility in its actual day-to-day enactment, there would be less
chance for intimate peer-like relationships to develop both with the
people with whom one is obliged to interact and also with colleagues at
work. Jobs with high *Social Requirements* involve interaction with persons in
reciprocal rather than *parallel* roles, between physician-patients, teacher-
students, lawyer-clients, and the like. These jobs may require too many
reciprocal obligations for friendships to develop from these relationships
themselves. Furthermore, these jobs generally do not allow for much
contact with others in a similar role position and may therefore stand in
the way of a person finding affiliative gratification from co-workers. In

law and in teaching there may be limits to the number of affiliative contacts of this kind. By way of contrast, in jobs low in *Social Requirements*—accounting, engineering—there is often great potential for people to seek out affiliative relationships with others doing parallel work. People who are in similar status, then, men who work *parallel* to other people at the same type of labor would seem to be the best targets for affiliative gratification because they offer the strongest bases for easy interchange. If this interpretation is accurate, perhaps one can say that men with a high affiliation motive would find their jobs particularly gratifying if they require parallel rather than reciprocal activity with others.

Thus, opposite types of predictions were kept in mind in thinking about the relationship between affiliation motivation and job satisfaction and dissatisfaction. We had reason to anticipate both great affiliative satisfaction and minimal affiliative satisfaction from jobs high in *Social Requirements*.

As mentioned above, we entertained the general hypothesis that men with high affiliation motivation are more likely to find affiliative gratification at work. The potential for finding both intensive and extensive friendship is usually, in part, up to the individual, although some jobs allow for greater and more extensive contact with people than others. Therefore, in most jobs men can find affiliative contact at work if they look for it. If a person has high affiliation motivation, he might be expected to look for such contact more than others; we would also expect him to interpret such contacts as satisfactions even if he actually tends to be unpopular. Therefore, it was felt that the prediction based on the sensitization principle, that a high motive produces high perception of motive-relevant satisfactions, might hold up best with affiliation motivation.

Achievement motivation and job reactions We began with the assumption that the prestige of an occupation reflects its level of difficulty and demands for individual decision-making. We were then led to the general hypothesis that men who had high achievement motivation and were in jobs with high *Prestige* would be more satisfied with their work than those with low achievement motivation, and that men with high achievement motivation in jobs with low *Prestige* would be more disgruntled than men with low achievement motivation in these same jobs. In other words, it was assumed that where the level of achievement motivation was congruent with the *Prestige* level of the job, there would be felt satisfaction, and where such motivation was incongruent with *Prestige*, there would be felt dissatisfaction. As evidence for this hypothesis, we note that Kornhauser and Reid (1965) reported in their survey of Detroit workers that men who were in the lowest strata of the occupational hierarchy and whose boyhood orientations included high vocational goals tended to have poor scores on their index of mental health.

We also assumed that jobs in which interpersonal activity was an essential part of successful performance of the work were not congruent with achievement gratification. Successful performance in such jobs is not based upon individual responsibility for effort, but instead is contingent upon the performance of another person. A teacher's feedback for good performance is contingent upon the skill or understanding acquired by the student. Therefore, we felt that in jobs requiring social interaction, those men with high achievement motivation would show less commitment and greater dissatisfaction than those with low achievement motivation.

A simple application of the sensitization principle seemed appropriate: the greater the achievement motivation the greater should be the potential for perceiving achievement gratifications and frustrations at work. This seems applicable to all jobs, but we expected it to be most applicable to jobs that are ambiguously structured for achievement.

Thinking of particular types of jobs, we felt that achievement satisfaction in work should most often be perceived by self-employed managers who are high in achievement motive. Atkinson and Hoselitz (1958) have suggested that the entrepreneurial role contains strong incentive for achievement gratifications, and McClelland (1961) also has theoretically and empirically established linkages between the entrepreneurial life and achievement motivation. We also assumed that the probability of experiencing achievement satisfactions at work should be strong in highly achievement-motivated men working at skilled jobs or farming. Both of these occupations had moderate *Prestige* ratings and hence their overall achievement potentials could be considered ambiguous. But in both of these jobs individual responsibility for decision-making remains a possible strong source of achievement gratification. This type of achievement satisfaction is one in which a person with high achievement motivation can focus his perceptions. Men with high achievement motivation caught in jobs with low achievement potential (unskilled labor, clerical work, semiskilled work) should express the most achievement dissatisfactions.

Power motivation and job reactions Conceiving of the power motive as a fear of weakness, we advanced the hypothesis that men in jobs where there was greatest potential for being considered weak would be most dissatisfied with their work. There are two ways that a man's job can be used to infer his power or influence. One way is by an evaluation of the prestige ascribed to the type of work a man does. A man can be judged weak if his job is not one that guarantees some community esteem and effect on the community; a man can be judged powerful if his job is prestigious. On this basis, we anticipated that a man in a job with low *Prestige* would be more disgruntled with work if he had a high power motive than if he had a low power motive.

The other way a man's job can act as a guide to his power or weakness depends on an evaluation of the influence he is able to exert in the actual job setting. Jobs that are high in *Supervisory Potential* would appear to permit the exertion of influence, but they are not necessarily congruent with a high power motive. If the potential to exert power is high *and* easily realized, a man with high power motive should be protected from feelings of weakness. This would mean that such jobs are congruent for men with high power motivation. Thus a man who has a job with high influence potential should be more satisfied if his power motivation is high rather than low. But when the exercise of influence is required on a job, there are often either actual or potential obstacles that can prevent success-ful use of influence. Under these conditions, it is possible to conclude that fear of weakness should be especially strong. From this perspective, a man in a job that requires but does not guarantee successful influence, would express greater disgruntlement with his work if he had high rather than low power motivation. Such jobs should include many that are high in *Supervisory Potential*, as well as other specific occupations that require, but do not guarantee, persuasive influence, such as the advising professions or sales jobs. Similarly, it is difficult to predict whether receiving close super-vision on the job is evidence for weakness or a protection against weakness. Power-motivated men who, in jobs with high *Supervision*, could either be very satisfied or very dissatisfied, depending on whether they interpret being supervised as indicating weakness or as protection against displaying their inability to influence.

To sum up, looking at the day-to-day job setting itself, we had opposite ways of thinking about the power implication of a man's work. We could view jobs that do not require influence assertion—jobs with low *Supervisory Potential*, jobs with high *Supervision*—as jobs with low potential for power gratification, and expect disgruntlement in men with high power motivation. On the other hand, we could view these same jobs as protective—men in these jobs can feel they are out of the public eye and safe from the possibility of failing to be influential when the opportunity exists. We would then expect satisfaction among men with high power motivation who have such jobs.

It is also hard to make direct predictions about the kinds of satis-factions and dissatisfactions to which subjects high in the power motive should be sensitized. The types of satisfactions and dissatisfactions that men report about their work can reflect either their sense of weakness at work or their sense of weakness in relationship to the rest of the community, or both. This should be especially true for older men who may take the mere fact of working at a job as a sign of their potential respect from the community. One intriguing, although highly speculative, idea about the effect of power motivation on the perception of job satisfactions seems worth considering. A man with high power motivation in a job with a low power potential may structure his job in affiliative terms in order to avoid thinking about the job's low influence potential. Taking these motives at face value, affiliative and power goals seem to be psychologically incompatible in the same interpersonal relationship. Thus, it may be that men with high power motivation in jobs with little potential to influence others seek out and report affiliative gratifications.

In light of all our tentative predictions, any consistent relationships found between power motive and job reactions should shed a great deal of light on the meaning of the power motive and/or the structure of certain jobs. With this motive, more than with the others, our research is more frankly exploratory.

MEASURES OF JOB REACTIONS

In this section we used the same sample of subjects and the same job classifications as in the previous section, on job selection. But here, we will relate the three motives to different job *reactions*, for subjects within each type of specific and general occupational classification. Seven different types of job reactions were measured. The questions on which they were based followed directly after those about parenthood. (See Appendix A, Section III, questions 52 through 66.)

We will first briefly describe the seven indices of job reactions, and then discuss our interpretation of each of them.

After ascertaining the type of job the subject held, the question used to measure *Job Dissatisfaction* was asked,

Taking into consideration all the things about your job, how satisfied or dissatisfied are you with it?

Replies to this question were coded into the following six-point scale, designed to reflect the intensity of dissatisfaction with the job:

1. Very satisfied (for example, "very good," "I like it very much," "couldn't be better")
2. Satisfied ("satisfied," "I like it," "pretty good")
3. Neutral ("It's O.K.," "average")
4. Ambivalent—respondent mentions both being satisfied and dissatisfied
5. Dissatisfied ("I'm not satisfied," "I don't like it," "not too good")
6. Very dissatisfied ("very unsatisfied," "terrible")

The next question was designed to determine the types of job satisfaction he experienced:

What things do you particularly like about the job?

The first two replies to this question were coded into various types of categories which were designed to make qualitative distinctions that would be important in studying the relationships of the motives of affiliation, achievement, and power to job adjustment. Three such categorizations were used here.[9] The *Affiliation* category included responses that mentioned liking, being with, or seeing the people with whom the person worked. The *Achievement* category included such responses as: "It gives you a sense of accomplishment," "It is interesting work," "It gives me a chance to express myself," "I like to do that kind of work." The *Economic* category included responses that described economic security or economic gains the person obtained from his job.

Three indices were derived from this coding of the first two sources of job satisfaction: *Affiliation Job Satisfaction*, *Achievement Job Satisfaction*, and *Economic Job Satisfaction*. Each of these indices was a two-point scale scored for: (1) no mention and (2) mention of that type of job satisfaction. Since most men described at least two things they liked about their job, we used a person's first two responses in constructing these indices. However this meant that a subject could have a high score on more than one of the three indices listed above, and these three types of job reactions are not mutually exclusive. We recognize that this introduces a methodological problem, since in a heterogeneous sample there may be a greater willingness or ability to give multiple responses in certain subgroups, but, as we said, most men did give more than one response. Had we employed two mentions on parallel codes of marriage and parenthood, we would have introduced more serious biases. We should also note that these three categories of job satisfaction are not exhaustive. Therefore, a small number of subjects who mentioned only other types of job satisfaction had low scores on all three variables.[10]

Parallel to the question asking about sources of job satisfaction, we next asked about dissatisfaction:

What things don't you like about the job?

[9]The original coding of replies to this question included several categories of influence-related satisfaction, such as "I like to be my own boss" and "I like teaching people things." Too few subjects made such responses to warrant using this category in systematic analyses.

[10]A small number of subjects ($N = 15$) were omitted from these three indices because they indicated that there was nothing about their job that they particularly liked.

The first two responses to this question were coded for types of dissatisfaction, and we selected two to examine for this study:[11] *Achievement* dissatisfactions, such as: "I find the work uninteresting," "I don't like doing the kind of work I'm doing," "It does not give me a chance to express myself," "It does not give me a chance to do the things I like to do," and *Economic* dissatisfactions, which included any mention of economic deprivation felt on the job; for example, "I don't make enough money; the pay is low." Two indices were derived from this coding of the first two replies, *Achievement Job Dissatisfaction* and *Economic Job Dissatisfaction*. Each was a two-point index scored: (1) for no mention and (2) for mention of that type of job dissatisfaction. Both of these indices could be applied only to respondents who reported some things about their job that they didn't like. Therefore, these variables were scored only for a subsample of employed men, the 87 percent who reported some job dissatisfaction.

Whether a person was satisfied or dissatisfied with his specific job, he still could be very committed to work itself. Therefore, we included the following question as another overall measure of job reaction:

If you didn't have to work to make a living, do you think you would work anyway?

Replies were simply coded (1) yes and (2) no, to yield the index of *Lack of Commitment*.

We will now present our interpretation of each of these measures of job reactions. The previous factor analysis of measures of subjective adjustment (Veroff et al., 1962b) is of limited use in interpretation because only one of the current measures (*Job Dissatisfaction*) was included in that analysis, and it did not correlate strongly with any of the factors. Instead, we will supplement our initial conceptions of these measures by considering the differential distribution of the measures of job reaction among the specific occupational groups (Table 5.d in Appendix B), the association between job reactions and the general occupational characteristics (Table 5.e in Appendix B), and the interrelationships among the measures of job reactions for men in jobs that are coded high in *Prestige* and for those in jobs that are coded low in *Prestige* (Table 5.f in Appendix B). We also obtained the interrelationships among the measures of job reactions separately for men in each of the ten specific occupational groups, and for men at the three age levels. These results will be cited only when they lead to different conclusions than those obtained from the analyses based on the two *Prestige* groups.

[11]The original coding scheme for sources of satisfaction and dissatisfaction were parallel, but only these two types of dissatisfaction occurred with sufficient frequency to use here.

Job dissatisfaction The major distinction in the *Job Dissatisfaction* index is the difference between feeling "very satisfied" and "satisfied." The percentage of men in any occupational group who reported being "dissatisfied" or "very dissatisfied" was small. (See Table 5.d in Appendix B.) However, there were a sufficient number of dissatisfied responses to allow us to consider them in the interpretation of this measure. The greatest job dissatisfaction was reported by the salesmen and clerical workers among white-collar workers, and by the unskilled workers among blue-collar workers. Since these are the men in "low" positions within the white-and blue-collar hierarchies, we were led to the conclusion that *Job Dissatisfaction* is in some way determined by the prestige of one's occupation relative to your major reference group, such as the blue- and white-collar groups.

Was such an interpretation of *Job Dissatisfaction* borne out in examining the relationship of general job characteristics to the job reaction? *Job Dissatisfaction* was significantly negatively related to *Prestige* and significantly positively related to *Supervision*. (See Table 5.e in Appendix B.) While both of these relationships might reflect the general interpretation we have made that *Job Dissatisfaction* reflects the prestige of a man's work relative to his reference group, there also appears to be an overall tendency for men in more prestigeful jobs to feel more satisfied with their work.

It is interesting that being closely supervised in one's work is generally associated with feelings of dissatisfaction, disregarding motivational state, while being in jobs where you supervise others is only minimally related to feeling satisfied. As the reader will recall, *Supervision* and *Supervisory Potential* were strongly associated with each other and with *Prestige*. Despite these relationships *Job Dissatisfaction* is most closely associated with *Supervision* (gamma = .30, $p < .01$ for tau beta), next to *Prestige* (gamma = $-.11$, $p < .01$ for tau beta), and only minimally to *Supervisory Potential* (gamma = $-.15$). Apparently, close supervision is specifically related to job dissatisfaction, but its mirror status—being a supervisor —is not specifically related to job satisfaction.

The above speculation about the meaning of *Job Dissatisfaction* gets even further corroboration when we look at the patterns of interrelationships of these various job reactions. (See Table 5.f in Appendix B.) The relationships between *Job Dissatisfaction* and the other measures of job reactions differ somewhat in the two *Prestige* groups. Most of the significant relationships between *Job Dissatisfaction* and other job reactions appeared for men whose jobs were low in *Prestige*. For this group, *Job Dissatisfaction* was significantly related to three other measures of job reactions: negatively to *Achievement Job Satisfaction* and positively to *Achievement Job Dissatisfaction* and to *Economic Job Satisfaction*. We will be interpreting each of these measures in keeping with their face validity. Thus for men in jobs with low *Prestige*, overall job satisfaction seems to be contingent upon a person's assessment of the possibilities for achievement gratification in his job. It is somewhat surprising that a man in a job low in *Prestige* who mentions economic rewards as a source of job satisfaction is more likely to be dissatisfied with his job than a man in a comparable job who does not mention economic rewards as a source of job satisfaction. It is as if dissatisfied men clutch at the economic satisfactions from their jobs, not because they are very pleased with their economic rewards, but because their job at least gives them some financial security, if nothing else.

For the men high in *Prestige*, there was also a tendency for achievement gratifications to be crucial for feelings of job satisfaction. But only the negative association between *Job Dissatisfaction* and *Achievement Job Satisfaction* was significant. Unlike the results for the low *Prestige* group, for the high *Prestige* group *Economic Job Satisfaction* was not related to *Job Dissatisfaction*. *Affiliation Job Satisfaction* was not associated with *Job Dissatisfaction* in either *Prestige* subgroup. The only group for whom feelings of job satisfaction seemed to be dependent on affiliative gratifications was the skilled workers, for whom there was a significant negative relationship between *Job Dissatisfaction* and *Affiliation Job Satisfaction*.

For some jobs, therefore, job satisfaction is more dependent on a sense of accomplishment or adequate social relations than on economic rewards. What is surprising here is that this conclusion seemed to be more compelling for men with jobs low in *Prestige* than for those with jobs high in *Prestige*. We interpret these findings as an indication that a man's level of *Job Dissatisfaction* reflects the extent to which work is a source of very personal gratification. *While the economic benefits from work are certainly important, they are not sufficient for job satisfaction.* This interpretation of the measure of *Job Dissatisfaction* is consistent with the finding in the factor analytic study that this variable did not correlate with the *Unhappiness Factor*, which we had interpreted as reflecting a passive evaluation of role difficulties.

In general, *Job Dissatisfaction* did not relate significantly to the next measure we will be discussing, *Lack of Commitment*. There was, however, a significant positive relationship for middle-aged men. We will discuss this result in our analysis of *Lack of Commitment*.

Lack of commitment   As stated previously, the percentage of people who said that they would discontinue work if they didn't have to work to earn a living was very small. (See Table 5.d in Appendix B.) In any one occupational group the largest percentage of men who would give up work if they were given a chance was 21 percent. There was relatively little difference among the specific occupational groups in the amount of work commitment, although within the white-collar workers, salesmen stand out as the least committed group, and the farmers reported the most commitment to work of any occupational group. *Lack of Commitment* also was not significantly related to any of the general occupational characteristics. (See Table 5.e in Appendix B.)

The measure of *Lack of Commitment* was, however, related to certain of the other job reactions. As reported above, *Job Dissatisfaction* and *Lack of Commitment* were significantly positively related for middle-aged men. It could be that for this age group our measure of commitment to work reflected a man's specific commitment to his particular job and therefore was directly associated with how satisfied or dissatisfied he was with his particular job. As we had mentioned earlier it might very well be that while young men are committed to finding a career, to finding a proper job, and older men are committed to maintaining themselves in the role of the worker, middle-age men may be committed to the specific job that they have consolidated for themselves over time. We therefore, might expect that relationships between motives and *Lack of Commitment* might parallel relationships between motives and *Job Dissatisfaction* for middle-aged men. For the other two age groups perhaps these two variables reflect somewhat different psychological reactions, and we might expect that each will generate slightly different results in relationship to the motives.

Lack of Commitment, like *Job Dissatisfaction*, seems to reflect the presence or absence of personal, motive-relevant gratifications, in addition to economic gratifications. For the total group of employed men there was a significant positive relationship between *Lack of Commitment* and *Economic Job Satisfaction*. Although this relationship was not significant within each of the *Prestige* groups, the same trend did exist in both groups. (See Table 5.f in Appendix B.) There was also a negative relationship between *Lack of Commitment* and *Achievement Job Satisfaction* in both *Prestige* groupings, although significantly so only for the men in jobs with low *Prestige*. Thus men who are committed to work are especially likely to mention achievement satisfactions and unlikely to mention economic satisfactions in their own job.

Among the specific occupational groups, *Lack of Commitment* was also significantly negatively related to *Achievement Job Satisfaction* for two groups: the self-employed managers, and the semiskilled workers. Men in these jobs perhaps require considerable individual initiative to set achievement standards and to find achievement gratifications. Explicit standards of evaluation are less available to men in these jobs than to lawyers, to bureaucratic managers, to skilled workers, or even to clerical workers. Self-employed managers must run a business in which the day-to-day achievement standards may not be apparent. So it is with semiskilled workers assigned a routine task. Achievement is not directly structured into the day-to-day operations of the jobs themselves. Men in such jobs who have been able to seek out and obtain achievement gratifications, therefore, are more likely to be those men who personalize their efforts and thus have a strong commitment to work.

There was one further significant relationship with *Lack of Commitment* in a specific occupational group: *Lack of Commitment* was negatively related to *Affiliation Job Satisfaction* among clerical workers. This suggests that clerical workers, when committed to their work, respond to interpersonal satisfactions.

In general, the results concerning the relationship between *Lack of Commitment* and other job reactions for specific occupational groups were different from the pattern of relationship with *Job Dissatisfaction*. This divergence once again suggests that a man's commitment to work may have different motivational significance than does his expressed satisfaction with his work.

Types of job satisfaction: Economic, Achievement, and Affiliation Of the three types of job satisfaction coded here, both *Affiliation Job Satisfaction* and *Achievement Job Satisfaction* were reported by a sizable proportion of the subjects, and thereby yielded fairly productive variables. (See Table 5.d in Appendix B.) The other measure of type of job satisfaction— *Economic Job Satisfaction*—and both measures of types of job dissatisfaction produced severely skewed variables, thereby limiting somewhat their potential variability among the specific occupational groups. Nevertheless, there were variations in all types of job satisfaction, for the specific and general occupational groupings.

In general, the data on the distribution of these satisfactions led us to conclude that the particular type of job satisfaction that is mentioned is determined by the specific nature of the work performed in particular jobs. *Achievement Job Satisfaction* seems to reflect the difficulty of the job within the prestige hierarchy. Salesmen expressed less *Achievement Job Satisfaction* than other white-collar workers. Among the blue-collar workers, the semiskilled and the unskilled workers were also noticeably low in reports of achievement gratifications. We also found that mentioning achievement satisfaction was significantly associated both with having a prestigious job and with having supervisory responsibilities. Thus it seems that mentioning achievement satisfaction as one of the things liked most about a job implies a lot of ego-involvement with one's job.

Affiliation Job Satisfaction seems to reflect more than one type of psychological gratification. It is associated both with jobs that involve clear power potential and with jobs that lack achievement gratification. Affiliative satisfactions were mentioned significantly more often by men who had jobs high rather than low in *Social Requirements*, at least among those men in the jobs of high *Prestige* for whom that variable was coded. In the specific occupational groups, none of the farmers cited affiliative relationships as a source of job satisfaction, while the professional advisers reported somewhat more affiliative satisfactions than any of the other group. Although affiliative satisfactions were mentioned more often by men in white-collar than in blue-collar jobs, this was not because of the different prestige of these two broad groups, since there was no relationship between *Prestige* and *Affiliation Job Satisfaction*. Therefore we looked more closely at the distribution of this variable in the specific occupations within the blue- and white-collar hierarchies. We noted that within each hierarchy *Affiliation Job Satisfaction* was most often mentioned by men in power positions (advisers and foremen) and was also often mentioned by men low in *Achievement Job Satisfaction* (salesmen and unskilled workers). This suggests that affiliative satisfaction can derive either from being in a position where you try to influence other people or as a compensation for lack of achievement gratifications.

There were relatively few differences between specific occupational groups in *Economic Job Satisfaction*, although the men who presumably receive the least financial rewards, the semiskilled and unskilled workers, were relatively high in reports of economic factors being what they liked most about their job. These results, along with the earlier reported positive relationships of *Economic Job Satisfaction* with *Job Dissatisfaction* and *Lack of Commitment*, suggest that the report of *Economic Job Satisfaction* is made when other, psychologically more important, sources of job satisfaction are absent. This is also consistent with the finding that *Economic Job Satisfaction* was significantly negatively associated with both *Prestige* and *Supervisory Potential*.[12] In this light, *Economic Job Satisfaction* is viewed as an indication of *extrinsic* involvement in work. Alternately, we interpret mentioning achievement gratification as a reflection of ego satisfaction. It will be recalled that mentioning economic satisfaction was generally associated with *Lack of Commitment*—that is, men who feel that monetary considerations are the most satisfying aspects of their job look at work as a forced role requirement rather than a role that actively engages the ego. By contrast, men who particularly like the achievement-related aspects of their job also are generally satisfied with their job and are committed to work as a role that has personal as well as economic rewards.

Types of job dissatisfaction: Economic and Achievement Reports of *Achievement Job Dissatisfaction* were uniformly low among blue-collar occupational groups, but varied in an interesting fashion among the

---

[12]The direct relationships among the three types of job satisfaction are not a good source of information on this point because these measures are not experimentally independent, and they were always significantly negatively related. However, it is interesting that the strongest negative relationship between any pair of these variables was between *Economic Job Satisfaction* and *Achievement Job Satisfaction* for the men low in *Prestige*.

white-collar workers. It seems to be both a reflection of lack of achievement gratifications and a measure of a high level of aspiration among men in white-collar jobs. *Achievement Job Dissatisfaction* was mentioned most by professional advisers, clerical workers, and salesmen, in that order. It seemed appropriate for the latter two groups of men, who are white-collar workers but not in very prestigious jobs, to feel dissatisfaction with the achievement aspects of their job, but it was surprising to obtain so much mention of discontent with achievement-related matters among men in the advising professions. This finding suggested the possibility that *Achievement Job Dissatisfaction* can be a measure of aspiration on the job as well as a measure of actual discontent with the achievement possibilities on the job.

Although reports of *Achievement Job Dissatisfaction* did not differ for the specific blue-collar occupations we had singled out for study, this type of dissatisfaction was important for men in low *Prestige* jobs. For them, *Job Dissatisfaction* was significantly positively associated with *Achievement Job Dissatisfaction*.

We should further note that *Achievement Job Dissatisfaction* tended to be associated with close rather than minimal supervision. Being closely supervised can increase either a man's aspirations or his achievement discontents: it can act as a thorn in his side to increase his discontent and as a positive incentive for feedback about performance. Its effect depends on the style of the supervisor. Men can feel watched and coerced by their supervision. Or men can feel that they are being positively evaluated for good performance. The former style could reflect deep discontent about the possibilities for independent accomplishment. The latter could indicate a high level of job aspiration. But this simple two-pronged interpretation of achievement dissatisfaction is not entirely satisfactory. We note that the managers were particularly low in mentioning achievement dissatisfaction. It is hard to think of them as being either contented with the achievement gratifications in their job or low in achievement aspirations. It may be that for these men and other men in highly achievement-oriented jobs, mentioning achievement dissatisfaction would reflect their own failure, *and so they avoid mentioning it.* For men in jobs of low achievement potential (particularly those with coercive supervisors), mentioning achievement dissatisfaction realistically reflects the lack of achievement potential in the job and its failure to provide stimulation. Thus one might be on the lookout for these different types of reactions whenever achievement dissatisfaction is particularly evident or absent. Some men may use one psychological framework for answering this question and others may use a second. Perhaps which one a worker will use is guided by the strength of his achievement motivation. We will be alert to this possibility.

Emphasis on dissatisfaction with economic aspects of the job also seems to have a dual interpretation. For men in bad economic straits, it is a measure of discontent. *Economic Job Dissatisfaction* was most often mentioned by unskilled workers and farmers. For men in prestigious jobs, it appears to be a measure of lack of commitment or involvement with *people* in their job. For these men *Economic Job Dissatisfaction* occurred more often in jobs with low *Social Requirements* than in jobs with definite requirements for social skills. One might assume that the more social interaction required of men in their work, the more emotionally attached they will be to their work. Therefore, men who work with things rather than with people can be more socially distant from their work and focus on economic dissatisfaction when asked about their complaints.

None of the relationships between types of satisfaction and types of dissatisfaction were significant. (See Table 5.f in Appendix B.) Although there was a potential artifactual relationship between mentioning economic satisfaction and dissatisfaction, the general negative relationship between these two measures was significant only among middle-aged men. It is possible, therefore, for a man both to be satisfied with earning enough for a living but dissatisfied with not earning as much as he wants.

Summary of conceptualizations of measures   Our concluding interpretations about the meaning of the measures, which stem from our initial ideas and the above results, can now be summarized as follows. *Job Dissatisfaction* is interpreted as an index of dissatisfaction that reflects achievement frustrations rather than economic frustrations, and under certain conditions, affiliative frustrations. *Lack of Commitment* has a similar interpretation, but in some instances we will take it to imply even more deeply personal frustrations, since it seems to reflect more directly a failure of men's attempts to find satisfactions at work when they are not immediately available from the nature of the job requirement. *Achievement Job Satisfaction* coincides with an ego-involvement with one's work. *Affiliation Job Satisfaction* reflects ego-involvement in high *Prestige* jobs, while in low *Prestige* jobs mentioning affiliative satisfaction can reflect a sense of failure or lack of accomplishment at work. *Achievement Job Dissatisfaction* can be a reflection of dashed aspirations, or of very high standards of excellence. *Economic Job Satisfaction and Dissatisfaction* among high *Prestige* groups generally will be interpreted as disengaged attitudes toward work which can come about from a lack of commitment to people at work. Among certain other groups—low status blue-collar workers and farmers—these measures will be interpreted as reflecting the generally barren economic reward possibilities in these jobs, as well as a more general discontent.

RESULTS CONCERNING MOTIVES AND JOB REACTIONS—IN SPECIFIC OCCUPATIONAL GROUPS

We turn now to the major focus of this section. We are interested in what the relationships are between motives and job reactions in particular types of job roles. In this section we will be looking at the results of this type of analysis within the ten specific occupational groups. In the next section we present a parallel analysis within the general occupational classifications.

In this section the data are presented separately for each motive (Tables 5.4–5.6). Each table presents the relationship between a given motive and a given job reaction for men in each of the ten specific occupational groups. Preceding the presentation of results for each motive we will orient the readers with capsule summaries, as we had done in the chapters on marriage and parenthood.

Affiliation motivation and job reactions in specific occupations. We had discussed two theoretically possible sources of affiliative gratification in the job role, one dependent on the social interaction required by the work activity and the other dependent on social interaction that was ancillary to the work activity itself. The results concerning the relationship between the affiliation motive and job reactions for men in different occupations strongly suggest that only the latter source is actually gratifying to men with strong affiliation motivation.

The sensitization principle was exemplified in the finding that clerical workers who had high affiliation motivation were significantly more likely to describe the affiliative relations at work as a primary source of job satisfaction than were clerical workers with low affiliation motivation.

The congruence principle was supported by two sets of relationships. First, men with high affiliation motivation in jobs with few parallel associates—the foremen and farmers—were significantly more dissatisfied with their jobs than men with low affiliation motivation. Second, men with high affiliation motivation in jobs with many parallel associates—the semiskilled and unskilled workers—were more satisfied with their jobs than men with low affiliation motivation, significantly so for the semiskilled workers.

The role of salesman emerges as a double problem for men with high affiliation motivation. Salesmen with high affiliation motivation reported significantly more economic job satisfaction and significantly less achievement job satisfaction than did salesmen with low affiliation motivation. We suggest that this pattern for the men with high affiliation motivation shows a certain amount of disengagement from their work. They may be so consistently frustrated in their search for affiliation in commercial relationships that they are unable to meet the achievement demands of the job. They thereby lose out on achievement satisfactions, too.

Among men in white-collar jobs, it was only among the lower-status groups that significant relationships between affiliation motivation and job reactions were obtained (Table 5.4). Salesmen who had high affiliation motivation reported significantly more *Economic Job Satisfaction* and less *Achievement Job Satisfaction* than those who had low affiliation motivation.[13] Men with high affiliation motivation who are in sales evidently view the

---

[13]Although these variables were negatively associated with each other, these relationships do not seem entirely attributable to that negative association. These two sources of job satisfaction showed opposite and significant relationships only to the affiliation motive and not to the achievement or power motives.

TABLE 5-4 THE RELATIONSHIP OF THE AFFILIATION MOTIVE TO JOB REACTIONS (WITHIN SPECIFIC OCCUPATIONS)

Job Reaction		Professional Advisers	Managers: Self-Employed	Managers: Not Self-Employed	Salesmen	Clerical Workers	Foremen	Skilled Workers	Semiskilled Workers	Unskilled Workers	Farmers
						Specific Occupation					
Job dissatisfaction	γ	−.28	.03	.01	.06	−.10	.36*	.02	−.28†	−.53	.41*
	(N)	(17)	(32)	(32)	(30)	(29)	(33)	(81)	(80)	(17)	(32)
Lack of commitment	γ	−.24	−.22	.10	−.30	−.03	−.11	.22	.02	−.77	.02
	(N)	(16)	(33)	(32)	(31)	(29)	(33)	(83)	(81)	(17)	(32)
Type of job satisfaction											
Economic	γ	−.67	−.12	−.12	.80†	.14	.10	.23	−.25	−.26	—a
	(N)	(17)	(32)	(31)	(30)	(28)	(33)	(80)	(77)	(16)	(31)
Achievement	γ	−.10	−.01	−.43	−.52†	−.18	−.04	−.13	.07	.27	−.20
	(N)	(17)	(32)	(31)	(30)	(28)	(33)	(80)	(77)	(16)	(31)
Affiliation	γ	.20	−.11	.37	−.16	.58*	−.05	.06	.20	−.62	—a
	(N)	(17)ᵇ	(32)	(31)	(30)	(28)	(33)	(78)	(77)	(16)	(31)
Type of job dissatisfaction											
Economic	γ	−.55	−.13	−.09	−1.00	.18	−.10	.21	.08	−.33	.22
	(N)	(15)	(24)	(26)	(26)	(25)	(24)	(64)	(62)	(12)	(26)
Achievement	γ	−.50	−1.00	−.38	.35	.39	.57	−.07	−.36	−.73	−.05
	(N)	(15)	(24)	(26)	(26)	(25)	(24)	(64)	(62)	(12)	(26)

Note: In this and subsequent tables in this chapter, entries are the gamma index of association between a given motive and job reaction or leisure activity for the specified occupational subgroup. Probability levels are reported for the tau-beta rank order correlation coefficient computed for the same relationship. For example, in this table the gamma for the relationship between the affiliation motive and Job Dissatisfaction was −.28 for the professional advisers, and .03 for the self-employed managers.

ᵃNot reported because of inadequate distribution.

*p < .05.

†p < .10.

250

gratification from the economic rewards that sales bring as more important than do salesmen with low affiliation motive. Perhaps men with strong motivation for social acceptance are particularly concerned about adequately providing for their families and therefore emphasize the economic rewards of their job since they are a means of satisfying their personal needs. The interpretation of *Economic Job Satisfaction* that we offered earlier, however, would suggest that reporting this kind of job satisfaction reflects a disengaged attitude toward the job and the absence of more personally meaningful sources of satisfaction. Why should salesmen with high affiliation motivation be disengaged from their job? Contact with people is a requirement of sales, but the kind of contact selling requires can be inimical to those interested in satisfying emotional relationships with people. Indeed, for salesmen there was a slight negative relationship between the affiliation motive and mentioning affiliative gratification at work. We will see later that it is the salesmen with high power motive who describe affiliative gratification in their jobs. At any rate, it seems that the interpersonal contact in sales is not the kind gratifying to a man with a high affiliation motive. Men who seek friendship in their commercial relationships may not only be disappointed in that quest, but because they focus on the potential affiliativeness of the contact may not be able to focus on the potential achievement in sales work. This may explain why men with high affiliation motivation in sales work are not likely to report achievement satisfactions. They may not perform their jobs well nor find their work interesting or suited to their ability.

In contrast, clerical workers with high affiliation motivation mentioned more affiliative job satisfactions than those who were low in this motivation. Clerical work requires very little in the way of social or reciprocal role relationships in the job enactment itself; but it is a job that often provides colleagues in parallel job status. This condition, where friendship can develop in the job situation but where it is not a part of the enactment of the job, may be the kind of flexible situation that a man can adapt to the goals of a strong affiliation motive. This conclusion will become even clearer as we discuss further results. At this point we would use this rationale to understand why men with high affiliation motivation may more easily obtain affiliative satisfaction in clerical work than in jobs such as sales or in the advising professions.

Among blue-collar workers there was a very interesting pattern of relationships between the affiliation motive and *Job Dissatisfaction*. For two groups, having a high affiliation motive seemed to interfere with job satisfaction: farmers or foremen who had high affiliation motive were significantly *more likely to be dissatisfied* with their jobs than those farmers and foremen who had low affiliation motive. For two other blue-collar groups, however, the reverse tended to be true: the semiskilled and

251

unskilled workers with high affiliation motive were *more likely to be satisfied* with their work than those with low affiliation motive. This relationship was significant only for the semiskilled.

We see this pattern of results with blue-collar workers as a good demonstration of the congruence principle. Foremen and farmers, in different ways, hold jobs that do not allow much in the way of affiliative gratification. Farmers do not have much potential for finding affiliative gratification because their job is a solitary one, their work activity requires self-responsibility without much contact with others. Therefore, men with high affiliation motive who are in farming jobs are apt to be disgruntled. Foremen also have major blocks in the way of finding affiliation gratification in their work. Any kind of supervisory relationship probably interferes with the development of friendship between supervisor and supervisee. Foremen may have additional blocks to affiliative satisfaction, since their supervisory relationships are likely to be with men with whom they once had affiliative contact as peers. In the new role of supervisor, a foreman symbolically wears a badge of identification with management, a badge that is a barrier to continued affiliative contact with the workers whom he now supervises, and with whom he once shared a common fate. Lieberman (1950) found that men who were promoted to the job of foreman in a large factory were more likely to become critical of the union than either the men whose status was maintained, or the men promoted to the job of steward for union affairs. Their new role as a foreman set them aside from the other men. The separation between former and present affiliative potential in their job is probably what makes the foremen with high affiliation motive feel dissatisfied with their work.

In the two blue-collar groups where the affiliation motive was negatively related to *Job Dissatisfaction*, the semiskilled and the unskilled, there is considerable freedom for affiliative contact at work. Men in these jobs, as in the clerical jobs, often work alongside a number of colleagues and peers and rarely are in supervisory positions. Fellow-workers are easy targets for affiliative interests. Men with high affiliation motive in such jobs should find this sort of work setting very gratifying. It is curious, in light of our interpretation, that the smiskilled and unskilled men with high affiliation motivation do not report more *Affiliation Job Satisfaction* than men low in affiliation motivation. There is a tendency in this direction for the semiskilled, but an opposite trend for the unskilled. These are curious results in light of our interpretation. It raises the possibility that the type of friendly contact made among unskilled workers is one that men with high affiliation motive may not be prone to verbalize. Affiliation is not manly in our society.

At any rate, the negative relationship found between affiliation motivation and *Job Dissatisfaction* in groups of semiskilled and unskilled workers and the positive relationship found between affiliation motivation and *Job Dissatisfaction* in foremen and farmers represent a pattern of results that we view as a clear demonstration of the congruence principle. Indeed it is the clearest verification of this principle that we have been able to obtain in the whole set of data presented so far in this book. A similar pattern of results will emerge when we look at the motive-job reaction interaction within some of the general job classifications in sections to follow.

Achievement motivation and job reactions in specific occupations. We had expected that the relationship between the achievement motive and job dissatisfaction would be conditioned by the difficulty, prestige, or opportunities for independence in different jobs. We found instead that the relationship was largely independent of occupational subgroupings: men with high achievement motivation expressed more dissatisfaction with their jobs than men with low achievement potential. Since this trend was generally true, although significant only among the skilled workers, we suggest that achievement motivation may underlie a continual striving for excellence that is expressed in lack of satisfaction with one's job, no matter how much potential achievement exists in the occupation.

This continual striving for excellence among men with strong achievement motivation may also help explain the general trend, which was significant for the semiskilled workers, for a positive association between the achievement motive and the report of dissatisfaction with the achievement gratifications in one's job. Men with strong achievement motivation seem to be sensitized to achievement inadequacies in their jobs. There were two occupational groups in which the opposite trend was found: strong achievement motivation was associated with the absence of achievement job dissatisfaction among clerical and unskilled workers. These are the occupational groups that occupy the low rung of their respective status hierarchies. Not only was the association with achievement job dissatisfaction negative for these groups, and significantly so for the clerical workers, but it was also in these groups that achievement motivation was positively related to achievement job satisfaction. This pattern of results suggests that these occupations produce defensive reactions in men with high achievement motivation. These men deny their achievement dissatisfaction and overreport their achievement satisfaction.

In all but one of the occupational groups (unskilled workers) there was a positive relationship between *Job Dissatisfaction* and the strength of the achievement motive; the higher the achievement motive, the more dissatisfaction at work (Table 5.5) The only group in which the relationship was significant was in the skilled workers, one of the largest samples in our study. Our immediate reaction to this result is that we have no direct support for the congruence principle. Using that guiding principle, we expected that persons with high achievement motivation would be dissatisfied in their work only if they were in jobs that were low in achievement potential. Therefore, we expected a positive relationship between

TABLE 5-5 THE RELATIONSHIP OF THE ACHIEVEMENT MOTIVE TO JOB REACTIONS (WITHIN SPECIFIC OCCUPATIONS)

Job Reaction		Professional Advisers	Managers: Self-Employed	Managers: Not Self-Employed	Salesmen	Clerical Workers	Foremen	Skilled Workers	Semiskilled Workers	Unskilled Workers	Farmers
						Specific Occupation					
Job dissatisfaction	γ	.52	.06	.19	.05	.07	.32	.22*	.22	-.50	.06
	(N)	(17)	(32)	(32)	(30)	(29)	(33)	(81)	(80)	(17)	(32)
Lack of commitment	γ	.10	-.10	.16	.05	-.14	-.46	-.12	.04	-.12	.35
	(N)	(16)	(33)	(32)	(31)	(29)	(33)	(83)	(81)	(17)	(32)
Type of job satisfaction											
Economic	γ	.39	.04	-.20	-.23	-.11	.06	.12	-.04	-.26	—[a]
	(N)	(17)	(32)	(31)	(30)	(28)	(33)	(80)	(77)	(16)	(31)
Achievement	γ	-.10	.41	-.21	.15	.52*	.18	-.21	.04	.68	.25
	(N)	(17)	(32)	(31)	(30)	(28)	(33)	(80)	(77)	(16)	(31)
Affiliation	γ	-.44	-.36	.12	.26	-.27	.20	-.01	.17	-.11	—[a]
	(N)	(17)	(32)	(31)	(30)	(28)	(33)	(78)	(77)	(16)	(31)
Type of job dissatisfaction											
Economic	γ	-1.00	-.23	-.55	.37	.27	-.07	-.12	.09	.33	.22
	(N)	(15)	(24)	(26)	(26)	(25)	(24)	(64)	(62)	(12)	(26)
Achievement	γ	.56	1.00	1.00	.24	-.73†	-.07	.16	.45*	-.33	.44
	(N)	(15)	(24)	(26)	(26)	(25)	(24)	(64)	(62)	(12)	(26)

[a]Not reported because of inadequate distribution.
*p < .10.
†p < .05.

achievement motivation and *Job Dissatisfaction* among the semiskilled or unskilled workers and a negative relationship between achievement motivation and *Job Dissatisfaction* in groups such as in the professional advisers, managers, and the skilled workers because they are highly prestigious jobs in their respective occupational hierarchies. But the relationships obtained in the latter groups were distinctly positive. These results and succeeding ones made us change our perspective about the relationship of achievement motive and satisfaction or dissatisfaction with the job.

We had assumed that certain jobs are high in achievement potential because they call for the exercise of individual skills and permit evaluation of effort in competition with standards (skilled workers, professional advisers, and even foremen). We further assumed that men with high achievement motivation would be satisfied with such jobs because they provide the conditions for achievement satisfaction. It seems apparent now that that assumption neglected the dynamic aspect of achievement motivation which leads to continual goal setting and increasing levels of aspiration after successful mastery. The achievement motive, therefore, could be a factor not only in determining the quality and development of aspirations before attaining a job but also throughout the course of job performance. Men with high achievement motive in any job might demand greater and greater accomplishment from themselves in their work and might demand more and more challenging work. *Perhaps men with high achievement motivation are never satisfied with their accomplishment.* The continual striving for excellence at work and the continual setting of higher goals that are characteristic of men with high achievement motivation could provide a basis for high levels of discontent. Men with low achievement motivation may be the ones who can accept their level of accomplishment, who do not demand more from their work, and who are more easily satisfied with their jobs. We look at this particular finding as one of the most important results in the whole study.

We expected that a high achievement motive would be associated with reporting both achievement satisfaction and dissatisfaction in most jobs and especially in those jobs ambiguously structured for achievement. But the results do not support this simple hypothesis. Instead the type of job is an important conditioner of these relationships.

For two groups—the clerical workers and unskilled workers—the achievement motive was positively related to *Achievement Job Satisfaction* and was negatively related to *Achievement Job Dissatisfaction* (although only the gammas for the clerical workers were significant). This was a surprising result since the clerical workers are at the bottom of the white-collar hierarchy and the unskilled workers are in the same low position in the blue-collar hierarchy. Men in both of these jobs are presumably finding minimal achievements that could be recognized by the world. Indeed among the unskilled workers we found the only negative correlation between achievement motivation and *Job Dissatisfaction*. And this correlation was very low, although positive, for the clerical workers. Perhaps these are indications that these men have easily given up finding achievement possibilities at work. And so we were startled to find that in these groups men with a high achievement motive were more likely to report achievement satisfaction and less likely to report achievement dissatisfaction than men with a low achievement motive. If the same pattern of results had emerged in other groups we might have considered it to be a reflection of positive achievement gratification in the job. In these two occupational groups, however, where there is relatively little opportunity or recognition on the job for independent accomplishment, we suggest that this combination of results may indicate a defensive reaction. A man who has high achievement motive but is in a job that offers very little in the way of achievement incentives, may state defensively that he is pleased by the possibilities for achievement when indeed there may be few such possibilities. He may be very loathe to admit to himself and to the world that the job itself is indicative of his inability to gain achievement gratification. He, therefore, may "over" report achievement gratifications and "under" report achievement dissatisfactions.

For semiskilled workers there was a positive relationship between *Achievement Job Dissatisfaction* and achievement motivation, a result that we originally expected from the sensitization principle. Perhaps among the semiskilled workers there is enough ambiguity about the achievement potential in a job that men with high achievement motive are more likely to see the achievement difficulties inherent to such jobs. Furthermore, not being in the lowest position in the blue-collar status hierarchy, these semiskilled workers are potentially more sensitive to their own possibility for achievement than are the unskilled workers.

In most of the other groups the direction of the relationship between the achievement motive and reporting achievement dissatisfaction was as we expected: a high achievement motive was associated with complaints about the achievement-relevant aspects of the job. This leads us to believe that the sensitization phenomena in the area of achievement usually operate more clearly when men report reasons for job dissatisfaction than when they report reasons for job satisfaction.

The entire pattern of results concerning achievement motivation led us to an interesting possible overall conclusion. Although not all the results neatly fit it, we present it as a guiding conclusion for further work. A person with a high achievement motive in a job that has some potential for achievement gratification may be operating with progessive goals for accomplishment that are never fully realized. Therefore, he is likely to be more oriented to the quality of his achievement discontent than he is to the quality of his contentment relevant to achievement. A person with a high achievement motive in a job with very low achievement potential can become so demoralized that he may forget about his achievement aspirations and take on the defensive style we have discussed above—overreporting potential achievement satisfactions at work and underreporting achievement dissatisfactions.

Power motivation and job reactions in specific occupations. Our data support the idea that power motivation can disrupt men's feelings about their worth if the job demands certain types of explicit influencing. Foremen and professional advisers were significantly more likely to report job dissatisfaction if they had high power motivation than if they had low power motivation.

One role—that of salesman—seems to be congruent with high power motivation. Salesmen were significantly more often committed to work and pleased with the interpersonal aspects of their job, and were significantly less often pleased with the economic aspects of their job if they had high rather than low power motivation. We would suggest this is so because salesmen have more leeway in their choice of targets and styles of influence than do foremen and professional advisers. Salesmen with high power motivation are sensitive to this influence potential in their interpersonal contacts.

Based on the general congruence principle, we had dual expectations for how the power motive might be related to job reactions in the various occupations. We expected fear of weakness to be reflected in dissatisfaction, both with jobs that did not allow for much influence or with jobs that demanded a considerable amount of influence in the job itself. The data in Table 5.6 lend more support to the latter alternative.

Men with high power motive who had jobs as foremen or as professional advisers were significantly more dissatisfied with their work than their counterparts with low power motive. Both of these jobs require influence activity in the day-to-day setting. Foremen and professional advisers are people who are expected to exert influence on others and for whom success or failure at influence attempts can be easily determined. In these jobs one might say that men have to offer a great public display of their influence. Professional advisers in law have to argue their cases for their clients in public, some cases are lost and some are won. Foremen have to keep production going and sometimes production may lag; their lack of influence can be easily seen. Put in such positions, men with fear of weakness (high power motive) might be particularly anxious about whether or not their influence will be effective. Being in such vulnerable positions from day-to-day may make the men who are high in power motive quite dissatisfied. Men who lack concern about their own weakness, those low in measured power motive, may be the men who cannot be easily disrupted by their lack of influence in the job setting.

TABLE 5-6 THE RELATIONSHIP OF THE POWER MOTIVE TO JOB REACTIONS (WITHIN SPECIFIC OCCUPATIONS)

Job Reaction		Specific Occupation									
		Professional Advisers	Managers: Self-Employed	Managers: Not Self-Employed	Salesmen	Clerical Workers	Foremen	Skilled Workers	Semi-skilled Workers	Unskilled Workers	Farmers
Job dissatisfaction	γ	.52*	−.18	.12	.17	.01	.40*	−.04	.12	.26	.15
	(N)	(17)	(32)	(32)	(30)	(29)	(33)	(81)	(80)	(17)	(32)
Lack of commitment	γ	.72	−.16	.11	−.73*	1.00	−.26	−.04	−.23	−.33	−.66
	(N)	(16)	(33)	(32)	(31)	(29)	(33)	(83)	(81)	(17)	(32)
Type of job satisfaction											
Economic	γ	1.00	.37	.26	−.56*	−.29	−.05	.02	−.11	.56	—[a]
	(N)	(17)	(32)	(31)	(30)	(28)	(33)	(80)	(77)	(16)	(31)
Achievement	γ	−.04	−.12	.36	.08	.00	.29	.09	.02	−.62	−.25
	(N)	(17)	(32)	(31)	(30)	(28)	(33)	(80)	(77)	(16)	(31)
Affiliation	γ	−.07	−.13	−.10	.52†	−.32	−.24	−.33	.14	.58	—[a]
	(N)	(17)	(32)	(31)	(30)	(28)	(33)	(78)	(77)	(16)	(31)
Type of job dissatisfaction											
Economic	γ	.00	−.06	−.21	.22	.54	−.27	.16	.32	.42	.34
	(N)	(15)	(24)	(26)	(26)	(25)	(24)	(64)	(62)	(12)	(26)
Achievement	γ	−.13	−1.00	.16	.13	−.23	.20	−.32	.18	1.00	−.84
	(N)	(15)	(24)	(26)	(26)	(25)	(24)	(64)	(62)	(12)	(26)

[a]Not reported because of inadequate distribution.
*p < .10.
†p < .05.

Where we do seem to find a meshing of the power motive with a job, a meshing that produces strong ego-involvement with work, is in the sales group. Salesmen with a high power motive were significantly more committed to their work, reported significantly less *Economic Job Satisfaction*, and reported significantly more *Affiliation Job Satisfaction* than salesmen with a low power motive. Salesmen with high power motivation seem to be gaining power satisfaction from their sales work. They de-emphasize the economic rewards of work and emphasize the social rewards, the contact with people that permits gratifications from influencing another. We should remember that there was a significant negative relationship between the affiliation motive and mentioning affiliative satisfactions among sales workers. Social gratifications that require influence in the commercial world thus seem particularly gratifying to a person concerned about his weakness and not at all gratifying to a person seeking an accepting emotional relationship with another individual. Camaraderie with a customer is usually transient. Salesmanship engages a salesman's public image, a salesman cannot easily feel his private self is ever known to a customer. Business dealings are institutionalized forms of influence—apparently enjoyed by men with high power motive and offering little for men with high affiliation motive. Thus we would see the positive relationship of power motivation to affiliative satisfaction as consistent with the sensitization principle, once the quality of affiliative contact in sales is taken into account.

From this discussion we might conclude that while the influence requirement in sales is congruent with power motivation, the influence requirement in professional advising and in the foreman's job is incongruent with power motivation. What is the difference between these kinds of jobs? Why isn't power motivation congruent with all jobs where influence is a major job requirement? The following speculations are suggested. In sales a person has some leeway in making decisions on how much he should approach or avoid an influence attempt with particular persons in the course of his job. For example, he can choose to attempt to influence through a "soft sell" or a more assertive "hard sell" technique. Foremen and professional advisers have no leeway as to whether an influence attempt has to be made with particular people. Lawyers, teachers, foremen have to exert influence publicly on particular people in order to be successful at work. Although a salesman's job is public also, in most instances a salesman has some option in dealing with the people whom he meets. He can attempt to influence those whom he sees as a reasonable target for an influence attempt. Furthermore, if he is unsuccessful he can move on to another customer; his failure need not remain in evidence. Professional advisers and foremen generally have more enduring relationships with the people whom they try to influence. Salesmen also have concrete products to sell, unlike teachers, lawyers, or foremen. As a result, salesmen can attribute difficulties in influence to the product, not so the public advisers or foremen. Thus one might say that the fear of weakness that seems to stimulate the dissatisfaction among men with high power motivation who are foremen or professional advisers may not seem to be as strong a factor in the power situation for salesmen. If such an interpretation is correct, we could conclude that conditions of congruence are in evidence for power-motivated men in sales jobs but that incongruence is reflected in the responses of power-motivated men in professional advising jobs or in foremen occupations.

It seems apparent that more detailed descriptions of any particular jobs would give us more clues about the potential for both the congruence and sensitization principles. In our discussion about sales personnel, for example, we assumed that there was some freedom of action for a salesman in choosing to make an influence attempt, a fact that allowed the sales person to be less fearful than a foreman or a professional adviser of displaying his weakness. But it might very well be that there is considerable public display of sales incapacities in certain sales jobs where there are no choices and no easy way to attribute difficulties in sales to a bad or expensive product. A person who is employed as a door-to-door salesman has quite different job demands from a sales person within an executive training program, or a sales person in a retail store. A closer look at any one of these occupations would yield a better assessment of the usefulness of the congruence principle. In this national survey we included a number of different jobs into one job classification that we have called sales, or foremen, or whatever. It is quite gratifying to find that there are some consistent patterns of motive-role interactions in these occupational classifications, in spite of the fact that these classifications do represent fairly gross groupings of various types of actual occupations.

RESULTS CONCERNING MOTIVES AND JOB REACTIONS—WITHIN GENERAL OCCUPATIONAL CHARACTERISTICS

In the previous section we had assumed that specific categories of occupations had certain role demands, gratification potentials, and ambiguities. Then, based on our assumptions about the ways that specific occupations differed, we investigated the effects of congruence between motives and role characteristics on job reactions. We will now consider whether each of the three motives shows different patterns of relationships to job reactions when the role characteristics are defined in terms of the general occupational classifications that we have singled out for study— namely, *Prestige, Social Requirements* in high *Prestige* jobs, *Supervision,* and *Supervisory Potential.* Here our assumption is that regardless of the specific occupational characteristics, certain role features, such as whether or not a person is closely supervised in his work, are more or less congruent with each of the motives. Some of the interpretations of the results for specific occupational groups were based on their shared *general* role characteristics. Since the same subjects are involved in specific and general occupational groupings, some of the results previously described under the *specific* occupational groups will reappear in more general form using the *general* job characteristics. We should be cautious in thinking of results that appear to be the generalized form of an earlier result as new, independent results.

The data are presented in Tables 5.7–5.10 for two of the major role reactions—*Job Dissatisfaction* and *Lack of Commitment*. Relationships to other role reactions will be discussed in the text when they are relevant. In each table, a separate general occupational characteristic is used, and the subjects are divided into two groups—those whose jobs were coded high on that occupational characteristic and those whose jobs were coded low. Within each of these two groups, then, the relationships between each motive and the two job reactions are presented separately for subjects at three age levels and for all subjects, disregarding age. The results are discussed separately for the four general occupational characteristics.

Motives and job reactions within jobs of high and low prestige. We had expected that prestigeful jobs would be congruent with high achievement and power motivation and that this general job characteristic would probably be irrelevant to the gratification of the affiliation motive. And we found that the categorization of subjects in terms of the prestige of their jobs produced no significant motive-role interactions for affiliation motivation but that there were significant relationships for both achievement and power motivation.

The sensitization principle was in evidence in the relationship found between achievement motivation and mentioning achievement satisfaction among young men in jobs high in prestige: these men with high achievement motivation significantly more often reported achievement job satisfactions than did their counterparts with low achievement motivation. This was not so for older men in high prestige jobs or for any of the men in low prestige jobs. We would suggest that young men with high prestige jobs might be the only group for whom the ultimate achievement potential is ambiguous. Thus, if they have high achievement motivation they become alerted to achievement satisfactions.

The relationship of achievement motivation to mentioning achievement dissatisfaction showed opposing trends at the two levels of job prestige: achievement dissatisfaction tended to be positively associated with achievement motivation in men whose jobs were high in prestige, and negatively associated in men whose jobs were low in prestige. This pattern confirmed an earlier interpretation of a similar contradiction to a direct sensitization principle: men with high achievement motivation who are caught in jobs that offered few achievement possibilities avoid mentioning their achievement dissatisfaction.

Earlier we suggested that being dissatisfied with one's job may reflect a high level of aspiration rather than discontent. In examining the different age groups within the two prestige levels, we found that such a conclusion seems justified only for the young men, for whom the limits on aspiration might still be at an unknown height. At both prestige levels young men were significantly more dissatisfied with their jobs if they had strong rather than weak achievement motivation.

For older men in high prestige jobs, the expression of job dissatisfaction was significantly associated with high power motivation, not with high achievement motivation. For these men we interpret job dissatisfaction not as high aspiration but as true discontent with the intrinsic aspects of work, for these men also under-report achievement dissatisfaction. And at all ages men with high power motivation in high prestige jobs tended to be highly alerted to economic job satisfaction, as if they were aware of the public consequences of their financial status rather than the nature of their work as such.

Men with high power motivation react differently if they enjoy the financial benefits of a prestigious job than if they have a job of low prestige. The power-motivated men with prestigious jobs were significantly more dissatisfied with their jobs, and tended to report more economic job satisfaction and less achievement job dissatisfaction than those with low power motivation. In jobs low in prestige, men with high power motivation tended to less often report economic job dissatisfaction than those with low power motivation. Thus in both types of jobs there was a focus on the economic benefits or liabilities rather than on intrinsic work activities. However, middle-aged men in jobs of low prestige showed a somewhat different pattern. Those with high power motivation were significantly more committed to their work and significantly more often satisfied with the achievement aspects of their job than those with low power motivation. For these middle-aged men, the mere fact of working seems to be a very important way to control feelings of weakness.

We had no expectations for the way that the *Prestige* of a man's job role should affect the relationship between affiliation motive and job reactions, and in fact, the affiliation motive did not relate significantly to any job reactions in the jobs of either high or low *Prestige* (Table 5.7). There was some tendency for a high affiliation motive to be associated with *Affiliation Job Satisfaction* in most groups, regardless of job *Prestige*, but none of these relationships was significant. Although the consistency of this trend across groups is interesting, we can conclude that the prestige of a job does not seem to be an important factor in determining whether or not men with a high affiliation motive will report affiliative satisfaction.

Our initial expectation was that high achievement motive would be congruent with high *Prestige* jobs and incongruent with low *Prestige* jobs. But the results within specific occupational groups suggested that this expectation was incorrect. The data in Table 5.7 corroborate the results that we have already reported for certain specific occupations; namely, regardless of the *Prestige* level of their job, men who had high achievement motivation tended to be more dissatisfied with their job than men with low achievement motivation. This positive relationship between the achievement motive and *Job Dissatisfaction* was significant within both *Prestige* levels for the young men, and also for the total groups, disregarding age. We had previously interpreted this type of relationship as reflecting the high level of job aspirations set by men with high achievement

TABLE 5-7 THE RELATIONSHIP (γ) OF MOTIVES TO SELECTED JOB REACTIONS IN JOBS HIGH AND LOW IN PRESTIGE (WITHIN AGE)

Job Reaction	Age	High Prestige				Low Prestige			
		Affiliation Motive	Achievement Motive	Power Motive	(N)	Affiliation Motive	Achievement Motive	Power Motive	(N)
Job dissatisfaction	Young	−.05	.49‡	.08	(56)	−.15	.25†	.00	(107)
	Middle	.08	.10	.04	(71)	−.17	.17	−.13	(83)
	Old	.07	.03	.39†	(61)	.03	−.05	.16	(77)
	All	.04	.22†	.17*	(188)	−.11	.14*	−.01	(268)
Lack of commitment	Young	.07	−.32	.13	(57)	−.09	.04	.12	(109)
	Middle	−.28	.16	.18	(71)	−.02	−.20	−.40*	(86)
	Old	.10	−.50	−.29	(61)	−.07	−.01	−.09	(77)
	All	−.07	−.16	.05	(189)	−.07	−.03	−.12	(272)

*p < .10.
†p < .05.
‡p < .01.

263

motive. Such an interpretation seems most appropriate for young men, whose early career phase means that their ultimate occupational success is still ambiguous, whether they are in jobs of recognized achievement potential or not.

For men with jobs high in *Prestige*, achievement motivation tended to be associated with commitment to work. Thus in high *Prestige* jobs men with high achievement motivation express work commitment and job dissatisfaction. This seems consistent with the view of these men as being involved in their work, but unsatisfied because they demand a lot from it. We suggest, therefore, that there is greater congruence between high achievement motivation and work in high *Prestige* jobs than there is in low *Prestige* jobs, as we originally hypothesized.

We had assumed that men with high achievement motivation generally would be sensitive to both the achievement satisfactions and dissatisfactions on the job. Faced with jobs with objectively poor achievement potential, such as jobs low in *Prestige*, it seemed that men with high achievement motivation should be sensitized to report achievement dissatisfactions. Faced with jobs with objectively high achievement potential, such as jobs high in *Prestige*, it seemed that men with high achievement motivation should be sensitized to report achievement satisfactions in their work. We did find support for the latter ramification of the sensitization principle, but not the former. There were generally consistent trends in all age groups for men with high *Prestige* jobs who had high achievement motivation to report achievement job satisfactions. This was clearest for young men; for this group there was a significant positive relationship (gamma = .37, $p < .10$ for tau beta) between the achievement motive and reporting *Achievement Job Satisfaction*. There were positive associative trends between the achievement motive and *Achievement Job Satisfaction* in young and old men in jobs low in *Prestige*, but these relationships were not significant, and the trend for middle-aged men was not consistent. We had previously suggested that the final evaluation of success at work accomplishment is most ambiguous for young men. Older men generally know what level of excellence they have attained already and what their future accomplishments are likely to be. We now suggest that this ambiguity is strongest for young men in jobs high in *Prestige*. Young men in a job of low *Prestige* generally are aware of its limitations, and if they are achievement-oriented they are as likely to think of increasing their achievement gratifications by changing jobs as they are to focus on the achievement possibilities in their current jobs.

The other direct application of the sensitization principle led us to expect that achievement motivation would be associated with reporting *Achievement Job Dissatisfaction*, and especially for men in jobs low in *Prestige*. Instead we found this general trend among men with jobs of high *Prestige*. Mentioning achievement dissatisfaction tended to be positively associated with achievement motivation in high *Prestige* jobs for young (gamma = .26) and old men (gamma = .61). For men in jobs low in *Prestige* there were negative trends of association with *Achievement Job Dissatisfaction* (gamma = −.27 for young men, gamma = −.40 for old men); these men in jobs with manifestly low achievement gratification potential were less likely to report dissatisfaction with the achievement aspects of their jobs if they had high rather than low achievement motivation. Although these opposite patterns for men in jobs high and low in *Prestige* do not confirm our original ideas in applying the sensitization principle, they do reinforce a general speculation we had made based on the relationships found within the specific occupations: mentioning achievement dissatisfaction reflects a positive attitude towards achievement in jobs that offer some potential for achievement, but mentioning such dissatisfaction in jobs that offer little potential for achievement may be tantamount to admitting total failure, particularly for those men who have a high achievement motive. Therefore the men who are most involved in achievement goals in low *Prestige* jobs, those high in achievement motive, would avoid mentioning these deficits.

The pattern of relationship of the power motive to job reactions showed an interesting differentiation within the two different levels of *Prestige*. In the high *Prestige* jobs, men with a high power motive were less satisfied with their jobs (significantly so for older men and the total group) than men with a low power motive. We interpret this job dissatisfaction, not as reflecting a high level of aspiration, but rather a high level of discontent with the work itself. We were influenced in this interpretation by the pattern of relationships between the power motive and the sources of job satisfaction and dissatisfaction. Men with high power motivation in jobs of high *Prestige* tended to have more often mentioned *Economic Job Satisfaction* as a thing they liked about their work (gamma = .25 for all men) and *less* often mentioned *Achievement Job Dissatisfaction* (gamma = −.14 for all men) than those with low power motivation. Thus, men with high power motive in prestigious jobs are more concerned about the relatively public consequences of their job, its economic rewards, than they are about what the work itself entails. And they did not report the kinds of dissatisfaction we had interpreted to mean setting standards of excellence at work (achievement dissatisfaction). Since feelings of satisfaction with the job itself are tied to the intrinsic qualities of the job, this focus on extrinsic job characteristics may account for their high levels of *Job Dissatisfaction*. This pattern of results suggests a picture of men who are interested in using the power that prestigious jobs bring as a means of reducing their own sense of weakness in relationship to others in their social community. For these men, being in a job recognized as prestigious

265

by others could be more important than other aspects of their job. The money obtained from jobs of high *Prestige* by men with high power motivation is perhaps an important symbol to them, a symbol that gives them influence in the community but it does not take them very far in attaining direct gratification from work.

In jobs of low *Prestige* we found a somewhat different pattern of results which both confirms this interpretation of what work could mean for men with high power motivation, and suggests an additional interpretation. Whereas men in jobs of high *Prestige* were alert to economic job satisfactions if they had high power motivation, in jobs of low *Prestige*, men with high power motivation were alert to *Economic Job Dissatisfaction* (gamma = .24 for all men). Thus we have further evidence that men with high power motivation might be attuned to the extrinsic influence potential of a job rather than its intrinsic value.

Work also seems to have another type of extrinsic meaning for some power-motivated men in jobs of low *Prestige*. Among the middle-aged men in these jobs, there was a significant negative relationship between *Lack of Commitment* and the power motive; men with a high power motive were more likely than those with low power motive to be committed to work for nonmonetary reasons. This relationship was in the same direction in the older age group, but was not significant. Middle-aged men with high power motive were also significantly more likely to mention achievement satisfactions at work than were those with low power motive (gamma = .30, $p < .10$ for tau beta). This commitment to work and focus on ego-involved aspects of their work among middle-aged men with high power motive could be an indication that the mere fact of working, even in jobs that are not very prestigious, becomes a guarantee of power. The power accorded men who hold a job may thus be an important signpost of the avoidance of weakness among certain social groups. Faced with the general assessment of one's job as low in status, a middle-aged man (for whom we assume work is still a primary focus of attention) should be especially concerned about boosting the importance of work if he has a high power motive.

These interpretations should be considered highly speculative. We had expected that concern about job maintenance would be most striking in the o dest age group of men who were in the low *Prestige* jobs, but the pattern of results suggests that this is not the case.

Our expectation that low *Prestige* would be incongruent with high power motivation, and therefore cause disgruntlement, does not seem to have been borne out. Jobs of low *Prestige* offer little potential for the exercise of power. If a man with high power motivation is concerned about influencing, then we would have expected some results indicating a lack of congruence between having high power motivation and being in a job of low *Prestige*. Such was not the case. This suggests perhaps that men with high power motivation are not as much concerned about influencing as they are avoiding the appearance of weakness.

Motives and job reactions within jobs of high and low social requirements. For men who held high prestige jobs, we distinguished those jobs that required social relations for adequate performance and those that did not in order to determine whether this distinction in role demands was associated with differential patterns of relationships between motives and job reactions. We had expected that the social requirements of a job could be relevant to all three motives, and the results supported this expectation.

In jobs with high social requirements men with high affiliation motivation tended to be more dissatisfied than men with low affiliation motivation, while in jobs without these requirements, high affiliation motivation tended to evoke job satisfaction. This pattern seems most explicable as an instance of the congruence principle if we assume here, as we had done after surveying the results for specific occupations, that a job obliging men to assume social functions in fact impedes affiliative gratification. On the face of it, however, this result seems to be a contradiction of the congruence principle.

In jobs with high social requirements, older men with high achievement motivation were significantly more committed to work, and reported somewhat more achievement dissatisfaction (at all ages) and significantly less economic dissatisfaction than men with low achievement motivation. This pattern suggests that men with high achievement motivation are strongly involved in work, but find it difficult to obtain gratification in these jobs. Perhaps social obligations stand in the way of finding achievement gratification. Among men holding jobs low in social requirements, high achievement motivation was positively related to mentioning achievement satisfaction, and was significantly negatively related to mentioning affiliation satisfaction. Thus, in these jobs lacking in social obligations, men with a high achievement motive can seek out achievement gratifications. These patterns in the two types of high prestige jobs are consistent with our expectation that jobs lacking in social requirements are more congruent with the goals of achievement motivation than jobs high in social requirements.

Jobs with strong social obligations also appear to be incongruent with the goals of the power motive. Men with high power motivation in such jobs were significantly more dissatisfied with their job than those with low power motivation. We suggest this is so because in such jobs their influence is on public display, a state of affairs that may be anxiety-provoking for strong power motivation. They truly do feel dissatisfied.

We had alternate expectations for whether high affiliation motive was congruent with jobs high in *Social Requirements* because we were not certain whether affiliative gratification could be best obtained from required role relationships or from peer-group associations. If job requirements for social relationships were satisfying to affiliative goals, then men with high affiliation motivation in jobs that are high in *Social Requirements* would be able to find more satisfaction than men with low affiliation motivation, and men with high affiliation motivation in jobs

TABLE 5-8 THE RELATIONSHIP (γ) OF MOTIVES TO SELECTED JOB REACTIONS IN JOBS HIGH AND LOW IN SOCIAL REQUIREMENTS (WITHIN AGE)

Job Reaction	Age	High Social Requirements				Low Social Requirements			
		Affiliation Motive	Achievement Motive	Power Motive	(N)	Affiliation Motive	Achievement Motive	Power Motive	(N)
Job dissatisfaction	Young	.10	.48†	.41*	(29)	−.47*	.50*	−.31	(27)
	Middle	.07	.12	.15	(49)	.39	.00	−.30	(22)
	Old	.23	.28	.18	(30)	−.06	−.19	.48†	(31)
	All	.06	.26†	.25†	(108)	−.08	.14	.07	(80)
Lack of commitment	Young	.55	−1.00	−.16	(30)	−.06	.04	.25	(27)
	Middle	−.50	.16	.19	(48)	.09	.16	.16	(23)
	Old	.09	−.68*	−.51	(30)	−.13	−.15	.12	(31)
	All	−.13	−.29	−.03	(108)	.01	.04	.15	(81)

Note: Includes only men in jobs high in Prestige.
*p < .10.
†p < .05.

with low *Social Requirements* would be less satisfied than men with low affiliation motivation. On the other hand, if jobs that required social relations were not gratifying to affiliative goals, or if jobs that required many social role obligations did not allow for many intimate colleague relationships, opposite predictions could also be made. Therefore, we could only view this analysis as exploratory. What we found is that in jobs with low *Social Requirements* young men with high affiliation motivation were significantly more satisfied than those with low affiliation motivation. There were no other significant results in relating affiliation motivation to any job reaction in either type of job role. In jobs that were high in *Social Requirements* there was a consistent trend at all age levels for men with a high affiliation motive to indicate more dissatisfaction with their jobs than men with a low affiliation motive.

What seems to be suggested by these results is that in jobs that are not specifically structured for social obligations in the work itself, men with high affiliation motive are likely to be more satisfied than those with low affiliation motive. Perhaps in these jobs with low *Social Requirements* men can easily work out intimate peer relationships, while such affiliation is less possible in jobs with high *Social Requirements*. If that is so, and if peer relations are the bases for affiliative gratifications, then jobs low in *Social Requirements* may be the very jobs that are *high* in affiliative gratification potential.

To indicate our conclusion regarding the affiliative gratification potential of jobs with required social relations, we will anticipate the finding concerning jobs with another type of social demand—supervising other people's work. There, too, a high affiliation motive predicts job satisfaction for the men who are in jobs that do *not* require them to supervise other people's work. All of these results are consistent with the interpretation we made of the results concerning specific occupations: men who are in jobs where there are very few reciprocal role requirements involving social obligations are in a better position to obtain affiliative gratifications resulting from parallel intimate relationships than men who are in jobs that require supervising, influencing, or some kind of social function to fulfill the requirements of the job. Social gratifications from the latter type of jobs, we said, were more tied to the power relationship than to the affiliative relationship. When a manager said, "I enjoy the people I work with," it was coded as an affiliative response, but it can have power implications. Not so when a factory worker says he enjoys the people with whom he works.

If this interpretation is correct it would have wide implications for appropriate job selections for different types of people. We have seen that persons with high affiliation motive tended to hold jobs with high *Social Requirements*. But here it is suggested that people with high affiliation motivation may be especially concerned about rejection and affiliation, and can be distressed in jobs that require social function in the job role itself. A man who finishes college and decides to go into "personnel work" because he "likes people" may, in fact, not find the job to his liking. A man who "likes people" may find his work more satisfying if he chooses a job that provides him with colleagues who do not have anything to do directly with his own performance at work, for they may be the major sources of affiliative gratification at work.

We had assumed that jobs requiring social relations for adequate performance would be incongruent with high achievement motivation because of the dependence upon other persons for successful performance, and that jobs lacking such social requirements would be congruent with achievement motivation. We found that in jobs that are high in *Social Requirements*, achievement motive was consistently positively related to *Job Dissatisfaction:* men with high achievement motive were more dissatisfied than men with low achievement motive (Table 5.8). These results were significant for young men, as well as the total group. In jobs that are low in *Social Requirements* also, young men with high achievement motive were significantly more dissatisfied with their jobs than those low in achievement motive, but in the other age groups this trend was absent or reversed. The trends in the middle and older groups lend the only slight support to the view that jobs without social demands are more congruent for men with high achievement motive. However, the positive relationships between *Job Dissatisfaction* and the achievement motive, especially for young men, may be nothing but a repetition of the previous findings (Table 5.6 and 5.7) that men with high achievement motivation expressed more *Job Dissatisfaction* than men with low achievement motivation regardless of their jobs.

There were other noteworthy consistent trends in examining the achievement motive in relationship to job reactions for job roles with high and low *Social Requirements*. Men with high achievement motivation in jobs that were low in *Social Requirements* tended to report more *Achievement Job Satisfaction* (for the total group, gamma = .23) and reported significantly less *Affiliation Job Satisfaction* (for the total group, gamma = −.68, $p < .10$ for tau beta) than those with low achievement motivation. Furthermore, men with high achievement motivation in jobs that are high in *Social Requirements* consistently mentioned more *Achievement Job Dissatisfaction* (for the total group, gamma = .25) and less *Economic Job Dissatisfaction* in these jobs, with the latter association being significant for the older men (gamma = −.89, $p < .05$ for tau beta) and the total group (gamma = −.39, $p < .10$ for tau beta). The younger and older men in these jobs of high *Social Requirements* were more committed to work if they had high achievement motive; the relationship was a significant one for older men (Table 5.8). This pattern of results suggests that a man with high achievement motivation in a job that requires a lot of social interaction to fulfill his role obligations is, in fact, at some disadvantage. He feels some dissatisfaction with his own accomplishment, but the fact that he mentions his concerns about these matters and that he remains more committed to his work than a man low in achievement motivation, suggests that he is still quite ego-involved in his work. It is as if he is finding difficulty in working out his achievement gratifications in the job but is constantly engaged in the search for such gratifications. In jobs low in *Social Requirements*, however, there is greater ease for those high in achievement motivation to fulfill their achievement aspirations because social obligations do not stand in their way; they become especially alerted to the achievement potential in such jobs. Perhaps it is the high *Prestige* job with low *Social Requirements* that comes as close as any to being a job high in potential achievement for men. Later results in the next two role analyses that we will do will corroborate this conclusion.

Because of the ambiguity about whether men with a high power motive are pleased or frightened by jobs that have high influence potential, we had no clear expectations about the congruence between power motivation and *Social Requirements*. The results with power motive therefore seem to be especially important to look at. The data in Table 5.8 generally support the view that situations that test one's influence ability are anxiety provoking to men with high power motive. In jobs high in *Social Requirements* there was a consistent positive association between power motive and *Job Dissatisfaction*. These relationships were significant for the young men and the total group. Many jobs with high *Social Requirements* involve reciprocal interpersonal role obligations that regularly involve making influence attempts. Foremen have to supervise; teachers have to teach. But they may not succeed at influencing. Such jobs may cause a man of high power concern to feel discontent. There were no other trends consistent across age groupings in jobs with high *Social Requirements*, but the middle-aged men with a high power motive did report *Economic Job Dissatisfaction* significantly less often than men with a low power motive (gamma $= -.59$, $p < .10$ for tau beta). In jobs where the *Social Requirements* were minimal, there was some tendency for young and middle-aged men with high power motivation to feel more satisfied with their jobs than men with low power motivation. In these jobs, men with a high power motive may be especially satisfied because they are not threatened by being required to deal with people. Unfortunately, this interpretation cannot be totally accepted because the older men in jobs of low *Social Requirements* showed the opposite relationship, which was significant: high power motivation was associated with dissatisfaction with one's job. This result was puzzling. It may, however, simply reflect the overall positive relationship between power motive and *Job Dissatisfaction* for older men in high *Prestige* jobs (Table 5.7). We expected that older men would be less concerned with the job itself, with its day-to-day evidences of their weakness or strength, and therefore the job conditions themselves might not affect their lack of satisfaction with their job. Having attained prestigious jobs, the older men with high power motivation might be dissatisfied with the lack of sustained impact the job had on their broader social influence in the community.

Motives and job reactions within jobs of high and low supervision. The extent of supervision received was expected to be an important influence on power motive-job role interaction, but its effect was expected to be dependent on whether close supervision was perceived as a threat or as a means of rationalizing one's lack of power. The results suggest that high levels of supervision are threatening to men with high power motivation. Young men with high power motivation who were supervised a lot were significantly more dissatisfied with their jobs and reported significantly fewer achievement job satisfactions, significantly more economic job dissatisfaction, and somewhat fewer achievement job dissatisfactions than those with low power motivation. The opposite relationships tended to occur for young men who received little supervision in their jobs. We take these findings to signify a greater congruence of high power motivation to jobs in which little supervision is received than to jobs in which there is much supervision. In the latter type of job, young men with high power motivation are sensitive to the lack of intrinsic job satisfactions and defensively focus on the more external economic dissatisfactions.

Once again, when the subjects were grouped on the basis of general job characteristics, affiliation motivation showed little relationship to the reactions in the job role. However, with the achievement motivation there was a noteworthy set of findings. Although our original expectations were that men with high achievement motive would prefer the independent activity of jobs with little supervision, the earlier results concerning job selection and the present data suggest that supervision can provide valuable feedback about the quality of performance. In jobs where there is close supervision men with high achievement motivation were significantly less likely to report economic satisfactions and more likely to report affiliation satisfactions than were men with low achievement motivation. In jobs where there was little supervision, the highly achievement-motivated men seemed to focus on economic rewards. This suggests that material rewards can be an important feedback about performance when a man lacks the interpersonal feedback from a supervisor, but the latter is important when available.

The extent of the supervision received and required were two characteristics of roles that we thought would be particularly important for the engagement of the power motive. Therefore, it is with the power motive that we expected the congruence and the sensitization principle to operate most clearly in these two different role distinctions. Although the other two motives were considered in relationship to the job reactions, we viewed these analyses only as explorations. We did find that there was some indications of the usefulness of the congruence and sensitization principles

TABLE 5-9 THE RELATIONSHIP (γ) OF MOTIVES TO SELECTED JOB REACTIONS IN JOBS HIGH AND LOW IN SUPERVISION (WITHIN AGE)

Job Reaction	Age	High Supervision				Low Supervision			
		Affiliation Motive	Achievement Motive	Power Motive	(N)	Affiliation Motive	Achievement Motive	Power Motive	(N)
Job dissatisfaction	Young	−.22	.29	.50†	(34)	−.09	.18	−.18	(34)
	Middle	−.28	.27	.04	(29)	−.33	.21	.07	(32)
	Old	.42	−.06	−.30	(22)	.29	−.04	.33	(26)
	All	−.12	.21*	.17	(85)	−.06	.15	.01	(92)
Lack of commitment	Young	.20	−.22	.07	(34)	−.29	−.32	.28	(34)
	Middle	−.33	−.37	.05	(30)	−.24	.18	−.20	(33)
	Old	−.00	−1.00	.38	(22)	.46	−.08	−.11	(25)
	All	−.08	−.30	.04	(86)	−.03	−.06	−.04	(92)

*p < .10.
†p < .05.

273

with the power motive when the role distinction of high and low *Supervision* was used (Table 5.9). Young men who were supervised a lot were significantly more dissatisfied with their jobs if they had high power motive than if they had low power motive. For young men who received little supervision there was a trend in the opposite direction; those with high power motive were somewhat more satisfied in their jobs than those with low power motive. Thus it appears that jobs with close supervision are not congruent with high power motivation, at least for young men.

The difficulties that face a young man with a high power motive in a job in which he is closely supervised are also seen in the sources of satisfaction and dissatisfaction he perceives. For the young men who were in jobs where they received a lot of *Supervision*, those with high power motive significantly less often mentioned *Achievement Job Satisfaction* than those with low power motive (gamma = $-.48$, $p < .10$ for tau beta). This same group of young men significantly more often mentioned *Economic Job Dissatisfaction* (gamma = $.86$, $p < .10$ for tau beta), a response which we have taken to mean a lack of involvement with work, a focus on an aspect of the job that is external to the work activity itself. In contrast, there was greater *Achievement Job Satisfaction* expressed by men with high power motive than with low power motive when in jobs where they received little *Supervision*. This association was significant when all age groups were combined (gamma = $.30$, $p < .10$ for tau beta); each age group showed the same trend, but none was significant by itself. Thus the power motive seems to sensitize men to the achievement gratification in jobs where they are not supervised, and interferes with it in jobs where men are closely supervised. It is as if the fear of weakness aroused when one is highly supervised is disruptive to feelings of achievement, to satisfaction with the work activities themselves. If there is no pressure from close supervision, there can be a protection from fear of weakness which can enhance a man's sense of accomplishment.

It is interesting that being closely supervised seems most disruptive for young men with high power motivation. We had speculated that close supervision could be interpreted by the job occupant either as evidence of lack of power or as protection against failure at tests of one's power. Young men with high power motivation may be less concerned with finding a job that provides a safe haven from evidences of weakness than older men. Young men should be at the height of their ambitions and search for a good job that will prove their worth.

The affiliation motive was not significantly related to any job reactions within this role distinction of *Supervision*. However, with the achievement motive there were some interesting results. When holding jobs where a lot of supervision is received, men high in achievement motive reported significantly more *Job Dissatisfaction* than those low in the achievement motive, when all age groups were combined. Similar trends, but not significant, were found for men in jobs with little supervision of their work. The general positive association between *Job Dissatisfaction* and achievement motive, therefore, was only slightly influenced by the amount of supervision a person received. However, the stronger relationships occurred, as we would expect from the discussion of the findings for jobs of high and low *Social Requirements*, in jobs where performance is dependent upon other persons. These seem to be jobs that are most dissatisfying for men with high achievement motive.

The amount of supervision received does seem to affect the sources of job satisfaction for men high and low in achievement motive. High achievement motivation appears to sensitize men to different sources of feedback about their performance in jobs with varying amounts of *Supervision*. Men with high achievement motivation who were in jobs where they received little supervision tended to express more *Achievement Job Satisfaction* than men who were low in achievement motivation in each age group. Opposite tendencies were found for men in jobs with close supervision; in those jobs achievement motivation was associated with not mentioning achievement-related aspects of the job as most satisfying. In jobs with high *Supervision* there was also a consistent negative association between achievement motivation and *Economic Job Satisfaction* (for the total group, gamma $= -.34$, $p < .10$ for tau beta): men with a high achievement motive were significantly less likely to mention *Economic Job Satisfaction* than those with a low achievement motive. The opposite relationship tended to be true for men in jobs that did not have much supervision. What does appear to be satisfying about their jobs for men with high achievement motive in high *Supervision* jobs are their affiliative relations, although significantly so only for middle-aged men (gamma $= .59$, $p < .10$ for tau beta).

Although our conclusions are tentative because not all the results were significant, the pattern does suggest that there are two important aspects of supervision. Supervision involves the evaluation of the supervisee's work as well as its direction. If men with high achievement motivation are in jobs in which they are supervised a lot, they can get feedback about their accomplishments. Supervisors can reward accomplishment by signs other than money—by praise and added responsibilities. But the achievement feedback is based on satisfactory interpersonal relations. However, if a man is in a job where there is very little supervision of his work, then in fact the material rewards, economic satisfactions, can provide important feedback about his own performance. Close supervision can also bring with it directions about how and when to perform the required work activities, and this may explain the relative absence of *Achievement Job Satisfaction* among men with high achievement motivation in such jobs. On the other hand, when they received little supervision, men with high achievement motivation expressed relatively greater pleasure in the intrinsic work activities, which were probably self-directed.

Motives and job reactions within jobs of high and low supervisory potential. The supervisory potential of a job was expected to be relevant to the motive-role interactions for all three motives. For power motivation we originally were uncertain whether high supervisory potential would act as a threat or a source of power to men with strong power motivation. The earlier results on job selection and the present data suggest that being required to exert influence is mainly a threat to a man motivated to avoid weakness. In all age groups there were consistent associations between the power motive and feeling dissatisfied with work in jobs that required supervising others, but not in jobs where the requirement to supervise others was absent. Thus, jobs with high supervisory potential did not appear to be congruent with high power motivation. Results relating power motivation to mentioning certain types of satisfaction corroborate the interpretation that men with high fear of weakness might be made anxious by being required to exert public influence especially at middle-age. In jobs requiring supervising, men with high power motivation concentrated on economic rewards rather than satisfactions in the work activities. In jobs not requiring supervising, power-motivated men enjoyed the achievement gratifications in the work itself.

In jobs of low supervisory potential, middle-aged men with high affiliation motivation expressed significantly greater job satisfaction and reported significantly more economic gratification from their work than their counterparts with low affiliation motivation. We would suggest that these men with high affiliation motive in jobs that do not require them to supervise are not involved with the job itself but are satisfied with their job because it does not interfere with the contact they make with their colleagues outside of work.

The repeated positive association of achievement motivation with job dissatisfaction was significant for young and middle-aged men in jobs of low supervisory potential. Younger achievement-motivated men in jobs where they do little supervising can devote themselves to setting higher and higher personal standards of excellence. The pattern was somehat different for older men: in jobs where they were not required to supervise others, older men with high achievement motivation, while tending to report less job dissatisfaction reported significantly less economic satisfaction and achievement dissatisfaction than their counterparts with low achievement motivation. In this sort of role older men with achievement goals perhaps no longer reach out for continuously higher goals. In jobs of high supervisory potential a consistent association was found at all ages between achievement motivation and commitment to work for nonmonetary reasons. The last result suggests that men with high achievement motivation are more likely to feel commitment to work when others depend on them than are men with low achievement motivation. We had previously found that men with high achievement motivation avoided supervisory jobs, but we see now that when they do hold jobs as supervisors they do become highly committed.

There were some consistent trends in all age groups for men with high power motive to be more dissatisfied with their jobs than men with low power motive, *if they were supervising others* (Table 5.10). In jobs that

TABLE 5-10 THE RELATIONSHIP OF (γ) MOTIVES TO SELECTED JOB REACTIONS IN JOBS HIGH AND LOW IN SUPERVISORY POTENTIAL (WITHIN AGE)

Job Reaction	Age	High Supervisory Potential				Low Supervisory Potential			
		Affiliation Motive	Achievement Motive	Power Motive	(N)	Affiliation Motive	Achievement Motive	Power Motive	(N)
Job dissatisfaction	Young	−.22	.10	.43	(22)	−.17	.33†	.14	(51)
	Middle	−.10	.14	.01	(31)	−.36*	.37*	−.06	(34)
	Old	.15	.73*	.40	(20)	.32	−.18	.08	(31)
	All	−.04	.20	.15	(73)	−.10	.20*	.06	(116)
Lack of commitment	Young	.14	−1.00	.13	(22)	.08	−.08	.08	(51)
	Middle	−.27	−.20	.24	(31)	−.12	.18	−.39	(35)
	Old	.11	−.45	−.30	(20)	.38	−.10	−.03	(30)
	All	−.10	−.44	.03	(73)	.11	.00	−.09	(116)

*p < .10.
†p < .05.

277

did not include supervising others, parallel results were smaller and not as consistent. There were two statistically significant relationships between the power motive and job reactions in jobs differing in *Supervisory Potential*. First, in jobs requiring the supervising of others middle-aged men with a high power motive reported significantly more *Economic Job Satisfaction* than those with low power motive (gamma = .66, $p < .10$ for tau beta). In contrast, this relationship did not emerge in jobs where such men did not have to supervise other people. Secondly, in jobs where they did not supervise, middle-aged men with a high power motive mentioned *Achievement Job Satisfaction* more often than did men with a low power motive (gamma = .48, $p < .10$ for tau beta). This would suggest that for men with high power motivation, being in the supervisory role can interfere with their enjoyment of the work itself and their own accomplishments, at least at middle-age. Such men can perhaps focus on the material benefits of work as major satisfactions and ignore their interpersonal anxieties. Middle-aged men who are not required to supervise and who have a high power motive are perhaps not anxious and are able to see the achievement possibilities at work. This interpretation is consistent with our previous interpretations of the power motive as a measure of fear of weakness. Men with high fear of weakness could easily feel some anxiety about their own performance in jobs that require them to supervise. In jobs requiring no supervising, such men might feel more comfortable and more satisfied with their performance.

What about affiliation and achievement motives? How do they bear on job reactions in these two different types of roles? We had expected that supervising others would not be congruent with the affiliation motive since supervisors are often disliked. We found that in such jobs there were no significant relationships between affiliation motivation and job reactions. In job roles that did not require supervising others, the affiliation motive was significantly negatively related to *Job Dissatisfaction* for middle-aged men. This same group of middle-aged men were significantly more likely to report *Economic Job Satisfaction* if they had high affiliation motive than if they had low affiliation motive (gamma = .52, $p < .10$ for tau beta). Perhaps these men with a high affiliation motive in jobs that do not require much supervising are more satisfied with their jobs than those with a low affiliation motive because they are getting gratification from the casual contact they have with other people. They are not especially involved with their work activity itself, and thus mention economic rather than achievement satisfaction. This interpretation agrees with our earlier suggestion that the potential for affiliation gratification is high in jobs that do not have strong social demands, whether in supervision or in other reciprocal role relationships with clients, customers, and so forth.

Our original expectations and the results concerning job selection led us to view jobs with high *Supervisory Potential* as incongruent with an achievement-motivated man's desire for excellence based on his own standards and accomplishments. However, we find here that in jobs that require supervising others the achievement motive was associated with reports of work commitment consistently in all age groups. This pattern of results suggests that when a man with high achievement motive is responsible for the work of others, he may feel commitment to work because others depend on him. Excellence in such job function requires organizational commitment. We should be reminded that men with a high achievement motive were unlikely to be in the supervisory role by their older years (see Table 5.3). But we should also be reminded that only for older men in jobs with high *Supervisory Potential* did we find a significant positive association between the achievement motive and *Job Dissatisfaction*. We might thus say that if men with high achievement motivation *do* select a job role with supervisory functions, they are likely to be committed workers.

A more general phenomenon may also be operating. Commitment to work seems generally to be associated with high achievement motive in jobs requiring one to work with other people: in jobs with high rather than low *Social Requirements*, in jobs with high rather than low *Supervision*, and in jobs with high rather than low *Supervisory Potential*. Perhaps the kind of work done in such jobs cannot be accomplished outside the formal job situation, and men interested in maintaining a sense of accomplishment in their chosen line of endeavor, as are men with high achievement motive, would need to continue working at their jobs. It is perhaps no wonder these men answered "yes" to a question asking them whether they would go on working if they did not have to work to make a living.

The pattern of results for men in jobs with low *Supervisory Potential* did generally support the idea that those jobs were more congruent with achievement motivation. There were significant positive relationships between achievement motivation and *Job Dissatisfaction* among those young and middle-aged men who do not have to supervise others. We assume that these relationships reflect the achievement-motivated men's high aspirations for accomplishment in the kinds of activities they are doing. In the jobs that do not require supervision of others, a person with high achievement motive can more clearly find the source of achievement in his own efforts. If this is so, there is little need for commitment to his work *as a job in the social organization;* he may be able to get the same mastery from his effort in work at home. He does not necessarily have to have a job to gain personal satisfaction. We can speculate further than when asked if he would go on working if he did not have to earn a living, a person with high motivation for accomplishment can say "no" if he is finding gratification from his own effort and not from his role in the organization. Perhaps

279

it is for this reason that *Lack of Commitment* was not associated with achievement motivation for men who do not supervise but was consistently negatively associated for men who do.

It is in the older age group of men in jobs where they are not supervising others that significant relationships appeared between achievement motive and sources of satisfaction and dissatisfaction. Older men with high achievement motive were *less* likely than older men with low achievement motive to mention either *Economic Job Satisfaction* (gamma $= -.55$, $p < .10$ for tau beta) or *Achievement Job Dissatisfaction* (gamma $= -.82$, $p < .10$ for tau beta), and were somewhat more likely to report *Achievement Job Satisfaction* (gamma $= .32$). We see this pattern as an instance of considerable involvement with work for these men. Perhaps at an older age highly achievement-oriented men can resolve for themselves how far they have come, only at jobs where they are autonomous and do not have to take care of other people. Seniority often implies a great deal of administrative supervision. Without the burden of supervision, an older man with high achievement motivation can come to terms with his final goals of accomplishment. It is interesting to note that it was only for the older men that there was a tendency for high achievement motivation to be associated with job satisfaction, but only in jobs where they are not required to supervise others. It may be that in this older group we find an instance of our initial simple congruence principle operating with respect to the achievement motive. That is, in jobs where men are not required to supervise others (which we will now assume to have higher achievement potential), achievement motivation and the job's potential for achievement are congruent and produce a *heightened* level of satisfaction, and a sensitivity to the intrinsic satisfactions in the work activity itself. In this sort of role, older men with high achievement goals perhaps no longer feel psychologically required to seek higher and higher aspirations.

REASSESSMENT OF MOTIVES IN THE CONTEXT OF WORK

We will now review and synthesize the results obtained in relating motives to job selection and job reactions within the specific occupations and within the general role classifications, with respect to each of the motives separately. By sorting out the apparent effects each of the motives might have on job choice or reactions to different kinds of job roles, we will also have some perspective on the effects that motives could have on leisure activity, a topic that is to follow in the next section.

AFFILIATION MOTIVATION AND THE JOB ROLE

Affiliation motivation seems to underly feelings of gratification from work if the primary job demands *do not include social functions*. Wherever the social relationships are integral to job functioning, wherever they are part of the job role, the role occupant may feel unable to enter into satisfying affiliative relationships with the coworkers or other people with whom he must interact in the course of performing this role. The *kind* of social relationships required in different jobs also seems critical to consider. In jobs that require supervising, in particular, the potential for affiliative gratification appears minimal. Men with high affiliation motivation are selected out of, or select themselves out of, such jobs by the time they reach the final stages of their job career. In the absence of supervisory demands, men with high affiliation motive are more satisfied with their jobs than men with low affiliation motive. In jobs where supervisory demands are primary, such as that of foremen, such demands conflict with affiliative goals and yield dissatisfaction with work, and disengagement from it among men with high affiliation motivation.

Jobs with other types of requirements for social activities are less easily characterized as having high or low potential for affiliative gratification. Men who have a high affiliation motive select jobs that involve contact with other people, as defined by our variable of *Social Requirements*, and avoid jobs, such as that of farmer, which lack potential for social relations. However, once in jobs that demand social relations (of diverse sorts such as selling, "helping" people, giving advice, teaching, supervising), there may be difficulty in using these interpersonal contacts as the basis for satisfying affiliative relationships. In jobs where the *role demands* do not include interpersonal activities, and where other people are available for social interaction, men are satisfied with their jobs if they have high affiliation motive. For example, clerical workers, whose primary role demands are asocial but who usually do not work alone, are pleased with the interpersonal aspects of their work if they have high affiliation motive. Similarly, semiskilled workers are satisfied with their jobs if they have high affiliation motivation. Farmers, however, who do not have other people available for interaction, are dissatisfied with their jobs if they have high affiliation motivation.

What psychological processes might underlie these conclusions about the potential for affiliative gratification in different types of jobs? We might suggest that in jobs that *require* social functioning there may be some ambiguity about what affiliative satisfactions are possible. As a result of the obtained pattern of results, we have suggested that affiliative gratifications from work are not ones that role occupants necessarily experience *in the job role itself*. A man's work can be the source of friendships *outside his work relationship*. It may be that men can find affiliative gratifications with people only when they also meet outside of the job setting itself. If this is so, then affiliative gratification from the job role is dependent on finding potential friendships with those who are *similar* to one's self—colleagues, peers. Supervisees and supervisors, clients and lawyers, patients and doctors, students and teachers, customers and salesmen—because of their reciprocal role obligations to each other—may not easily enter into friendships on the job or outside of the job. As a result, a man may perceive that a job requiring social responsibilities might fulfill his affiliative needs, but when he is on the job, he may discover an affiliative vacuum. Among those he cannot easily interact with as peers in his home are those people with whom he has reciprocal role relationships.

ACHIEVEMENT MOTIVATION AND THE JOB ROLE

Achievement motivation underlies a feeling of disquiet at work, a disquiet that reflects a man's continual desire to set aspirations for himself and to strive to meet the standards of excellence that these aspirations imply. That this disquiet does not stem simply from failure to excel is seen in the fact that men with high achievement motive attain jobs of higher social prestige by the final stages of their job career than do men with low achievement motive. But regardless of how prestigious a man's job is, regardless of how successful or unsuccessful a man has been in the social system, his achievement motivation seems to lead to job dissatisfaction.

Achievement satisfactions and gratifications, however, seem to be more forthcoming from jobs that do not require people to enter into social obligations at work either in influencing clients, in supervising coworkers, or in being supervised. Indeed, men with high achievement motive are not likely to be found in jobs where they supervise others. The man on his own, however, the man who is self-employed, does not seem to be the person who is most unambiguously able to follow through on achievement strivings. Rather, a man in some kind of bureaucratic organization, perhaps even given some kind of supervision, where he is able to get feedback about his own performance and feels that he is doing well does seem able to carry out achievement strivings. If a man is required to be the ultimate resource for evaluating performance of his employees, he will often find it difficult to evaluate his own accomplishment. There is some hint that economic rewards are used by men to gain achievement gratifications if they are in situations where interpersonal supervision does not give them any feedback about their performance.

Since there is evidence in the research literature to suggest that men with high achievement motivation will not perform well under constant external surveillance, we might conclude that achievement motivation is best enacted in jobs with *moderate* supervision, where the person is neither left entirely to his own internal standards nor kept under incessant supervision. Neither the creative artist operating on his own, unresponsive to the standards of his time, nor the factory worker whose rate of production is consistently checked, are models for men with high achievement motivation. Rather, a good model might be the bureaucratic manager—a man who decides for himself but is occasionally responsible to others.

Achievement motivation seems to be entering into job reactions no matter where on the status hierarchy one looks, although there are some qualitative differences between reactions of men with high achievement motivation in different jobs. Our simple expectations from the congruence principle with respect to achievement motivation does not seem to apply. Whether they are in low or high status jobs, men with high achievement motive are more likely to be dissatisfied with work than men with low achievement motivation. Men in low status rungs of white and blue-collar hierarchies, however, do seem to be more defensive about their achievement gratifications than men in higher positions. In many different contexts, therefore, achievement motivation seems to be important in determining reactions to work. Indeed, achievement motivation remains as a major underpinning to a man's sense of identity at work.

POWER MOTIVATION AND THE JOB ROLE

The overwhelming evidence of our results relating power motivation to job selection and job reactions points to the interpretation of the motive measure as one of fear of weakness. Men with high power motivation seem to be both discontent with being influenced and anxious about their own influence capacities in jobs where they are required to influence. What seems important in jobs for a man high in power motivation, therefore, is to avoid any public awareness of the person's own weakness in roles that perhaps require him to be influenced or to influence. Thus we find that all types of jobs with supervisory demands, and the occupations of foremen and salesmen, are more likely to be held by men with low rather than high power motive. For men with high power motivation, prestige, especially if accompanied with money, provides the symbols of power. If this prestige is not forthcoming, the mere fact of holding a job may be the important factor in avoiding weakness. In only one case, in the role of salesman, does power motivation seem to be a motivation strong enough to commit a man to the work activity itself. This suggests that the power motive is the motive that finds its gratification in contact with the world outside of the job. With a more directly positive measure of power motivation, such as has been suggested by Uleman (1966), perhaps there can be more evidence of direct gratifications of power motivation from the day-to-day activity *at work*. We have evidence, both in marriage and parenthood, that the power motive can be effective in producing certain types of gratification of power in the interpersonal setting outside of work. We can perhaps expect the power motive to show relationships to the use of leisure time. We will return to the consideration of this topic in the next section.

MOTIVES AND LEISURE

THEORETICAL BACKGROUND

In this section we will explore the potential impact these motives have on the way men spend their leisure time. As we stated earlier in this chapter, there is some reason to believe that if men are becoming disengaged from work, they may be finding motivational gratifications in leisure that were perhaps once found at work. In the national survey, we were able to ask a number of questions that pertained to leisure activity and from these questions we derived five measures that we related to the three motives. We anticipated that the relationships of the three motives to these measures would be strongest when men felt that what they were doing at work offered very little in the way of fulfillment of motives. We thought that the motives would relate to leisure reactions for men who, feeling the lack of gratification at work, would turn to outside activity for gratification. For this analysis, therefore, we used the high and low *Prestige* as a control for the relationships of motives to leisure activities. We anticipated that the relationship between motives and leisure should be higher in the jobs of low *Prestige* than in the jobs of high *Prestige* because the latter presumably offer more in the way of ego-gratification. There is some evidence for the major assumption of our hypothesis. Kornhauser and Reid (1965) report that routine semiskilled workers in Detroit are more likely to indicate that the job sector of their life is dissatisfying and less likely to report that the leisure sector of their life is dissatisfying, when compared to men in other less routine occupations.

To amplify our general hypothesis, we expected that men in jobs of low *Prestige* in particular should find affiliation motivation satisfied in social activity and social organizations, achievement motivation gratified in leisure-time activities spent in constructive individual performance, and power motivation gratified in social contact with friends, and in formal social organizations. These, then, were the original hypotheses with which we began the analysis of this section.

MEASURES OF LEISURE ACTIVITY

In the initial section of this interview in the national survey, a number of questions were asked about the way people spent their time. For the present analysis, five measures were derived from these questions.

The first question in the interview was the basis for two measures of leisure activity, *Leisure Spent in Achievement* and *Leisure Spent in Affiliation:*

One of the things we'd like to know is how people spend their time. For instance— how do you usually spend your time when your work is done—what kinds of things do you do, both at home and away from home?

The first-mentioned leisure activity was coded into one of three categories: (a) achievement, which included any individual activity or hobby, where the respondent has to create something or construct something—for example, gardening, building and fixing things, creative arts and home-making hobbies, collecting things, an extra job; (b) affiliation, which included leisure activities where the major focus was the time spent in the company of other people—for example, visiting the family or friends, playing with children, playing cards, going to organized social clubs, doing church or social welfare work; (c) all other activities. Only the first response was coded to avoid biasing the codes in favor of those respondents who are able to give more responses about the types of leisure activities in which they indulge. Both measures, then, *Leisure Spent in Affiliation* and *Leisure Spent in Achievement*, are dichotomized variables coded (1) for no mention or (2) for mention of the specified type of leisure activity. A subject could not receive a high score on both measures, although he could receive a low score on both.

The measure of *Leisure Spent in Achievement* was meant to include the kinds of activities that were of interest as possible substitutes for achievement gratifications on the job. The measure of *Leisure Spent in Affiliation* was designed to include all interpersonal activities that could provide alternate routes to affiliative or power gratifications.

The measure of *Membership in Organizations* was based on replies to the first question, described above, as well as the subsequent one:

Are you a member of any (other) clubs or organizations like a lodge, PTA, a community group or any other kind of group.
(IF YES) What are they?

The total number of different organizations mentioned in reply to both questions was coded into a six-point scale. The range of organizational membership coded was from zero to five, with code category five including persons belonging to five or more organizations. This measure was included as a possible indicator of either affiliative or power interests.

Frequency of Socializing was based on replies to the following question:

About how often do you get together with your friends or relatives—I mean, things like going out together or visiting in each other's homes—more than once a week, once a week, a few times a month, once a month, less than once a month?

The fixed alternatives presented to the subject were the bases for this five-point scale of how often the respondent got together with friends or relatives. Affiliative gratifications were assumed to be sought in these contacts.

The measure of *Has Enough Friends* was based on the last question in the series:

Do you feel you have as many friends as you want, or would you like to have more friends?

The two alternates presented to the subject determined this dichotomous variable: (1) would like more friends, or (2) has as many friends as wants. A person who was coded as not having enough friends was assumed to be dissatisfied with his affiliative gratifications. This measure, then, unlike the above four, was not, strictly speaking, a measure of leisure activity but a response to it, and possibly a response to job activity, as we have previously discussed.

RESULTS CONCERNING MOTIVES AND LEISURE

The five measures of leisure activity were related to each of the three motives, first for all full-time employed men, the same total group of subjects used in the previous sections, and then separately for men who held jobs with high and low *Prestige*, controlling on age. We will first present the highlights of these results for the more casual reader; and then discuss them in greater detail.

Affiliation motivation appears to be directly expressed in leisure activities, but it has different associations with leisure at different parts of a man's life cycle. Furthermore, these associations are very much affected by the status of a man's work. Younger men with high affiliation motive seem to seek gratifying relationships through membership in social organizations if they have jobs low in prestige. As men move on to middle and older age they appear to require more intimate contact to satisfy their affiliative goals. For men at middle-age who were in jobs of high prestige, affiliation motivation was significantly associated with saying that one does not have enough friends; the same trend existed in all middle-aged and older groups. The middle-aged men who were in low prestige jobs were significantly more likely to report leisure spent in achievement if they had high rather than low affiliation motivation. We suggest that during middle-age this type of person, disengaged from his work, can become family-oriented, making and doing things that please his family. The younger and older men perhaps work out their affiliative striving with friends. Among these age groups, the men in low prestige jobs were significantly more likely to report affiliative leisure activities if they had high rather than low affiliation motivation.

The most fascinating finding that emerged from the relationships of the achievement motive to leisure is the absence of any direct relationship to leisure spent in achievement for any group. In fact, the achievement motive was significantly negatively related to achievement spent in leisure for men in high prestige jobs. We would suggest that these men look for achievement in their jobs and find it. They avoid it in leisure. For men in low prestige jobs leisure spent in achievement cannot often compensate for lack of achievement at work. We suggest that all men keep a strong achievement investment in their work, regardless of its prestige, and cannot easily transfer this investment to leisure activities.

The power motive appears to find direct expression in social forms of leisure activities only for older men. For old men in high prestige jobs the power motive was significantly related to membership in social organizations and to the absence of leisure spent in achievement activities. We can conjecture a picture of an old man, concerned with his own potential loss of influence on his job, attempting to wield influence in the community—probably through the money his prestigious job has given him. In contrast, old men from the low prestige group were significantly more likely to be active in informal socializing if they had high power motivation. We assume that this is the way that these men, concerned with the impotence of advancing age, with their lack of influence in society, reassure themselves of their effectiveness.

In general, the results do not support a position that makes leisure the focus for gratification of men's motives. Achievement in leisure, in particular, does not seem to compensate for frustrated achievement strivings at work.

We first considered the relationships of motives to leisure activities for all men regardless of prestige group or age. There were only two significant relationships, both with the affiliation motive. The affiliation motive was related positively to *Leisure Spent in Affiliation* (gamma = .18, $p < .10$ for tau beta) and negatively to *Has Enough Friends* (gamma = $-.15$, $p < .05$ for tau beta). There were no significant overall relationships between the achievement or the power motive and leisure activities. These relationships suggest that the kinds of leisure activities on which we obtained information serve mainly to provide affiliative gratification.

Our major interest, however, is in the presumed relationship between the presence or absence of motivational gratification in the job and in leisure. It is therefore important to recall that social contacts demanded by one's job were not conducive to satisfying job reactions among men with high affiliation motive. Therefore, we were interested in pursuing the link between a man's leisure time and his job as inferred from the relationships between motives and leisure activities in jobs varying in social prestige. We looked at the separate age groups within the high and low *Prestige* categories. These data are reported in Table 5.11. The results are discussed below separately for each motive.

Affiliation motivation and leisure The overall significant relationship between affiliation motivation and seeking affiliative leisure activity appeared to be largely a function of the low *Prestige* groups. The positive relationship between affiliation motive and *Leisure Spent in Affiliation* was significant only for young and old men in low *Prestige* jobs. Furthermore, young men in low *Prestige* jobs also showed a significant positive relationship for affiliation motivation and the number of organizations to which they belonged.[13] These results suggest that men with high affiliation motive

---

[13]This may not be an independent result since, if a social organization was the first-mentioned leisure activity, it could be coded both in *Leisure Spent in Affiliation* and in *Memberships in Organizations*.

TABLE 5-11 THE RELATIONSHIP (γ) OF MOTIVES TO LEISURE ACTIVITIES IN JOBS HIGH AND LOW IN PRESTIGE (WITHIN AGE)

Leisure Activity	Age	High Prestige				Low Prestige			
		Affiliation Motive	Achievement Motive	Power Motive	(N)	Affiliation Motive	Achievement Motive	Power Motive	(N)
Leisure spent in achievement	Young	−.18	−.21	.16	(57)	−.10	−.11	.29*	(108)
	Middle	−.15	−.35	−.26	(71)	.40*	.18	.07	(85)
	Old	−.10	−.17	−.47†	(57)	.15	.18	−.24	(76)
	All	−.14	−.25†	−.11	(185)	.09	.03	.08	(271)
Leisure spent in affiliation	Young	.25	.33	−.22	(57)	.66‡	−.28	−.15	(108)
	Middle	.06	.11	−.31	(71)	−.11	−.30	−.13	(85)
	Old	−.33	.42	.13	(57)	.43*	.20	.12	(76)
	All	.03	.25	−.15	(185)	.27*	−.13	−.05	(271)
Memberships in organizations	Young	−.02	.00	.13	(56)	.21*	−.24*	.04	(108)
	Middle	.03	−.05	−.16	(71)	−.04	.04	−.07	(86)
	Old	.15	−.01	.48‡	(60)	−.15	.02	−.18	(75)
	All	.05	−.03	.14	(187)	.04	−.09	−.06	(269)
Frequency of socializing	Young	−.07	−.04	−.14	(56)	−.08	.07	−.04	(108)
	Middle	.03	−.15	−.09	(72)	−.03	−.13	−.04	(86)
	Old	.18	.17	−.09	(61)	−.10	.12	.25†	(77)
	All	.05	.00	−.09	(189)	−.06	.00	.05	(271)
Has enough friends	Young	.08	.09	.06	(57)	.01	−.07	−.18	(109)
	Middle	−.57‡	−.00	−.21	(72)	−.16	−.07	−.18	(85)
	Old	−.21	−.26	−.11	(60)	−.17	.18	.28	(76)
	All	−.28†	−.06	−.13	(189)	−.07	−.03	−.06	(270)

*p < .10.
†p < .05.
‡p < .01.

288

in a low *Prestige* job perhaps seek affiliative gratifications not at work, but in leisure, more so than similarly motivated men in high *Prestige* jobs. The less prestigious jobs, usually devoid of many social obligations, disallow affiliative gratification from the work task itself, but in these less prestigious jobs, men are likely to be in parallel associations with men and women with whom they work. Such parallel associations can be the basis for developing intimate contact with people at work. Although there had been generally positive relationships between affiliation motivation and *Affiliation Job Satisfaction* in both high and low *Prestige* jobs, none of these relationships was significant (Table 5.7). In jobs low in *Prestige*, the availability of parallel work associates may permit a man to engage in social activity with his colleagues on the job, but perhaps more important is that it provides easy targets for establishing affiliative gratifications during leisure time activities. Not so with men in more prestigious jobs. There are many psychological restrictions that men feel in such jobs about fraternizing with men who are above or below them in a supervisory hierarchy or who operate in some reciprocal role obligations to them. Without an easy source of friendships in their work, these men are perhaps less likely to establish intimate personal ties with other men—the type that permit affiliative gratification.

We have been talking about the relationships between affiliation motivation and leisure activities as if they were equally valid for all age groups. But there were some variations by age. None of the above results was true for the middle-aged group, and the positive relationship between affiliation motivation and *Membership in Organizations* was true only for young men. How do we account for these variations?

Middle-aged men with high affiliation motive who held jobs low in *Prestige* did not spend their leisure time in affiliative activities, as did the younger and older men. Instead, they were significantly more likely than their counterparts with low affiliation motive to report *Leisure Spent in Achievement*. Why not affiliative activities as the other age groups do? Our only speculation is that during middle age, this type of person can become family-oriented and with his skills provide his family with things and services that please them. Perhaps the younger man and the older man work out their affiliative ties with friends rather than with family— the younger man because his family is not yet old enough to engage his affiliative interests—the older man because his children have left him with an affiliative void. We raised such possible distinction when we discussed the significance of parenthood at different points of the life cycle for different social strata. (See Chapter 4.)

Why was it only the young men with high affiliation motivation who were likely to be members of many organizations? Again, we can only speculate. We have said that young men with high affiliation motivation in low *Prestige* jobs would turn to social activity with friends, possibly co-workers, rather than family. In early adulthood it is perhaps more important for men to turn to organizations as a vehicle for affiliative gratification. This may be part of establishing new adult status in the social world. But the promise of affiliative satisfactions in organizational membership may not be easily realized. Groups often preclude intimacy and gestures of acceptance that would affect a man with affiliative longings. As men get older, perhaps they come to recognize this more clearly and thus turn to other social relations. Alternately, it is possible that memberships in organizations do provide the basis for intimate friendships. But once established, these friendships may not be dependent upon organizational ties and indeed, may flourish better under less formal conditions.

It will be recalled that there was an overall finding that men who had high affiliation motivation, in contrast to those low in affiliation motivation, more often said that they did not have as many friends as they would like to have. This relationship is interpreted as indicating the dissatisfaction that men with high affiliation motives feel about their affiliative gratification. This association was also affected by the *Prestige* of a man's job and his age. The relationship between affiliation motivation and discontent with friendships was maintained only for middle-aged and older men at both levels of *Prestige* and was significant only for middle-aged men in the occupations of high *Prestige*. We interpret these results to imply that for younger men the affiliation motive is perhaps centered more around the possibility of affiliation through social organizations, and not around friends in the intimate sense. As men move to middle age and later to older age, they perhaps demand more of social intercourse if they have high affiliation motivation. More intimate or more enduring friendships may be desired and pleasant acquaintances may no longer be satisfying. Why is this most striking for middle-aged men in high *Prestige* occupations? Could it be that these occupations in general provide less chance for fraternizing with coworkers? Jobs high in *Prestige* are very likely to require the type of reciprocal role obligations which we have argued do not permit the kind of intimacy required by men with high affiliative motive. These jobs may also make heavier demands upon the time and energy of the job holder, and especially at middle age, when men are attempting to reach the pinnacle of their career, the prestigious job may interfere with social activities. Older men with high affiliation motivation, having gone through this career stage, may be less limited by their work than middle-aged men.

Achievement motivation and leisure In Table 5.11 we see that the achievement motive did not seem very relevant to leisure time activities, even when we distinguished subjects according to the *Prestige* of their jobs and their age. There was a consistent trend at all age levels for men with high achievement motivation in jobs of high *Prestige* not to spend their time in achievement activity, which was significant for the total group disregarding age. There was also a consistent trend for these men to spend their leisure time in affiliative activity. These results are provocative even though they are not all significant. They lead us to speculate that men in prestigious jobs are getting sufficient achievement gratification at work so that the pressure for achievement in leisure time is absent. Another way of looking at it is to suggest that the domain for achievement is limited to the job for these men and does not easily encompass pursuits of leisure. Perhaps the job is a less unique focus for the achievement goals of men with less prestigious jobs.

The one significant relationship between achievement motive and leisure activities for men in low *Prestige* jobs was for young men, for whom there was a negative relationship between the achievement motive and *Memberships in Organizations*. These young men, perhaps, are still trying to consolidate their achievement aspirations at work and hence they perceive that developing attachments to social organizations may stand in the way of their career goals. There is another way to think about these men. Men who have a high achievement motive but end up in jobs of low achievement potential in the eyes of the world may be particularly anomic men. They have adopted the value system of higher status groups but have attained or selected a job without status. This suggests that they may be particularly unintegrated men—full of conflicts in their sense of identity, unable to give of themselves to social groups, and avoiding membership in such groups.

The most important overall conclusion we can draw about the relationships that achievement motive bears to leisure is that the motive does not seem potent in determining the social and achievement activities performed by men outside the job. We must perhaps reconsider our expectation that men with high achievement motivation who are in jobs that have been automated, or that are frustrating to their personal needs, would find achievement gratifications in their leisure activities. Regardless of how much depersonalization has occurred in the area of work, regardless of how meaningless a job might be to many men, perhaps it is still through their work that men engage their achievement motivation in our society. The role of work perhaps absorbs so much of men's achievement concerns that their evaluations of themselves and their own capacity for performance are primarily relegated to their appraisal of what they do or do not do at work. No matter how much encouragement there is for do-it-yourself leisure activities or mastery experiences in sporting activities, men seek to achieve aspirations mostly at work. This conclusion reaffirms the conclusion that Kornhauser and Reid (1965) came to in their discussion of the great investment that men of all social strata have in job performance.

Power motivation and leisure In contrast to the achievement motive, the power motive showed a number of interesting relationships to men's leisure activity, but only when the *Prestige* level of their job was taken into account. Let us look at each of the prestige levels separately.

In high *Prestige* jobs, among older men high power motivation was significantly associated with the absence of *Leisure Spent in Achievement* activity and relatively more *Memberships in Organizations*. Achievement activity is primarily asocial and membership in organizations is primarily social. It is therefore easy to reason that power gratifications can be enacted in membership in organizations but not in achievement activity at leisure. However, our previous analysis of the job role suggested that men perhaps will retreat from influence demands if they have high power motive, that is, if they are particularly concerned about their weakness. For men in this age group who hold prestigious jobs, perhaps retreat is not the appropriate means of coping with a high power motive. As the reader can recall from our analysis of how the power motive is engaged in high *Prestige* jobs, we noted that economic gratifications can be a symbol of power that can come from work. For older men especially, monetary signs of influence are probably very potent. One way to wield this power is in giving or threatening not to give money to social organizations. We can picture a man concerned about weakness, who has a prestigious job, who has earned a lot of money, and who then turns to fulfilling power gratifications by his advice and his pocketbook in the affairs of the community college, church groups, political organizations, and the like. He can wield the influence that money has brought him.

In contrast, older men who, by virtue of the job they hold, have relatively low *Prestige* in the community, might be especially concerned about their potential weakness. For this group of older men, concern about just maintaining their jobs may be especially strong. They need reassurance. They need other people to tell them they are not weak. This may explain why older men with high power motivation in jobs with relatively low *Prestige* socialize significantly more than their counterparts with low power motivation. Such socialization with family and friends perhaps is a way that men with a high power motive, but little influence in society, can reassure themselves that they perhaps are not inadequate. They still can find influence in the interpersonal setting. These men are perhaps avoiding the more formal social arenas where their less prestigious occupational attainments would put them at a disadvantage. They seek out the informal social contacts to reassure themselves that they are not socially inadequate.

There was one other significant result relating power motivation to leisure. Young men in low *Prestige* jobs with high power motivation were more likely to mention achievement types of leisure activity than were men with low power motivation. We would think that young men, especially those in jobs that are not prestigious, are not in a position to wield power in the community and therefore may retreat to solitary achievement activity in leisure to demonstrate mastery, a control over nature perhaps as a substitute for their lack of control over social matters. This relationship is opposite to that found between power motivation and *Leisure Spent in Achievement* for older men, especially those in high *Prestige* jobs. We view the contrast in these relationships as reflecting the contrasting age and social status in these groups. This is a very speculative interpretation, but again, perhaps, is in keeping with our interpretation that the power motive measure taps a fear of weakness rather than a positive power motivation.

These, then, were the results that we found in relating the three motives to leisure time activities among men with full-time jobs. In general, the results do not corroborate our position that leisure has become the focused arena for men's gratifications of these motives. Affiliation and power motives do seem to enter into the types of leisure time activities chosen by men, but the achievement motive does not seem to be a very salient motive for activities in leisure. Achievement in leisure does not seem to compensate for lack of gratification of achievement on the job.

REASSESSMENT OF THE JOB ROLE

We have looked at the motives of affiliation, achievement, and power in relationship to job selection, job reactions, and leisure activities. In each of the sections covering these topics we found some significant and provocative results that differentiate men according to the kind of job role they hold. The prestige of a man's occupation and the specific type of social requirements a man engages in at work seem to be important factors in determining both the capacity for finding affiliative gratifications at work and outside of work, and for finding the job a potential symbol of power that the man can use to combat his own fear of weakness. The job role seems to incite the achievement motive more than leisure activities.

What then can we conclude about the job role? As we did in the previous chapters on marriage and parenthood, we integrate our analyses of motives and the job role by assessing what we have learned about demands, gratifications, and ambiguities in the job role. Our examination of men's affiliative reactions at work, their achievement strivings, and their attempts to maintain a sense of power from their occupations, all have added some information to the tentative characterizations of the job role with which we begin the investigation (cf. Chapter 1).

ROLE DEMANDS

A major conclusion from our analysis of men's work and leisure reactions as a function of their achievement motivation, is that the pressure men feel to perform at some kind of job, the pressure men feel to demonstrate that they can achieve at work, is such a potent role demand for all types of job roles that performance in realms other than work—leisure, social roles—cannot compensate for inadequate job performance. Our moral attitude toward work probably is too pervasive for men to break away from their glorification of work as a justification of their masculinity. With such social sentiments, our society has established a guaranteed, built-in stimulation of men's achievement strivings in their work.

Furthermore, we have concluded that in *any* job, most men, if they have strong achievement interests, will continually set new levels of aspiration. Our guess is that even if a job does not seem difficult, men will find ways to excel in their performance at work, or aspire to types of jobs that would be more demanding. A conclusion worth exploring in future studies of the job role is that a major role demand experienced in *any* work situation by the American male with strong achievement motivation is "to do the best one can." This is not a new insight about high status jobs, but it was an unexpected view of the role demands for low status jobs.

If a primary demand of the specific job role a man holds explicitly involves reliance on other people, either as a supervisor or in other interpersonal relationships, then there also seems to be an investment in the goals of the organization, or the social enterprise, and a reliance upon it. But such social commitments at work to a relatively depersonalized social system seem to interfere both with feelings of personal achievement and also with feelings of power.

In thinking about the conflict between social expectations in a man's work and his achievement goals, we were stimulated to think about the role of work in general in modern society. There is no direct evidence for what we are about to say, but it is not hard to conceive of the possibility that in modern organizational settings, and in any job that requires social performance, there is a strong implicit demand for men to sacrifice personal accomplishment and power for the sake of the social good, for the sake of the social benefits directly affected by his work. A foreman or a teacher, each has to retreat from what he might have wanted in the way of personal accomplishment and power, and to enjoy the social benefits offered by the industry (in the case of the foreman) and the accomplishments of his students (in the case of the teacher). Perhaps, then, it is well to conceive of almost any organizational job as a role that involves, by definition, a conflict of demand between achievement and social goals.

ROLE GRATIFICATIONS

One of the most provocative ideas emerging from our analysis of the work and leisure reaction of men with different motives is that the gratifications that are possible and are obtained from work are dramatically different for men at different ages: young men seek the satisfaction attendant to having reached a certain type of occupation; middle-aged men seek gratification directly from the particular qualities of their job; and older men attempt to find satisfaction from the symbolic significance work has for their broader life goals, especially as it reflects the capacity to maintain a sense of activity, a sense of usefulness. For both younger and older men the job role implicates other social reactions. For them, working seems to be the route for obtaining major social gratification from other activities, *not in the job itself, but outside the job*. Men obtain power and influence from being in prestigious jobs, or merely holding down a job, or they make friends with people they meet at work. For the middle-aged man, there seems to be a greater capacity for obtaining gratifications from what the job role itself explicitly offers.

The type of social gratification a man directly gets from his work itself seems more likely to come from jobs where men still exercise choice about their social behavior. If men are *required* to be social or to be influential on their job, they seem less likely to get affiliation or power gratification from it than they would if they were in a job where the sociability and influence behavior is up to them. Salesmen seem to enjoy influence more than foremen. Salesmen are freer to choose whom they influence than are foremen. Unskilled workers or clerical workers seem to get more affiliation satisfaction from their work than lawyers and teachers. Clerks and unskilled workers can choose with whom they are to be social; lawyers and teachers have less freedom in this regard. We are thus led to the conclusion that a sense of personal choice perhaps underlies the social gratification possible in men's work.

ROLE AMBIGUITIES

Jobs vary in how much they require men to be social. What seems to be clear from our analysis is that jobs that have explicit social demands for one type of motivational system can often be *ambiguous* for another social motive. How much friendship can evolve between a supervisor and his supervisee? Teacher and student? Doctor and patient? Foreman and worker? How much power can and does a social worker wield? These are all questions that make these social roles that explicitly demand certain types of social behavior actually very ambiguous with regard to other social behaviors.

Another role ambiguity concerns the mechanisms available to

evaluate the excellence of performance, as required to satisfy achievement-motivated behavior. This may be particularly problematic for the self-employed: when have they done well? The entrepreneur role seems most clearly structured for achievement gratifications when there is some explicit feedback from a supervisor. The question of when a man has done a good job will probably always be answered ambiguously in the minds of men. In most jobs there is no end to men's achievement aspirations. One of the most important findings in this study was that men with high achievement motivation in both high and low status jobs were discontented. Men are always in search of higher goals that they set for themselves. In such a view, demands and gratifications for performance in all jobs will always be ambiguously characterized, because men's standards of excellence will be constantly shifting.

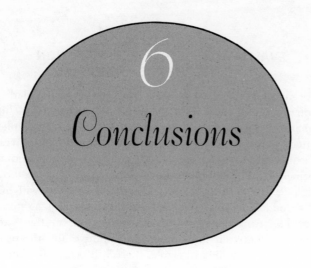

6

Conclusions

What can we now say about the general proposition of
this book—that the strength of a man's motives will have a
bearing on the way he reacts to marriage, parenthood, and work? What
can we now say about our guiding principles con-
cerning motive-role interaction? Does the strength of a man's motives
affect his role perceptions or his reactions to his life roles? What characteristics of the affiliation, achievement, or power motives help
to explain the bases of their interaction with social
roles? And what are the important characteristics of roles that
interact with motives? We will try to answer each
of these questions in turn in this chapter. These will be tentative
answers—ones that will hopefully provide a
basis for future motive-role investigations.
Because we undertook this investigation
as an exploratory study, we will try to specify research
proposals suggested by our conclusions. In each major section to
follow, therefore, we will suggest some research that
might test some of our major conclusions more directly than was
possible in our exploratory research.

EVALUATION OF THE SENSITIZATION
AND CONGRUENCE PRINCIPLES

We began our study with only a partially articulated position on the interaction of motives and roles. We tried to define roles and personality independently and argued that the effects of one on the other in interaction would have predictable consequences. In investigating these consequences, we were guided by the sensitization and the congruence principles. The sensitization principle asserts that in motivationally ambiguous roles, the strength of a man's motives will affect the quality of demands, frustrations, and gratifications that he perceives in these roles. The congruence principle asserts that, to the extent that congruence exists between the strength of a motive and the possibilities for the motive to be gratified in a role, there will be satisfaction and ease in role performance, and to the extent that there is poor meshing, there will be problems in the way an individual reacts to the role. These two principles were not employed to implement a logically deductive research investigation. Rather, we used them as the conceptual framework for this exploratory venture. How well did they serve us? We now turn to an evaluation of the usefulness of each principle. For this purpose we will emphasize similarities rather than differences among the motives or roles. From these evaluations, we hope to be in a better position to anticipate the future heuristic value of such global theoretical formulations about personality-role interaction.

THE SENSITIZATION PRINCIPLE

In Table 6.1, results supporting the sensitization principle are summarized. Not all results that could be interpreted as instances of the sensitization principle are included in the table. Only those that we discussed as sensitization effects are used. In previous chapters the reasons were given for considering these relationships as consistent with the sensitization principle. We are summarizing these relationships here in order to determine whether certain consistencies are discernible when the three social roles and three motives are considered simultaneously. We will not discuss all results listed in the table, but only highlight the consistencies.

At first glance these results may seem scattered and not very definitive, especially in light of the many relationships that might have emerged to support the sensitization principle. This would suggest dropping this approach to the study of personality-role interaction. But we do not view the data in Table 6.1 as random, rather the pattern of results suggested to us that a modified version of the sensitization principle would be a useful basis for investigating motive-role interaction. From our retrospective view of the data, it seems as if two additional phenomena have to be taken into account before any sensitization phenomenon becomes apparent in the analysis of motive-role interaction. First, some notion of *motive arousal* has to be employed. And secondly, the level of gratification of the motive in the role has to be considered. Let us see how we arrived at these additional conditions for the operation of the sensitization principle in the context of motive-role interaction.

First of all, we note that there appear to be more results supporting the sensitization principle when the motive in question is obviously very salient in the particular role—for example, the power motive in the marital role and the achievement motive in the job role. This suggests that a motive must be strongly salient in a role before any sensitization effects occur.

What do we mean by saying that these motives are salient in the roles? We have defined "motive" as a disposition to find certain goal states attractive. For example, people with a high achievement motive are assumed to have a strong disposition to be attracted to competition according to standards of excellence. By referring to a motive as a disposition, we wish to imply that it is a *latent* state, one that is not always directly or indirectly evidenced in behavior. Before a motive can determine a person's behavior in a situation, he has to become aware (although not necessarily consciously) that the motive is relevant to that situation. He has to become aware that the goal state of the motive is potentially attainable in that situation. When a person expects that the goal state of a particular motive may possibly be attained or frustrated in a given situation, we speak of his motive as being salient in that situation. This expectancy is independent of the expected probability of success or failure at efforts to reach a given goal state. Veroff (1965) and Crandall (1968) have more fully discussed this distinction. When there is general consensus that a given goal is relevant to a specific situation, we can speak of that motive as being generally salient in the situation. In such situations we would expect to be able to show that the behavior of persons for whom that motive is strong is different from that of persons for whom that motive is weak.

Under what conditions does a motive become generally salient in a role? Under what conditions would most people agree that a position requires its occupant to attend to the goals of the motive? Obviously there are very idiosyncratic interpretations of roles which would promote particular saliences for particular people. A woman can set specific achievement goals for her social relationship with her husband; she may strive for perfection in her conversational ploys or her lovemaking techniques. And yet these strivings seem like idiosyncratic adaptations to the marital role, ones not clearly inherent in the normative role demands and gratifications of marriage. We are asking how particular motives become

TABLE 6-1 SUMMARY OF FINDINGS SUPPORTING THE SENSITIZATION PRINCIPLE

Motive	Marital Role Reaction	Parental Role Reaction	Job Role Reaction
Affiliation	+ *Relationship Satisfaction* (grade-school-educated wives)	+ *Tolerance Inadequacy* (trends college-educated mothers of school-age and adolescent children) − *Parental Restrictiveness* (grade-school-educated fathers of preschoolers; trends all fathers of preschool and school-age children) + *Parental Restrictiveness* (grade-school-educated fathers of adults)	+ *Affiliation Satisfaction* (clerical jobs; trends in jobs of high social requirements)
Achievement	+ Career Achievement Motivation to *Marital Restrictiveness* (college-educated wives) + *Relationship Satisfaction* (high-school-educated wives)	− *Parental Distancing* (college-educated mothers of preschoolers) + *Parental Distancing* (high-school-educated mothers of preschoolers; high-school-educated fathers of school-age children)	+ *Achievement Satisfaction* (clerical jobs; trend unskilled jobs; trends in jobs of high prestige, significant for young men; trends in jobs of low social requirements and for old men in jobs of low supervisory potential) + *Affiliation Satisfaction* (middle-aged men in jobs of high supervision) − *Economic Satisfaction* (jobs of high supervision; old men in jobs of low supervisory potential) + *Achievement Dissatisfaction* (semiskilled jobs; trends in jobs of high prestige; trends in general)

TABLE 6-1 *continued*

Power		
+ *Relationship Satisfaction* (trends grade-school-educated wives; grade-school-educated husbands)	+ *Parental Distancing* (high-school-educated mothers of adults; trends high-school and college-educated mothers of school-age children; grade-school-educated fathers of school-age children)	− *Achievement Dissatisfaction* (clerical jobs; trend unskilled jobs; old men in jobs of low supervisory potential)
− *Marital Restrictiveness* (young college-educated wives)	− *Parental Restrictiveness* (high-school-educated mothers of adults)	+ *Affiliation Satisfaction* (salesmen)
+ *Marital Restrictiveness* (old college-educated husbands; older childless husbands)	+ *Affiliation Inadequacy* (mothers of adults)	− *Economic Satisfaction* (salesmen; trends in jobs of high prestige)
		+ *Achievement Satisfaction* (jobs of low supervision; middle-aged men in jobs of low supervisory potential)
		− *Achievement Satisfaction* (young men in jobs of high supervision)

Note: Entries indicate the direction of the relationship between the motive specified to the left and the role reaction specified in the body of the table. All relationships entered were significant unless entered as trend.

301

generally salient to marriage, parenthood, or work for most people who enact these roles. A motive becomes generally salient in a role when *primary role demands clearly implicate that motive, when all role occupants have to come to terms with the goals of this particular motive because the role requires them to behave in certain ways that automatically affect the gratification or frustration of the goals of the motive in question.*

Now let us return to the findings that led us to be concerned about the salience of motives in roles. In our analysis of motives and roles, we seem to have two instances of a motive being so generally salient in a role that the sensitization principle has a consistent chance to operate. These are two instances when the role demands clearly engage a particular motive, and that motive seems to play a strong part in the role perceptions when conditions of gratification are ambiguous.

The first instance is the power motive in marriage. We would argue that men and women have to establish a basis for influence in their marital interaction, no matter what else they do. Although it might be argued that power problems in decision-making are an essential element in *all* interpersonal interactions, they seem particularly unavoidable in American marriages. Other roles have some bases for avoiding issues of power. In parenthood, a mother can relegate all issues pertaining to the parent-child power struggle to the father, or vice versa. In marriage power issues seem unavoidable, while the other motives we have been considering do not seem to be necessarily intrinsic to the marital relationship. Certain groups, of course, do prescribe the presence or absence of strong affiliative bonds between husbands and wives as a basic part of the marital situation; however, in general, husbands and wives can avoid friendship-oriented interaction (affiliation). Similarly, couples can avoid performance goals in their interaction with each other (achievement). But there seems to be no way to avoid confrontation in a marriage over the issue of the relative influence of husband over wife and vice versa. There is no way to avoid evolving some means of dealing with the relative power of the husband and wife. Thus, most marriages in America automatically implicate the power motive and, hence, we might expect that persons high in this motive are more likely to be sensitized to certain aspects of marriage than persons high in the other motives.

The second such instance of a particular motive being automatically salient in a role is the achievement motive and the job role. There is some minimal standard of excellence that a man has to meet merely to hold a job. *All men have to establish a basis for evaluating their performance at work.* They can ignore their colleagues (affiliation), and the organizational power structure (power), but they cannot avoid evaluations of their job performance (achievement).

Thus, psychological imperatives for the engagement of the influence goals of a man or woman exist when the married position is attained and, similarly, a man's achievement goals are engaged when he enters the position of a job-holder. Perhaps this is why the sensitization principle seems most strongly in evidence for these particular motives in these specific roles.

Why was there no such clear application of the sensitization principle in American parenthood? With our new perspective on the sensitization principle—that it operates only when the motive is salient in the role—we would have to conclude that achievement, power, or affiliation are not automatically salient to the American view of fatherhood or motherhood. How reasonable is this conclusion? Can we say that there is no continuous functional necessity for friendship, power, or achievement demands in parenthood? Perhaps with the wisdom of hindsight, we might say that these motives are not automatically salient to the parental role because parenthood in America has increasingly become a shared role. There are *two* parents. Mothers and fathers can both act to nurture and influence, regulated according to the respective skills required of each at different points in the family life cycle and according to their particular personal interests. Within certain subgroups, there may be strong demands that do implicate a particular motive. But, in general, there is no *necessary* implication of one of the motives—affiliation, achievement, or power—in the role of mother or father, although these motives are obviously engaged in the role of parent. Parents have to socialize and nurture, but if the mother handles one or both of these functions, the father can relax, and vice versa.

These considerations led us to amend the sensitization principle to state that *the strength of a motive will affect perceptions of the quality of frustrations and gratifications in roles when the motive is necessarily engaged in role enactment because of some primary role demands and when the likelihood of frustration or gratification is ambiguous.* Once the motive becomes engaged, it can then affect perceptions. Without assured engagement, it is difficult to ascertain sensitization.

In asserting that primary role demands must be relevant to a motive for the sensitization principle to operate, we are requiring that a motive be salient in the role. Although in theory the sensitization principle can operate whenever a motive is aroused or salient in the role for a particular individual, the only instances in our present research when we are assured of arousal in a whole category of role occupants is when the motive is *generally* salient in the role. In our present research, idiographic analyses are minimized. Our evidence for the sensitization principle is therefore limited to cases where a motive is engaged by the *primary* role demands. This aspect of the refinement of the sensitization principle is needed for analyses of motives in interaction with a *general* role, such as marriage or parenthood.

In making this assertion that motives must be salient in a role for the principle of sensitization to operate in motive-role interaction, we are introducing the general idea of motivational "arousal" as a basis for understanding the results. We are saying that before a motive can influence perception, the motive has to be engaged.[1] Role demands can uniformly provide such engagement, because only under such circumstances is there sufficient orientation to role characteristics relevant to the motive among role occupants high in that motive. In other words, there has to be some characteristic of the role that acts as a stimulus to direct the attention of the role-occupant to the motivationally relevant class of incentives available in that role. Once the motive is aroused, then the other critical role characteristic we originally postulated—the ambiguity of gratification of the motive in that role—should be important in determining whether or not the aroused motivational state of the person affects the kinds of gratifications and frustrations he perceives.

We still recognize that there has to be some ambiguity about gratification or frustration for any sensitization to occur. In some instances the role demand will engage the motive because the role calls for behaviors that are expected to lead to goals compatible with the motive. The demand elicits positive expectancies. In other instances the role demand will engage the motive because it calls for behaviors that are probably incompatible with the goals of the motive. The demand elicits negative expectancies. But in many instances the role demand calls for behaviors whose specific outcome is not clear. The outcome may be compatible or incompatible with the goal of the motive, but not irrelevant to it. The role occupant is not assured of motive gratification or motive frustration if the motive is salient in a role. He is just assured that the goal is relevant, that it is likely to be gratified or frustrated if he performs certain role behaviors. For the sensitization principle to have any meaning, however, the role still has to be somewhat ambiguous as to its gratification potential for the motive, in spite of the motive being clearly salient in the role. Power is clearly salient to marriage, achievement is clearly salient to work, but the gratification of each of these motives is still ambiguously structured in most marriages or in most jobs. Being married means that one must make and receive attempts to influence, but it doesn't necessarily mean that one will succeed or fail as an influencer. Working incorporates evaluation of performance but the outcome of the evaluation is not clear.

Let us consider one specific example from the research findings. For the college-educated wife, being married makes primary demands on her

---

[1]The assumption concerning arousal is important because we, like others concerned with motivation theory (Atkinson, 1964), have been operating without such an "energizing" principle. In subsequent sections, it will become more apparent that this assumption about arousal is essential to our conclusion about motive-role interaction.

decisions with regard to problems of mutual support, sexual gratification, and her relationship to her children. The existence of these demands activates expectancies about her influence and thus arouses her power motive. Since the potential for the gratification of her power motive in the companionate marital role is ambiguous, her aroused power motive can sensitize her to perceiving the power affects of her marriage. And indeed we find that college-educated wives with high power motivation are more likely to see their marriages as being unrestrictive than those with low power motivation.

Another pattern is discernible from the data in Table 6.1 that led us to a further refinement of the sensitization principle. There were several instances where, in roles that we had assumed were clearly *lacking* in the potential for motive-relevant satisfactions, strong motivation seemed to result in a distorted sensitization—in the report of those role satisfactions that we had assumed were difficult to obtain. This kind of relationship between motivation and role reactions occurred in three specific contexts: affiliation motivation and emphasizing relationship satisfaction in marriage for grade-school-educated wives; achievement motivation and stressing active, self-involved (nondistancing) satisfactions in motherhood for college-educated mothers of preschool children; and achievement motivation and focusing on achievement satisfaction, but not on achievement dissatisfaction, in work for clerical workers. What do each of these findings suggest? Each of these relationships seems somewhat at variance with the assumed gratification potential of these specific roles. We have assumed that the sensitization principle operates best when there is ambiguity about the potential for frustrating or gratifying a particular motive in that role. In the above instances, the gratification potential does not seem to be ambiguous at all. It seems clearly low. Traditional marriages were not expected to be satisfying to persons seeking friendship-like relationships with their spouses. College-educated mothers with strong achievement goals were expected to find childrearing an unsatisfactory outlet for such desires. The relatively low status of clerical workers in the white-collar prestige structure was expected to be distressing to men with high achievement motivation.

We might argue that each of these roles in some way represents a situation where the role occupants are faced with role demands that disallow the gratification of certain motives. The gratification potential of these roles is not ambiguous at all; *enactment of these roles leads to consistent frustration with respect to the motives in question.* With such frustration, role occupants can become defensive.

One mechanism for handling frustration under certain circumstances is to deny dissatisfaction. For example, a person can change the quality of his goals, accentuate small gratifications, even hallucinate gratifications, or combine any of these reactions. The relationship between these kinds of reactions and frustration is a basic assumption of the psychoanalytic theory of perception (Rapaport, 1959) and of modern theories of defensive behavior (Miller and Swanson, 1960; Parsons, 1959; Parsons and Shils, 1952). In these instances of the sensitization principle, we see motives leading to *distorted* perceptions of role possibilities when a person feels deeply committed to a role that both engages the motive and leads to its frustration. We had previously thought that a motive would operate to sensitize individuals only in roles in which gratification potential was ambiguous. We now see how it might operate in situations in which motivational goals are clearly frustrated.

Let us look at the three instances of this special sort of sensitization that seemed to appear in our data. We would suggest that as a consequence of marriage, women with a grade-school education are gradually faced with an absence of affiliative satisfactions. The traditional marriage role precludes a companionate relationship between mates. Throughout the book we have suggested that marriage in lower status groups means sharply delineated sex-role boundaries. Men provide, and women take care of the home. Furthermore, men should ideally be the major decision-makers, although often they are not. We can only surmise that companion-ship is not easily attained in such marriages and instead is relegated to relationships with same-sex friends and family. Clearly, for this group of women, the primary marital role demands disallow affiliative satisfactions in the marital relationship. After marriage, these women may be forced to give up many dreams about their future social contacts with the world. Marriage, once a potential salvation for them, probably is found lacking on many grounds. Komarovsky's interview study of working-class spouses (1964) emphasizes that women in working-class marriages apparently have low aspirations about what they expect from marriage. Nor would we expect them to derive much affiliative gain from other life circumstances.

Given this characterization of the traditional marriages of grade-school-educated wives, how do we account for the positive association between affiliation motivation and reports of relationship satisfactions? According to our previous discussion, the sensitization principle is opera-tive only when the motive is salient in the role. The affiliation motive seems to be salient in the marital role for grade-school-educated wives, not because the primary role demands directly engage the affiliation motive, but because affiliative satisfactions are so explicitly limited in enactment of this role, while at the same time such gratifications are difficult to obtain in other ways. Men who are parties to a traditional marriage at least have contacts with colleagues at work that can promote affiliative gratification. Women are more restricted to their homes by their children, and while they may have intense relationships with their children and their families of origin, we have previously argued that such relationships are not adequate means of satisfying affiliative goals because of their obligatory nature and the status differentials in the participants. Thus the affiliation motive is salient in the marital role for these women because it is intensely ungratified. For women with high affiliation motivation, such a marriage could be intensely limiting and unsatisfying. And yet it is a role to which they *have to be committed* to live up to general sex-role expectations. There are few psychological alternatives for these women, and they have grounds for defensive sensitization. Caught in such a position, these women could easily try to "make the best of things" by minimizing their expectations for affiliative marriage satisfactions. A woman who has strong affiliation motivation might, in such a situation, be especially likely to focus on the ways in which very minimal expectations for affiliation with her spouse are met. She may exaggerate the joy she experiences in her relationship with her spouse because she does not, in general, expect much from it. Marriage in other classes is perhaps less clearly limited in affiliation potential for women, especially as it takes on some of the more egalitarian perceptions of the personal relationships of husband and wife. Therefore, among the more-educated, the press for defensive sensitization is not evident.

The above description of the marital role for grade-school-educated wives has certain similarities to the characterization of parenthood for college-educated women. A woman who remains in the educational stream through college is socialized in a masculine world where career-oriented ambitions are fostered. After marriage, a college-educated woman often has to abandon worldly ambition for diapers and the P.T.A. She turns to the parental role with efforts to excel at the task of childrearing, but finds herself involved in an unsatisfying role to which she has to be committed. Social pressures for mothering are unavoidable. College women, therefore, often make creative childrearing a primary parental role demand, which in turn engages the achievement expectancy and motive. The achievement motive becomes salient in the parental role for these women, but it is not easily gratified. The achievement possibilities in childrearing are limited. These women seem to be trying to make the best of their fate, but they are often frustrated, and being frustrated, they become defensively sensitized to the achievement potential in the role. The achievement gratification is perhaps less decisively and dramatically salient in parenthood to mothers from other educational backgrounds and parenthood may be less frustrating to any achievement aspirations they might have had. Their goals for excellence in childrearing may be less difficult to attain. Thus, they may not get defensively engaged by motherhood.

Now we will examine the third instance of defensive sensitization. We have said that achievement goals are salient in all jobs. Hence, we will assume that clerical workers have their achievement motivation engaged at work. But we have found clerical workers to be a particularly distressed group that is characterized by the lack of fulfillment of high aspirations (Gurin et al., 1960, p. 162). This is perhaps due to an emasculating quality in male clerical work not found in even the most unskilled manual jobs. Men in clerical jobs probably have hoped for, or been trained for, better occupational positions. Then they find themselves in a job that requires commitment and achievement evaluation, but clearly does not permit satisfaction of their ambitions or use of their uniquely masculine talents. When the enactment of such an unsatisfying role is coupled with high achievement motivation, with all that it implies about commitment to work and ambition for successful accomplishment, there is a similar situation to that of the lower-status wives and the upper-status mothers. These men have to make the best of things; they defensively report achievement satisfaction in their job.

We would thus suggest that each of these three roles produces defensive maneuvers for adjustment. In these special groups the role clearly demands behavior relevant to the motive. For the grade-school-educated woman, marital demands explicitly prescribe against expectancies for affiliation, and yet she has no other good alternative for affiliation. For the college-educated woman, parental demands to rear a child properly, to raise a successful child clearly evoke expectancies about achievement. For the clerical worker, as for other men, his job demands for competent performance evoke achievement concerns, but the clerical worker is often frustrated in his ambitions. As such, each role is likely to engage a person's motivational pattern. And in each case, the motivational goal is extremely difficult to attain. If a man has high achievement motivation in a clerical job, he will defend against extreme frustration of his achievement desires in work by emphasizing the possible achievement gratifications in his work. If a comparable situation occurs for someone with high affiliation motivation in his friendships, for example, affiliation-relevant defenses will be engaged by emphasizing the possible social gratifications in friendship. The same holds true for power motivation in marriage.

It may not be farfetched to see these results as a complex example of what theorists in cognitive dissonance have been discussing (Brehm and Cohen, 1962). Experiments in cognitive dissonance have shown that subjects committed to an undesirable activity and thus confronted with dissonant cognitive states tend to handle this dissonance by overevaluating the activity. We suggest that a similar phenomenon is operating in these three cases. Men and women praise those qualities of their life circumstances that are in fact not very gratifying but are instead the very aspects of the roles that lead to frustration. They react this way because they are strongly committed to the role. They are combating a primary role requirement that evokes expectancies about the motive in a situation where the role is so structured that it leads to motivational frustration.

These considerations led us to a further refinement of the sensitization principle. Our earlier statements concerning this principle, both here and in Chapter 1, specified that motivational sensitivity occurred only under conditions of ambiguity in the gratification potential of a role. It was proposed that strong motivation could increase the perception of motivationally relevant aspects of a role only when expectations about motive gratification or frustration are not clear. Now we feel able to describe another condition under which perceptual selectivity can be predicted. *Strong motivation will enhance motive-specific positive evaluations of a role when the motive is necessarily salient in role enactment because of primary role demands and when the role occupant feels trapped in the role—committed to the role but severely limited by the potential it has to fulfill his goals and expectations for life.* The motive is aroused, but it is consistently frustrated. With such frustration, the person becomes defensive. We are thus led to take another psychological phenomenon into account when using the sensitization principle—the level of motivational frustration in performing the role. Where we previously viewed sensitization as occurring only under conditions of ambiguity about gratification, we now think that it can operate under conditions of explicit frustration.

What if role demands consistently lead most role-occupants to focus on the gratification of a particular motive? It seems to us that the sensitization principle may be meaningless under these conditions, since all role-occupants could recognize and realize such gratifications regardless of their motivation. Alternatively, under these conditions gratifications may be "taken for granted," and most persons may even become insensitive to them. But we recognize that even when there is apparent clarity in the gratification potential of a role because its enactment appears relevant to the satisfaction of only one motivational interest, certain men, because of their motives, can have special doubts. Men with a certain motivational pattern may be sensitive to the potential frustration of that motive in a role, although the role may appear to outside observers to clearly have a high potential for the gratification of that motive. These men may defensively see great ambiguity about potential gratification when there is "realistically" little ambiguity. Generally, when we speak of ambiguity we have reference to an objective or consensual assessment of the certainty for gratification, but we do recognize that certain men create their own subjective ambiguities.

Perhaps it is impossible for the gratification potential in a role to be totally unambiguous to all role occupants, no matter how clearly structured the role is for gratification of a given motive. Indeed, there were certain roles that we, as outside observers, assumed to have clear gratification potential for a given motive but which appeared to elicit sensitization from role occupants who were strong in that motive. For example, we assumed that prestigious jobs would generally and consistently allow for achievement gratification. And yet there seems to be sufficient ambiguity about it so that not all men mentioned achievement satisfactions. Men with high achievement motivation seem to be sensitized to achievement satisfactions in such job roles more than are men with low achievement motivation. We can explain these results in two ways. Men with high achievement motivation may be so sensitive to the possibilities for frustration of their achievement desires that they do not take achievement gratifications for granted, even in jobs where they are readily obtained; some ambiguity always exists. They therefore describe these gratifications as important aspects of their job while their counterparts with low achievement motivation do not emphasize these apparent features of their jobs. Alternatively, we might say that even these prestigious jobs can realistically be judged ambiguous in their achievement gratification potential, in the sense that a number of different motive-incentive systems can easily be gratified in these job roles, and the men with higher achievement motive are sensitized to the achievement incentives. Or we could use both explanations. In either case, our explanation assumes that sensitization occurs as a result of ambiguity about gratification, despite the observer's judgment of clarity in the gratification potential of the role.

In general, however, we would expect that when a role unambiguously provides certain motivational gratifications, the sensitization principle would not be useful in understanding the attention persons in that position direct to these gratifications. Under such conditions, most individuals may report the same type of general satisfaction, or most may be insensitive to it. We would contend that qualities of the role more highly specific than the ones we undertook to analyze, and not personality differences, may determine individual differences in types of role gratification under these conditions. For example, teaching, as an advising profession, may generally present power rewards, whether a person is high or low in power motivation. Most teachers might describe the pleasure derived from the exercise of influence inherent in teaching, or most might ignore this obvious feature of their job, depending on how they were questioned about their role gratifications. Variations in a teacher's reactions to his job may depend, under these conditions, not on the strength of his power motive, but on more specific influence-related aspects of his job—such things as the degree of personal contact permitted him, the size of the classes assigned to him, the amount of supervision he is given, the degree of freedom he is allowed in curriculum planning—rather than on his power motivation. Thus we are saying that personality factors play an important part in determining reactions to roles when role gratification potentials are ambiguous. When gratifications for a particular motive are clearly present, the role structures, by themselves, are the major determinant of role reactions.

Let us consider what these conclusions might mean for social scientists interested in modern industrial organization and, in particular, those interested in such matters as commitment and gratification of personnel in industry. We have said that when role requirements unambiguously lead to certain gratifications, individual differences in role reactions can become more a function of variations in the structure of the role itself than a function of personality-role interactions. We would expect, therefore, that when slight changes in organizational policy appear effective in changing the feelings of satisfaction or commitment of business executives, it is probably because the underlying basic individual motives (achievement and power in particular) have been gratified in these job roles. Furthermore, we have said that when role gratification is more uncertain, personality variables may have a great deal to do with individual differences in role reactions. When slight organizational changes have little effect, we would expect it is because some basic motives have either not been gratified at all or are inconsistently gratified. Changes in organizational policy cannot easily change basic personality differences. Argyris' (1964) general pessimism about the potential effectiveness of minor revisions in organizations perhaps stems from this implicit problem. He suggests a far more radical revision in organization that truly would affect the overall gratification potential of the role-occupant.

Although we recognize now that sensitization can occur under conditions of consistent frustration and that it may even occur under conditions of consistent gratification, we are still convinced that this principle is most applicable when a role is neither frustrating enough for a given motive to evoke a defensive sensitization, nor clearly gratifying enough to evoke desensitization. We would suggest that motives would be observed to have strong affects on the perceptions of the gratifications and frustrations in a role when the role is not consistently expected to lead to gratification nor frustration of a given motive. Three instances of this phenomenon can be cited: (1) the positive association between achievement motivation and mentioning achievement gratifications as job satisfactions for young men in prestigious jobs; (2) the positive association between power motivation and reporting relationship satisfactions in marriage for grade-school-educated husbands; and (3) the positive association between achievement motivation and reporting dissatisfaction with achievement aspects of the job by semiskilled workers. All of these are possible examples of sensitization to motive-gratifying or frustrating qualities of a role in which gratification or frustration of that motive is possible but not automatic. The last example probably reflects a sensitization to the motive-relevant aspects of a role that has the potential to be consistently frustrating, but in this case the role is not so totally devoid of motivational gratification that defensive perceptions are elicited.

All of the foregoing may be a way of saying that with regard to the sensitization principle, a personality-role interaction analysis may be especially fruitful when the theorist takes into account the level of frustration or gratification of the goals of motives that are salient in the roles. First the motive must be salient in the role. Once it is salient, then the motive can lead to defensive distortion if the goals are consistently frustrated. It can lead to very direct sensitization to either frustration or satisfaction if there is some ambiguity about whether the goals can be gratified or not.

In summary, we would suggest that *personality characteristics may strongly determine role reactions when that personality characteristic is salient in the role and when a person is defensive about this role, or when he finds that the potential gratifications in his role are ambiguous.* We have further suggested that *specific role demands may strongly determine role reactions when a person is particularly gratified and is not defensive, and hence when he is psychologically open to the objective stimuli coming from the role characteristics themselves.* We believe these are important insights we have had about personality-role interaction. We hope that these further refinements of our general statement of the sensitization principle can be pursued in further work.

Before proceeding to a discussion of the type of research that is suggested by these conclusions, we would like to call attention to the way our discussion of defensive sensitization relates to certain previous research or theory about role-personality interaction. In Argyris' treatment of *Personality and Organization* (1957), there was a clear recognition of the possibility of defensive denial occurring when an organization continually frustrated the needs of individuals. Argyris assumes that all organizations will be frustrating and, hence, that all individuals resort to one defensive maneuver or another in adapting to organizations. The denial maneuver—the one we have accentuated here—is just one of many possibilities that Argyris notes. Although Argyris generally is talking about needs or motives common to all men—self-actualization and independence—and not about individual variations in these needs, we are suggesting here that his statements about defensive reactions for men in general may also be true for men with specific motivational patterns.

Parsons and Shils (1952) have also been concerned with defensive reactions to personality-role interaction. These theorists draw a distinction between mechanisms of defense—the way an individual handles his intrapsychic conflicts—and mechanisms of adjustment—the way he handles his interpersonal or role-personality conflicts. Although this distinction breaks down when an individual begins to incorporate role expectations as part of his own internal system and to experience role-personality conflicts intrapsychically, generally speaking, we have discussed defensive sensitization as a mechanism of adjustment that may be independent of a person's characteristic way of handling internal conflict. On this score we have followed the lead of Parsons and his group.

The particular defensive maneuver that we were highlighting—overaccentuation of gratifications and underaccentuation of frustration when confronted with frustration—is a maneuver noted by others in different contexts. Sears (1940) long ago noted in studies of level of aspiration that some children increase their level of aspiration following failure. Recently Coleman and his colleagues (1966) pointed to the high evaluation placed on school and studying by Negro students who in fact were consistently poor performers in school. Are not these both instances of distorted perceptions of present or future performance to keep the child from recognizing frustration? Part of Atkinson's thinking about achievement motivation (1964) is that some people concerned about failure will overaspire to avoid confronting realistic failure. It is as if the person says, "If I fail, it is excusable. It was so hard." But what we are suggesting is somewhat different. We are proposing that with consistent failure a person may in fact feel satisfied. He may fool himself into thinking that he really is finding success.

A recent study by Lowe and Steiner (1968) indicates that this sort of denial in the face of frustration does not only occur in the achievement sphere. Their female subjects were asked to make ratings of attraction to a person who had been described to them and who was going to be their blind date. Then the subjects received additional negative information about the prospective blind date. After receiving the additional information, their ratings became more extreme in either the positive or negative direction. It is this unexplained increase in variability that interests us. Why do some college women, faced with a prospective blind date, increase their attraction to the date after being given negative information? Why do others act more "rationally" and decrease their attraction? We would suggest that the increase in attraction is attributable to the subjects' commitment to enact the role and to the engagement of a motive—affiliation, perhaps—by the blind-date role. One subject, about to go on a blind date with a man about whom she has a certain impression from previous information, can distort new negative information by making it positive, if the motive engaged by the blind date is one that is strong for her. Another subject, whose motivation has not been aroused, may simply revise her attraction downward in keeping with the new information.

Suggested research The perspective we have developed on the sensitization principle suggests some specific ways of investigating this principle in role-personality studies in the future. Two points seem paramount—

research should control for the salience of the motive in the role and also for the gratification potential of the motive in the role. Both of these factors should have an important impact on the relationship found between a motive and perceptions of the demands and gratifications in the role.

Let us concentrate on some potential research dealing with the control of the gratification potential in a role. There are two ways to control for gratification potential, either through the person's responses about level of gratification, or through some independently measured role characteristic from which the social scientists could infer a gratification difference in roles. The latter seems preferable, since reported levels of gratification can also be subject to distortion. This is one reason why we did not control for the amount of expressed satisfaction at work or in marriage when we correlated motives and perceptions of specific gratifications, in addition to the fact that the number of subjects in any particular analysis of this sort would have been much too small.

In any future research on the sensitization principle, the study should be specifically designed to control for the gratification potential of roles. A study of achievement motivation as it affects job role perceptions in different organizational settings would seem most promising. For such a study we would suggest sampling at least three types of organizations: those that consistently gratify achievement goals; those for which the gratification potential for achievement goals is uncertain; and those that consistently frustrate achievement goals. Within each of these types of organizations a researcher could look for the effects that assessed achievement motive might have on perceptions of achievement satisfactions and dissatisfactions. Ideally, the men in each type of organization would do approximately equivalent work. For the definition of the potential of an organization to gratify achievement goals, we could make use of some of the information we will be discussing in our integration of the results about achievement motivation in a subsequent section. We would hypothesize that with high achievement motivation there should be sensitization to realistic achievement possibilities or frustrations in the organizations that have a moderate or ambiguous level of achievement potential, a minimum sensitization at the high level of achievement potential, and distortion of the achievement possibilities at the low level of achievement potential.

A similar study could be made of the marital role. To do it well, you would have to obtain data from *couples*. A researcher could use the expectations of the person's spouse to define the affiliative or power potential of marriage, or the researcher could use the actual time a person spends with his spouse to define the affiliation potential of a particular marriage, and the success of observed influence attempts to define his

314

potential for power gratification. Having identified the level of gratification possible in a marriage, the researcher could then relate the affiliation and power motives to the types of satisfactions and frustrations that the person reports. We felt very much handicapped in delineating the marital role in the present study because we lacked responses from the spouses of our subjects. Such responses would have given us a better basis for inferring the role demands and gratification potentials for a given subject. If such data were available, a study of marriages parallel to the proposed organizational study could be accomplished. It would be important to see whether the general statements we made about sensitization in motive-role interaction have relevance for several motives and roles. It would thus be crucial to develop a workable research investigation of marriage or some other interpersonal role to parallel the study of business organizations.

We should also note that marital role expectations from spouses can also be used as a way to control for the salience of a motive in a role. We might find that affiliation motivation correlated more clearly with role reactions in marriages in which the spouse either strongly encouraged or forbade companionate activity in marriage.

Of course, laboratory studies could also be devised in which the experimenter manipulated the assignment of positions to subjects, the salience of a motive to role enactment, as well as the expectancies for successful goal attainment. We have not focused on that type of study because our major interest in the present study is the applicability of motivational concepts in natural settings.

Let us now turn to our findings on the congruence principle. Are there any general conclusions about it? And, if so, how can these conclusions be tested in further studies?

THE CONGRUENCE PRINCIPLE

In Table 6.2 are summarized the major findings that support the congruence principle. Again, not all results that could be interpreted as instances of the congruence principle are presented. We have listed only those discussed in previous chapters. There was not overwhelming support for the congruence principle; instead, the principle seemed useful only for certain groups, certain motives, and certain roles. Nevertheless, the results are enlightening. We will not discuss all the results listed in this table, but will try to point out major trends.

We seem to have found results that support the congruence principle in roles where the demands and gratifications pertaining to a particular motive are especially explicit and where such demands and gratifications are either clearly available or unavailable. If the demands, gratifications,

TABLE 6-2 SUMMARY OF FINDINGS SUPPORTING THE CONGRUENCE PRINCIPLE

Motive	Marital Role Reaction	Parental Role Reaction	Job Role Reaction
Affiliation	− *Marital Unhappiness* (grade-school and high-school-educated wives; all mothers) + *Marital Unhappiness* (young grade-school-educated husbands) − *Marital Problems* (trends grade-school-educated wives)	+ *Negative Orientation* (trends mothers of preschool, school-age, and adolescent children) + *Parental Problems* (high-school-educated fathers of adolescents)	+ *Job Dissatisfaction* (foremen and farmers; trends in jobs of high social requirements) − *Job Dissatisfaction* (semiskilled jobs; trend unskilled jobs; young men in jobs of low social requirements; middle-aged men in jobs of low supervisory potential)
Achievement	+ *Marital Inadequacy* (young grade-school-educated wives) + *Marital Problems* (young high-school-educated husbands) − Home Achievement Motivation to *Marital Unhappiness* (grade-school-educated wives) − *Marital Problems* (young high-school-educated wives)	− *Parental Inadequacy* (college-educated mothers of school-age children; trends fathers of school-age, adolescent children) + *Parental Inadequacy* (college-educated mothers of preschoolers; fathers of preschoolers) + *Negative Orientation* (trends fathers of preschoolers, significant for high-school-educated; grade-school-educated fathers of adults) − *Negative Orientation* (housewives-mothers of adolescents)	− *Lack of Commitment* (trends in jobs of high prestige) − *Job Dissatisfaction* (trend old men in jobs of low supervisory potential)

316

TABLE 6-2 continued

Power			
− *Marital Inadequacy* (grade-school-educated wives)	− *Parental Inadequacy* (college-educated mothers of pre-schoolers; trends fathers of pre-schoolers)	+ *Job Dissatisfaction* (professional advisers and foremen; young men in jobs of high supervision; jobs of high social requirements; old men in jobs of high prestige; trends in jobs of high supervisory potential)
− *Marital Problems* (college-educated wives)	+ *Parental Inadequacy* (high-school-educated mothers of preschoolers; trends employed mothers of school-age and adolescent children)	− *Lack of Commitment* (salesmen)
− *Marital Unhappiness* (young college-educated wives)	+ *Negative Orientation* (trend college-educated mothers of adults)	
+ *Marital Problems* (college-educated husbands)	− *Negative Orientation* (high-school-educated mothers of adults; trends fathers of preschoolers, significant for college-educated)	
	+ *Parental Problems* (grade-school-educated fathers of adults)	

Note: Entries indicate the direction of the relationship between the motive specified to the left and the role reaction specified in the body of the table. All relationships entered were significant unless entered as a trend.

and frustrations are explicit, then more predictable role reactions are obtained from role occupants with specific motives. Let us look at each role in turn with this in mind.

For marriage, the congruence principle seemed to predict the role reactions of grade-school-educated men and women and college-educated men and women, all of whom experienced fairly explicit role demands— the traditional marital status for the lowest educational strata and the egalitarian marital arrangement in the college-educated groups. For the grade-school-educated group the congruence principle operated indirectly. The traditional marital role can be a help or a hindrance to affiliative gratification outside the marriage. From our analysis of the situation, the traditional marital role was congruent with the less-educated women's affiliation motivation in general, but incongruent with that of less-educated men. For the college-educated, the explicit demand for shared decision-making was congruent with the power motivation of wives and incongruent with that of husbands.

The congruence principle was useful in understanding the parental role reactions of fathers in three main instances: first, achievement motivation appeared incongruent to the paternal role when children were of preschool age, a time when the majority of skills required for child care are explicitly feminine; second, achievement motivation seemed congruent to the father's role when children were of school age or were adolescents ages when fathers are explicitly expected to teach performance skills; and third, power motivation appeared to be congruent with the paternal role when children were of preschool age, a time in which fathers are explicitly expected to exert their influence to socialize the child.

The congruence principle also was applied to the parental role reactions of mothers in three main situations: first, affiliation motivation appeared incongruent with the maternal role when children were young— at preschool or school age—a period when mothers are clearly expected to spend a lot of time with their children and when interaction with other adults is severely restricted; second, power motivation seemed congruent with their role when children were preschoolers, a time when mothers are explicitly expected to mold the character of their children; third, the power motivation of college-educated women appeared incongruent with the maternal role when children were older, a time when these mothers are expected to complete the final socialization of their children, and yet allow them to become autonomous.

In the job role, we found the congruence principle useful where the role had explicit motive-relevant demands or potentials for gratification: first, the explicit limits to gratification of affiliation motivation for men in the role of farmer or foreman result in role reactions emphasizing the incongruence with respect to affiliation motivation in these roles; second, the achievement rewards clearly available in jobs with high prestige result in reactions from high achievement motivated men that suggest that these jobs are congruent with their motives; third, the threat posed to gratification of power motivation by jobs in which men are very vulnerable to public failure, as when one is closely supervised or required to influence others, results in role reactions that seem to characterize an incongruence between power motivation and being in such positions.

This leads us to an important general conclusion: *we will find support for the congruence principle in investigations of personality-role interaction only when the motivational gratifications or lack of gratifications available in that role are explicit.* Where the roles are somewhat ambiguous or where it is possible to reinterpret the role in terms more congruent with one's motives, then these distortions can affect apparent congruence. Our best guess is that a researcher working with more clearly defined roles than those we have been dealing with will find that the congruence principle is very possibly the essential explanation for personality-role interaction. It is not surprising that two of the most specific occupations that we have dealt with, foreman and farmer, yielded more support for the congruence principle than other less strictly defined job classifications.

We have stated that the congruence principle might be evidenced only when there are clear-cut demands, gratifications, and frustrations in roles. When these are ambiguous or flexible, the door is open for men and women to restructure the role in the way that is most congruent with their own particular motivational pattern. Cognitive theorists recently have been emphasizing just this type of restructuring. Heider (1958) and Newcomb (1959), when they discuss imbalance, and Festinger (1957) and Brehm and Cohen (1962), when they discuss dissonance, have been especially provocative in suggesting that people use various adjustive mechanisms to bring about a conceptual harmony where disharmony previously existed. People can level and sharpen or distort their perceptions about the world, about sources of information, and about the value of people or ideas. These theories of cognitive reorganization do not specify the psychological processes that dictate *which* adjustive mechanism will occur, although in experimental situations the possibilities of adjustment are often limited so that predictions can be made. In the natural setting, many different adjustive devices can be used, especially if there is ambiguity about the role demands, what performance is required to meet role demands, or the kinds of activity that will satisfy certain goals. Furthermore, some of these adjustments made by the subjects in our study obviously took place long before the interview, in which we assessed whether the person was experiencing inadequacy, lack of satisfaction, or some other kind of difficulty in his role performance. Thus, when we looked for evidence of motive-role congruence or incongruence, it was hard to find.

Suggested research Our discussion of the congruence principle suggests

319

two conditions that should be met in designing research to test this principle of role-personality interaction: (1) role enactment clearly frustrates or gratifies the goals of a motive, and (2) the person has had little time to invoke adjustive means of handling incongruence.

This last condition suggests research that contrasts role occupants who have had inadequate time to get adjusted to a role and those who have had sufficient time. The relationship between motives and role reactions should be different in the beginning stages of a role than in the later stages. We are not referring to the age of the subject as the critical conditioning variable. Rather we are contrasting the early and late adjustment period in a role. This would be helpful in thinking about personality interaction with the marital role (during the first year of marriage as opposed to subsequent years), with the parental role (during the first year of a first child's life, as opposed to time thereafter), or with the job role (during the first year or so at a job, and thereafter). Our data do not allow for such a refined analysis of time spent in a role, but certainly research studies can be set up that specifically focus on such comparisons. Newcomb (1961) has contrasted early and late perceptions of dormitory mates. This is the kind of contrast that is needed for the roles we have discussed.

The idea that the congruence principle might be effective only when role demands or gratifications are explicit may be useful in future research on social change. As any role demand or role gratification is clarified by external intervention of one sort or another—changes or formalization of rules, changes in a person who is in a reciprocal relationship to the role occupant, changes brought about by therapy, changes in social milieu—then the possibility for motive-role congruence or incongruence is increased. For example, psychotherapy for one or both members of a marriage sometimes leads to newfound marital gratification and in other cases to divorce. Assuming that therapy sharpens the perception of role demands and gratifications, the client's motives would be made to appear more congruent or more incongruent with his marriage. The former may lead to heightened gratification, the latter to divorce. This observation is one well worth exploring in marriage or in other roles. Another illustration may be found in the recent popularity of sensitivity training, which suggests that people are increasingly interested in explication of feelings, both to enhance gratifications and to clarify frustrations. Studies of couples, families, or members of business organizations before and after sensitivity training might be enlightening. We would predict that some relationships between motives and role adjustment that were negligible prior to sensitivity training might become stronger after sensitivity training increases clarity of role perceptions.

Our hypothesis—the more specific the role is in its requirements, the more likely it is that the congruence principle would apply—also suggests another type of research. It would be interesting to categorize people in similar general social positions on the basis of the *specificity* of their role requirements and see whether motives (relevant to the dimension on which some roles are seen as more specific and other roles are seen as less specific) are more strongly related to role adjustment for persons in the more specific roles than in the less specified ones.

Let us try this idea out in a proposed study of marriage. If we assume that companionship in marriage is what is relevant to the affiliation motive, then the more specific a person's spouse is about being a companion in marriage, the more the person's level of affiliation motivation will affect how he reacts to the marriage. In order to test this reaction, both members of a marriage pair would have to be interviewed. From the subject, estimates of level of marital satisfaction and dissatisfaction would be obtained. From the subject's spouse, careful probing about companionship in marriage could enable a researcher to classify marriages into those for which the spouse had more detailed or differentiated views about the nature of marital companionship and ones that were less detailed (undifferentiated). We would then expect to find a stronger relationship between affiliation motive and marital reactions of satisfaction or dissatisfaction for subjects whose marriages had more differentiated requirements concerning companionship than for the subjects classified as participating in marriages with relatively undifferentiated requirements.

Such studies could also be done about specific types of job roles. For example, the relationship of power motivation and job satisfaction could be compared for foremen whose specific job role included very specific rules for regulating supervisee behaviors and foremen whose specific job had more general or ambiguous role specifications. Again we would expect that the motive would be a better predictor of adjustment in the more specified role. In this instance, high power motivation in foremen would be related more clearly to their feelings of adequacy or satisfaction, if they were in the more specified roles than in the less specified ones. The direction of the relationships would depend on the type of regulations that were prescribed; specific role requirements could lead to clear evidence of either congruence or incongruence.

NEW PERSPECTIVES ON THE MOTIVES FROM THE STUDY OF MOTIVE-ROLE INTERACTION

We did not view this investigation as solely dependent on the evaluation of the two guiding principles. The personality-role interaction approach fostered the consideration of unanticipated results as ways to clarify characteristics of the specific personality dimensions or of the specific roles investigated in this study. Therefore, we were able to expand our understanding of the meaning of affiliation, achievement, and power motivation, especially as they operate in social behavior, and to revise our conceptions of the significance of marriage, parenthood, and work in our society. These conclusions were put forth within the context of each of the roles, in the integration and summary of results for each chapter. We shall now review these summaries in an effort to integrate them from two perspectives—first, to define the common themes about affiliation, achievement, and power motivation that run through each of the roles, and second, to compare the psychological significance of the three roles. We will attempt these two broad integrations in this and the subsequent section.

We entered this study with some questions about the definitions of the goals implied by each of the motives we explored. Was achievement motivation guided totally by internal standards? How relevant was the social sphere of behavior for evaluation of achievement? What type of individual best elicits a positive emotional response from a person with high affiliation motivation? Does a person with high power motivation seek out overt ways to display his influence? There were many other such questions, but these are ones about which we gained some clarification from our study of motive-role interaction and we will highlight these questions below in a separate discussion of each motive.

THE AFFILIATION MOTIVE

From our study of affiliation motivation in marriage, parenthood, work, and leisure, we concluded that a person of similar status is the most appropriate object to gratify the goal of the affiliation motive—to be liked and to avoid being rejected. Several paths led us to this conclusion. First, we noted that affiliation motivation was not often significantly associated with marital role reactions. Apparently, the marital relationship is not often the interpersonal context for satisfying or frustrating the affiliation motive. The complementary features of marital union—sexual and affectionate behavior between men and women—usually preclude the attainment of affiliative gratification in marriage itself. The attainment of the position of a married man or woman does seem to be required for the feeling of acceptance by others, which is the goal of the affiliation motive. Thus, especially in groups where traditional marriages are the norm, a man or woman can feel that he or she is a lovable or likable individual by avoiding the unmarried status. But beyond the initiation into the role, affiliation motivation does not seem to underlie many marital reactions.

Like the marital relationship, the parent-child relationship does not appear to be an appropriate means for gratifying the affiliation motive. We viewed this inappropriateness as reflecting the divergent statuses, the differential strength, authority, and knowledge of parent and child. But it is not uncommon for parents to seek affiliative satisfactions through their relationships with their children. Many parents, in attempting this, give up their responsibility to socialize their children and, instead, try to become "friends" with them. Other parents try to increase the similarity between their children and themselves by identifying with their children. Through this identification, a parent can become attached to the child as an *affiliative* choice. Such parents try to live through their children. The fathers in our sample seemed to be attempting the latter more than the mothers. Perhaps the interpersonal *obligations* of motherhood are so dominant that they prevent the attempt to make a child one's peer. We feel that redefinition of the parent-child relationship may be a misguided choice for ultimate satisfaction of affiliative goals. Even the fathers' efforts seem unsuccessful. As children reach maturity, fathers with high affiliation motivation seem to be especially disappointed in their search for affiliative gratification.

The results on motive-role interaction in work suggested that affiliation gratification is most probable when one's job role provides colleagues who engage in parallel activity. For example, foremen with high affiliation motivation were likely to be dissatisfied with their jobs, but semiskilled workers with high affiliation motivation were prone to be satisfied with their jobs. Thus, it seems that for semiskilled workers, whose intrinsic work activity does not require interaction with persons of different status, there are possibilities for friendships to develop with one's coworkers. These friendships may extend outside the job role. Such is not the case for the foremen, who *have to manage* men of lower status and who have minimal opportunities for colleagueship at work.

Results from analyses of affiliative motivation in the context of leisure support the conclusions drawn about affiliative motivation in the job role. Affiliation motivation seems to be an important determinant of the kinds of leisure activities typical of men in jobs with relatively low prestige, for whom the amount of social gratification from the work enterprise itself may be severely limited. We might suggest that for lower status men there is a good chance of finding colleagues at work who will be their friends at leisure. Men in lower status jobs are likely to be in *parallel* relationships with many other men. Men in higher status jobs are more likely to be in reciprocal relationships with people with whom they work.

Thus, our analysis of each role led to similar conclusions about the kinds of people who are gratifying affiliative objects and to the further inference that, in their social relations, men and women who are highly motivated to affiliate will seek out persons of similar social positions and attitudes. Byrne, Clore, and Worchel (1966) have called attention to the importance of similarity for general attraction to people. That this type of attraction is part and parcel of affiliative interests has not been clearly established here or elsewhere. Indeed, one previous study by Byrne (1961a) suggests that the relationship between affiliation motivation and the attraction to similarity may be more complex than what we are suggesting here. Much work needs to be done on this problem. Recent work on social comparison processes suggests that affiliative choices occur more often with similar others when threat is also involved. When a person is unthreatened, he begins to orient himself to people different from himself. (See the *Journal of Experimental Social Psychology Supplement*, 1966, which was devoted to this problem.)

Despite these cautionary notes, we are willing to propose the hypothesis that affiliation motivation is a strong force in the direction of choosing interpersonal relations that are familiar. Similarity is just a fairly reliable way of gauging feelings of familiarity, although we think of the push for familiarity as the major push for affiliative concerns. However, such a force can lead men and women to distort their social relationships, to perceive similarity where there is none, to make the unfamiliar, familiar. This distortion can occur most easily in parenthood, when there are no clear expectations for what children should be like.

We became aware of another feature of the affiliative incentive in our analyses. Parallel activity at work not only cuts back on status differences between people, but it also cuts back on obligatory affiliation. These are two different facets of colleagueship. A person who is obliged by role requirements to behave in an affiliative manner does not appear to be an appropriate incentive to gratify an individual's affiliative goals. One basis for this conclusion was a set of negative findings—the absence of relationships between affiliation motivation and reactions to parental, marital, and certain job roles. The parental role, because it *obliges* mothers and fathers to be nurturant with their children, who in turn are obliged to love their parents, the marital role, because it *obliges* the husband and wife to nurture and love one another, jobs with high social requirements, because they *oblige* men to be social with their coworkers or clients, were roles that did not seem to engage affiliation motivation. If a man desires an affiliative relationship with another person, he may be unsatisfied if he perceives that this other person is accepting and friendly towards him only because that person feels some obligation to be affiliative, if he perceives that the other person would behave differently if there was some freedom to choose. Interpersonal relationships in work, marriage, and parenthood can all partake of this sense of affiliative duty rather than affiliative sincerity. Although the interpersonal relations in these roles may provide genuine affiliative gratification, a mistrust of the relationship can frequently occur. This dual interpretation of the personal relations in these roles may preclude finding strong statistical relationships between affiliation motivation and any particular role reaction. These considerations led us to propose a more general hypothesis—the satisfaction of the affiliation motive depends on establishing a sense of trust in the sincerity of an interpersonal relationship.

Suggested research The two hypotheses we suggested—that a sense of trust in the sincerity of an interpersonal relationship is essential for satisfactory affiliative relations, and that affiliation motivation underlies the attraction to similar others because they are familiar—could lead to new directions in research on affiliation motivation. In addition to investigating these two hypotheses separately, it would be important to study the effects of joint variations in trust and similarity because it might very well be that affiliative gratification cannot occur without both these features in the relationship, or that either one might be sufficient. These considerations lead us to suggest investigations of the affiliative potential of an interpersonal role based on its potential for invoking both a sense of the familiar or the meeting of "like minds," and a sense of trust in the sincere intentions of the participating parties.

One direction that could be taken in the investigation of the affiliative potential in role relationships would be to assess the degree of similarity in the *functions* of activities required of role partners. This is quite a different approach to the affiliative potential in a role from the more traditional one of assessing the degree of interpersonal contact required in the role. A mother and child can share a lot of companionate activity, a foreman and a worker can spend a lot of time talking with each other, a man and his wife can engage in a great deal of decision-making together, but we have seen how these characteristics in role relationships do not seem to guarantee gratification for men and women with high affiliation motivation. What does seem necessary is a perceived sense of colleagueship in role relationships, an equalization of power, a participation in the same kinds of activities. Some parents and young children may never be able to see their relationships this way. Certain reciprocal roles in industrial organizations may never permit this type of relationship, although reciprocal roles such as teacher and student or related types of professional advisers and their clients may be more flexible in this regard. Thus we are saying that any role can be characterized for its potential to elicit perceived similarity in the people involved, although there might be some variability in this perception between different people in the same role. A researcher could try to determine for various role relationships—between a husband and wife, or a parent and child, or two friends, or coworkers—how much of the interactive activity represents parallel activity in which each person is not only engaging in the same type of behavior, but is also fulfilling the same perceived function. Objective job information would help to categorize job roles in this way. Indeed, men in specific jobs are often assumed to share values and attitudes. Nevertheless, we think information probably would be required from the participants to get a reasonable assessment of this characteristic in job and especially in marital or parental role activities. This type of information would be a good first step in assessing one of the two major characteristics of affiliative relationships that our motive-role explorations have suggested.

Our focus on the importance of a sense of trust in affiliative relationships can also lead to a new type of assessment about relationships. The motive-role analyses suggest that future research in affiliation account for a role occupant's perceived freedom from being obliged to maintain affability in that relationship. We have assumed that some roles include demands for sociability—parent to child, husband to wife, teacher to student, doctor to patient, and vice versa—and that because of these formal sanctions about affiliation, signs of affection or acceptance obtained in such roles may be mistrusted by people with high affiliation motivation. Of course, this is not necessarily the case, and what we would like to see is some more direct assessment of this perceived obligation for affiliative behavior in role relationships. We would suggest that the perception that the affiliative behaviors of a role partner are rooted in a role demand for an affiliative role relationship implies a restricted perception of the relationship, one that is limited to that role. We would suggest further that when a person is able to perceive that the other person relates to him according to his many different roles, then the sense of obligatory affiliation is minimized. It is only after a person believes that another person cares about him in ways that have nothing to do with their specific role relationship that the other person's behavior toward him can be gratifying to his affiliation goals.

How could this characteristic be assessed? From the subject himself we could ascertain how much contact he thought the other person has or would like to have with him outside their significant role relationship. Or, to avoid relying on assessments from the subjects themselves, the spouse, child, or coworker could be asked such questions about their attitudes toward and contacts with the other person in these reciprocal role relationships. These data could then be used to infer the degree of trust that such interest by the other would engender in the subject.

Much attention would have to be given to the methodological problems in assessing the degree of trust and similarity in role relationships. But we would contend that these would be the essential aspects of affiliative goals to which a person with high affiliation motivation would attend. Furthermore, because these are such personal characteristics of relationships, we feel that research on affiliation motivation in relatively impersonal life situations in the laboratory—with strangers, whose potential sincerity for affiliative contact would be unknown to the subject—

would be comparatively fruitless. Controlled studies of friends, marital partners, parents and children, and actual coworkers might be more fruitful. In summary, the two dimensions of affiliative relationships that we have been highlighting—trust and familiarity—require either some naturalistic observations in long-term interpersonal settings or some very ingenious ways of observing these settings in the laboratory.

THE ACHIEVEMENT MOTIVE

The achievement motive is most clearly satisfied or frustrated in a man's job role. Only in studying the role of parenthood did we get any indication that the goal of the achievement motive can generalize beyond the usual performance sphere of work and engage feelings about *social* performance. This motive seems to be relevant to marriage only in the sense that marriage can interfere with achievement strivings in other spheres. Furthermore, achievement motivation does not seem to be relevant to the leisure activities of adult American men.

The data from some mothers and fathers did give some indication that they set and gratify achievement goals within the social role of parenthood. The duties and obligations of parenthood are sometimes more explicit than those of marriage. Thus, a parent can measure his performance in the way he is raising his children or in the way he is providing for his family against some standard of excellence. This type of performance evaluation would be more difficult for a husband or a wife to make, in spite of Sunday supplement attempts to measure marital adequacies in ten questions or less. In parenthood, furthermore, there is some indication that it is possible to derive vicarious achievement gratification through one's children. A possibly important, but tentative, conclusion about achievement motive seems to be that one can attain achievement gratification by identifying with another person and his achievements. This was not in evidence for wives in their relationship to their husbands, but it did apply to some parents in their relationship to their children. Perhaps this difference occurred because the demands in the parental role to influence the performance of one's child are more explicit than the demands in the marital role to influence one's spouse. Since part of the parent's function is to influence the child, he can more easily experience the child's accomplishments as his own.

Although we found some provocative relationships between achievement motivation and parental response, it is the job role that seems most relevant to the achievement motive. This relevance exists throughout the status hierarchy; high achievement motivation distinguished men's reactions to the job role in both high status and low status jobs. From the data on motive-job role interaction, we were led to three important conclusions about the achievement motive: (1) it is not very easily gratified since it seems to lead a person to continually revise and increase his achievement aspirations; (2) while close supervision seems to preclude direct achievement satisfactions in the work itself, supervision can provide useful feedback that may aid in evaluating one's arrival at an achievement goal; (3) achievement gratification is most possible in situations where the person is not required to engage in social interaction, and in particular, where he is not required to supervise the work of other people.

Our first conclusion is not particularly relevant to social interaction at work. The other two conclusions are. The receipt of social feedback can be an important aid to attaining achievement gratification, but being the conveyor of social feedback does not facilitate one's achievement satisfactions. Although supervisors with high achievement motivation tend to feel commitment to their work, they do not develop achievement satisfactions in their particular job. It is as if supervising others forces a person to give up his own achievement goals and substitute the goals of the organization at large. The achievement-motivated person is dependent on others to set standards for his own goals, but is frustrated when he has to establish standards for others, or when he has to rely upon others to meet his own goals. In a certain sense one might think of the achievement motive as a *selfish* motive. Achievement gratification requires that the person *receive* evaluations from standards set by others, while achievement frustration emerges when a person sets standards for others and must rely on them to meet those standards. We feel that this is an important insight about the achievement motive derived from our exploration of this motive and the job role.

Suggested research   The most intriguing area for further investigation of the achievement motive in interaction with social roles has to do with the effect that social relationships might have on the gratification of achievement strivings. From our current data, we became interested in asking under what conditions and to what extent can the achievements of *another* person be an incentive for achievement aspirations? We also became curious to know whether social feedback contingent on good performance is necessary for achievement goal states and, if so, what kind of social feedback is required? Let us consider a number of ideas about research on each of these questions.

First, can achievement strivings be gratified by another person's behavior? In the social roles we were dealing with, we could ask: Can a husband's achievements vicariously gratify his wife's achievement motivation? Can a child's achievements gratify his parent's achievement motivation? Can a supervisee's achievements gratify his supervisor? College-educated women seemed to be reacting to the parental role in this vicarious fashion, especially in the early stages of parenthood. However, this did not seem to be the way women were reacting to marriage, nor the way supervisors were reacting to their role. In each of these cases we would suggest that what is crucial is the person's perception that he himself has had some influence on the behaviors that are instrumental to the other person's achievement goal attainment. But this is mere supposition. These ideas should be tested empirically.

We are suggesting that vicarious achievement gratification can occur in social roles when there is a perceived connection between the self and the other person's performance. In intensive interviews a researcher could discover whether vicarious achievement satisfactions were particularly common for women with a strong sense of personal effectiveness in rearing their children, or for wives who nurture the achieving behaviors of their husbands, or for supervisors who feel that their quality control has an important influence on their supervisees. Such studies could be done. They would, however, present some severe methodological hurdles. How does one measure the strength of vicarious achievement gratifications or their importance? One approach to such measurement is to ask a person to rank order the importance of various goals in his role. An item describing vicarious achievement gratification could be embedded in a list of other, similar socially desirable gratifications which the subject must rank. For example, a mother could be asked: "When would you be more pleased—when your son does well in school or when he is cooperative with another person?" Let us assume that we could adequately assess the strength of vicarious achievement gratifications. Then, we could determine if the relationship between the strength of such gratification and the achievement motive was greater when mothers had a strong sense of effectiveness about the consequences of their parental role performance on their child's accomplishments than when this sense of effectiveness was weak. We would expect that this would be the case.

Experimental analogues of these questions could be devised for the laboratory. Children or adults, grouped as high and low in achievement motivation according to standard testing procedures, could be placed in situations in which there was a clearly perceived connection between their skill and the consequent performance of another person and situations in which this connection was not clearly perceived. We would predict larger differences between the behaviors and satisfactions of the high and low motive groups under conditions where their skills were clearly linked to the other person's performance than in situations where this linkage was not clearly perceived.

Now let us turn to the second type of research question toward which our present analysis of the achievement motive directs us: Is social feedback contingent on performance necessary to sustain achievement strivings? One approach that is suggested is a set of experimental studies of the persistence behavior of subjects with high or low achievement motivation under various conditions of social and nonsocial feedback about performance, with no feedback of any sort being a baseline condition. Mechanical, asocial feedback (for example, through a machine) can be compared with social feedback, with each emitted at different frequencies over a set of trials. Our prediction would be that men with high achievement motivation would be more persistent under social rather than asocial feedback conditions, but that high levels of social feedback may be less conducive to effective performance than moderate or low levels. The first part of the prediction stems directly from an assumption that social feedback reflects more effective evaluation than asocial feedback. The latter part of this prediction is based on the assumption that high frequencies of social feedback may be interpreted by the individual as manipulation and interfere with a sense of personal accomplishment. The performance of men with low achievement motivation would not be expected to differ under the conditions of social and asocial feedback. Whatever the outcome, the results would give us the type of information that seems so important in understanding the expression of the achievement motive in social roles.

A similar study could be done in the work setting—comparing performance measurements for men with high and low achievement motivation under different types of feedback systems. This might mean comparing different organizations that use different kinds of feedback, but it also could mean comparing men within one organization who have different types of supervisors.

THE POWER MOTIVE

Although there were instances in our analysis of motive-role interaction in which the goal of the power motive seemed to be the pursuit of the pleasure of power, in most cases the goal seemed to be the avoidance of anticipated feelings of weakness. The power motive seems to be expressed in a fear of weakness in social behavior where failure to influence or to avoid being influenced would clearly be visible—especially in job relationships and in influence relationships with older children. In the early years of parenthood, power motivation has less avoidant overtones. Furthermore, only in the distressed marital reactions of college-educated men with high power motivation do we get direct evidence of avoidant reactions to marriage by those with power concerns. Our conclusion is that the power motive is mostly incited by fears of weakness, but sometimes by the pleasure of power. But more important, it seems that *the more public a person's power or lack of it in a role, the more likely it is that the negative features of the motive will be engaged in role behavior.*

In our study, certain job roles required very visible displays of influence. In these jobs, public influence is an essential role requirement, although resistance to influence can occur. The roles of foreman and public adviser are the best examples of this. Men with high power motivation in these jobs are especially likely to be dissatisfied.

The parental role with older children is similar; the parent can feel a threat to the required exercise of power. Adolescents defy their parents in a highly visible manner. Fathers of older children seem especially vulnerable to feelings of dismay if they have high power motivation. Mothers with high power motivation seem to be more likely to get pleasurable power gratification. It is as if a mother's major role function to nurture her children cushions the effects of her lack of influence on them. Even a public display of failure to influence is not as threatening to mothers as it would be to fathers. Yet even mothers with high power motivation begin to share the fathers' concern about power failure when the children mature to adult status and can exercise their own powers of decision.

In marital relationships there is little public recognition of the dominance-submission behavior of husbands over wives or vice versa. It is for this reason that high power motivation may underlie satisfaction or pleasure at power assertion in marriage, as well as lead to avoidant concerns. Indeed, for some women in both the lowest and highest social strata, power motivation seemed to underlie a distinctly positive view of the role. The same might be said about the lowest social strata of men. For different reasons, each of these groups can perhaps enjoy their power position in marriage: grade-school-educated women can enjoy the traditional wifely role which protects them from feelings of weakness, since it does not require them to be openly influential; college-educated women can enjoy the egalitarian role which gives sanction to influence attempts, increases their influential status, and makes power assertion more feasible; grade-school-educated husbands can enjoy the dominant male role provided by a traditional definition of marriage. Nevertheless, in all of the roles we find a pattern of reactions that can best be understood if we interpret power motivation as a fear of weakness, although there are these exceptions mentioned above. Even in leisure activities, power motivation seemed to underlie attempts to maintain the illusion of power, especially in older groups. Further use of the measure of power motive in personality-role analysis should take this interpretation into account.

Suggested research Our interpretation of the power motive as primarily a fear of weakness directed at avoiding states of clear vulnerability directs our attention to the conditions that we would expect to induce power *avoidant* behaviors and those that we would expect to induce direct power *assertive* behaviors. We have suggested that under conditions of public vulnerability, avoidant behaviors occur in people high in power motivation, and under conditions of less public or private vulnerability, assertive behaviors occur in these people.

Terhune (1968) has recently reported that men dominated by high power motivation are exploitative in a game-like situation in which their power assertion cannot be challenged and there is no commitment for future public relationships. This is in keeping with our hypothesis about what happens to power-motivated people under private conditions, when vulnerability is very low. Now suppose the conditions are changed so that power assertion exposes the person to possible exploitation by others. The situation used by Terhune, the Prisoner's Dilemma game, could be so arranged. For example, each player could be led to assume that his partner may react to his exploitation in future encounters. Partners could be maintained for a second experiment involving personal evaluation. Under these conditions we would not expect Terhune's results to obtain, rather we would expect extremely low levels of exploitative behavior among the highly power-motivated men.

Using a similar idea in a study of marriage, we would suggest comparing public and private decision-making by marital partners. We have suggested that marriage usually is a good arena for working out power motivation concerns by assertive behavior because the marital relationship generally is very private. The opposite might be true when the marital relationship and the influence process is clearly open to public scrutiny. It would be very intriguing to see whether in fact this is so—whether under the usual private conditions of marriage there was more assertive influence in men and women with high power motivation than in men and women with low power motivation, and whether the difference disappeared under public confrontation. One way to investigate this hypothesis would utilize a short-term longitudinal design where it could be determined whether the spouse who wielded more influence in a public decision involving some *later* action that would actually occur was also more influential when the actual decision was made. For example, husbands and wives could publicly resolve their differences on a topic such as how to spend a vacation. Then, follow-up interviews could assess their actual decision in private life when vacation time rolled around, to determine whether their conflicts were resolved in the same or in a different direction. We would expect the spouse with high power motivation to wield more influence than his spouse with low power motivation in the private condition, but not in the public condition.[2]

For another reason, as well, our present data alerted us to the importance of longitudinal information for understanding power motive-

[2]Marital partners could be categorized into four groups differing in patterns of power motivation: husband and wife both high; husband high—wife low; wife high—husband low; husband and wife both low. Our predictions hold only for the two kinds of couples who have one member high and one member low in power motivation. We have no clear predictions for the couples who are either both high or both low in power motivation.

role interactions. To explain the effect of power motivation on certain role reactions, we adopted certain speculations about the power potential of a given role. In particular, we recognized that a critically important way to specify a person's vulnerability to attacks on his power is to set some gauge of his power potential at that moment in time, *compared to some other point in time*. A person with a high power motive is most likely to be reactive to sudden changes in power and vulnerability. For example, we discussed the problems of parents who are suddenly confronted with autonomous teenagers. This stage in the parental role is often, but not always, threatening to a parent with high power motive. We suggested that whether threat occurs depends on the power relationship of the parent and child prior to adolescence. A father who has granted a lot of autonomy to his preschool of his grade-school-age child will not be as vulnerable to adolescent metamorphsis as one who has been running a tight ship and demanding respect and obedience. We would also suggest that a highly power-motivated father who was able to grant early autonomy to his children might not be disrupted by his adolescent child, but the power-motivated father who ran the tight ship might find his adolescent child very disturbing. This is only one of many transitional power problems in the parental cycle that could be better understood through longitudinal investigations of shifts in power relations and concomitant shifts in parental reactions.

In the same way, other roles could benefit from longitudinal studies. Researchers should explore transitions in job status or changes in the marital power structure affected by such shifts as retirement, the birth of a child, or children leaving home. We would expect people to adapt to their vulnerable power relationships over time so that an analysis of the effects of power motivation might be most productive at a point in time when role shifts involve a confrontation with new sources of vulnerability.

A COMPARISON OF ROLES: AMERICAN MARRIAGE, PARENTHOOD, AND WORK

From our study of the interaction of motives with three important roles in modern American society, we are now in a position to attempt an evaluation of the comparative psychological significance of these roles for men and for women—a comparison of marriage and parenthood for women, and a comparison of marriage, parenthood, and work for men. Having looked at motive-role interaction within different social strata and different age groupings of men and women in our society, we are also in a position to attempt an evaluation of the importance of these distinctions for role adjustments and role perceptions. This we will do in the final sections of this chapter.

In discussing the results in support of or contrary to the congruence and sensitization principles, we drew some important conclusions about roles from the patterns of both significant and nonsignificant results. When we found that the achievement motive was related to feelings of parental inadequacy in college-educated mothers but not in the other educational groups, we concluded that parenthood is a *relevant* arena for the achievement motivation of college-educated mothers, although not for the other groups of mothers. This type of interpretation has two important consequences: (1) It provides a basis for evaluating the meaning of motherhood for different groups, and (2) it alerts us to the need to account for the degree to which a role *arouses* thoughts about a particular incentive—about affiliation, achievement, or power—in our study of motive-role interaction. The assumption that the presence or absence of a pattern of relationships between a given motive and reactions to a particular role is a reflection of the salience of the goals of that motive to that role was important in our discussion of the sensitization principle. This assumption is basic to our discussion in this section as well.

A COMPARISON OF MARRIAGE AND PARENTHOOD FOR WOMEN

The marital and parental roles seem to differ in their relevance for motivational gratification and frustration for the more-educated and less-educated women. Our data lead us to suggest tentatively that among the more-educated women the maternal role engages more personal gratification than the marital role, while the reverse is true for the less-educated women. We had expected that the achievement motivation of women might be connected to their functions as a housewife, but this seemed to be true only for the wives from lower educational strata. And even for these women, achievement motivation was only minimally relevant. We had expected the affiliation motivation of women to be related to their marital reactions, but this was true only for reports of marital happiness among the less-educated women.

The more-educated women seem to find a clear achievement goal in being good mothers, but not in being good wives. Furthermore, there seems to be some evidence that these women turn to their children for "friendship" and affiliative gratification. But despite the companionate activity prescribed in the egalitarian marriages of college-educated groups, the affiliation motive is irrelevant to marital role reactions. Perhaps the companionate activity in these marriages is dictated more by obligatory role prescriptions than is the companionate activity prescribed by the parental role. The prescription for mutuality and sharing called for in marriages of the college-educated seems to lead to the arousal of power goals for the more-educated women. Perhaps what is being shared is influence and authority rather than companionship.

Thus, for more-educated women power seems to be the major source of personal gratification in marriage. It should be noted that this gratification may occur at some cost to the marriage, since the more-educated husbands are particularly frustrated in their own power goals. Power also seems to be a major source of maternal gratification for more-educated women, but in this role, unlike marriage, the gratification may not have negative consequences. Children do feel vulnerable to maternal power assertion, but their relationships with peers often supplant their family relationships and can soften the negative consequences of maternal power assertion. A mother's power can exist as an uncomplicated motivational gratification more easily than can a wife's power.

What all this suggests is that in more-educated groups the marital relationship, despite its presumed intimacy, does not offer women many personal gratifications. Motherhood still remains a role in which an educated women can find the personal gratification she needs to justify her existence. A highly educated American woman's investment in her children seems more deeply personalized, more richly rewarding and, perhaps as a result, more intensely frustrating than are her commitments to her husband. This may occur because these women can easily learn to be indifferent to their marriages. Even if they find their interpersonal marital gratifications wanting, they usually feel well provided for and can adopt an air of indifference to their mates. But they will generally find it impossible to maintain an indifferent attitude to their children. No matter how much they may want to escape, the responsibilities of parenthood are too demanding. The techniques of childrearing that have figured so importantly in twentieth-century thinking about parenthood are their charge. We are reading between the tables, so to speak. Nowhere in the study are these roles directly compared. But the relationship that each of the motives bears to the marital and parental role adjustments strongly suggests that highly-educated women may desperately need to be married, but motherhood rather than marriage seems to be the role that engages their deepest personal core.

For the lower status wife and mother, the opposite pattern seems to be true. Affiliation, achievement, and even power gratifications in marriage seem more directly tied to the individual's needs than do these gratifications in parenthood. For these women, parenthood does not seem to be a central concern. The ability of a mother to mold her children into successful personalities is not emphasized in the less-educated groups. Consequently, the relevance of achievement and power goals in parenthood is minimal. We have already discussed what marriage means to a lower-status woman when we analyzed the sensitization principle. We concluded that marriage defensively engages this woman, that she tends to view it positively, but that her situation is very confining. She can never become completely indifferent to her marriage, because it makes her feel limited and wanting. A woman expects to find her outlets to the rest of the world and her sources of comfort in marriage. A lower status woman will most likely find that her marriage, as a tie to the world, severely limits her horizons, and, as a means of satisfying her needs, is deficient—if not in physical provision, then in social stimulation. After marriage, she may spend the rest of her life attempting to "make the best" of the situation. Her children are seen as traditional accoutrements of the marital relationship. Although she cannot escape the psychological demands of motherhood, the lower status woman rarely invests herself deeply in the parental role. She takes children as a matter of course and follows social role prescriptions for parenthood without many personal investments.

Suggested research   The conclusions we drew in the previous section suggest a study of the salience of various life roles for women from different status backgrounds. We know of three studies in which such a comparison was made.

Elder (1968) in *Children of the Great Depression* contrasted the preferences for activities involved in different life roles for women from economically deprived backgrounds and women from nondeprived backgrounds. He found that women from disadvantaged backgrounds generally gave higher ratings to activities within the family role, in contrast to nonfamily roles, such as that of friend. However, Elder did not distinguish between marriage and parenthood in the family role.

Havighurst's (1957) intensive interview study of middle-aged people residing in Kansas City is also relevant. In examining the social competence of subjects divided into six groups, varying in social status, Havighurst rated social performance in nine life roles, including that of spouse, parent, and worker. These ratings were based on a conglomeration of factors including quality of performance and the amount of satisfaction felt about role performance. The six groups showed *generally* greater or lesser competence in *all* roles rather than patterns of competence in certain roles. The upper middle-class groups received higher competence scores than the working-class groups in most of the social roles. Havighurst draws no conclusions about the differential meaning of the roles of spouse, parent, and worker based on this study, but perhaps some notion of the importance of the role can be partialed out of his overall measure of competence.

A third relevant investigation of the differential salience of roles is a study of time use in America by Converse and Robinson.[3] These researchers asked a representative sample of Americans how they spend their time and how much satisfaction each type of activity provides for

---

[3]P. Converse and J. Robinson, Personal communication, 1968.

them. The marital and the parental roles provide a great deal of satisfaction, according to over 70 percent of the sample. We would be interested in data on the differential satisfaction experienced in these two roles by persons with varying educational and other social backgrounds, which at this date were not available to us.

The aforementioned national survey will provide a good deal of important information, but our interest in role salience would require other ways of assessing the salience of roles, in addition to that inferred from preferences in spending time in these roles. Three types of assessment can be suggested. One approach would be to ask subjects about their feelings concerning the legitimacy of not enacting the role—not being married, not being a parent, not working, not having many friends. We would assume that the more salient a role is to a subject, the more negative would be his description of someone who rejects the role.

Another approach to the description of the salience of a role would be to ask subjects about the extent to which they think they can differentiate persons according to the positions they occupy. We had asked such a question about a man and his job: "Some people say that you can tell a lot about a man by the kind of job that he has. Other people say that a job isn't that important. How do you feel about this?" Similar or more direct questions could be asked of women about mothers and wives.

Another way to get at salience would be to assess the degree of differentiation the subject has about her own particular children or spouse. We would assume that the more salient the role is, the more differentiations the person would make about the person who is in a reciprocal relationship to her in that role.

From our perspective then, an ideal study about the major social roles of women in our society would be based on a nationally representative sample. It would be designed to assess the differential salience of parenthood and marriage, defined and measured in the above ways, in different status groups, along with the three social motives. In that way it would be possible to test the hypothesis that for women with lower status, and especially those with lower educational levels, marriage is more salient than parenthood, while the reverse is true of highly-educated women. As a follow-up of this general hypothesis we would be interested in examining the correlation between various other kinds of demographic factors and role salience. For example, religious differences might be critical determinants of role salience. In such a study it would also be possible to test the hypothesis that personality variables are strongly related to role reactions when that role is highly salient to the individual.

A COMPARISON OF MARRIAGE, PARENTHOOD, WORK, AND LEISURE FOR MEN

Work and leisure appear to be the two life situations that most strongly engage a man's interest. Marriage and parenthood are necessary for full adult status, but they act as supporting roles to what men see as the main theater for their behavior.

The achievement strivings of men do not seem to be regularly engaged outside the job role—in marriage, parenthood, or leisure activities. Only during certain stages of parenthood—in middle childhood when fathers are called upon to be the transmitters of skills and knowledge—does there seem to be clear achievement goals directed outside the job role. Standards of excellence are not easily attached to concrete performances in social roles, at least not as easily as in work. Where there were some significant relationships between achievement motivation and marital reactions for men, they seemed to stem from the effects that marital behaviors have on achievement or lack of achievement at work or vice versa. It seems safe to conclude that a social role will be relevant to the achievement motive of men only to the extent that it is also indirectly relevant to the job role. The evaluation of how good a husband or a father a man is to his family is to some extent based on how good a worker he is.

Most of the data concerning the marital role suggest that when affiliation or power motivation do become relevant to this role, they are not easily gratified in role behaviors. In some groups, husbands with high affiliation or power motivation were more likely to report problems and dissatisfaction with marriage rather than to report feeling of contentment. Does this relationship mean that men, although strongly impelled into marriage by social motives, feel socially trapped by it? Much of what novelists write about "the human condition" in the twentieth century is a description of man's desperate search for love. Marriage is an institution that makes love legitimate for women. Thus, it is an institution that women need and men must follow. Idealized concepts of modern marriage focus on the potential intimacy and joy to be found in the marital relationship—characteristics designed to fulfill the search for love by men and women. However, these characteristics seem to be role *demands* that are not yet easily translated into role *gratifications*. We have hypothesized that companionate marriages that are designed to make men and women affiliative with each other would have to become somewhat desexualized to meet this aim. Marriage as a vehicle for companionship would require that men and women love each other as *similar* people, while sexuality requires complementary differentiation of attitudes and behaviors. With desexualization in marriage, some new kinds of dissatisfactions can accrue. Companionate marriages can threaten men's power. Thus, the companionate, egalitarian conception of marriage can backfire; it can be very threatening to men's feelings of power and sexual adequacy. As a result, men's capacities for finding affiliative gratification within the marital relationship may be impaired.

If marriage is frustrating to men with high power motivation, and possibly those with high affiliation motivation as well, it is no wonder that many of them may turn to the parental role as a potential resource for social gratification. Men, like women, seem to be working out some important affiliative and power motivations with their children. Younger men are even caught up with parenthood as a potential arena of achievement.

But it is not in parenthood or in marriage that social motivations seem best expressed for men. It is in friendships and in relationships with colleagues at work and with the larger social community that men seem to find their affiliative and power motivations satisfied. These motivations seem related to a number of different aspects of men's leisure activities. Marriage and parenthood are prescribed ways for him to anchor his life, to establish his adult validity, but it is in day-to-day contact with the business world and the social world outside of the home that men seem to seek their broad interpersonal gratifications. A man without a wife or without children has no anchor, but a man without friends is deprived of his daily social satisfactions.

Suggested research Studies comparable to the ones suggested to examine the salience of different life roles for women can also be instituted for men. Elder (1968) has some evidence that regardless of economic background, men prefer work activities to activities in other roles, as we would predict. However, that study was done on a very limited sample, and a large-scale study is now needed.

Although we would propose a similar study for men and for women, we would like to distinguish the salience of a role for men according to its *overall value* and its *daily value*. The overall value a man places on a role could be measured by his ability to tolerate the absence of the role. The daily value a man gives to a role could be measured by his activity preferences and cognitive differentiations within roles. Our hypothesis is that men would perhaps find family roles and the job role equal in overall value, but that the job role and leisure activities would have higher daily value.

One further point—a more detailed investigation of men's leisure activities seems called for. We had only minimal data on the problem. It would be desirable to obtain interviews with more intensive probing about feelings of accomplishment, sociability, and power in leisure activities to test our conclusion that men's major investments are in the job role, in spite of pressures to make leisure more salient.

In considering the proposed studies for both men and women, we must remember that the data from the present study were obtained in 1957. Significant shifts in general role salience can occur. Our conclusions about role salience in 1957 might not apply a decade or two later. We doubt that radical changes have occurred, but we should be aware of the possibility. Periodically conducted cross-sectional and longitudinal studies of the kind we have outlined are needed to reach firm conclusions about the ideas we presented about role salience.

TWO IMPORTANT VARIABLES TO BE CONTROLLED IN RESEARCH IN MOTIVE-ROLE INTERACTION

Throughout this chapter, when we were discussing conclusions suggested by the present research and designs for future work, we often had to qualify general statements about role-personality interaction to account for age and educational differences. We would like to highlight these variables at the very end of this book, because so often when researchers go out to attack these problems about role-personality interaction they are not fortunate enough to be dealing with a large representative sample. Instead, in most instances, the sample is drawn from a restricted population group that includes persons in only a certain age range or a particular social status category. Our experience emphasizes the need to take these variables into account before generalizing conclusions about motive-role interaction. Let us now describe the consequences of social status and age-related distinctions for our conclusions about motive-role interaction.

THE IMPORTANCE OF SOCIAL STATUS IN THE DEFINITION OF ROLES

Nothing we said about marriage, parenthood, work, and leisure applied equally well to persons at all social-status levels. We have made distinctions about an individual's social position in society in all of the roles—using either educational level or job prestige as indirect measures of social status. These distinctions have been critical, but we would hope that in future research other means of gauging social status can also be obtained, and the differential implications of different aspects of social status can be assessed. Let us see how educational differences have affected our results.

In our comparison of marriage and parenthood for women, we noted that women at the lowest educational level are likely to be more engaged by marriage than by motherhood, which they take as a matter of course, and that the reverse is comparatively true for highly educated women. The egalitarian premise of marriage found in upper-status groups seems to present a problem for these women. They step away from marriage and move into the parental role as a means of finding personal gratification. This conclusion about the differential meaning of the marital role in two social groups is very important, for this difference in the meaning of marriage has important ramifications for social class differences in other aspects of motive-role interaction.

The egalitarian view of marriage at the upper educational levels seems to entail role demands that interfere with the potential the role has for personality enactment for both men and women. The traditional expectations of male assertiveness and female submissiveness at the lowest educational levels seem to act as binding forces. The new look at marriage in modern society, advocated among the more educated, seems to create forces that interfere with motivational gratifications. The achievement gratifications for women and the power gratifications for men seem to be greatly reduced by the new view of the marital role. We have speculated that expecting the traditional marital relationship to be a friendship relationship may play havoc with the potential that the marital role has to permit satisfying sexual and interpersonal activity. That is mere speculation. But if it is so, then it presents a strong conflict for men and women in this role and has effects on their other roles as well. In upper-status marriages, men and women who are expected to share their lives openly and extensively, have to work at maintaining their individuality. In these marriages, men may turn to their jobs and women to their maternity as distinctive roles that preserve their specialized contributions to marriage. It may be that for this reason work is so very important to the highly-educated man and parenthood so important to his wife. As a result, there may be a greater chance for parenthood and work to affect the marital relationship itself. To the extent that these other roles are still masculine and feminine, to the extent that work is a man's role and parenthood a woman's role, then the investment in each by a man or woman is a means of protecting sexual uniqueness, not only in marriage but also in relation to a general sense of adequacy. At any rate, we have seen how a gauge of social status differences is extremely significant in considering the marital role.

What about the parental role? Are social status differentiations necessary to an understanding of motive-role relationships in parenthood? Our answer is most clearly in the affirmative for women. The lower-status groups, we have suggested, treat motherhood with relatively little active personal investment, while women at upper educational levels have defensive investments in being good mothers. Furthermore, mothers with moderate educational attainment seem to view the parent-child relationship with the same motivational significance as their children mature as when their children are young. In contrast, the motives of mothers at both higher and lower educational levels seem to determine different reactions to their role as their children reach independent adult status. These social class differences in the significance of the maternal role might be very important to pursue in future research.

For fathers there do not seem to be strong differences among the educational strata in the way that motives interact with parenthood. There is a suggestion that fathers from different social strata get their most direct satisfaction of motivation at different stages of the parental cycle. The grade-school-educated father seems to be most involved and satisfied when he has young children and most disturbed by his parental role when his children are adults; the high-school-educated father is most actively satisfied with children during middle childhood; there are trends to indicate that the college-educated father is most involved with his children when they are adolescents or adults. We would think that a man's social position would in some way determine how much respect he is given by his children, especially as they grow older and become more aware of social status in general. It is not hard to accept the idea that the more status a man has in his community, the longer he will receive unwavering respect from his children, all other things being equal. The lower the status of the father, the earlier the child feels able to assert his independence. And thus we might conclude that the investment that a grade-school-educated father has in his children would occur when his children are particularly young, because he is most likely to receive satisfactory reciprocation at this stage. The highly-educated father, whose career-involvement prepares him for the task-oriented activities of school-aged and older children, may find that his social status also enables him to continue to maintain an influential role with his children as they mature.

How important to the job role was the prestige accorded men on the basis of occupational attainment? We conclude that this distinction in social status is less critical in accounting for motivational involvement in job role reactions than are particular job role characteristics. We did find some support for the idea that a more prestigious job forces a man to commit himself to his work and thereby allows him to get more important gratifications from it. We also did get some support for the idea that men in jobs low in prestige will more often turn to leisure for different kinds of personality gratifications than will men in prestigious jobs. However, what we tended to find was that when the prestige distinction did begin to explain a pattern of results, we could better account for this same pattern by looking at more specific job characteristics. We therefore conclude that future motive-role analyses in the work area would be most fruitful if particular jobs were examined rather than general occupational characteristics such as prestige.

THE IMPORTANCE OF AGE-RELATED DISTINCTIONS IN MOTIVE-ROLE INTERACTION

We cannot emphasize enough the importance of accounting for a person's age in thinking about the role demands and gratifications in each of the roles we have investigated. We had assumed that age distinctions were important when we began our investigation, and the data bear out our assumption.

What specific age distinctions are important in the study of motive-role interaction? Several generalizations seem to cut across the various findings from the previous chapters. One interesting possible distinction concerns the coincidence of young adulthood and a period of initiation into roles. This period of adjustment, of learning about the roles of marriage, parenthood, or work, sets up certain demands and gratifications that are quite distinct from role demands and gratifications that exist when a person is older and already deeply immersed in a role. We found this particularly important in thinking about the job role. In that context, a distinction was made between men grappling with decisions about which job is best for them and which provides a satisfactory place for fulfilling their needs, and men's later adjustment to the specific demands of the particular jobs to which they have committed themselves. This distinction was based upon the way the motives related to job reactions for middle-aged men as compared to younger men. For older people in all the roles—marriage, parenthood, and work—motives seem to relate to role reactions in a pattern suggesting one general interpretation: role reactions reflect behaviors designed to *maintain* a person's sense of gratification in life situations to which he adapted earlier in life. Older men who are working wish to maintain their position, power, and achievements. Men and women, who are fathers and mothers of children who are themselves adults, wish to maintain their status as parents and maintain some contact with their children. Men and women whose marriages persist through the later years want to maintain a sense of interpersonal ties through marriage, in the face of the loss of ties in other social relationships. Their children move away and disassociate themselves from their parents; friends or relatives close to them die. Marriage thus becomes a major source of social stability for older men and women.

This general position concerning age-relevant distinctions in motive-role interactions can be summarized as follows: young adulthood in all roles is a time for men and women to *adapt* to roles; middle age in all roles is a time for men and women to *experience* particular gratifications or frustrations attendant to the specific role demands; and old age in all roles is a time for men and women to *maintain* their positions and sense of contentment.

But at any of these age periods, we have found that accounting for a person's motives, his role demands and gratifications, and for the interaction between the two has consequences for the way people react to these roles in American society. Sometimes their reactions are quite predictable, sometimes not so predictable. In any case, we were again made fully aware that people's individuality alone cannot account for their behavior. Nor can the constraint of the social world. Only by a complex examination of individuals and their society in interaction, can we accelerate the future study of men's and women's significant behavior in the social world around them.

REFERENCES

Andrews, J.D.W. "The Achievement Motive and Advancement in Two Types of Organizations," *Journal of Personality and Social Psychology*, **6** (1967), pp. 163–168.

Argyris, C. "Human Relations in a Bank," *Harvard Business Review*, **32** (1954), pp. 63–73.

Argyris, C. *Personality and Organization.* New York: Harper and Row, 1957.

Argyris, C. *Interpersonal Competence and Organizational Effectiveness.* Homewood, Ill.: Dorsey Press, 1962.

Argyris, C. *Integrating the Individual and the Organization.* New York: John Wiley, 1964.

Atkinson, J.W. "Studies in Projective Measurement of Achievement Motivation." (Doctoral dissertation, University of Michigan) Ann Arbor, Mich.: University Microfilms, 1950. No. 50-1945.

Atkinson, J.W. "Motivational Determinants of Risk-taking Behavior," in J.W. Atkinson (ed.), *Motives in Fantasy, Action, and Society.* Princeton, N.J.: Van Nostrand, 1958, pp. 322–339. (a)

Atkinson, J.W. (ed.), *Motives in Fantasy, Action, and Society.* Princeton, N.J.: Van Nostrand, 1958. (b)

Atkinson, J.W. *An Introduction to Motivation.* Princeton, N.J.: Van Nostrand, 1964.

Atkinson, J.W. and Feather, N.T. (eds.), *A Theory of Achievement Motivation.* New York: John Wiley, 1966.

Atkinson, J.W., Heyns, R.W., and Veroff, J. "The Effect of Experimental Arousal of the Affiliation Motive on Thematic Apperception," *Journal of Abnormal and Social Psychology*, **49** (1954), 405–410.

Atkinson, J.W., and Hoselitz, B.F. "Entrepreneurship and Personality," *Explorations in Entrepreneurial History*, **10** (1958), pp. 107–112.

Atkinson, J.W. and McClelland, D.C. "The Projective Expression of Needs: II. The Effect of Different Intensities of the Hunger Drive on Thematic Apperception," *Journal of Experimental Psychology*, **38** (1948), pp. 643–658.

Atkinson, J.W. and O'Connor, Patricia. "Neglected Factors in Studies of Achievement-oriented Performance: Social Approval as Incentive and Performance Decrement," in J.W. Atkinson and N.T. Feather (eds.), *A Theory of Achievement Motivation.* New York: John Wiley, 1966, pp. 299–325.

Atkinson, J.W. and Raphelson, A.C. "Individual Differences in Motivation and Behavior in Particular Situations," *Journal of Personality*, **24** (1956), 349–363.

Atkinson, J.W. and Reitman, W.R. "Performance as a Function of Motive Strength and Expectancy of Goal-Attainment," in J.W. Atkinson (ed.), *Motives in Fantasy, Action, and Society.* Princeton, N.J.: Van Nostrand, 1958, pp. 278–287.

Atkinson, J.W. and Walker, E.L. "The Affiliation Motive and Perceptual Sensitivity to Faces," *Journal of Abnormal and Social Psychology*, **53** (1956), pp. 38–41.

Axelrod, M. "Urban Structure and Social Participation," *American Sociological Review*, **21** (1956), pp. 13–18.

Backman, C.W. and Secord, P.F. "The Self and Role Selection." Paper presented at the meeting of the American Sociological Association, Chicago, September 1965.

Baldwin, A.L. "The Effect of Home Environment on Nursery School Behavior," *Child Development*, **20** (1949), pp. 49–61.

Baruch, R. "The Achievement Motive in Women: Implications for Career Development," *Journal of Personality and Social Psychology*, **5** (1967), pp. 260–267.

Becker, H.S. "Personal Change in Adult Life," *Sociometry*, **27** (1964), pp. 40–53.

Becker, W.C. and Krug, R.S. "A Circumplex Model for Social Behavior in Children," *Child Development*, **35** (1964), pp. 371–396.

Bell, R.Q. and Costello, Naomi. "Three Tests for Sex Differences in Tactile Sensitivity in the Newborn," *Biologia Neonatorium*, **7** (1964), pp. 335–347.

Bell, R.Q. and Darling, Joan F. "The Prone Head Reaction in the Human Neonate: Relation with Sex and Tactile Sensitivity," *Child Development*, **36** (1965), pp. 943–949.

Bermann, E.A. "Stability and Compatibility in Interpersonal Relationships." (Doctoral dissertation, University of Michigan) Ann Arbor, Mich.: University Microfilms, 1964. No. 64-12,559.

Biddle, B.J. and Thomas, E.J. *Role Theory: Concepts and Research.* New York: John Wiley, 1966.

Bion, W.R. *Experiences in Groups.* New York: Basic Books, 1961.

Blood, R.O. "A Situational Approach to the Study of Permissiveness in Childrearing," *American Sociological Review*, **18** (1953), pp. 84–87.

Blood, R.O. and Wolfe, D.M. *Husbands and Wives.* Glencoe, Ill.: The Free Press, 1960.

Bordin, E.S. and Beale, Lynette. "The Development and Personality of Engineers," *Personnel and Guidance*, **43** (1964), pp. 23–32.

Borgatta, E.F. "Role Playing Specification, Personality, and Performance," *Sociometry*, **24** (1961), pp. 218–234.

Borgatta, E.F., Cottrell, L.S., and Meyer, H.J. "On the Dimensions of Group Behavior," *Sociometry*, **19** (1956), pp. 223–240.

Bott, Elizabeth. *Family and Social Network.* London: Tavistock Publications, 1957.

Bowerman, C.E. and Elder, G.H. "Variations in Adolescent Perception of Family Power Structure," *American Sociological Review*, **29** (1964), pp. 551–567.

Brehm, J.W. and Cohen, A.R. *Explorations in Cognitive Dissonance.* New York: John Wiley, 1962.

Brim, O.G., Jr. "The Parent-Child Relation as a Social System: I. Parent and Child Roles," *Child Development*, **28** (1957), pp. 343–364.

Brim, O.G., Jr. "Socialization Through the Life Cycle," in O.G. Brim, Jr. and S. Wheeler, *Socialization After Childhood: Two Essays.* New York: John Wiley, 1966, pp. 3–49.

Brophy, A.L. "Self, Role, and Satisfaction." (Doctoral dissertation, Columbia University) Ann Arbor, Mich.: University Microfilms, 1957. No. 57-21,631.

Browning, R.P. "Businessmen in Politics: Motivation and Circumstance in the Rise to Power." Unpublished doctoral dissertation, Yale University, 1961.

Burdick, H.A. "The Relationship of Attraction, Need Achievement, and Certainty to Conformity Under Conditions of a Simulated Group Atmosphere."

(Doctoral dissertation, University of Michigan) Ann Arbor, Mich.: University Microfilms, 1956. No. 56-17,419.

Burnstein, E., Moulton, R., and Liberty, P., Jr. "Prestige vs. Excellence as Determinants of Role Attractiveness," *American Sociological Review*, **28** (1963), pp. 212–219.

Byrne, D. "Interpersonal Attraction and Attitude Similarity," *Journal of Abnormal and Social Psychology*, **62** (1961), pp. 713–715. (a)

Byrne, D. "Interpersonal Attraction as a Function of Affiliation Need and Attitude Similarity," *Human Relations*, **14** (1961), pp. 2383–2389. (b)

Byrne, D., Clore, G.L., Jr., and Worchel, P. "Effect of Economic Similarity-Dissimilarity on Interpersonal Attraction," *Journal of Personality and Social Psychology*, **4** (1966), pp. 220–224.

Byrne, D., McDonald, R.D. and Mikawa, J. "Approach and Avoidance Affiliation Motives," *Journal of Personality*, **31** (1963), pp. 21–37.

Caplow, T. *Principles of Organization.* New York: Harcourt, Brace & World, 1964.

Catton, W.R., Jr. "The Development of Sociological Thought," in R.E.L. Faris (ed.), *Handbook of Modern Sociology.* Chicago: Rand McNally, 1964, pp. 912–950.

Child, I., Storm, T., and Veroff, J. "Achievment Themes in Folk Tales Related to Socialization Practice," in J.W. Atkinson (ed.), *Motives in Fantasy, Action, and Society.* Princeton, N.J.: Van Nostrand, 1958, pp. 479–492.

Christie, R. "Acquiescence and Education." Unpublished manuscript, Columbia University, 1958.

Coleman, J.S., Campbell, E.Q., Hobson, C.J., McPartland, J., Mood, A.M., Weinfeld, F., and York, R.L. *Equality of Educational Opportunity.* Washington: U.S. Government Printing Office, 1966.

Crandall, Virginia. "Sex Differences in Expectancy of Intellectual and Academic Performance," in C.P. Smith (ed.), *Achievement-related Motivation in Children.* New York: Russell Sage Foundation, 1969.

Crockett, H.J., Jr. "Achievement Motivation and Occupational Mobility in the United States." (Doctoral dissertation, University of Michigan) Ann Arbor, Mich.: University Microfilms, 1961. No. 61-1734.

Crockett, H.J. "Achievement Motive and Mobility," *American Sociological Review*, **27** (1962), pp. 191–204.

Duvall, Evelyn M. "Conceptions of Parenthood," *American Journal of Sociology*, **52** (1946), pp. 193–204.

Elder, G. "Children of the Great Depression," Unpublished manuscript, 1968.

Elder, R.A. "Traditional and Developmental Conceptions of Fatherhood," *Marriage and Family Living*, **11** (1949), pp. 98–101.

Etzioni, A. *A Comparative Analysis of Complex Organizations: On Power and Involvement and Their Correlates.* New York: The Free Press of Glencoe, 1964.

Feld, Sheila. "Feelings of Adjustment," in F.I. Nye and Lois W. Hoffman (eds.), *The Employed Mother in America.* Chicago: Rand McNally, 1963, pp. 331–352.

Feld, Sheila. "Studies in the Origins of Achievement Strivings." (Doctoral dissertation, University of Michigan) Ann Arbor, Mich.: University Microfilms, 1960. No. 60-1759.

Feld, Sheila, and Smith, C.P. "An Evaluation of the Method of Content Analysis," in J.W. Atkinson (ed.), *Motives in Fantasy, Action, and Society*. Princeton, N.J.: Van Nostrand, 1958, pp. 234–241.

Festinger, L. *A Theory of Cognitive Dissonance*. Evanston, Ill.: Row Peterson, 1957.

Fishman, D.B. "Need and Expectancy as Determinants of Affiliative Behavior in Small Groups," *Journal of Personality and Social Psychology*, **4**, (1966), pp. 155–164.

Fortune Survey, The. "Women in America," *Fortune*, **34** (1946), 5–6 ff.

French, Elizabeth G. "Motivation as a Variable in Work-Partner Selection," *Journal of Abnormal and Social Psychology*. **53** (1956), pp. 96–99.

Getzels, J.W. and Guba, E.G. "Social Behavior and the Administrative Process," *School Review*, **65** (1957), pp. 423–441.

Goodman, L.A., and Kruskal, W.H. "Measures of Association for Cross-Classifications," *Journal of the American Statistical Association*, **49** (1954), pp. 732–764.

Goodman, L.A. and Kruskal, W.H. "Measures of Association for Cross-Classification: III. Approximate Sampling Theory," *Journal of the American Statistical Association*, **58** (1963), pp. 310–364.

Goodman, P. *Growing Up Absurd*. New York: Random House, 1960.

Groesbeck, B.L. "Toward Description of Personality in Terms of Configuration of Motives," in J.W. Atkinson (ed.), *Motives in Fantasy, Action, and Society*. Princeton, N.J.: Van Nostrand, 1958, pp. 383–399.

Gross, N., Mason, W.S., and McEachern, A.W. *Explorations in Role Analysis*. New York: John Wiley, 1958.

Gurin, G., Veroff, J., and Feld, Sheila. *Americans View Their Mental Health: Joint Commission on Mental Illness and Health. Monograph Series No.* 4. New York: Basic Books, 1960.

Hare, A.P. and Bales, R.F. "Seating Position and Small Group Interaction," *Sociometry*, **26** (1963), pp. 480–487.

Havighurst, R. "The Social Competence of Middle-aged People," *Genetic Psychology Monographs*, **56** (1957), pp. 298–375.

Heider, F. *The Psychology of Interpersonal Relations*. New York: John Wiley, 1958.

Herbst, P.G. "The Measurement of Family Relationships," *Human Relations*, **5,** (1952), pp. 3–35.

Hess, R.D. and Handel, G. *Family Worlds*. Chicago: University of Chicago Press, 1959.

Hoffman, Lois W. "The Decision to Work," in F.I. Nye and Lois W. Hoffman (eds.), *The Employed Mother in America*. Chicago: Rand McNally, 1963, pp. 18–39.

Hoffman, Lois W. and Lippitt, R. "The Measurement of Family Life Variables," in P.H. Mussen (ed.), *Handbook of Research Methods in Child Development*. New York: John Wiley, 1960, pp. 945–1013.

Hughes, E.C. *Men and Their Work*. Glencoe, Ill.: The Free Press, 1958.

Jackson, E.F. "Status Consistency and Symptoms of Stress," *American Sociological Review*, **27** (1962), pp. 469–480.

Jackson, E.F. and Burke, P.J. "Status and Symptoms of Stress: Additive and Interaction Effects," *American Sociological Review*, **30,** (1965), pp. 556–564.

Jacobson, Allvar H. "A Study of Conflict in Attitudes Toward the Roles of the Husband and Wife in Marriage," *American Sociological Review*, **17** (1952), pp. 146–150.

Journal of Experimental Social Psychology, 1966, Supplement 1, pp. 1–102.

Kahn, R.L., Wolfe, D.M., Quinn, R.P., and Snoek, D.J. *Organizational Stress: Studies in Role Conflict and Ambiguity*. New York: John Wiley, 1964.

Kelly, E.L. "Consistency of the Adult Personality," *The American Psychologist*, **10** (1955), pp. 659–682.

Kendall, M.G. *Rank Correlation Methods*. 2nd ed.; New York: Hafner, 1955.

Klein, G.S. "Need and Regulation," in M.R. Jones (ed.), *Nebraska Symposium on Motivation*. Lincoln, Neb.: University of Nebraska Press, 1954, pp. 224–274.

Koenig, Kathryn E. "Social Psychological Correlates of Self-Reliance." (Doctoral dissertation, University of Michigan) Ann Arbor, Mich.: University Microfilms, 1963. No. 63-4978.

Kohn, M.L. "Social Class and the Exercise of Parental Authority," *American Sociological Review*, **24** (1959), pp. 252–366.

Kohn, M.L. and Carroll, Eleanor E. "Social Class and the Allocation of Parental Responsibilities," *Sociometry*, **23** (1960), pp. 372–392.

Komarovsky, Mirra. "The Homemaker: A Comparative View," *Journal of the American Association of University Women*, **55,** (1962), pp. 226–229.

Komarovsky, Mirra. *Blue Collar Marriage*. New York: Random House, 1964.

Kornhauser, A. and Reid, O.M. *Mental Health of the Industrial Worker: A Detroit Study*. New York: John Wiley, 1965.

Lansing, J.B. and Heyns, R.W. "Need Affiliation and Frequency of Four Types of Communication," *Journal of Abnormal and Social Psychology*, **58** (1959), pp. 365–372.

Leary, T.F. *Interpersonal Diagnosis of Personality*. New York: Ronald Press, 1957.

Lieberman, S. "The Effects of Changes in Roles on the Attitudes of Role Occupants," *Human Relations*, **9** (1950), pp. 385–403.

Lindman, H.A. "Study of Motives and Vocational Preference in High School Students." Unpublished honors thesis, The University of Michigan, 1958.

Lindner, M.E. and Courtney, D. "The Human Life Cycle and Its Interruption," *American Journal of Psychiatry*, **109** (1953), pp. 906–915.

Linton, R. *The Cultural Background of Personality*. New York: Appleton-Century-Crofts, 1945.

Lowe, Rosemary H., and Steiner, I.D. "Some Effects of the Reversibility and Consequences of Decisions on Postdecision Information Preferences," *Journal of Personality and Social Psychology*, **8** (1968), pp. 172–179.

Mahone, C.H. "Fear of Failure and Unrealistic Vocational Aspiration," *Journal of Abnormal and Social Psychology*, **60** (1960), pp. 253–261.

McClelland, D.C. *The Achieving Society*. Princeton, N.J.: Van Nostrand, 1961.

McClelland, D.C., Atkinson, J.W., Clark, R.A., and Lowell, E.L. *The Achievement Motive*. New York: Appleton-Century-Crofts, 1953.

McClelland, D.C., Clark, R.A., Roby, T.B., and Atkinson, J.W. "The Projective Expression of Needs: IV. The Effect of Need for Achievement on Thematic Apperception," *Journal of Experimental Psychology*, **39** (1949), pp. 242–255.

McClelland, D.C. and Liberman, A.M. "The Effect of Need for Achievement on Recognition of Need-related Words," *Journal of Personality*, **18** (1948), pp. 236–251.

Mead, G.H. *Mind, Self, and Society from the Standpoint of a Social Behaviorist*. (edited by C.W. Morris) Chicago: University of Chicago Press, 1934.

Mead, Margaret. "What Women Want," *Fortune*, **34** (1946), 172ff.

Miller, D.R., and Swanson, G.E. *The Changing American Parent*. New York: John Wiley, 1958.

Miller, D.R., and Swanson, G.E. *Inner Conflict and Defense*. New York: Holt, Rinehart & Winston, 1960.

Moos, R.H. and Speisman, J.C. "Group Compatibility and Productivity," *Journal of Abnormal and Social Psychology*, **65** (1962), pp. 190–196.

Morse, Nancy C. and Weiss, R.S. "The Function and Meaning of Work and the Job," *American Sociological Review*, **20** (1955), pp. 191–198.

Murray, H.A. *Thematic Apperception Test and Manual*. Cambridge: Harvard University Press, 1943.

Nachmann, Barbara. "Childhood Experience and Vocational Choice in Law, Dentistry, and Social Work," *Journal of Counseling Psychology*, **7** (1960), pp. 243–250.

National Opinion Research Center. "Jobs and Occupations: A Popular Evaluation," in R. Bendix and S.M. Lipset (eds.), *Class, Status, and Power*. Glencoe, Ill.: The Free Press, 1953, pp. 411–426.

Newcomb, T.M. "Individual Systems of Orientation," in S. Koch (ed.), *Psychology: A Study of a Science*. New York: McGraw-Hill, 1959, pp. 384–422.

Newcomb, T.M. *The Acquaintance Process*. New York: Holt, Rinehart & Winston, 1961.

O'Connor, Patricia, Atkinson, J.W., and Horner, M. "Motivational Implications of Ability Grouping in Schools," in J.W. Atkinson and N.T. Feather (eds.), *A Theory of Achievement Motivation*. New York: John Wiley, 1966, pp. 231–248.

Parsons, T. "An Approach to Psychological Theory in Terms of the Theory of Action," in S. Koch (ed.), *Psychology: A Study of a Science*. New York: McGraw-Hill, 1959, pp. 612–712.

Parsons, T. and Bales, R.F. *Family, Socialization and Interaction Process*. Glencoe, Ill.: The Free Press, 1955.

Parsons, T., and Shils, E.C. *Towards a General Theory of Action*. Cambridge: Harvard University Press, 1952.

Parsons, T. and White, W. "The Link Between Character and Society," in S.M. Lipset and L. Lowenthal (eds.), *Culture and Social Character*. New York: The Free Press of Glencoe, 1961, pp. 89–135.

Preiss, J.J. and Ehrlich, H.J. *An Examination of Role Theory: The Case of the State Police*. Lincoln, Nebraska: University of Nebraska Press, 1966.

Rapaport, D. "The Structure of Psychoanalytic Theory: A Systematizing Attempt," in S. Koch (ed.), *Psychology: A Study of a Science*. New York: McGraw-Hill, 1959, pp. 55–183.

Rapoport, Rhona and Rapoport, R.N. "New Light on the Honeymoon," *Human Relations*, **17** (1964), pp. 33–56.

Ricciuti, H.N. *The Prediction of Academic Grades with a Projective Test of Achievement Motivation: I. Initial Validation Studies.* Princeton, N.J.: Educational Testing Service, 1954.

Ricciuti, H.N., and Sadacca, R. *The Prediction of Academic Grades with Projective Test of Achievement Motivation: II. Cross Validation at the High School Level.* Princeton, N.J.: Educational Testing Service, 1955.

Reisman, D., Glazer, N., and Denney, R. *The Lonely Crowd: A Study of the Changing American Character.* Garden City, N.Y.: Doubleday, 1953.

Roe, Anne, *The Psychology of Occupations.* New York: John Wiley, 1956.

Rosenfeld, H.M. and Franklin, S.S. "Arousal of Need for Affiliation in Women," *Journal of Personality and Social Psychology,* 3 (1966), pp. 245–248.

Rosenthal, Irene. "Distribution of the Sample Version of the Measure of Association, Gamma," *Journal of the American Statistical Association,* 61 (1966), pp. 440–453.

Ross, I. and Zander, A. "Need Satisfactions and Employee Turnover," *Personnel Psychology,* 10 (1957), pp. 327–339.

Rossi, Alice S. "Transition to Parenthood." Paper presented at the meeting of the American Orthopsychiatric Association, Washington, D.C., March 1967.

Rossi, Alice S. "Transition to Parenthood," *Journal of Marriage and the Family,* 30 (1968), pp. 26–39.

Schachter, S. *Psychology of Affiliation.* Stanford, Calif.: Stanford University Press, 1959.

Schaefer, E.S. "Converging Conceptual Models for Maternal Behavior and for Child Behavior," in J.C. Glidewell (ed.), *Parental Attitudes and Child Behavior.* Springfield, Ill.: Charles C. Thomas, 1961, pp. 124–146.

Schaie, K.W. "A General Model for the Study of Developmental Problems," *Psychological Bulletin,* 64 (1965), pp. 92–107.

Schutz, W.D. *Firo: A Three-Dimensional Theory of Interpersonal Behavior.* New York: Holt, Rinehart, & Winston, 1958.

Sears, Pauline S. "Levels of Aspiration in Academically Successful and Unsuccessful Children," *The Journal of Abnormal and Social Psychology.* 35 (1940), pp. 498–536.

Segal, S.J. "A Psychoanalytic Analysis of Personality Factors in Vocational Choice." *Journal of Counseling Psychology,* 8 (1961), pp. 202–210.

Shipley, T.E. and Veroff, J. "A Projective Measure of Need for Affiliation," *Journal of Experimental Psychology,* 43 (1952), pp. 349–356.

Simmel, G. *Conflict and Web of Group Affiliation.* Glencoe, Ill.: The Free Press, 1955.

Skolnick, Arlene, "Motivational Imagery and Behavior Over Twenty Years," *Journal of Consulting Psychology,* 30 (1966), pp. 463–478.

Smelser, W.T. "Dominance as a Factor in Achievement and Perception in Co-operative Problem Solving Interactions," *Journal of Abnormal and Social Psychology,* 62 (1961), pp. 535–542.

Smelser, N. and Smelser, W.T. (eds.), *Personality and Social Systems.* New York: John Wiley, 1963.

Stendler, Celia B. "Sixty Years of Child Training Practices," *Journal of Pediatrics,* 36 (1950), pp. 122–134.

Straus, M.A. "Power and Support Structure of the Family in Relation to Socialization," *Journal of Marriage and the Family*, **26** (1964), pp. 318–326.

Sundheim, Betty Jean M. "The Relationships Among 'N' Achievement, 'N' Affiliation, Sex-Role Concepts, Academic Grades, and Curricular Choice." (Doctoral dissertation, Columbia University) Ann Arbor, Mich.: University Microfilms, 1963. No. 63-1528.

Survey Research Center. *Manual for Interviewers*. rev. ed; Ann Arbor: The University of Michigan, 1960.

Swanson, G.E. "Routinization of Love: Structure and Process in Primary Relations," in S. Klausner (ed.), *The Quest for Self Control*. New York: The Free Press of Glencoe, 1965, pp. 160–209.

Terhune, K.W. "Motives, Situation, and Interpersonal Conflict Within 'Prisoner's Dilemma'," *Journal of Personality and Social Psychology*, **8** (Monogr. Suppl. 3, 1968).

Thomas, E.J. "Social Role, Personality, and the Individual." Unpublished paper, School of Social Work, The University of Michigan, 1966.

Thorndike, R.L. *Personnel Selection*. New York: John Wiley, 1949.

Trow, D.B. "Autonomy and Job Satisfaction in Task-oriented Groups," *Journal of Abnormal and Social Psychology*, **54** (1957), pp. 204–210.

Uleman, J.S. "A New TAT Measure of the Need for Power." (Doctoral dissertation, Harvard University) Ann Arbor, Mich.: University Microfilms, 1966. No. 66-12,884.

U.S. Bureau of the Census. *1950 Census of Population: Alphabetical Index of Occupations and Industries*. rev. ed.; Washington: U.S. Government Printing Office, 1950.

U.S. Bureau of the Census. *Current Population Reports, Series P-60, No. 53: Income in 1966 of Families and Persons in the United States*. Washington: U.S. Government Printing Office, 1967.

U.S. Bureau of Employment Security. *Dictionary of Occupational Titles: Vol. 1. Definitions of Titles*. 2nd ed.; Washington: U.S. Government Printing Office, 1949.

Veroff, J. "Power Motive in Two-Person Influence Situations." Unpublished paper, Princeton University, 1956.

Veroff, J. "Development and Validation of a Projective Measure of Power Motivation," *Journal of Abnormal and Social Psychology*, **54** (1957), pp. 1–8.

Veroff, J. "A Scoring Manual for the Power Motive," in J.W. Atkinson (ed.), *Motives in Fantasy, Action, and Society*. Princeton, N.J.: Van Nostrand, 1958, pp. 219–233.

Veroff, J. "Thematic Apperception in a Nationwide Sample Survey," in J. Kagan & G.S. Lesser (eds.), *Contemporary Issues in Thematic Apperceptive Methods*. Springfield, Ill.: Thomas, 1961, pp. 83–118.

Veroff, J. "Theoretical Background for Studying the Origins of Human Motivational Dispositions," *Merrill-Palmer Quarterly of Behavior and Development*, **11** (1965), pp. 1–18.

Veroff, J., Atkinson, J.W., Feld, Sheila, and Gurin, G. "The Use of Thematic

Apperception to Assess Motivation in a Nationwide Interview Study," *Psychological Monographs*, **74** (12, Whole No. 499) 1960.

Veroff, J., Feld, Sheila, and Crockett, H. "Explorations into the Effects of Picture Cues on Thematic Apperceptive Expression of Achievement Motivation," *Journal of Personality and Social Psychology*, **3** (1966), pp. 171–181.

Veroff, J., Feld, Sheila, and Gurin, G. "Achievement Motivation and Religious Background," *American Sociological Review*, **27** (1962), pp. 205–217. (a)

Veroff, J., Feld, Sheila, and Gurin, G. "Dimensions of Subjective Adjustment," *Journal of Abnormal and Social Psychology*, **64** (1962), pp. 192–205. (b)

Veroff, Joanne P.B. "An Exploratory Study of Parental Motives, Parental Attitudes, and Social Behavior of Children." (Doctoral dissertation, University of Michigan) Ann Arbor, Mich.: University Microfilms, 1959. No. 59-2189.

Vogel, M.D. "An Investigation of the Affiliation Motive in College-Age Women Using Low Cue Strength Pictures." Unpublished honors thesis, The University of Michigan, 1954.

Vroom, V.H. "Some Personality Determinants of the Effect of Participation," *Journal of Abnormal and Social Psychology*, **59** (1959), pp. 322–327.

Walker, E.L. and Atkinson, J.W. "The Expression of Fear-related Motivation in Thematic Apperception as a Function of Proximity to an Atomic Explosion," in J.W. Atkinson (ed.), *Motives in Fantasy, Action, and Society*. Princeton, N.J.: Van Nostrand, 1958, pp. 143–159.

Weinstein, E.A. and Deutschberger, P. "Some Dimensions of Altercasting," *Sociometry*, **26** (1963), pp. 454–467.

Weller, G.M. and Bell, R.Q. "Basal Skin Conductance and Neonatal State," *Child Development*, **36** (1965), pp. 647–657.

Wheelis, A. *The Quest for Identity*. New York: Norton, 1958.

Wilensky, H.L. *Intellectuals in Labor Unions*. Glencoe, Ill.: The Free Press, 1956.

Williams, L.K. "The Measurement of Risk-taking Propensity in an Industrial Setting." (Doctoral dissertation, University of Michigan) Ann Arbor, Mich.: University Microfilms, 1961. No. 61-1810.

Winch, R.F. *Mate-selection: A Study of Complementary Needs*. New York: Harper, 1958.

Winter, D. G. "Power Motivation in Thought and Action." (Doctoral dissertation, Harvard University.) Cambridge, Massachusetts: University Microfilms, 1967.

Yarrow, L.J., and Yarrow, Marian R. "Personality continuity and change in the family context," in P. Worchel and D. Byrne (eds.), *Personality Change*. New York: Wiley, 1964, pp. 489–523.

Zelditch, M., Jr. "Family, marriage and kinship," in R.E.L. Faris (ed.), *Handbook of Modern Sociology*. Chicago: Rand McNally, 1964, pp. 680–733.

Zimbardo, P.G., and Formica, L.A. "Emotional Comparison and Self-esteem as Determinants of Affiliation," *Journal of Personality*, **31** (1963), 141–162.

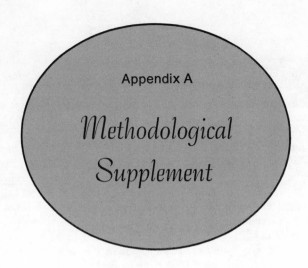

Appendix A

Methodological Supplement

I. SAMPLING PROCEDURES[1]

The individuals interviewed in this survey were a representative cross-section of adults, twenty-one years of age or older, living in private households in the United States. Households on military reservations were excluded; also excluded (because their unusual nature calls for special treatment) were all households in which persons had living arrangements of some type different from the usual family dwelling, for example, persons living in hotels and large rooming houses, dormitories for students or workers, barracks, or living quarters for inmates of institutions.

The sample was selected by a probability method with procedures known as area sampling.[2] By this method, every member of the population sampled has a known chance of being selected. Stratification insured that the sample had the same characteristics as the total population. The population to be sampled was first sorted into several groups, or strata, on the basis of geographic location and relevant social and economic variables. Units within each of these strata were selected for the sample, thus insuring that the sample reflected the diversity of the population with respect to these variables.

[1]The design and selection of the sample was executed by the Sampling Section of the Institute for Social Research, The University of Michigan, under the direction of Leslie Kish.

[2]In probability samples, the chance of drawing a specific element (dwelling unit, individual) into the sample can be calculated for every element of the population. Probability samples have the distinction of yielding measurable results; that is, the precision of estimates from probability samples can be measured objectively in terms of the sampling errors calculated from the sample.

The county was used as the stratification unit and 66 strata were formed from all the counties in the United States. The 12 largest metropolitan areas and their suburbs accounted for 12 of the strata and contained about 30 percent of the population. From each of the remaining 54 strata a random selection of one county unit was made to represent the stratum. Thus, there were 66 primary sampling units in the survey, one unit from each of the 66 strata. Within each primary sampling unit some subsampling was necessary. In the 12 largest metropolitan areas, each of the 12 central cities was included in the sample. From a list of the cities, towns, and suburban areas surrounding these central cities, a sample of these places was drawn. The sampling of dwelling units within the central cities and the suburban places followed procedures similar to those described below for cities and towns in the remaining 54 primary units.

Within each of the 54 primary sampling units outside the large metropolitan areas, a rather general urban-rural[3] stratification was established. The urban areas were further subdivided by size of place before a probability selection was made to represent each subgroup. Similarly, the rural part of the primary sampling unit was divided into two categories according to the density of population—rural congested areas and open country areas—and selections from each were made by probability-sampling techniques.

To select the specific dwelling units where interviews were taken, three different procedures were used: (1) In places where an up-to-date city directory was available, addresses were selected from the street addresses section of the directory. These directory addresses were supplemented by an area sample to insure that dwelling units that were not located at directory addresses also had the appropriate probability (greater than zero) of selection for the survey. (2) In all rural areas, and in some urban places where blocks could be easily subdivided, a probability sample of small geographic areas or segments was selected for interviewing. (3) For the remaining urban places, which included almost all of the central cities in the large metropolitan areas, a sample of blocks was selected and sent to the interviewers for prelisting. The listed addresses for each block were returned to the central office where a subselection of addresses was made by probability sampling techniques and sent to the interviewers for inclusion in the survey. The interviewers were also instructed to interview at any unlisted dwelling unit located between a sample address and the next listed address. This procedure, known as the "half-open" technique, provides for the inclusion of a proper sample of new construction addresses and addresses missed at the time of block listing.

Within each sample dwelling unit, only one adult was interviewed for this study. The respondent was designated by an objective procedure of selection,[4] and no substitutions were allowed. If the respondent was not at home on the first call, from three to ten callbacks were made in an attempt to reach him. However, even after repeated calls, a small proportion (5 percent) of the designated indi-

[3] Briefly, places of 2500 or more population at the time of the 1950 Census are classified as urban.

[4] Leslie Kish, "A Procedure for Objective Respondent Selection Within the Household," *Journal of the American Statistical Association*, 44 (1949), 380–387.

viduals were not found at home and some (8 percent) refused to be interviewed. Thus, a total of 87 percent of the selected sample were interviewed.

Although each dwelling unit had an equal chance of selection into the sample, the adults within the sample dwelling units had different probabilities of selection; people living in households with a large number of adults had a smaller chance of being interviewed than people in one or two-adult households. Happily, these differences in probabilities of selection were not great; about five-sevenths of the households had two adults, about one-seventh had one adult, and the remaining one-seventh had three to six adults, with three being the majority category in this group. Although the differences can be adjusted through a weighting procedure, this was not done; instead, both the weighted and unweighted estimates were computed for a number of critical items. When compared, these estimates showed only small differences relative to the sampling errors. Consequently, the bias resulting from the use of unweighted data is regarded as negligible, and all tabulations in the report have been made from unweighted data.

The overall study used three interview forms, each assigned randomly to one-third of the respondents throughout all primary sampling units. The use of three schedules permitted the employment of a greater variety of questions. The present study was based mainly on questions included in two forms of the interview schedule (Forms A and B). Since the assignment of respondents to forms was strictly random, this subsample has the same characteristics as the total sample.

II. SAMPLING ERROR OF PERCENTAGES

Although most of the data reported here are presented in terms of the gamma index of association, certain tables include percentage figures. In order to estimate the size of difference between percentages required for statistical confidence, Table A.1 has been included here. Table A.1 provides an estimate of the "significance" of the difference between percentages based on two *different subgroups*. Such

TABLE A-1 APPROXIMATE SAMPLING ERROR DIFFERENCES FOR PERCENTAGES FROM 35% TO 65%

N	500	300	200	100	75	50	25
500	6.3–8.8	7.2–10.1	8.4–11.8	11.0–14.8	12.3–16.2	14.8–19.2	20.5–26.1
300		8.2–11.5	9.1–12.7	11.5–15.6	12.9–17.0	15.4–19.7	20.8–26.5
200			10.0–14.0	12.2–16.7	13.4–17.9	15.8–20.7	21.2–27.2
100				14.1–19.0	15.2–20.1	17.3–22.4	22.4–28.6
75					16.2–21.2	18.2–23.5	23.1–29.4
50						20.0–25.7	24.5–31.1
25							28.3–35.8

Note: The values shown are the differences required for significance (two standard errors) in comparisons of percentages derived from two different subgroups of the current survey. Two values—low and high—are given for each cell. The lower estimates are based on simple random samples. The higher values are based on the computation of individual sampling errors carried out on the current study data and allow for the departure from simple random sampling in the survey design, such as stratification and clustering.

an estimate is necessary in evaluating differences between two sample figures since both sample percentages are subject to sampling errors, and the "true" values of each will not necessarily coincide exactly with the obtained values. Each cell of the table contains two figures—a "high" and a "low" estimate of the sampling error. The low values represent the lower bounds of the sampling errors and are computed from the standard simple random sample formulas. The high values represent the upper bounds of the sampling errors and are derived from estimates of the additional sampling error caused by clustering; these estimates are based on actual calculations of data from this study and were available to us for percentages, but not for other statistics. Most of the sampling errors computed for particular sample values lie between these limits.

III. INTERVIEW SCHEDULE

STUDY OF MODERN LIVING

Legend: Where no letter precedes the question number, this question appears on all forms of the questionnaire.

    a.   These questions appear on Forms A and B of the questionnaire.

    b.   These questions appear on Forms B and C of the questionnaire.

    c.   These questions appear on Forms A and C of the questionnaire.

    d.   These questions appear on Form A of the questionnaire.

    e.   These questions appear on Form C of the questionnaire.

    *   These questions were used in the present study.

One of the things we'd like to know is how people spend their time.

*1.   For instance—how do you usually spend your time when your work is done—what kind of things do you do, both at home and away from home?

    1a.   What other things do you do in your spare time?

    1b.   Do you have any other hobbies, or anything like that, that you do regularly in your spare time?

    1c.   (If Yes) What sort of things do you do?

*2.   Are you a member of any (other) clubs and organizations—like a lodge, PTA, a community group, or any other kind of group?

    *2a.   (If Yes) What are they?

*3.   About how often do you get together with friends or relatives—I mean things like going out together or visiting each other's homes? More than once a week; once a week; few times a month; once a month; less than once a month.

*4.   Do you have as many friends as you want, or would you like to have more friends?

    As many friends as wants; would like more friends.

    (Picture Stories. Show set of male pictures to men, female pictures to women.) Another thing we want to find out is what people think of situations that may come up in life. I'm going to show you some pictures of these situations and ask you to think of stories to go with them. The situations won't be clearly one thing or another—so feel free to think of any story you want to. (Show Picture 1.) For example, here's the first picture. I'd like you to spend a few moments thinking of a story to go with it. To get at the story you're thinking of, I'll ask you questions like: Who are these people? What do they want? and so on. Just answer with anything that comes to mind. There are no right or wrong answers.

* *a*5. Who are these people? What are they doing?

    5a. What had led up to this—what went on before?

    5b. What do they want—how do they feel?

    5c. What will happen—how will it end?

* *a*6. (Show Picture 2.) Who are these people? What are they doing?

    6a. What had led up to this—what went on before?

    6b. What do they want—how do they feel?

    6c. What will happen—how will it end?

* *a*7. (Show Picture 3.) Who are these people? What are they doing?

    7a. What had led up to this—what went on before?

    7b. What do they want—how do they feel?

    7c. What will happen—how will it end?

* *a*8. (Show Picture 4.) Who is this person? What is (he, she) doing?

    8a. What has led up to this—what went on before?

    8b. What does (he, she) want—how does (he, she) feel?

    8c. What will hap pen—how will it end?

* *a*9. (Show Picture 5.) Who are these people? What are they doing?

    9a. What has led up to this—what went on before?

    9b. What do they want—how do they feel?

    9c. What will happen—how will it end?

**a*10. (Show Picture 6.) Who are these people? What are they doing?

    10a. What has led up to this—what went on before?

    10b. What do they want—how do they feel?

    10c. What will happen—how will it end?

One of the things we're interested in is what people think about these days.

11. Everybody has some things he worries about more or less. What kinds of things do you worry about most?

12. Do you worry about such things a lot, or not very much?

13. If something is on your mind that's bothering your or worrying you, and you don't know what to do about it, what do you usually do?

    13a. (If doesn't mention "talk it over") Do you ever talk it over with anyone?

    13b. (If not mentioned) Who is that?

14. Now I'd like you to think about your whole life—how things are now, how they were ten years ago, how they were when you were a little (boy) (girl). What do you think of as the happiest time of your life? (I don't mean just a particular day or single happening, but a whole period of your life.)

    14a. (If mentions "present" time as happiest) Why is this a happy time— what are some of the things that you feel pretty happy about these days?

    14b. (If mentions "past" time as happiest) Why was that a happy time—

what are some of the things about it that you like to remember?

14c. (If mentions "past" time as happiest) How about the way things are today—what are some of the things you feel pretty happy about these days?

15. Everyone has things about their life they are not completely happy about. What are some of the things that you're not too happy about these days?

16. Thinking now of the way things were in the *past*, what do you think of as the most unhappy time of your life?

16a. Why do you think of that as an unhappy time?

17. Taking things all together, how would you say things are these days— would you say you're *very happy*, *pretty happy*, or *not too happy* these days?

18. Compared to your life today, how do you think things will be five or ten years from now—do you think things will be happier for you than they are now, not quite as happy, or what?

18a. (If "happier") How is that?

19. One of the things we'd like to know is how people face the unhappy periods in their lives. Thinking of unhappiness you've had to face, what are some of the things that have helped you in those times?

We're interested in how people react to certain typical situations. I'd like to ask you to think about times in your own life when these things happened and tell me what you did.

*b*20. For instance, when you wanted very much to do something well, and tried hard but failed:

20a. How did you feel?

20b. What did you do about it?

20c. What was it?

20d. (If "never failed") If you had failed, how would you have felt?

20e. (If "never failed") What would you do?

*b*21. When you like people a lot and try to make friends with them, but they aren't friendly to *you*:

21a. What do you do?

21b. How do you feel?

*b*22. How about when you get angry at someone you're very close to? Think of the last time someone close did something or said something that really made you angry:

22a. What did you do?

22b. How did you feel *then*?

22c. What was it about?

*b*23. Suppose you moved into a new neighborhood and made some new friends. They like you but they criticize certain of your habits and manners. You know that they will like you better if you change.

23a. How would you feel?

23b. What would you do?

Now we'd like to ask you some other questions about yourself.

24. People are the same in many ways, but no two people are exactly alike. What are some of the ways in which you're different from most other people?

Many people, when they think about their children, would like them to be different from themselves in some ways.

25. (Ask men) If you had a son, how would you like him to be different from you?

    (Ask women) If you had a daughter, how would you like her to be different from you?

26. How about your good points? What would you say were your strongest points?

Now I'd like to ask you some questions about marriage.

* 27. (Ask men) First, thinking about a man's life—how is a man's life changed by being married?

    (Ask women) First, thinking about a woman's life—how is a woman's life changed by being married?

Now here are a couple of questions I'd like you to use your imagination on.

c28. (Ask men) Suppose all you knew about a man was that he didn't want to get married. What would you guess he was like? (If answer in terms of lack of opportunity, never asked, never met a woman to marry, etc.: Well, suppose he had plenty of chances to get married but just didn't want to?)

    (Ask women) Suppose all you knew about a woman was that she didn't want to get married. What would you guess she was like? (If answer in terms of lack of opportunity, never asked, never met a man to marry, etc.: Well, suppose she had plenty of chances to get married but just didn't want to?)

    28a. (Ask men) Do you think he could live a happy life, or do you think he probably wouldn't be happy?

    (Ask women) Do you think she could live a happy life, or do you think she probably wouldn't be happy?

* 29. Are you married, single, widowed, divorced, or separated?

    (If "presently married" ask questions 30 through 37.)

* 30. We've talked a little about marriage in general. Now, thinking about your own marriage, what would you say were the nicest things about it?

* 31. Every marriage has its good points and bad points. What things about your marriage are not quite as nice as you would like them to be?

c32. (Ask men) Even in the happiest marriages there are often some things about the husband or wife that we're not completely satisfied with. If you could change one thing about your wife, what would you want to change?

    (Ask women) Even in the happiest marriages there are often some things about the husband or wife that we're not completely satisfied with. If you could change one thing about your husband, what would you want to change?

c33. (Ask men) What are some of the ways in which she is a good wife?

    (Ask women) What are some of the ways in which he is a good husband?

34. Taking things all together, how would you describe your marriage— would you say your marriage was *very happy, a little happier than average, just about average,* or *not to happy?*

    (If "very happy," "a little happier than average," or "just about average," ask questions 34a through 34f.)

34a. Even in cases where married people are happy there have often been times in the past when they weren't too happy—when they had problems getting along with each other. Has this ever been true for you?

34b. (If Yes) What was that about?

34c. What happened—how did you work it out?

34d. (If "outside help" not mentioned in 34b or 34c) Did you and your wife (husband) work it out yourselves or did you get any advice or help from others?

34e. (If "got advice or help") Where did you go for help?

34f. How did it work out?

(If "not too happy" ask questions 34g through 34l.)

34g. Have you tried to do anything about the things in your marriage that you're not too happy with?

34h. (If Yes) What have you tried to do?

34i. How did it work out?

34j. (If "outside help" not mentioned in 34h or 34j) Did you and your wife (husband) try to work it out yourselves or did you get any advice or help from others?

34k. (If "got advice or help") Where did you go for help?

34l. How did it work out?

* 35. (Ask men) Many men feel that they're not as good husbands as they would like to be. Have you ever felt this way?

(Ask women) Many women feel that they're not as good wives as they would like to be. Have you ever felt this way?

35a. (If Yes) What kinds of things make you feel this way?

*35b. Do you feel this way a lot of times, or only once in a while?

c36. (Ask men) What are some of the ways you've been a *good* husband?

(Ask women) What are some of the ways you've been a *good* wife?

* 37. We've asked you several questions about your marriage. Is this your first marriage?

37a. (If Yes) How long have you been married?

37b. (If No) How long have you been married to your present wife (husband)?

*37c. Did your first marriage end by death or divorce?

(If "divorced" or "separated" ask questions 38 through 40.)

38. We've talked a little about marriages in general. Now, thinking about your own marriage, what would you say were some of the nicer things about it?

39. What were some of the problems in your marriage?

40. What did you and your wife (husband) try to do to work things out?

40a. (If "outside help" mentioned) How did it work out?

40b. (If "outside help" not mentioned) Did you and your wife (husband) try to work it out yourselves, or did you try to get any help from others?

40c. (If "tried to get help") Where did you go for help?

40d. How did it work out?

And now I'd like to ask you some questions about children.

* 41. (Ask men) First, thinking about a man's life, how is a man's life changed by having children?

   (Ask women) First, thinking about a woman's life, how is a woman's life changed by having children?

* 42. What would you say is the nicest thing about having children?

   *42a. What other kinds of things do you think of?

   c43. Some people say that a parent's happiest time is when the children are very little. Others say the happiest time is when the children are older. Which of these times would you say a parent would be happiest? (Show card)

   (1) When the children are very little babies.

   (2) When the children are about three or four years old and haven't started school yet.

   (3) When the children are going to grade school, around the ages of eight or nine.

   (4) When the children are teen-agers, around high school age.

   (5) When the children are grown up and ready to go out on their own.

   43a. Why do you think that's the happiest time?

   43b. Which of these would you say is the *least* happy time for a parent?

(Ask people who are married or were ever married questions 44 through 51, as directed.)

* 44. Do you have any children?

   *44a. (If Yes) How many children have you had?

   *44b. Would you tell me whether they're boys or girls, how old they are, and whether they're living with you or away from home?

   45. Do you expect to have any (more) children?

(If ever had children ask questions 46 through 48.)

* 46. Most parents have had some problems in raising their children. What are the main problems you've had in raising your children?

   46a. What did (do) you do when things like that came (come) up?

*c47. (Ask men) Many men feel that they're not as good fathers as they would like to be. Have you ever felt this way?

   (Ask women) Many women feel that they're not as good mothers as they would like to be. Have you ever felt this way?

   *47a. (If Yes) What kinds of things have made you feel this way?

   *47b. Have you felt this way a lot of times, or only once in a while?

   c48. (Ask men) What are some of the ways you've been a *good* father?

   (Ask women) What are some of the ways you've been a *good* mother?

(Ask women with children aged sixteen or under questions 49 through 51.)

   c49. For every parent, there are times when you enjoy your children more than other times, or things that you enjoy most doing for them. Here is a list of different things and times with children that parents have told us they enjoyed. I'd like you to look this list over and tell me the *two* that you have found nicest about little children. (Show card)

   (1) When they listen to what you tell them to do.

   (2) When they are clean and neat.

   (3) When they are polite and well behaved with other people.

(4) When they hug and kiss you.

(5) When they play nicely with other children.

(6) When they learn to do something after they have tried for a long time.

(7) Playing with them.

49a. Which two would you say are the next nicest?

Now I have a number of questions which have to do with things you might expect from a child, and when you would expect him to learn them. After I read each one to you, let me know about what age you would think a son of yours should have learned it.

*e*50. How about

    (a) to try new things for himself without asking for help—at about what age would you think a son of yours should have learned that?

    (b) to be able to lead other children and assert himself in children's groups?

    (c) to make his own friends among children his own age?

    (d) to do well in school on his own?

    (e) to make decisions for himself, such as how he spends his pocket money, what books he reads, what movies he sees?

51. Have you ever tried to get any help in raising your child(ren) by talking to other people, or reading books, or things like that?

    51a. (If Yes) How do you mean—whom have you talked to and what are some of the books you've read?

    51b. Just how much help has that been—would you say it's been a lot of help, some help, or not much help?

Now I'd like to talk to you about your work.

* 52. What kind of work do you do?

    52a. (If "housewife") Do you do any part-time or full-time work for pay outside the home?

    52b. (If Yes) What kind of work do you do?

    52c. (If "retired") What kind of work did you usually do before you retired?

    52d. (If "unemployed") What kind of work do you usually do?

(Ask all people working "full time" or "part time" questions 53 through 55.)

* 53. Taking into consideration all the things about your job, how satisfied or dissatisfied are you with it?

* 54. What things do you particularly like about the job?

* 55. What things don't you like about the job?

(Ask men employed part time or full time questions 56 through 66.)

56. How long have you been doing this kind of work?

57. Have you ever done any other kind of work?

    57a. (If Yes) What was that?

* 58. Do you work for yourself or for someone else?

    58a. (If works for someone else) About how many people does your company employ—under 100, or over 100?

    58b. (If self-employed) Do you have any people working for you?

    58c. (If Yes) About how many?

* 59. Regardless of how much you like your job, is there any other kind of work you'd rather be doing?
    59a. (If Yes) What is that?
    59b. Why would you like that better than the work you're doing now?
    59c. Have you ever done anything about getting into this kind of work?
    59d. (If Yes) What happened?
    59e. (If No) Why is that?
* 60. If you didn't have to work to make a living, do you think you would work anyway?
    60a. (If Yes) What would be your reasons for going on working?
  61. Have you ever had any problems with your work—times when you couldn't work, or weren't getting along on the job, or didn't know what kind of work you wanted to do?
    61a. (If Yes) What was that about?
    61b. What did you do about it?
    61c. (If "outside help" not mentioned) Did you go to anyone for advice or help about it?
    61d. (If Yes) Whom did you go to?
    61e. How did it work out?
    61f. (If "Outside help" mentioned) How did it work out?
(If not "self-employed" ask questions 62 through 64.)
*d62. Do you work under anyone—a supervisor or anyone in charge of your work?
    *62a. (If Yes) Just how much does he (she) have to do with you and your work?
    62b. What kind of a person is he (she) to work for?
*d63. Do you have any people working under you?
    *63a. (If Yes) How many?
d64. Outside of the people working over you or under you, do you work with any other person or people?
    *64a. (If Yes) How do you like the people you work with?
c65. What does it take to do a really good job at the kind of work you do?
    65a. How much *ability* do you think it takes to do a really good job at the kind of work you do?
    65b. How good would you say you are at doing this kind of work—would you say you were *very good, a little better than average, just average,* or *not very good?*
b66. Some people say that you can tell a lot about a man by the kind of job that he has. Other people say that a job isn't that important. How do you feel about this?
    66a. How do you mean?
(Ask women employed part time or full time questions 67 and 68.)
a67. Regardless of how much you like your job, is there anything else you'd rather be doing?
    67a. (If Yes) What is that?
    67b. (If mentions "other kind of work") Why would you like that better than the work you're doing now?

67c. Have you ever done anything about getting into this kind of work?

67d. (If Yes) What happened?

67e. (If No) Why is that?

*a*68. If you didn't need the money that you get from working, do you think you would work anyway?

69a. (If Yes) What would be your reasons for going on working?

(If "full-time housewives," ask questions 69 through 72.)

69. Different people feel differently about taking care of a home—I don't mean taking care of the children, but things like cooking and sewing and keeping house. Some women look on these things as just a job that has to be done—other women really enjoy them. How do you feel about this?

70. Do you get much chance to spend time with other people during the day?

71. Have you ever wanted a career?

71a. (If Yes) What kind of career?

72. Are you planning to go to work in the future?

72a. (If Yes) Women have different reasons for working. What would be your main reason for working?

72b. What kind of work do you think you will do?

(If "retired" ask questions 73 through 77.)

73. Why did you retire?

73a. (If not clear) Did you have to retire, or is this something that you wanted to do?

74. In what way has retirement made a difference in your life?

74a. Could you tell me more about these changes and what they have meant in your life?

75. When you think of the days when you were working, what do you miss most?

76. Does the fact that you aren't earning a salary make a difference?

76a. (If Yes) How is that?

77. Did anyone do anything for you in connection with your retirement?

77a. (If Yes) What did they do?

77b. (If necessary) Who?

(If "unemployed" ask questions 78 through 82.)

78. Is there any other kind of work you'd like better than the work you usually do?

78a. (If Yes) What is that?

78b. Why would you like that better than the work you usually do?

78c. Have you ever done anything about getting into this kind of work?

78d. (If Yes) What happened?

79. When did you leave your last job?

80. What happened—why did you leave it?

81. Do you expect to have much trouble getting another job?

81a. (If Yes) Why do you expect to have trouble?

82. Have you gone to anyone for advice or help during the time you've been out of work?

82a. (If Yes) Whom have you gone to?

82b. Did they help in any way? How is that?

Now some questions about your health.

83. Do you have any particular physical or health trouble?
    83a. (If Yes) What is that?
84. Have you had any long illnesses in the past?
    84a. (If Yes) What was that?
85. Have you ever had the following diseases?
    (a) Asthma (If Yes) When was that?
    (b) Hay fever (If Yes) When was that?
    (c) Skin trouble (If Yes) When was that?
    (d) Stomach ulcer (If Yes) When was that?

Now I am going to hand you a sheet which tells about different troubles and complaints people have. After each one, would you check the answer which tells how often you have had this trouble or complaint?

86.	Nearly all the time	Pretty often	Not very much	Never
a. Do you ever have any trouble getting to sleep or staying asleep?				
b. Have you ever been bothered by nervousness, feeling fidgety and tense?				
c. Are you ever troubled by headaches or pains in the head?				
d. Do you have loss of appetite?				
e. How often are you bothered by having an upset stomach?				
f. Do you find it difficult to get up in the morning?				

	Many times	Some-times	Hardly ever	Never
g. Has any ill health affected the amount of work you do?				
h. Have you ever been bothered by shortness of breath when you were not exercising or working hard?				

	Many times	Some- times	Hardly ever	Never
i. Have you ever been bothered by your heart beating hard?				
j. Do you ever drink more than you should?				
k. Have you ever had spells of dizziness?				
l. Are you ever bothered by nightmares?				
m. Do you tend to lose weight when you have something important bothering you?				
n. Do your hands ever tremble enough to bother you?				
o. Are you troubled by your hands sweating so that you feel damp and clammy?				
p. Have there ever been times when you couldn't take care of things because you just couldn't get going?				

87. Here are some more questions like those you've filled out. This time just answer "Yes" or "No."
    87a. Do you feel you are bothered by all sort of pains and ailments in different parts of your body?
    87b. For the most part, do you feel healthy enough to carry out the things that you would like to do?
    87c. Have you ever felt that you were going to have a nervous breakdown?
    87d. (If Yes) Could you tell me about when you felt this way? What was it about?
    87e. What did you do about it?
88. Now here is something different. I have some statements here that describe the way some people are and feel. I'll read them one at a time and you just tell me how true they are for you—whether they're *very true for you, pretty true, not very true,* or *not true at all.*
    (Show card listing alternatives)
    (a) I have always felt pretty sure my life would work out the way I wanted it to.
    (b) I never have any trouble making up my mind about important decisions.
    (c) I often wish that people would listen to me more.

(d) I often wish that people liked me more than they do.

(e) I nearly always feel pretty sure of myself even when people disagree with me.

Problems often come up in life. Sometimes they're personal problems—people are very unhappy, or nervous and irritable all the time. Sometimes they're problems in a marriage—a husband and wife just can't get along with each other. Or sometimes it's a personal problem with a child or a job. I'd like to ask you a few questions now about what you think a person might do to handle problems like this.

89. For instance, let's suppose you had a lot of personal problems and you're very unhappy all the time. Let's suppose you've been that way for a long time, and it isn't getting any better. What do you think you'd do about it?

89a. (If "outside professional source" mentioned) If this didn't work, is there anywhere else you would go to get help? Where is that?

89b. (If "no outside professional source" mentioned) Do you think you would go anywhere to get some help with these problems? Where would you go?

89c. (If "outside professional source" still not mentioned) Suppose these problems didn't get better no matter what you tried to do about them yourself, and you felt you had to have some outside help. Do you know of anyone or any place around here where you could go for help?

89d. (If Yes to question 89c) Where would you go?

89e. Suppose you didn't know of any places yourself. Do you know of anywhere you might go, or anyone you might talk to, where you could find out where to go for help? Where is that?

89f. (If No to question 89c) Do you know of anywhere you might go, or anyone you might talk to, where you could find out where to go for help? Where is that?

(If "married now" ask question 90)

90. Suppose it was a problem in your marriage—you and your (wife) (husband) just couldn't get along with each other. What do you think you would do about it?

90a. (If "no outside professional source" mentioned) Do you think you would go anywhere to get some help with this problem? Where would you go?

90b. (If "outside professional source" mentioned) If this didn't work, is there anywhere else you would go to get help? Where is that?

Sometimes when people have problems like this, they go someplace for help. Sometimes they go to a doctor or a minister. Sometimes they go to a special place for handling personal problems—like a psychiatrist or a marriage counselor, or social agency or clinic.

91. How about you—have you ever gone anywhere like that for advice and help with any personal problems?

91a. (If Yes) What was that about?

91b. Where did you go for help? (Probe for specific names of social agencies.)

91c. How did you happen to go there?

91d. What did they do—how did they try to help you?

91e. How did it turn out—do you think it helped you in any way?
(If No to question 91 ask 92)
92. Can you think of anything that's happened to you, any problems you've had in the past, where going to someone like this might have helped you in any way?
92a. (If Yes) What do you have in mind—what was it about?
92b. What did you do about it?
92c. Who do you think might have helped you with that?
92d. Why do you suppose that you didn't go for help?
92e. (If No to question 92) Do you think you could ever have a personal problem that got so bad that you might want to go someplace for help—or do you think you could always handle things like that youself?
93. There are a lot of other kinds of places that people go to with their problems. I have a list of places here. I'll read them off to you one at a time, and you tell me whether you've ever gone to a person or place like this with any personal problems?
93a. How about a lawyer, I mean for a personal problem, not a legal problem?
93b. (If Yes) What was that about?
93c. What did he do about it—how did he try to help you?
93d. How did it work out—did he help you in any way?
93e. How about a policeman, judge, or someone in the courts?
93f. (If Yes) What was that about?
93g. What did they do about it—how did they try to help you?
93h. How did it work out—did they help you in any way?
93i. How about an astrologer, fortuneteller, or palmist?
93j. (If Yes) What was that about?
93k. What did they do about it—how did they try to help you?
93l. How did it work out—did they help you in any way?
93m. (If has school-age children) Did you ever talk to a teacher or someone else at school about any problems your child was having?
93n. (If Yes) What was that about?
93o. How did it turn out?
94. Have you ever gotten any help from reading a book or a newspaper columnist who advises on personal problems?
94a. (If Yes) What book or newspaper columnist was that?
94b. How did they help you?

Now we have finished the regular part of the interview. We need a few facts about you, like age, education, and so on, so that we can compare the ideas of men with those of women, older people with younger people, and one group with another. (Personal Data)

*PD1. (By observation) Sex: male, female.
*PD2. (By observation) Race: white, Negro, other (specify).
PD3. (Ask only if R is *not* head of household) What kind of work does (head of household) do?

PD3a (If head is unemployed) What kind of work does he usually do?

PD3b. (If head is retired) What kind of work did he usually do before he retired?

*PD4. About how old are you?

21–24; 25–29; 30–34; 35–39; 40–44; 45–49; 50–54; 55–59; 60–64; 65 or over.

*PD5. What was the highest grade of school you completed?

1; 2; 3; 4; 5; 6; 7; 8; 9; 10; 11; 12; more than 12.

* PD5a. (If more than 8) Have you had any other schooling?

* PD5b. (If Yes) What other schooling have you had?

* PD5c. (If attended college) Do you have a college degree?

PD6. What is your religious preference?

Protestant, Catholic, Jewish, other (specify).

PD6a. (If Protestant) What religious denomination is that?

PD7. About how often do you usually attend religious services?

More than once a week; once a week; two or three times a month; once a month; a few times a year or less; never.

PD8. Where were you born? (If U.S., get state.)

PD8a. (Do not ask of Negroes or foreign born) Were both your parents born in this country?

PD8b. (If Yes) What country did your parents' people originally come from?

PD8c. (If No) In which country was your father born?

PD8d. In which country was your mother born?

PD9. What kind of work did your father do for a living while you were growing up?

PD10. Were you brought up mostly on a farm, in a town, in a small city, or in a large city?

PD11. How long have you lived in (present community)?

PD12. Do you think (present community) is a *friendly* place, or an *unfriendly* place?

PD13. Did you always live together with both of your *real* parents up to the time you were sixteen years old?

PD13a. (If No) What happened?

PD13b. How old were you when it happened?

PD13c. (If step-parent not mentioned) Did your mother (father) remarry?

PD13d. (If had step-parent) How old were you when your mother (father) remarried?

PD13e. How well did you get along with your stepfather (stepmother)?

*PD14. About what do you think your total income will be this year for yourself and your immediate family?

Under $1,000; $1,000–1,999; $2,000–2,999; $3,000–3,999; $4,000–4,999; $5,000–5,999; $6,000–6,999; $7,000–7,999; $8,000–9,999, $10,000–14,999; $15,000 or more.

Length of interview.

IV. SPECIAL PROBLEMS IN ASSESSING MOTIVES THROUGH THEMATIC APPERCEPTION IN A NATIONAL SURVEY[5]

A. SPECIAL CODING CONVENTIONS

The following coding conventions were used to supplement the standard scoring manuals presented by Atkinson (1958b, Ch. 12, 13, 14).

AFFILIATION MOTIVATION

Instrumental activity $(I+, I?, I-)$ Engaging in convivial activity is considered as an end in itself, and hence should be scored $I+$ rather than $I?$, though no statement of outcome is made. Score $I+$ for the following: "The fellows are chewing the fat after dinner at a card game . . . ."; "Everyone feels in a talkative mood . . . so they sit down and talk . . . ."; "They will talk for a while, then play cards . . . ." These are instances of convivial, companionate activity. The outcome is inferred from this kind of affiliative small talk, which is an end in itself.

Anticipatory goal states $(Ga+, Ga-)$ In order to score Ga, a character in the story must be thinking either of the happiness or unhappiness accompanying an affiliative relationship or some affiliative activity, or of the activity itself. The thought need not have future reference in order to be scored as Ga. Recollecting a past goal state or goal activity is also scored Ga. In keeping with this procedure, current thinking about an attained goal state or goal activity is scored Ga, since it can be viewed as a current recollection of a past state; for example, "She is thinking about his neglect of her," is scored $Ga-$; "He thinks of his family . . . what they mean to him in sharing his success," is scored $Ga+$.

Affective states $(G+, G-)$ Anger can be considered an affect about affiliation, but it must be clear that the person who is angry is angry because of the disruption to the relationship, rather than because there is a difference of opinion. For example, if a woman is angry at her husband because he has been inconsiderate, score $G-$. If a woman is angry at her husband because he has spent too much money, do *not* score $G-$.

Affiliation thema (Th) Score Th whenever affiliation motivation is the *dominant* theme of the story. It is possible to score Th when there is *some* nonaffiliation content in the story. However, if the nonaffiliation content appears equally central to the story, or if the story is about the nonaffiliation content as much as or more than the affiliation content, do *not* score Th.

ACHIEVEMENT MOTIVATION

Achievement imagery $(Ach\ Im)$ Score Ach Im when the emphasis is on *creation* of a product and not the product itself. Do *not* score Ach Im if there is no emphasis

---

[5]The data described in this section are fully presented in: Veroff, J., Atkinson, J. W., Feld, S. C., and Gurin, G. "The Use of Thematic Apperception To Assess Motivation in a Nationwide Interview Study," *Psychological Monographs*, **74** (12, Whole No. 499) 1960.

on the process of creation, for example, "They want a nice dinner party" or "They want a good pie."

Similarly, satisfaction with work is insufficient evidence of Ach Im if there is no indication that the satisfaction comes from *accomplishment*. Do *not* score—"She is happy because the chair looks nice."

POWER MOTIVATION

Power imagery (Pow Im) Since Criterion 3 states that a story may be scored for Pow Im if there is some evidence for the enactment of a superior-subordinate role relationship, there might be an immediate tendency to score all parent-child stories for Pow Im under this criterion. This is not the case. The following criteria should be used as limitations for scoring parent-child stories for Pow Im. (a) If there is a direct imperative in the story, then the story is scored: for example, "The father told the child to sit down." The imperative does not have to be severe. All that has to be clear is that the parent is trying to *change* the behavior of the child in some way. Not scored under this criterion, then, are statements of teaching and explanation, unless they are scorable under Criterion 1 or 2. For example, "The father told the boy that it was a picture of a dinosaur," is not scored for Pow Im. (b) Punishment—scolding, reprimanding, lecturing, bawling out, etc.—should be considered a special case of the imperative, and hence scored for Pow Im.

For Criterion 3 to be met, the relevant evidence for the behavioral enactment of the power relationship implicit in superior-subordinate relations can come from the behavior of the superior or the subordinate. That is, if a story describes a worker behaving deferentially to his boss, this would be sufficient evidence for behavioral enactment of a superior-subordinate relationship to score the story for Pow Im.

The *formal* teacher-student relationship should be considered a superior subordinate relationship, and hence the scorer needs only the minimal cues for role enactment to score this kind of story for Pow Im under Criterion 3. But informal teacher-student relationships, such as may exist between friends, or between relatives, are not culturally defined in superior-subordinate terms, hence they require imagery scorable under Criterion 1 or 2.

Instrumental activity (I) Only when instrumental activity is in the active voice is it scored—"They are arguing." The passive voice or impersonal statements are not scored—"There is an argument."

B. PROCEDURES FOR COMPUTING CODING RELIABILITIES

Each coder's total scoring task was divided into three nearly equal sections (about 1,080 stories to be scored within each section). Furthermore, each coder scored the protocols in a different order, never scoring two stories from the same S in sequence. These three sections each represent a coding period for which check-coding procedures were done. Within each third of the coding, a set of 30 protocols were designated as reliability checks. The particular stories that were to be coded by the "expert coder"[6] were unknown to the coders. The "expert coder" did not

---

[6] The authors.

know how the original coders had rated the stories. From these protocols, we estimated the reliabilities. The total score reliability was based on the Spearman rank-order correlation between total motivation scores derived from the three coders' ratings and from the ratings of an "expert" scorer. For the achievement motive, the coding reliability was .89, .77, and .81; for affiliation it was .91, .76, and .76; and for the power motive it was .72 and .73.[7]

A second set of reliability coefficients were computed *after* the coder and the expert check-coder had discussed every instance of disagreement and had come to a consensus about final coding. Correlations between the coders' original scorings and the consensus-scores were uniformly higher, thus indicating that, at times, it was agreed the "expert" had been in error. The postdiscussion score reliabilities for first, second, and third checks were: achievement—.91, .94, .88; affiliation—.94, .84, .81; and power—.77, .77.

C. PROCEDURES FOR CORRECTING MOTIVE SCORES FOR THEIR CORRELATION WITH STORY LENGTH

Before applying correction procedures, we simplified our considerations of the motivation scores by putting the achievement, affiliation, and power scores on the same scale within each sex. There is no legitimate basis for making direct comparisons of raw scores between men and women on a particular motive or between the raw motivation scores within each sex. To an unknown degree, the varying means and standard deviations of raw scores for each sex and on each motive were a function of the pictures. Percentile ranks were assigned to each motivation score (for men and women separately), and each distribution of percentile ranks was normalized. Percentile ranks were converted to normal deviate scores based on a mean of 50 and a standard deviation of 10 (T scores). These T score conversions of percentile ranks effectively removed the differences between average motivation scores for both men and women. These normalized scores were used in correcting for the effect of story length.

Theoretically, the best possible correction would be one based on the average of correlations between scores for many kinds of motives and the length of protocol. This average correlation would indicate the systematic relationship between length of protocol and score on any motive. Some types of motivation might be meaningful determinants of the length of a story. For example, a person highly motivated to achieve might want to try to tell a long and complete story in order to tell the best possible story. The correlation between achievement motivation score and length of protocol might then be expected to be higher than the correlation between some other types of motivation and length of protocol. But the average of all possible correlations would reflect the extent to which longer stories provide greater opportunity for motivational imagery of any sort to appear.

In this study, the stories have thus far been coded for only three motives. Hence the average of the three correlations provides the nearest estimate that can be made of the extent to which length of story influences opportunity to get a

---

[7]Due to a misadventure with the coding sheets for power from the first time-period, no first period reliability figures are available. These figures were similar to those attained in the second and third reliability checks.

high score. The average of the three correlations is .22 for men and .24 for women.[8] For each sex, this average correlation was used to determine a regression line of motivation scores on length of protocol. The average "expected" motivation score was determined for each of 10 length-of-protocol intervals. The average expected score at each interval was then subtracted from the obtained average score for the whole sample on each motive separately. This difference score (obtained for each motive separately) was then used as a constant correction for all individual scores within particular intervals of length. Thus, a correction factor was added to scores that were too low because protocols were short, and a correction factor was subtracted from scores that were too high because of very lengthy protocols.

D. TESTING THE EFFECTS OF INTERVIEWER DIFFERENCES ON MOTIVE SCORES

We tried to design a post-facto study of interviewer differences that would be least subject to criticism. In a natural setting, we grossly confound interviewers and characteristics of respondents. Our analysis undoubtedly still can be criticized on this score. But in any case, a violation of the assumption that the respondents of each interviewer represent a random sample of the population should in most cases contribute to an overestimation of interviewer effects. As a result, the estimates to be described can probably be viewed as *maximal* estimates of interviewer differences.

Possible interviewer effects were examined in a limited sample of the total population of interviewers. The limitations introduced to approximate the assumption of equivalence among respondents for each interviewer were that the interviewer was a white female who had interviewed in nonmetropolitan sampling points, that she had interviewed at least four male respondents, and/or four female respondents who gave story protocols judged adequate for motivational analysis, and that she should have interviewed in a primary sampling unit in which there was another qualified interviewer. The restrictions on sex, race, and place were related to the tendency for greater nonrandom assignment procedures to be found among the eliminated interviewers. The limitations concerning the number of interviewees and interviewers in a given primary sampling unit were imposed in order to obtain more reliable data on interviewer effects.

These conditions were met by 8 pairs of interviewers for male Ss and 15 pairs of interviewers for female Ss. Each pair represents a different primary sampling unit. An analysis of variance of motivation scores was used to determine the components of variance attributable to Ss (or individual differences), interviewers, and primary sampling units.[9] The component variance attributable to interviewers was segregated from the S variance and its percentage contribution to S variability estimated. Separate analyses of variance were conducted for male and female Ss for each of the three motives. In these analyses, we estimated the significance of the variance assignable to interviewer effects. A "possible" inter-

---

[8]These were the correlations based on the T scores. The correlations based on raw scores, were all within $\pm$ .01 of these correlations.

[9]For a discussion of this design, see: Anderson, R. L., and Bancroft, T. A. *Statistical Theory in Research.* New York: McGraw-Hill, 1952.

viewer effect on motivation scores was statistically significant ($p < .05$) in three instances: achievement motivation scores for women and power motivation scores for both men and women. Then, the component variance for interviewers was specifically segregated and its effect on score variability was estimated as an intraclass correlation, from which we derived the proportion of variance in motivation scores possibly contributed by interviewer differences.[10] These were negligible for men except for power motivation, where the percentage increase in variance was 29. Among women, the percentage increase was negligible for affiliation, but 18 for achievement and power motivation. Since we consider these as maximal estimates, we feel safe in concluding that we have achieved a fair degree of standardization in interviewing techniques for these measures of motivation.

Similar analyses of variance were run, using number of words in the protocol as the dependent variable. For both men and women respondents, there was a substantial interviewer effect on length of protocol. The effect was especially strong among male Ss. The correction of motivation scores to eliminate the effect of differences in length of protocol had removed most of the possible interviewer effect on these scores.

[10]The intraclass correlation is described in: Snedecor, G.W. *Statistical Methods*. Ames, Iowa: Iowa State College Press, 1946, p. 243.

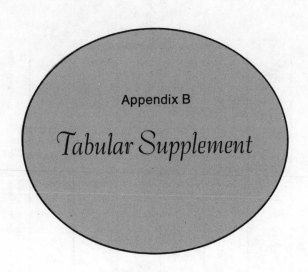

Appendix B

Tabular Supplement

TABLE 3-a SIZE OF SAMPLE FOR CHAPTER THREE ANALYSES, WITHIN THREE EDUCATIONAL BACKGROUNDS, THREE AGE LEVELS, AND TWO PARENTAL STATUS CATEGORIES

Status Characteristic	Wives	Husbands
Highest Educational Level attained		
Grade school	118	127
High School	304	222
College	92	112
	514	461
Age		
Young (21–34)	198	159
Middle (34–49)	201	147
Old (50 and older)	113	158
	512	464
Parental Status		
No children	66	63
Children	447	398
	513	461

Note: Except as noted, includes all subjects from the total sample who met all three of the following criteria: white, currently married, and adequate responses to motive measures. (Does not include: 3 men whose education was unknown; 2 women whose age was unknown; 3 men and 1 woman whose parental status was unknown.)

TABLE 3-b INTERRELATIONSHIPS AMONG MEASURES OF MARITAL REACTIONS (WITHIN SEX)

Marital Reaction	Spouse	B γ	(N)	C γ	(N)	D γ	(N)	E γ	(N)	F γ	(N)
A. Restrictiveness	Wives	.26‡	(508)	.24‡	(490)	.12*	(489)	−.05	(491)	−.11	(364)
	Husbands	.10	(449)	.03	(441)	−.10	(440)	−.11	(446)	−.04	(246)
B. Unhappiness	Wives			.40‡	(495)	.04	(494)	−.28‡	(496)	−.18	(368)
	Husbands			.32‡	(450)	.00	(447)	−.13	(453)	−.05	(248)
C. Problems[a]	Wives					.35‡	(478)	−.18*	(481)	−.15	(350)
	Husbands					.36‡	(440)	−.05	(445)	.11	(243)
D. Inadequacy	Wives							.17†	(478)	.33	(354)
	Husbands							.16*	(446)	.18	(243)
E. Relationship satisfaction	Wives									−.02	(354)
	Husbands									−.02	(246)
F. Self-dissatisfaction[b]	Wives										
	Husbands										

[a] Here and in subsequent tables, this variable does not include 6 men and 17 women who reported that their marriage was "not too happy."
[b] Here and in subsequent tables, this variable includes only those persons who mentioned something about their marriages that was not quite as nice as they would like them to be.
*p ∨ .10.
†p ∨ .05.
‡p ∨ .01.

| | Status Characteristics | | | | | | | |
| | Education | | | Age | | | Parental Status | |
Marital Reaction	grade school	high school	college	young	middle	old	no children	children
Restrictiveness	$\gamma = -.11$			$\gamma = -.11*$			$\gamma = .28\dagger$	
No responses	18%	16%	24%	13%	19%	23%	30%	16%
Some responses	30	39	35	37	37	32	35	36
All responses	52	45	41	50	44	45	35	48
	100%	100%	100%	100%	100%	100%	100%	100%
(N)	(118)	(299)	(92)	(197)	(198)	(112)	(66)	(442)
Unhappiness	$\gamma = -.30\ddagger$			$\gamma = .10*$			$\gamma = .09$	
Very happy	39%	45%	61%	49%	49%	38%	51%	46%
Little happier average	9	22	17	19	16	21	17	18
Average	41	32	22	29	33	34	29	33
Not too happy	11	1	0	3	2	7	3	3
	100%	100%	100%	100%	100%	100%	100%	100%
(N)	(118)	(304)	(92)	(198)	(201)	(113)	(66)	(447)
Problems	$\gamma = .09$			$\gamma = .22\ddagger$			$\gamma = .30\dagger$	
No	53%	46%	46%	41%	49%	59%	61%	46%
Yes	47	54	54	59	51	41	39	54
	100%	100%	100%	100%	100%	100%	100%	100%
(N)	(105)	(299)	(92)	(192)	(197)	(105)	(64)	(431)
Inadequacy	$\gamma = .30\ddagger$			$\gamma = .33\dagger$			$\gamma = .01$	
Never	58%	41%	26%	31%	43%	59%	42%	42%
Sometimes[a]	35	46	63	51	49	34	49	46
Often	3	3	3	6	2	1	0	4
A lot	4	10	8	12	6	6	9	8
	100%	100%	100%	100%	100%	100%	100%	100%
(N)	(114)	(293)	(88)	(191)	(193)	(109)	(65)	(429)
Relationship Satisfaction	$\gamma = .38\ddagger$			$\gamma = -.08$			$\gamma = -.21$	
No	73%	56%	41%	56%	55%	64%	48%	58%
Yes	27	44	59	44	45	36	52	42
	100%	100%	100%	100%	100%	100%	100%	100%
(N)	(116)	(290)	(91)	(190)	(194)	(111)	(65)	(431)
Self-Dissatisfaction	$\gamma = .38$			$\gamma = .25$			$\gamma = 14$	
Not self	99%	94%	93%	94%	93%	93%	96%	94%
Self	1	6	7	3	7	7	4	6
	100%	100%	100%	100%	100%	100%	100%	100%
(N)	(82)	(219)	(68)	(147)	(147)	(73)	(47)	(321)

[a]Two categories combined here.
*p < .10.
†p < .05.
‡p < .01.

Marital Reaction	Education			Age			Parental Status	
	grade school	high school	college	young	middle	old	no children	children
Restrictiveness	γ = −.23‡			γ = −.14†			γ = .12	
No responses	15%	24%	31%	17%	24%	28%	30%	22%
Some responses	36	38	40	37	43	35	36	39
All responses	49	38	29	46	33	37	34	39
	100%	100%	100%	100%	100%	100%	100%	100%
(N)	(121)	(220)	(110)	(158)	(144)	(152)	(61)	(390)
Unhappiness	γ = −.21‡			γ = .03			γ = .17	
Very happy	43%	50%	57%	49%	50%	50%	60%	49%
Little happier average	20	29	30	30	27	23	19	28
Average	34	20	13	20	22	24	19	22
Not too happy	3	1	1	1	1	3	2	1
	100%	100%	100%	100%	100%	100%	100%	100%
(N)	(126)	(221)	(111)	(159)	(146)	(156)	(63)	(395)
Problems	γ = .12			γ = .28‡			γ = .34†	
No	63%	51%	54%	46%	52%	68%	69%	53%
Yes	37	49	46	54	48	32	31	47
	100%	100%	100%	100%	100%	100%	100%	100%
(N)	(123)	(218)	(110)	(158)	(145)	(151)	(62)	(389)
Inadequacy	γ = .05			γ = −.20‡			γ = .21*	
Never	55%	46%	47%	41%	48%	57%	56%	48%
Sometimes[a]	35	39	47	46	38	35	41	40
Often	2	5	0	5	4	1	0	3
A lot	8	10	6	8	10	7	3	9
	100%	100%	100%	100%	100%	100%	100%	100%
(N)	(121)	(219)	(110)	(157)	(144)	(152)	(61)	(398)
Relationship Satisfaction	γ = .23‡			γ = −.01			γ = −.09	
No	64%	61%	45%	57%	58%	58%	54%	58%
Yes	36	39	55	43	42	42	46	42
	100%	100%	100%	100%	100%	100%	100%	100%
(N)	(125)	(219)	(111)	(158)	(145)	(155)	(61)	(394)
Self-Dissatisfaction	γ = .09			γ = .07			γ = .34	
Not self	82%	91%	79%	88%	83%	86%	92%	84%
Self	18	9	21	12	17	14	8	16
	100%	100%	100%	100%	100%	100%	100%	100%
(N)	(55)	(127)	(67)	(97)	(84)	(70)	(36)	(213)

[a]Two categories combined here.
*p < .10.
†p < .05.
‡p < .01.

TABLE 3-e RELATIONSHIPS (γ) IN WHICH PARENTS AND CHILDLESS SPOUSES SHOWED DIFFERENT PATTERNS OF ASSOCIATION BETWEEN MOTIVES AND MARITAL REACTIONS (WITHIN AGE AND SEX)

Correlated Variables		Control Variables				
Motive	Marital Reaction	Sex	Age	Parental Status	γ	(N)
Affiliation	Restrictiveness	Wives	<45	No children	−.34*	(45)
Affiliation	Restrictiveness	Wives	<45	Children	−.01	(283)
Affiliation	Restrictiveness	Wives	all ages	No children	−.31†	(66)
Affiliation	Restrictiveness	Wives	all ages	Children	.04	(442)
Affiliation	Unhappiness	Wives	<45	No children	.03	(45)
Affiliation	Unhappiness	Wives	<45	Children	−.13*	(287)
Affiliation	Unhappiness	Wives	all ages	No children	−.10	(66)
Affiliation	Unhappiness	Wives	all ages	Children	−.15†	(447)
Achievement	Restrictiveness	Husbands	<45	No children	−.01	(35)
Achievement	Restrictiveness	Husbands	<45	Children	−.15*	(218)
Power	Restrictiveness	Husbands	45+	No children	.48*	(26)
Power	Restrictiveness	Husbands	45+	Children	.02	(172)

*p < .10.
†p < .05.

TABLE 4-a SIZE OF SAMPLE FOR CHAPTER FOUR ANALYSES, WITHIN THREE EDUCATIONAL BACKGROUNDS AND FOUR PARENTAL STAGES

Status Characteristic	Mothers	Fathers
Highest Educational Level attained[a]		
Grade school	154	129
High school	319	201
College	90	100
	563	430
Stage of Parenthood[b]		
Preschool	57	71
School age	155	118
Adolescent	110	75
Adult	152	111
	474	375

Note: Except as noted, includes all subjects from the total sample who met all three of the following criteria: white, has living children, and adequate response to motive measures.
[a]Does not include 1 mother and 3 fathers whose educational levels were not ascertained.
[b]Does not include 90 mothers and 58 fathers whose parental life cycle presented a different pattern.

TABLE 4-b INTERRELATIONSHPS AMONG MEASURES OF PARENTAL REACTIONS (WITHIN SEX)

Parental Reaction	Parent	B γ	(N)	C γ	(N)	D γ	(N)	E γ	(N)	F γ	(N)	G γ	(N)
A. Negative orientation	Mothers	.82‡	(553)	−.04	(273)	.13*	(548)	.07	(159)	−.27*	(159)	.08	(501)
	Fathers	.86†	(423)	−.01	(200)	.02	(414)	−.17	(91)	−.19	(91)	.03	(388)
B. Restrictiveness	Mothers			−.03	(269)	−.12	(544)	.09	(157)	−.46‡	(157)	.03	(498)
	Fathers			.06	(200)	.03	(413)	.03	(91)	−.07	(91)	.11	(387)
C. Inadequacy	Mothers					.28†	(273)	−.16	(150)	.05	(150)	−.07	(246)
	Fathers					.45‡	(205)	.03	(88)	.07	(88)	−.05	(185)
D. Problems	Mothers							.02	(159)	−.34	(159)	−.02	(496)
	Fathers							−.60*	(91)	−.16	(91)	.03	(385)
E. Tolerance inadequacy[a]	Mothers											.09	(145)
	Fathers											−.46*	(81)
F. Affiliative inadequacy[a]	Mothers											.03	(145)
	Fathers											−.12	(81)
G. Distancing	Mothers												
	Fathers												

[a]The relationship between Tolerance Inadequacy and Affiliative Inadequacy is not reported because the coding of these two indices was not independent. Here and in subsequent tables, these variables include only those persons with some reported Parental Inadequacy.
*p < .10.
†p < .05.
‡p < .01.

TABLE 4-c THE RELATIONSHIP OF MOTHERS' PARENTAL REACTIONS TO THEIR EDUCATION AND PARENTAL STAGE

Parental Reaction	Status Characteristic						
	Education			Parental Stage			
	grade school	high school	college	pre-school	school age	adoles-cent	adult
Negative Orientation	$\gamma = -.13\ddagger$			$\gamma = .22\ddagger$			
Very positive	7%	7%	13%	5%	5%	11%	12%
Positive	45	48	40	35	37	42	53
Ambivalent[a]	6	16	21	15	24	16	15
Neutral	15	12	13	19	14	10	11
Negative	27	17	13	26	20	21	9
	100%	100%	100%	100%	100%	100%	100%
(N)	(151)	(315)	(90)	(57)	(154)	(110)	(147)
Restrictiveness	$\gamma = -.10$			$\gamma = -.16\ddagger$			
No responses	30%	31%	30%	21%	26%	32%	38%
Some responses	33	41	47	44	45	38	39
All responses	37	28	23	35	29	30	23
	100%	100%	100%	100%	100%	100%	100%
(N)	(150)	(313)	(89)	(57)	(151)	(110)	(147)
Inadequacy	$\gamma = .19\dagger$			$\gamma = -.13$			
Never	55%	41%	32%	59%	27%	42%	55%
Sometimes[b]	29	41	46	31	56	30	34
Often	6	5	12	5	8	14	4
A lot of times	10	13	10	5	9	14	7
	100%	100%	100%	100%	100%	100%·	100%
(N)	(77)	(158)	(41)	(22)	(75)	(52)	(75)

(*Continued on Next Page*)

(*Continued from Page 381*)

TABLE 4-c THE RELATIONSHIP OF MOTHERS' PARENTAL REACTIONS TO THEIR EDUCATION AND PARENTAL STAGE

	Status Characteristic						
	Education			Parental Stage			
Parental Reaction	grade school	high school	college	pre-school	school age	adoles-cent	adult
Problems	$\gamma = .11$			$\gamma = -.18$†			
No	26%	20%	20%	29%	14%	20%	31%
Yes	74	80	80	71	86	80	69
	100%	100%	100%	100%	100%	100%	100%
(N)	(151)	(315)	(88)	(56)	(153)	(109)	(148)
Tolerance Inadequacy	$\gamma = .26$†			$\gamma = -.36$†			
No	82%	71%	64%	50%	60%	91%	74%
Yes	18	29	36	50	40	9	26
	100%	100%	100%	100%	100%	100%	100%
(N)	(34)	(97)	(28)	(8)	(58)	(32)	(34)
Affiliative Inadequacy	$\gamma = .07$			$\gamma = .45$‡			
No	82%	80%	79%	87%	91%	59%	71%
Yes	18	20	21	13	9	41	29
	100%	100%	100%	100%	100%	100%	100%
(N)	(34)	(97)	(28)	(8)	(58)	(32)	(34)
Distancing	$\gamma = -.12$			$\gamma = .02$			
No responses	16%	13%	16%	18%	10%	9%	19%
Some responses	36	53	49	57	52	48	44
All responses	48	34	35	25	38	43	37
	100%	100%	100%	100%	100%	100%	100%
(N)	(140)	(280)	(84)	(51)	(138)	(102)	(132)

ᵃFour categories of ambivalence combined here.
ᵇTwo categories combined here.
†p < .05.
‡p < .01.

TABLE 4-d THE RELATIONSHIP OF FATHERS' PARENTAL REACTIONS TO THEIR EDUCATION AND PARENTAL STAGE

| | | Status Characteristic | | | | | |
| | Education | | | Parental Stage | | | |
Parental Reaction	grade school	high school	college	pre-school	school age	adoles-cent	adult
Negative Orientation	$\gamma = -.04$			$\gamma = -.01$			
Very positive	5%	10%	7%	13%	7%	8%	8%
Positive	63	58	63	58	55	52	62
Ambivalent[a]	5	6	3	1	10	9	12
Neutral	17	15	17	20	11	23	12
Negative	10	11	10	8	17	8	6
	100%	100%	100%	100%	100%	100%	100%
(N)	(123)	(200)	(98)	(71)	(116)	(75)	(105)
Restrictiveness	$\gamma = -.02$			$\gamma = -.03$			
No responses	34%	35%	34%	39%	29%	28%	40%
Some responses	36	35	42	34	39	38	40
All responses	30	30	24	27	32	34	20
	100%	100%	100%	100%	100%	100%	100%
(N)	(122)	(200)	(98)	(71)	(116)	(74)	(105)
Problems	$\gamma = .00$			$\gamma = -.08$			
No	32%	30%	33%	37%	25%	27%	40%
Yes	68	70	67	63	75	73	60
	100%	100%	100%	100%	100%	100%	100%
(N)	(125)	(196)	(98)	(68)	(117)	(74)	(106)

(*Continued on Next Page*)

Appendix B

(*Continued from Page 383*)

TABLE 4-d THE RELATIONSHIP OF FATHERS' PARENTAL REACTIONS TO THEIR EDUCATION AND PARENTAL STAGE

| | Status Characteristic | | | | | | |
| | Education | | | Parental Stage | | | |
Parental Reaction	grade school	high school	college	pre-school	school age	adoles-cent	adult
Inadequacy	$\gamma = .18$†			$\gamma = .21$†			
Never	67%	54%	48%	79%	55%	55%	49%
Sometimes[b]	21	28	36	12	26	35	35
Often	2	3	10	3	7	0	4
A lot of times	10	15	6	6	12	10	12
	100%	100%	100%	100%	100%	100%	100%
(N)	(61)	(92)	(52)	(34)	(57)	(31)	(55)
Tolerance Inadequacy	$\gamma = -.15$			$\gamma = -.36$			
No	83%	86%	89%	86%	69%	100%	88%
Yes	17	14	11	14	31	0	12
	100%	100%	100%	100%	100%	100%	100%
(N)	(18)	(44)	(28)	(7)	(26)	(15)	(28)
Affiliative Inadequacy	$\gamma = .48$†			$\gamma = -.02$			
No	89%	64%	50%	71%	69%	27%	76%
Yes	11	36	50	29	31	73	24
	100%	100%	100%	100%	100%	100%	100%
(N)	(18)	(44)	(28)	(7)	(26)	(15)	(28)
Distancing	$\gamma = .02$			$\gamma = .06$			
No responses	11%	16%	6%	18%	8%	10%	13%
Some responses	49	53	55	48	59	55	48
All responses	40	31	39	34	33	35	39
	100%	100%	100%	100%	100%	100%	100%
(N)	(110)	(187)	(95)	(65)	(110)	(69)	(97)

[a]Four categories of ambivalence combined here.
[b]Two categories combined here.
†p < .05.
‡p < .01.

TABLE 5-a DISTRIBUTION OF GENERAL OCCUPATIONAL CHARACTERISTICS WITHIN 10 SPECIFIC OCCUPATIONS

General Occupational Characteristic	Professional Advisers	Managers: Self-employed	Managers: Not Self-employed	Salesmen	Clerical Workers	Foremen	Skilled Workers	Semiskilled Workers	Unskilled Workers	Farmers
Prestige										
High	100%	100%	97%	0%	0%	100%	0%	0%	0%	94%
Low	0	0	3	100	100	0	100	100	100	6
(N)	100% (17)	100% (33)	100% (32)	100% (29)	100% (31)	100% (33)	100% (83)	100% (81)	100% (17)	100% (32)
Social Requirements										
High	100%	64%	100%	—ᵃ	—ᵃ	100%	—ᵃ	—ᵃ	—ᵃ	0%
Low	0	36	0			0				100
(N)	100% (17)	100% (33)	100% (31)			100% (33)				100% (30)
Supervision										
High	33%	—ᵇ	27%	36%	50%	31%	48%	65%	88%	0%
Low	67		73	64	50	69	52	35	12	100
(N)	100% (6)		100% (15)	100% (11)	100% (12)	100% (16)	100% (31)	100% (40)	100% (8)	100% (2)
Supervisory Potential										
High	17%	—ᵇ	77%	33%	23%	94%	39%	8%	13%	50%
Low	83		23	67	77	6	61	92	87	50
(N)	100% (6)		100% (12)	100% (12)	100% (13)	100% (18)	100% (33)	100% (40)	100% (8)	100% (2)

ᵃNot coded for Social Requirements; only high Prestige occupations coded.
ᵇNot coded for Supervision or Supervisory Potential; relevant questions not asked of self-employed men.

TABLE 5-b INTERRELATIONSHIPS AMONG GENERAL OCCUPATIONAL CHARACTERISTICS

Occupational Characteristic	Social Requirements[a]		Supervision[b]		Supervisory Potential[b]	
	γ	(N)	γ	(N)	γ	(N)
Prestige	.12	(190)	−.32‡	(178)	.65‡	(189)
Social requirements[a]			−.54†	(60)	.47	(65)
Supervision[b]					−.43‡	(176)
Supervisory potential[b]						

[a]Here and in subsequent tables, this variable is reported only for men in jobs high in Prestige.
[b]Here and in subsequent tables, these variables are reported only for those men who were not self-employed and who received the one interview form on which the relevant questions were asked.
†p < .05.
‡p < .01.

TABLE 5-c SIZE OF SAMPLE FOR CHAPTER FIVE ANALYSES, WITHIN VARIOUS JOBS CHARACTERISTICS AND THREE AGE LEVELS

Characteristic	Classification	Size of Sample
Specific Occupation (Coders, categorization based on modification of U.S. Bureau of the Census classification scheme — excluding jobs that do not fit this classification scheme)	Professional advisers	17
	Managers: self-employed	33
	Managers: not self-employed	32
	Salesmen	29
	Clerical workers	31
	Foremen	33
	Skilled workers	53
	Semiskilled workers	81
	Unskilled workers	17
	Farmers	32
		358
Prestige (NORC survey of public prestige of job categories, supplemented by Crockett's ratings)	High prestige	192
	Low prestige	274
		466
Social requirements[a] (Authors' judgment of whether job category requires interaction with other persons to fulfiill major role functioning — only for high prestige jobs)	High social requirements	109
	Low social requirements	81
		190
Supervision[b] (Subject's statement of whether or not supervisor has a lot or little to do with his work — excluding self-employed)	High supervision	86
	Low supervision	92
		178
Supervisory Potential[b] (Subject's statement whether or not he does any supervising — excluding self-employed)	High supervisory potential	73
	Low supervisory potential	116
		189
Age	Young (21–34)	166
	Middle-aged (35–49)	159
	Old (50 and older)	141
		466

Note: Except as noted includes all male subjects from the total sample who met all three of the following criteria: white, employed full-time, and adequate response to motive measures.
[a]Does not include 2 men in high Prestige jobs whose jobs could not be categorized for social requirements.
[b]Does not include nonself-employed subjects with missing data on these variables.

TABLE 5-d DISTRIBUTION OF JOB REACTIONS WITHIN 10 SPECIFIC OCCUPATIONS

Job Reaction	Specific Occupation									
	Professional Advisors	Managers: Self-Employed	Managers: Not Self-Employed	Salesmen	Clerical Workers	Foremen	Skilled Workers	Semiskilled Workers	Unskilled Workers	Farmers
Job Dissatisfaction										
Very satisfied	41%	28%	34%	17%	10%	27%	26%	30%	12%	19%
Satisfied	35	56	41	38	50	49	48	45	47	53
Neutral	0	0	13	10	10	6	5	8	6	6
Ambivalent	18	6	6	17	13	18	11	6	12	13
Dissatisfied[a]	6	10	6	18	17	0	10	11	23	9
(N)	100% (17)	100% (32)	100% (32)	100% (29)	100% (30)	100% (33)	100% (81)	100% (80)	100% (17)	100% (32)
Lack of Commitment										
Committed	88%	91%	91%	79%	84%	79%	83%	86%	82%	94%
Not committed	12	9	9	21	16	21	17	14	18	6
(N)	100% (16)	100% (33)	100% (32)	100% (29)	100% (31)	100% (33)	100% (83)	100% (81)	100% (17)	100% (32)

388

TABLE 5-d (continued)

Type of Satisfaction[b]										
Achievement — No	47%	47%	42%	68%	40%	36%	42%	62%	69%	42%
Yes	53	53	58	32	60	64	58	38	31	58
Economic — No	94%	88%	84%	79%	80%	91%	82%	73%	75%	100%
Yes	6	12	16	21	20	9	18	27	25	0
Affiliation — No	29%	66%	45%	50%	43%	57%	76%	73%	62%	100%
Yes	71	34	55	50	57	43	24	27	38	0
(N)	(17)	(32)	(31)	(28)	(30)	(35)	(78)	(77)	(17)	(31)
Type of Dissatisfaction[c]										
Achievement — No	53%	96%	92%	72%	65%	87%	84%	81%	83%	92%
Yes	47	4	8	28	35	13	16	19	17	8
Economic — No	87%	79%	88%	72%	92%	79%	78%	82%	50%	46%
Yes	13	21	12	28	8	21	22	18	50	54
(N)	(15)	(24)	(26)	(25)	(26)	(24)	(64)	(62)	(12)	(26)

[a]Two categories of "dissatisfied" combined here.

[b]Here and in subsequent tables, these variables include only those men with some reported job satisfaction. Each subtype totals to 100%, and for each, N is the same.

[c]Here and in subsequent tables, these variables include only those men with some reported job dissatisfaction. Each subtype totals to 100%, and for each N is the same.

389

	Occupational Characteristic							
	Prestige		Supervision		Supervisory Potential		Social Requirements	
Job Reaction	γ	(N)	γ	(N)	γ	(N)	γ	(N)
Job Dissatisfaction	−.17‡	(455)	.30‡	(176)	−.15	(188)	.10	(188)
Lack of Commitment	−.08	(461)	−.04	(178)	−.16	(189)	.01	(189)
Type of Job Satisfaction								
Economic	−.27‡	(447)	.21	(173)	−.52‡	(184)	.09	(187)
Achievement	.34‡	(447)	−.19	(173)	.30*	(184)	−.19	(187)
Affiliation	−.01	(447)	−.01	(173)	.18	(184)	.89‡	(187)
Type of Job Dissatisfaction								
Economic	−.07	(356)	−.24	(138)	−.15	(147)	−.38*	(144)
Achievement	−.04	(356)	.35	(138)	.09	(147)	.00	(144)

TABLE 5-e RELATIONSHIPS BETWEEN GENERAL OCCUPATIONAL CHARACTERISTICS AND JOB REACTIONS

*p < .10.
‡p < .01.

TABLE 5-f INTERRELATIONSHIPS AMONG MEASURES OF JOB REACTIONS (WITHIN JOBS HIGH AND LOW IN PRESTIGE)

Job Reaction	Prestige	B γ	(N)	C γ	(N)	D γ	(N)	E γ	(N)	F γ	(N)	G γ	(N)
A. Job dissatisfaction	High	.12	(187)	−.03	(185)	−.23*	(185)	.08	(185)	.04	(142)	.18	(142)
	Low	.08	(267)	.31‡	(257)	−.27‡	(257)	−.08	(255)	.06	(209)	.48‡	(209)
B. Lack of commitment	High			.46	(186)	−.14	(186)	.03	(186)	.00	(143)	.08	(143)
	Low			.26	(260)	−.46†	(260)	−.08	(260)	−.30	(212)	−.03	(212)
C. Economic satisfaction	High					−.60‡	(187)	−.46*	(187)	−.48	(142)	−1.00	(142)
	Low					−.75‡	(260)	−.53‡	(260)	−.18	(203)	.31	(203)
D. Achievement satisfaction	High							−.60‡	(187)	−.27	(142)	−.07	(142)
	Low							−.41‡	(260)	−.04	(203)	.19	(203)
E. Affiliation satisfaction	High									.15	(142)	−.08	(142)
	Low									.04	(203)	−.10	(203)
F. Economic dissatisfaction	High											−.72*	(144)
	Low											−.40*	(212)
G. Achievement dissatisfaction	High												
	Low												

*p < .10.
†p < .05.
‡p < .01.

Author Index

Subject Index